D0347443

Income tax rates

	2014–15	2013–14	2012–13
	%	%	%
Basic rate	20	20	20
Higher rate	40	40	40
Additional rate	45	45	50
Rate on non-dividend savings income	10/20/40/45[1]	10/20/40/45[2]	10/20/40/50[3]
Rate on dividend income	10/32.5/37.5[4]	10/32.5/37.5[4]	10/32.5/42.5[4]
Trust rate	45	45	50
Dividend trust rate	37.5	37.5	42.5
	£	£	£
Basic rate band	1–31,865	1–32,010	1–34,370
Maximum at basic rate	31,865	32,010	34,370
Higher rate band	31,866–150,000	32,011–150,000	34,371–150,000
Maximum at higher rate	118,135	117,990	115,630

Notes

[1] The rate of tax on non-dividend savings income is 10% up to £2,880, 20% for basic rate taxpayers, 40% for higher rate taxpayers and 45% for additional rate taxpayers.

[2] The rate of tax on non-dividend savings income is 10% up to £2,790, 20% for basic rate taxpayers, 40% for higher rate taxpayers and 45% for additional rate taxpayers.

[3] The rate of tax on non-dividend savings income is 10% up to £2,710, 20% for basic rate taxpayers, 40% for higher rate taxpayers and 50% for additional rate taxpayers.

[4] The dividend ordinary rate (up to basic rate limit) is 10%, the dividend higher rate (up to higher rate limit) is 32.5% and the dividend additional rate (above higher rate limit) is 42.5% for 2011–12 and 2012–13, and 37.5% for 2013–14 and 2014–15.

Income tax reliefs

	2014–15 £	2013–14 £	2012–13 £
Personal allowance			
– born after 5 April 1948	10,000	9,440	8,105[1]
– born after 5 April 1938 but before 6 April 1948	10,500	10,500	10,500[2]
– born before 6 April 1938	10,660	10,660	10,660[2]
Married couple's allowance			
– entitlement partner born before 6 April 1935	8,165	7,915	7,705
Minimum amount of allowance	3,140	3,040	2,960
Maximum income before abatement of:			
– Personal allowance	100,000	100,000	100,000
– reliefs for older taxpayers	27,000	26,100	25,400
Abatement income ceilings			
Single – born after 5 April 1948	120,000	118,880	116,210[3]
– born after 5 April 1938 but before 6 April 1948	28,000	28,220	30,190[4]
– born before 6 April 1938	28,320	28,540	30,510[5]
Married – born after 5 April 1948	37,050	35,850	34,890[3]
– born after 5 April 1938 but before 6 April 1948	38,050	37,970	39,680[4]
– born before 6 April 1938	38,370	38,290	40,000[5]
Blind person's allowance	2,230	2,160	2,100
'Rent-a-room' limit	4,250	4,250	4,250

Notes

[1] For 2012–13 and earlier years, entitlement to the basic personal allowance was by reference to age under 65 in the tax year. Individuals born after 5 April 1948 were aged under 65 on 5 April 2013 and remain entitled to only the basic allowance from 2013–14 onwards.

(2) For 2012–13 and earlier years, entitlement to higher age related personal allowances was based on attaining age 65–74, or age 75 and over, in the tax year. Individuals born before 6 April 1948 but after 5 April 1938 attained age 65–74 during 2012–13 and individuals born before 6 April 1938 attained age 75 or over during 2012–13. Entitlement to either the age 65–74 or 75 and over higher personal allowance continues (but the amounts are frozen) for those individuals so entitled at 5 April 2013.
(3) Claimant aged under 65 in the tax year.
(4) Claimant aged 65–74 in the tax year.
(5) Claimant aged 75 or over in the tax year.

National Insurance contributions

Class 1 primary (employee) contributions	2014–15	2013–14
Lower earnings limit (LEL)	£111 weekly	£109 weekly
Primary threshold	£153 weekly	£149 weekly
Upper earnings limit (UEL)	£805 weekly	£797 weekly
Upper accrual point (UAP)	£770 weekly	£770 weekly
Rate on earnings up to primary threshold	0%	0%
Not contracted-out rate	12% (£153.01–£805); 2% above £805	12% (£149.01–£797); 2% above £797
Contracted-out rate	10.6% (£153.01–£770); 12% (£770.01–£805); 2% above £805	10.6% (£149.01–£770); 12% (£770.01–£797); 2% above £797
Reduced rate	5.85% (£153.01–£805); 2% above £805	5.85% (£149.01–£797); 2% above £797

Class 1 secondary (employer) contributions	2014–15	2013–14
Secondary earnings threshold (ST)	£153 weekly £663 monthly £7,956 yearly	£148 weekly £641 monthly £7,696 yearly
Not contracted-out rate	13.8% on earnings above ST	13.8% on earnings above ST
Contracted-out rate	10.4% for salary related (COSR) schemes on earnings from ST to UAP (plus 3.4% rebate on earnings from LEL to ST), then 13.8% above UAP.	10.4% for salary related (COSR) schemes on earnings from ST to UAP (plus 3.4% rebate on earnings from LEL to ST), then 13.8% above UAP.
Employment Allowance	£2,000 (per year, per employer)	–

Class 2 – Self-employed	2014–15	2013–14	2012–13
	£	£	£
Small earnings exemption limit (annual)	5,885	5,725	5,595
Weekly rate	2.75	2.70	2.65
Class 3 – Voluntary contributions	**2014–15**	**2013–14**	**2012–13**
	£	£	£
Weekly rate	13.90	13.55	13.25

Class 4 – Self-employed	2014–15	2013–14	2012–13
	£	£	£
Annual earnings limit – upper	41,865	41,450	42,475
– lower	7,956	7,755	7,605
Rate	9% (£7,956–£41,865); 2% above £41,865	9% (£7,755–£41,450); 2% above £41,450	9% (£7,605–£42,475); 2% above £42,475

Taxation of capital gains

	Individuals %	Trustees and PR's %
2014–15		
- Gains eligible for entrepreneurs' relief	10	10
- Standard rate (within income tax basic rate band)	18	28
- Higher rate (above income tax basic rate band)	28	
2011–12 to 2013–14		
- Gains eligible for entrepreneurs' relief	10	10
- Standard rate (within income tax basic rate band)	18	28
- Higher rate (above income tax basic rate band)	28	
2010–11		
23 June 2010 to 5 April 2011		
- Gains eligible for entrepreneurs' relief	10	10
- Standard rate (within income tax basic rate band)	18	28
- Higher rate (above income tax basic rate band)	28	
6 April 2010 to 22 June 2010		
- Standard rate	18	18

Exemptions and reliefs	2014–15	2013–14	2012–13	2011–12
	£	£	£	£
Annual exempt amount	11,000	10,900	10,600	10,600
Chattel exemption (max. sale proceeds)	6,000	6,000	6,000	6,000

Inheritance tax

Gross cumulative transfer (on or after 6 April 2014)	Gross rate of tax	
	Transfers on death	Lifetime transfers
	%	%
£1–£325,000	Nil	Nil
£325,000 upwards	36/40	20

Note
Estate on death taxed as top slice of cumulative transfers in the seven years before death. Most lifetime transfers (other than to discretionary trusts) are potentially exempt, only becoming chargeable where death occurs within seven years.

Annual exemption	£3,000
Small gift exemption (to the same person)	£250

Taxation of companies

Financial year	2014	2013	2012
Main rate[2]	21%	23%	24%
Small companies' (SC) rate[1][2]	20%	20%	20%
Profit limit for SC rate	£300,000	£300,000	£300,000
Marginal relief fraction (SC rate)	1/400th	3/400	1/100
Intellectual property rate	10%	10%	–

Note

[1] The small companies' rate is not available to 'close investment-holding companies'.

[2] Main rate on ring fence profits (CTA 2010, s. 276) is 30%, small profits rate is 19% and the marginal relief ring fenced fraction is 11/400ths.

VAT

Standard rate	
From 4 January 2011	20%
1 January 2010–3 January 2011	17.5%
1 December 2008–31 December 2009	15%
1 April 1991–30 November 2008	17.5%
Annual registration limit – taxable supplies (from 1 April 2014)	£81,000
De-registration limit – taxable supplies (from 1 April 2014)	£79,000
VAT fraction	
For standard rate of 20%	1/6
For standard rate of 17.5%	7/47
For standard rate of 15%	3/23

Bank base rates

Date effective		Rate %	Date effective		Rate %
2009	5 March	0.50	**2006**	9 November	5.00
	5 February	1.00		3 August	4.75
	8 January	1.50	**2005**	4 August	4.50
2008	4 December	2.00	**2004**	5 August	4.75
	6 November	3.00		10 June	4.50
	8 October	4.50		6 May	4.25
	10 April	5.00		5 February	4.00
	7 February	5.25	**2003**	6 November	3.75
2007	6 December	5.50		10 July	3.50
	5 July	5.75		6 February	3.75
	10 May	5.50	**2001**	8 November	4.00
	11 January	5.25		4 October	4.50

PREFACE

Now in its 45th edition, *Hardman's Tax Rates & Tables* contains the numerical and factual data in everyday use by the tax practitioner. The material is conveniently arranged in twenty one chapters:

- Principles of income tax
- Taxation of business profits
- Taxation of investment income
- Taxation of earnings
- Taxation of capital gains
- Inheritance tax
- Taxation of companies
- Capital allowances
- National Insurance contributions
- Tax credits
- State benefits and statutory payments
- General
- Stamp taxes
- Value added tax
- Insurance premium tax
- Landfill tax
- Aggregates levy
- Climate change levy
- Air passenger duty
- Vehicle excise duty
- Scottish taxes

This Edition takes full account of the Autumn Statement 2014. These provisions may be affected by amendments made during their passage through Parliament.

Cross-references to CCH's *Tax Reporter* and *VAT Reporter* are included.

The data in this book is maintained by Sarah Arnold of Elucidate Tax and CCH's team of tax writers: Mark Cawthron, Julie Clift, Stanley Dencher, Trevor Johnson, Stephen Relf and Meg Wilson.

Every effort has been taken to include, within the constraints of available space, the information of greatest use to the practitioner. A number of changes have been made in the light of suggestions received from users of previous years' editions. CCH welcomes further suggestions as to material which might be inserted in future editions.

Paul Robbins

December 2014

Note: the late Philip Hardman was the original editor of *Hardman's Tax Rates & Tables*. CCH gratefully acknowledges the considerable help and guidance that he provided.

Disclaimer

This publication is sold with the understanding that neither the publisher nor the authors, with regard to this publication, are engaged in rendering legal or professional services. The material contained in this publication neither purports, nor is intended to be, advice on any particular matter.

Although this publication incorporates a considerable degree of standardisation, subjective judgment by the user, based on individual circumstances, is indispensable. This publication is an 'aid' and cannot be expected to replace such judgment.

Neither the publisher nor the authors can accept any responsibility or liability to any person, whether a purchaser of this publication or not, in respect of anything done or omitted to be done by any such person in reliance, whether sole or partial, upon the whole or any part of the contents of this publication.

Legislative and other material

While copyright in all statutory and other materials resides in the Crown or other relevant body, copyright in the remaining material in this publication is vested in the publisher.

The publisher advises that any statutory or other materials issued by the Crown or other relevant bodies and reproduced and quoted in this publication are not the authorised official versions of those statutory or other materials. In the preparation, however, the greatest care has been taken to ensure exact conformity with the law as enacted or other material as issued.

Crown copyright legislation is reproduced under the terms of Crown Copyright Policy Guidance issued by HMSO. Other Crown copyright material is reproduced with the permission of the controller of HMSO. European Communities Copyright material is reproduced with permission.

Telephone Helpline Disclaimer Notice

Where purchasers of this publication also have access to any Telephone Helpline Service operated by Wolters Kluwer (UK), then Wolters Kluwer's total liability to contract, tort (including negligence, or breach of statutory duty) misrepresentation, restitution or otherwise with respect to any claim arising out of its acts or alleged omissions in the provision of the Helpline Service shall be limited to the yearly subscription fee paid by the Claimant.

ISBN: 978-1-84798-924-6
CCH Code: UP/TRT2-BI14001

British Library Cataloguing-in-Publication Data.

A catalogue record for this book is available from the British Library.

Typeset by Innodata Inc., India

Printed and bound in the UK by Hobbs the Printers Ltd.

About the Publisher

CCH is part of the Wolters Kluwer Group. Wolters Kluwer is the leading international publisher specialising in tax, business and law publishing throughout Europe, the US and the Asia Pacific region. The Group produces a wide range of information services in different media for the accounting and legal professions and for business.

All CCH publications are designed to be practical and authoritative reference works and guides and are written by our own highly qualified and experienced editorial team and specialist outside authors.

CCH publishes information packages including electronic products, loose-leaf reporting services, newsletters and books on UK and European legal topics for distribution worldwide. The UK operation also acts as distributor of the publications of the overseas affiliates.

Wolters Kluwer
145 London Road
Kingston upon Thames
KT2 6SR
Telephone: 0844 561 8166
Facsimile: +44 (0)208 247 2637
Email: cch@wolterskluwer.co.uk
Website: www.cch.co.uk

Acknowledgements

Certain material in this publication is Crown Copyright and is reproduced with the kind permission of the Controller of Her Majesty's Stationery Office.

CCH acknowledges the endorsement of this publication by the Chartered Institute of Taxation and the Tax Faculty of the Institute of Chartered Accountants in England and Wales.

THE CHARTERED INSTITUTE OF TAXATION

The Association of Taxation Technicians

PRINCIPLES OF INCOME TAX

INCOME TAX RATES

Note: See ¶26-100 for rates applicable in Scotland from April 2016

[¶1-005] Income tax rates: 2015–16

(*Finance Act* 2014)

(Tax Reporter: ¶148-075ff.)

2015–16

	Taxable income band £	Tax rate %	Tax on band £
Basic rate	1–31,785	20	6,357
Higher rate	31,786–150,000	40	47,286
Additional rate	Over 150,000	45	

Rate on non-dividend savings income	0% up to £5,000[(1)] 20% up to basic rate limit 40% up to higher rate limit 45% thereafter
Dividend ordinary rate (effective rate with tax credit)	10% up to basic rate limit 0%
Dividend upper rate (effective rate with tax credit)	32.5% up to higher rate limit 25%
Dividend additional rate (effective rate with tax credit)	37.5% above higher rate limit 30.6%
Trust rate	45%[(2)]
Dividend trust rate	37.5%[(2)]

Notes

[(1)] The starting rate is available for savings income only. If an individual's taxable non-savings income (i.e. after deduction of their personal allowance) exceeds the starting rate limit, then the starting rate is not be available. From 6 April 2015, the starting rate for savings income will be reduced to 0% and the maximum amount of an individual's income that can qualify for this starting rate will increase to £5,000.

[(2)] The special trust rates do not apply to the first £1,000 slice of the 'trust rate income'. Instead, the normal income tax rates (currently the basic rate and dividend ordinary rate) apply as appropriate (ITA 2007, s. 491(1)–(3)).

[¶1-006] Income tax rates: 2014–15

(FA 2014, s. 1; ITA 2007, s. 6–15)

(Tax Reporter: ¶148-075ff.)

2014–15

	Taxable income band £	Tax rate %	Tax on band £
Basic rate	1–31,865	20	6,373
Higher rate	31,866–150,000	40	47,254
Additional rate	Over 150,000	45	

Rate on non-dividend savings income	10% up to £2,880[1] 20% up to basic rate limit 40% up to higher rate limit 45% thereafter
Dividend ordinary rate (effective rate with tax credit)	10% up to basic rate limit 0%
Dividend upper rate (effective rate with tax credit)	32.5% up to higher rate limit 25%
Dividend additional rate (effective rate with tax credit)	37.5% above higher rate limit 30.6%
Trust rate	45%[2]
Dividend trust rate	37.5%[2]

Notes

[1] A 10% starting rate applies to the first £2,880 of non-dividend savings income. The starting rate does not apply if non-savings income exceeds the personal allowance plus £2,880.

[2] The special trust rates do not apply to the first £1,000 slice of the 'trust rate income'. Instead, the normal income tax rates (currently the basic rate and dividend ordinary rate) apply as appropriate (ITA 2007, s. 491(1)–(3)).

[¶1-008] Income tax rates: 2013–14

(FA 2013, s. 3; ITA 2007, s. 6–15)

(Tax Reporter: ¶148-075ff.)

2013–14

	Taxable income band £	Tax rate %	Tax on band £
Basic rate	1–32,010	20	6,402
Higher rate	32,011–150,000	40	47,196
Additional rate	Over 150,000	45	

Rate on non-dividend savings income	10% up to £2,790[1] 20% up to basic rate limit 40% up to higher rate limit 45% thereafter
Dividend ordinary rate (effective rate with tax credit)	10% up to basic rate limit 0%
Dividend upper rate (effective rate with tax credit)	32.5% up to higher rate limit 25%
Dividend additional rate (effective rate with tax credit)	37.5% above higher rate limit 30.6%
Trust rate	45%[2]
Dividend trust rate	37.5%[2]

Notes

[1] A 10% starting rate applies to the first £2,790 of non-dividend savings income. The starting rate does not apply if non-savings income exceeds the personal allowance plus £2,790.

[2] The special trust rates do not apply to the first £1,000 slice of the 'trust rate income'. Instead, the normal income tax rates (currently the basic rate and dividend ordinary rate) apply as appropriate (ITA 2007, s. 491(1)–(3)).

[¶1-009] Income tax rates: 2012–13

(ITA 2007, s. 6–15)

(Tax Reporter: ¶148-075ff.)

2012–13

	Taxable income band £	Tax rate %	Tax on band £
Basic rate	1–34,370	20	6,874
Higher rate	34,371–150,000	40	46,252
Additional rate	Over 150,000	50	

Rate on non-dividend savings income	10% up to £2,710[1] 20% up to basic rate limit 40% up to higher rate limit 50% thereafter
Dividend ordinary rate (effective rate with tax credit)	10% up to basic rate limit 0%
Dividend upper rate (effective rate with tax credit)	32.5% up to higher rate limit 25%

Dividend additional rate (effective rate with tax credit)	42.5% above higher rate limit 36.1%
Trust rate	50%[(2)]
Dividend trust rate	42.5%[(2)]

[(1)] A 10% starting rate applies to the first £2,710 of non-dividend savings income. The starting rate does not apply if non-savings income exceeds the personal allowance plus £2,710.

[(2)] The special trust rates do not apply to the first £1,000 slice of the 'trust rate income'. Instead, the normal income tax rates (currently the basic rate and dividend ordinary rate) apply as appropriate (ITA 2007, s. 491(1)–(3)).

[¶1-010] Income tax rates: 2011–12

(ITA 2007, s. 6–15)

(Tax Reporter: ¶148-075ff.)

2011–12

	Taxable income band **£**	**Tax rate** **%**	**Tax on band** **£**
Basic rate	1–35,000	20	7,000
Higher rate	35,001–150,000	40	46,000
Additional rate	Over 150,000	50	

2011–12

Rate on non-dividend savings income	10% up to £2,560[(1)] 20% up to basic rate limit 40% up to higher rate limit 50% thereafter
Dividend ordinary rate (effective rate with tax credit)	10% up to basic rate limit 0%
Dividend upper rate (effective rate with tax credit)	32.5% up to higher rate limit 25%
Dividend additional rate (effective rate with tax credit)	42.5% above higher rate limit 36.1%
Trust rate	50%[(2)]
Dividend trust rate	42.5%[(2)]

[(1)] A 10% starting rate applies to the first £2,560 of non-dividend savings income. The starting rate does not apply if non-savings income exceeds the personal allowance plus £2,560.

[(2)] The special trust rates do not apply to the first £1,000 slice of the 'trust rate income'. Instead, the normal income tax rates (currently the basic rate and dividend ordinary rate) apply as appropriate (ITA 2007, s. 491(1)–(3)).

[¶1-020] Income tax rates: 2010–11

(ITA 2007, s. 6–15)

(Tax Reporter: ¶148-075ff.)

2010–11

	Taxable income band £	Tax rate %	Tax on band £
Basic rate	1–37,400	20	7,480
Higher rate	37,401–150,000	40	45,040
Additional rate	Over 150,000	50	

Rate on non-dividend savings income	10% up to £2,440[(1)] 20% up to basic rate limit 40% up to higher rate limit 50% thereafter
Dividend ordinary rate (effective rate with tax credit)	10% up to basic rate limit 0%
Dividend upper rate (effective rate with tax credit)	32.5% up to higher rate limit 25%
Dividend additional rate (effective rate with tax credit)	42.5% above higher rate limit 36.1%
Trust rate	50%[(2)]
Dividend trust rate	42.5%[(2)]

(1) A 10% starting rate applies to the first £2,440 of non-dividend savings income. The starting rate does not apply if non-savings income exceeds the personal allowance plus £2,440.

(2) The special trust rates do not apply to the first £1,000 slice of the 'trust rate income'. Instead, the normal income tax rates (currently the basic rate and dividend ordinary rate) apply as appropriate (ITA 2007, s. 491(1)–(3)).

[¶1-100] Personal allowances and reliefs

(ITA 2007, s. 35–46)

(Tax Reporter: ¶155-000ff.)

Finance Act 2012 made changes to the main income tax personal allowances. From 2013–14, there are still three main personal allowances, but availability is by reference to date of birth rather than age in the tax year (as it was for years up to and including 2012–13). The higher allowances for those born before 6 April 1948 have not been increased since the 2012–13 rates and will be removed from the statute book when the personal allowance for those born after 5 April 1948 catches up.

Existing legislation within ITA 2007 requires the Government to increase personal allowances and rate limits (except the £150,000 higher rate limit, £100,000 personal allowance income limit and since 2013–14 the personal allowances for people born before 6 April 1948) by the annual percentage increase in the Retail Prices Index (RPI) for the year to September preceding the new tax year (indexation). *Finance Act* 2014 sets for 2015–16 the basic rate limit at £31,785 (overriding the amount that would otherwise have been set by the 2014 indexation order). Prospective amendments have also been made in *Finance Act* 2014 to remove references to the personal allowance for those 'born after 5 April 1938 but before 6 April 1948' with effect from 2015–16 and to amend the category of allowances for individuals 'born after 5 April 1948' to become 'born after 5 April 1938', leaving only one category of higher allowance for those 'born before 6 April 1938'.

Autumn Statement 2014 announced that the personal allowance for those born after 5 April 1938 will be set at £10,600 for 2015–16 (overriding the amount previously announced).

At Budget 2011, the Government announced its intention to move the underlying indexation assumption for all direct taxes to the Consumer Price Index (CPI). This transition began in April 2012 and *Finance Act* 2014 prospectively amends ITA 2007 to give effect to the CPI change for income tax allowances and limits, with effect for the tax year 2015–16 and subsequent tax years.

Transferable tax allowances for married couples

Legislation introduced in *Finance Act* 2014 provides that from the 2015–16 tax year, a spouse or civil partner who is not liable to income tax because their income is below their personal allowance or who is liable to income tax at the basic rate, dividend ordinary rate or the starting rate for savings will be able to elect to transfer £1,060 of their personal allowance to their spouse or civil partner (i.e. 10% of the personal allowance for those born after 5 April 1938). There will be a corresponding reduction to the transferring spouse's personal allowance. A spouse or civil partner who is liable to income tax at the basic rate, dividend ordinary rate or the starting rate for savings will receive the transferred personal allowance. The transferred allowance will be given effect as a reduction to the recipient's income tax liability at the basic rate of tax. Married couples or civil partners entitled to claim the married couple's allowance will not be entitled to make a transfer.

Type of relief	2015–16[10] £	2014–15 £	2013–14 £	2012–13 £	2011–12 £	2010–11 £	2009–10 £
Personal allowance[3]							
– born after 5 April 1948	10,600	10,000	9,440	8,105[1]	7,475[1]	6,475[1]	6,475[1]
– born after 5 April 1938 but before 6 April 1948	10,600	10,500	10,500	10,500[2]	9,940[2]	9,490[2]	9,490[2]
– born before 6 April 1938	10,660	10,660	10,660	10,660[2]	10,090[2]	9,640[2]	9,640[2]
Married couple's allowance[4][5]							
– born before 6 April 1935 and age 75 & over	8,355	8,165	7,915	7,705	7,295	6,965	6,965
– minimum amount of allowance	3,220	3,140	3,040	2,960	2,800	2,670	2,670
Maximum income before abatement of:							
– personal allowance	100,000	100,000	100,000	100,000	100,000	100,000	–
– reliefs for older taxpayers	27,700	27,000	26,100	25,400	24,000	22,900	22,900

Type of relief	2015–16[10] £	2014–15 £	2013–14 £	2012–13 £	2011–12 £	2010–11 £	2009–10 £
Abatement income ceilings							
Personal allowance:							
– born after 5 April 1948	121,200	120,000	118,880	116,210	114,950	112,950	–
– born after 5 April 1938 but before 6 April 1948	27,700	28,000	28,220	30,190[2]	28,930[2]	28,930[2]	28,930[2]
– born before 6 April 1938	27,820	28,320	28,540	30,510[2]	29,230[2]	29,230[2]	29,230[2]
Married couples allowance							
Entitlement partner born before 6 April 1935;							
Relevant partner born after 5 April 1948	37,970	37,050	35,850	34,890[6]	32,990[6]	31,490[6]	31,490[6]
Relevant partner born after 5 April 1938 but before 6 April 1948	37,970	38,050	37,970	39,680[7]	37,920[7]	37,520[7]	37,520[7]
Relevant partner born before 6 April 1938	38,090	38,370	38,290	40,000[8]	38,220[8]	37,820[8]	37,820[8]
Blind person's allowance	2,290	2,230	2,160	2,100	1,980	1,890	1,890
Life assurance relief (policies issued before 14 March 1984)[9]	–[9]	12.5% of premiums	12.5% of premiums	12.5% of premiums	12.5% of premiums	12.5% of premiums	12.5% of premiums
'Rent-a-room' limit	4,250	4,250	4,250	4,250	4,250	4,250	4,250

Notes

(1) For 2012–13 and earlier years, entitlement to the basic personal allowance was by reference to age under 65 in the tax year. Individuals born after 5 April 1948 were aged under 65 on 5 April 2013 and remain entitled to only the basic allowance from 2013–14 onwards.

(2) For 2012–13 and earlier years, entitlement to higher age related personal allowances was based on attaining age 65–74, or age 75 and over, in the tax year. Individuals born before 6 April 1948 but after 5 April 1938 attained age 65–74 during 2012–13 and individuals born before 6 April 1938 attained age 75 or over during 2012–13. Entitlement to either the age 65–74 or 75 and over higher personal allowance continues (but the amounts are frozen) for those individuals so entitled at 5 April 2013.

(3) From April 2010, the personal allowance is gradually withdrawn for income over £100,000 at a rate of £1 of allowance lost for every £2 over £100,000 until it is completely removed (ITA 2007, s. 35).

(4) Relief is given as a tax reduction at a rate of 10%.

(5) The married couple's allowance is available only where at least one partner reached the age of 65 before 6 April 2000, i.e. was born before 6 April 1935. That partner will have become 75 at some point during 2009–10 and, therefore, will be entitled to the higher amount of the allowance for that tax year and subsequent tax years, i.e. for those aged 75 or over.

(6) Relevant partner aged under 65 in the tax year.

(7) Relevant partner aged 65–74 in the tax year.

(8) Relevant partner aged 75 or over in the tax year.

(9) By relief at source. Abolished for payments becoming due and payable on or after 6 April 2015, and payments becoming due and payable before 6 April 2015 but actually paid on or after 6 July 2015 (FA 2012, s. 227 and Sch. 39, para. 23).

(10) Rates per Autumn Statement 2014.

Personal allowances and rate limits (except the £150,000 higher rate limit, the £100,000 personal allowance income limit and since 2013–14 the personal allowances for people born before 6 April 1948) are indexed by the annual percentage increase in CPI (rather than RPI) for the year to September preceding the new tax year from 2015–16.

[¶1-110] High income child benefit charge

(ITEPA 2003, s. 681B–681H)

(Tax Reporter: ¶490-075)

The high income child benefit charge applies from 7 January 2013 to individuals whose income exceeds £50,000 who are themselves, or whose partner is, in receipt of child benefit. The charge is levied on the partner with the highest income, irrespective of which partner claims the child benefit. The charge is calculated as the 'appropriate percentage' of child benefit payments received during the tax year (but for 2012–13 restricted to amounts received after 7 January 2013 only) which equates to 1% of the amount of child benefit received for every £100 of income over £50,000. From 2013–14, coding out of the charge is possible.

Adjusted Net Income	Appropriate percentage
£60,000 and over	100%
£50,001–£59,999	$\frac{ANI - L}{X}\%$
Up to £50,000	Nil

Where:

ANI = Adjusted Net Income
L = £50,000
X = £100

Adjusted Net Income is calculated as:

- Net income (total income charged to income tax less income tax reliefs)
- Less grossed up (at basic rate) gift aid donations
- Less gross pension contributions (before deduction of basic rate tax)
- Add back any relief for payments to trade unions or police organisations (ITEPA 2003, s. 457 or 458) deducted in calculating net income.

Child benefit[(1)]	2015–16[(2)] £/week	2014–15 £/week	2013–14 £/week	2012–13 £/week
Eldest qualifying child	20.70	20.50	20.30	20.30
Each other child	13.70	13.55	13.40	13.40

Note

(1) Individuals who elected not to continue to receive child benefit before 7 January 2013 were not liable for the charge for 2012–13 and individuals who opted out by 28 March 2013 were not liable for the charge for 2013–14. For 2014–15, individuals who opt out and whose payments stopped before the beginning of the tax year will not be liable for the charge and will otherwise be liable only for the period until payments stop.

(2) Rates per Autumn Statement 2014.

[¶1-120] Cap on income tax relief

(ITA 2007, s. 24A)

(Tax Reporter: ¶148-450)

From 6 April 2013, a limit applies to the amount of certain income tax reliefs that may be deducted from income under the *Income Tax Act* 2007, s. 24. The limit does not apply to charitable reliefs.

From	Amount of cap
6 April 2013[(1)]	greater of: – £50,000; or – 25% of adjusted total income

Note

[(1)] The limit applies for the tax year 2013–14 and subsequent tax years, and additionally, where loss relief is claimed for a tax year before 2013–14 in relation to losses made in 2013–14 or a later year. However, the limit does not apply in relation to property loss relief arising from a loss made in 2012–13 where the loss is claimed for relief against general income in the tax year 2013–14.

Limited reliefs	Legislation
Trade loss relief against general income (excluding relief for losses attributable to overlap relief and Business Premises Renovation Allowances (BPRA)) [and excluding deductions so far as made from profits of the trade or business to which the relief relates – see next table]	ITA 2007, s. 64
Early trade loss relief (first four years of trade, profession or vocation; excluding relief for losses attributable to overlap relief and BPRA) [and excluding deductions so far as made from profits of the trade or business to which the relief relates – see table below]	ITA 2007, s. 72
Post-cessation trade relief (qualifying payments or qualifying events within seven years of the permanent cessation of the trade) [and excluding deductions so far as made from profits of the trade or business to which the relief relates – see table below]	ITA 2007, s. 96
Property loss relief against general income (property business losses arising from capital allowances or agricultural expenses; excluding relief for losses attributable to BPRA) [and excluding deductions so far as made from profits of the trade or business to which the relief relates – see table below]	ITA 2007, s. 120
Post-cessation property relief (qualifying payments or qualifying events within seven years of the permanent cessation of the UK property business) [and excluding deductions so far as made from profits of the trade or business to which the relief relates – see table below]	ITA 2007, s. 125
Employment loss relief against general income (certain circumstances where losses or liabilities arise from employment)	ITA 2007, s. 128
Former employees deductions for liabilities (payment made by former employees for which they are entitled to claim a deduction from their general income in the year in which the payment is made)	ITEPA 2003, s. 555

Limited reliefs	Legislation
Share loss relief on non EIS/SEIS/SI shares (capital losses on the disposal, or deemed disposal, of certain qualifying shares)	ITA 2007, Pt. 4, Ch. 6
Losses on deeply discounted securities (losses on gilt strips and on listed securities held since at least 26 March 2003)	ITTOIA 2005, s. 446, 454(4)
Qualifying loan interest (interest paid on certain loans including loans to buy an interest in certain types of company or to invest in a partnership)	ITA 2007, Pt. 8, Ch. 1

Excluded reliefs	Legislation
Deductions attributable to business premises renovation allowances	CAA 2001, Pt. 3A
Deductions so far as made from profits of the trade or business to which the relief relates in respect of: • trade loss relief; • early trade loss relief; • post-cessation trade relief; • property loss relief; • post-cessation property relief.	ITA 2007, s. 64, 72, 96, 120 and 125
Deductions so far as attributable to a deduction for overlap relief profit in final tax year or on change of accounting date (allowed under ITTOIA 2005, s. 205 or 220) in respect of: • trade loss relief; • early trade loss relief.	ITA 2007, s. 64 and 72
Deductions for amounts of relief for share losses: • where the shares in question are qualifying shares to which EIS relief is attributable; • where SEIS relief is attributable to the shares in question; • where SI tax relief is attributable to the shares in question.	ITA 2007, Pt. 4, Ch. 6 ITA 2007, s. 131(2)(a) ITA 2007, Pt. 5A ITA 2007, Pt. 5B

[¶1-150] Gifts of assets

Nature of asset	Legislation	Effect of relief
Stock manufactured or sold by trader that is given to charity, etc. (Tax Reporter: ¶226-650)	CTA 2009, s. 105; ITTOIA 2005, s. 108	No amount is brought into account as trading receipt as result of the donation
Plant and machinery used by trader given to a charity, etc. (Tax Reporter: ¶238-235)	CAA 2001, s. 63	Disposal value is nil for capital allowances purposes
Stock manufactured or sold by trader that is given to a designated educational establishment and qualifies as plant or machinery in the donee's hands. (Tax Reporter: ¶226-650)	CTA 2009, s. 105; ITTOIA 2005, s. 108	No amount is brought into account as a trading receipt as result of the donation
Plant or machinery used by trader that is given to a designated educational establishment and qualifies as plant and machinery in the donee's hands. (Tax Reporter: ¶238-235)	CAA 2001, s. 63	Disposal value is nil for capital allowances purposes

Nature of asset	Legislation	Effect of relief
Listed shares and securities and securities dealt with on a recognised stock exchange, units in unit trusts, etc. interests in land, that are given to a charity. (Tax Reporter: ¶115-575; ¶716-640)	CTA 2010, s. 203; ITA 2007, s. 431	Full value of gift is deductible in calculating profits for IT or CT purposes
Property settled by gift on a UK trust which has a charity as a beneficiary and the settlor retains an interest (Tax Reporter: ¶356-450)	ITTOIA 2005, s. 628	The trust income allocated to the settlor is reduced by an amount equal to the income paid to the charity in the year

[¶1-200] Gifts to the nation

(FA 2012, Sch. 14)

For the tax year 2012–13 and subsequent tax years, a reduction in income tax and/or capital gains tax is available where an individual makes a gift of pre-eminent property to be held for the benefit of the public or the nation. The tax reduction is 30% of the value of the gift. A gift offer must be made and registered in accordance with the scheme and relief is available against the individual's liability for the year in which the gift offer is registered and/or any of the succeeding four tax years.

Pre-eminent property includes any picture, print, book, manuscript, work of art, scientific object or other thing that is pre-eminent for its national, scientific, historic or artistic interest, collections of such items and any object kept in a significant building where it is desirable that it remain associated with the building.

ADMINISTRATION

[¶1-250] Submission dates for 2014–15 personal tax returns

(TMA 1970, s. 8)

(Tax Reporter: ¶180-125)

TMA 1970, s. 8 contains provisions concerning submission dates for returns issued on or after 6 April 2015 which relate to 2014–15, as follows:

- paper returns (whether or not HMRC is to calculate the tax liability) must be filed by 31 October 2015; and
- online returns must be filed by 31 January 2016.

There are the following exceptions:

Circumstances	Filing date
Return issued after 31 July 2015 but before 31 October 2015	Three months from the date of issue (paper returns); 31 January 2016 (online returns)
Return issued after 31 October 2015	Three months from date of issue

Circumstances	Filing date
Taxpayer wishes underpayment (below £3,000) to be coded out under PAYE in a subsequent year (paper returns)	31 October 2015
Taxpayer wishes underpayment (below £3,000) to be coded out under PAYE in a subsequent year (online returns)	30 December 2015

Withdrawing a notice to file a self-assessment return

(TMA 1970, s. 8B and 12AAA)

With effect in respect of returns for the tax year 2012–13 and subsequent tax years, HMRC will withdraw a notice to file a return, on request in certain circumstances, where they agree a self-assessment return is not required and cancel any late filing penalty already issued in respect of the outstanding return. Requests must be made within two years beginning with the end of the relevant year of assessment or period in respect of which the return is required or, in exceptional circumstances, such extended period as HMRC may agree.

[¶1-300] Payment dates 2014–15

(TMA 1970, s. 59A, 59B)

(Tax Reporter: ¶182-725ff.)

Tax is paid on 31 January next following the year of assessment as a single sum covering capital gains tax and income tax on all sources. Interim payments on account may be required. No interim payments are required if:

- the tax paid by assessment was less than £1,000; or
- more than 80% of the tax due the previous year was collected at source.

A payment on account can never exceed 50% of the net tax for the preceding year, even though it may already be clear, at the time the payments are made, that the actual liability for the year will exceed that for the preceding year. Net tax is the excess of assessed tax over tax deducted at source (incl. tax credits on dividends). For 2014–15, the following due dates apply:

First interim payment	31 January 2015
Second interim payment	31 July 2015
Final balancing payment	31 January 2016

Note

If a return is not issued until after 31 October 2015 and the taxpayer has notified chargeability by 5 October 2015, the due date for the final payment becomes three months from the issue of the return (TMA 1970, s. 59B).

[¶1-350] Main penalty provisions 2014–15

Offence	Penalty[1][2]		
Late return for 2010–11 and later years (FA 2009, Sch. 55; Tax Reporter: ¶181-500)[3]			
Failure to submit by the filing date (by 31 October 2015 for paper return; by 31 January 2016 for online return)	£100		
Failure continues three months after the filing date (1 February 2016 for paper returns; 1 May 2016 for online returns) by HMRC notice	£10 per day for a period up to 90 days beginning with the date specified in the notice (maximum £900)		
Failure still continues six months after the filing date (1 May 2016 for paper return; 1 August 2016 for online return)	The greater of £300 or 5% of the liability to tax shown by the return		
Failure still continues after 12 months (1 November 2016 for paper return; 1 February 2017 for online return)	The greater of relevant percentage of liability shown by the return and £300		
	Relevant percentage		
	Category 1	Category 2	Category 3
• withholding information deliberate and concealed	100%	150%	200%
• withholding information deliberate but not concealed	70%	105%	140%
• any other case	5%	5%	5%
Reductions for disclosure (maximum reduction weighted according to quality of disclosure determined as:	Standard penalty	Prompted disclosure Minimum	Unprompted disclosure Minimum
• 30% for telling,	70%	35%	20%
• 40% for helping, and	105%	52.5%	30%
• 30% for giving access)	140%	70%	40%
	100%	50%	30%
	150%	75%	45%
	200%	100%	60%
Late return for years up to and including 2009–10 (TMA 1970, s. 93)[3][4]:			
• if paper return not filed by the deadline	£100		
• if paper return still not filed six months after the deadline	£100		
• for continuing delay	Up to £60 per day (not restricted to the liability shown by the return)		
• failure continues beyond the anniversary of the filing date	Tax geared		

Offence	Penalty[1][2]				
Failure to notify chargeablility For failures after 1 April 2010 (FA 2008, Sch. 41; Tax Reporter: ¶181-350)	Percentage of potential lost revenue				
	Category 1	Category 2		Category 3	
• failure deliberate and concealed	100%	150%		200%	
• failure deliberate but not concealed	70%	105%		140%	
• any other case	30%	45%		60%	
Reductions for disclosure (maximum reduction weighted according to quality of disclosure determined as:	Standard penalty	Prompted disclosure Minimum[5]		Unprompted disclosure Minimum[5]	
• 30% for telling; • 40% for helping; and • 30% for giving access).		Case A	Case B	Case A	Case B
	30%	10%	20%	0%	10%
	45%	15%	30%	0%	15%
	60%	20%	40%	0%	20%
	70%	35%		20%	
	105%	52.5%		30%	
	140%	70%		40%	
	100%	50%		30%	
	150%	75%		45%	
	200%	100%		60%	
Failure to notify chargeablility For failures before 1 April 2010 (TMA 1970, s. 7; Tax Reporter: ¶181-525)	Tax geared up to 100% of the tax, subject to mitigation				
Failure to keep and retain tax records (TMA 1970, s. 12B; Tax Reporter: ¶181-900)	Up to £3,000 per year of assessment				
False statements to reduce interim payments (TMA 1970, s. 59A[6]; Tax Reporter: ¶182-725)	Up to the difference between the amount correctly due and the amount paid				
Failure to produce documents required to check a person's tax position or obstructing an inspection (FA 2008, Sch. 36, para. 39 and 40; Tax Reporter: ¶186-550ff.)					
• standard amount	£300				
• continued failure	daily penalty of £60				
Tax-related penalty where significant tax is at risk (FA 2008, Sch. 36, para. 50)	tax geared amount decided by Upper Tribunal				
Errors in returns Errors in returns for periods starting 1 April 2008 where return is filed on or after 1 April 2009 (FA 2007, Sch. 24; Tax Reporter: ¶184-850)[6]	Percentage of potential lost revenue				
	Category 1	Category 2		Category 2	
• careless action	30%	45%		60%	
• deliberate but not concealed action	70%	105%		140%	
• deliberate and concealed action	100%	150%		200%	
Reductions for disclosure (maximum reduction weighted according to quality of disclosure determined as:	Standard penalty	Prompted disclosure Minimum		Unprompted disclosure Minimum	
• 30% for telling; • 40% for helping; and • 30% for giving access).	30%	15%		0%	
	45%	22.5%		0%	
	60%	30%		0%	
	70%	35%		20%	
	105%	52.5%		30%	
	140%	70%		40%	
	100%	50%		30%	
	150%	75%		45%	
	200%	100%		60%	

Offence	Penalty[1][2]
Incorrect return or accounts (fraudulently or negligently); periods starting before 1 April 2008 where return is filed before 1 April 2009 (TMA 1970, s. 95, 95A; Tax Reporter: ¶184-875)	Tax geared up to 100% of the tax, subject to mitigation

Notes

(1) Interest is charged on penalties not paid when due. The due date is 30 days after the notice of determination of the penalty is issued.

(2) A defence of 'reasonable excuse' may be available.

(3) Late return penalties are cumulative, e.g. for a return six months late there are two penalties.

(4) The two fixed £100 penalties are reduced if the total tax payable by assessment is less than the penalty which would otherwise be chargeable.

(5) The case A minimum applies if HMRC become aware of the failure less than 12 months after the time when the tax first becomes unpaid by reason of the failure, otherwise the case B minimum applies.

(6) No penalty for inaccuracies that occur despite taking reasonable care.

[¶1-360] Offshore penalties – territory categories

The table below shows which territories are classified in 'category 1' and 'category 3' for the purposes of penalties for offshore non-compliance. Territories not listed here (other than the UK) are in 'category 2'. Penalties for domestic (UK) matters fall into category 1.

Category 1	Category 3[1]
Anguilla	Albania
Aruba	Algeria
Australia	Andorra
Belgium	Bonaire, Sint Eustatius and Saba
Bulgaria	Brazil
Canada	Cameroon
Cayman Islands	Cape Verde
Cyprus	Colombia
Czech Republic	Congo, Republic of the
Denmark (not including Faroe Islands and Greenland which are in category 2)	Cook Islands
Estonia	Costa Rica
Finland	Curacao
France	Cuba
Germany	Democratic People's Republic of Korea
Greece	Dominican Republic
Guernsey (includes Alderney and Sark)	Ecuador
Hungary	El Salvador
Ireland	Gabon
Isle of Man	Guatemala
Italy	Honduras
Japan	Iran
Korea, South	Iraq
Latvia	Jamaica
Lithuania	Kyrgyzstan
Malta	Lebanon
Montserrat	Macau (China and Hong Kong are in category 2)

Category 1	Category 3[1]
Netherlands (not including Bonaire, Sint Eustatius and Saba)	Marshall Islands
New Zealand (not including Tokelau)	Micronesia, Federated States of
Norway	Monaco
Poland	Nauru
Portugal (includes Madeira and the Azores)	Nicaragua
Romania	Niue
Slovakia	Palau
Slovenia	Panama
Spain (includes the Canary Islands and other overseas territories of Spain)	Paraguay
Sweden	Peru
Switzerland (from 24 July 2013)	Seychelles
United States of America (not including overseas territories and possessions of the United States of America which are in category 2)	Sint Maarten
	Suriname
	Syria
	Tokelau
	Tonga
	Trinidad and Tobago
	United Arab Emirates
	Uruguay

Notes

[1] Before 24 July 2013, category 3 territories included additionally:

- Antigua and Barbuda
- Armenia
- Bahrain
- Barbados
- Belize
- Dominica
- Grenada
- Mauritius
- Saint Kitts and Nevis
- Saint Lucia
- Saint Vincent and the Grenadines
- San Marino

[¶1-400] Penalties for late payment of tax 2014–15

(FA 2009, Sch. 56)

(Tax Reporter: ¶182-875)

A new penalty regime for late payments under income tax self-assessment was introduced by FA 2009, Sch. 56. This applies from 6 April 2011 to payments for the tax year 2010–11 and later years.

Tax overdue	Penalty
30 days	5% of tax overdue
6 months	further 5% of tax overdue
12 months	further 5% of tax overdue

These penalties will be issued automatically and are in addition to the interest that will be charges on all outstanding amounts, including unpaid penalties, until payment is received.

Penalties apply to:

- final tax payments on self-assessments (this includes any amounts due as interim payments which remain unpaid);
- tax on inspector's amendments to a self-assessment made during or as a result of an audit; and
- discovery assessments.

[¶1-450] Interest 2014–15

(FA 2009, s. 101–105 and Sch. 53 and 54)

(Tax Reporter: ¶182-925; ¶182-975)

A new harmonised regime for interest on overdue and overpaid tax was introduced by FA 2009, s. 101–105 and Sch. 53 and 54, with effect in relation to any self-assessment amount payable or repayable on or after 31 October 2011.

Interest is payable from the 'late payment interest start date':

Payment	Late payment interest start date
First interim payment(1)	31 January 2015
Second interim payment	31 July 2015
Final payment(2)	31 January 2016
Tax due on an amendment to a return	31 January 2016
Tax due on determination of appeal	31 January 2016

Notes

(1) Where the taxpayer has provided HMRC in good time with the information required to issue a statement of account ahead of the payment date of 31 January, but no statement is received before 1 January, interest on the tax to be paid will run from 30 days after the taxpayer is actually notified rather than from 31 January.

(2) Where notice to make a return is issued after 31 October following the end of the tax year, provided there has been no failure to notify chargeability under TMA 1970, s. 7, the date from which interest is payable becomes the last day in the period of three months beginning with the day notice to make a return was given.

Repayment interest runs from the date of payment (deemed to be 31 January following the tax year in respect of tax deducted at source) to the date on which the order for the repayment is issued.

For periods prior to self-assessment, the relevant period was:

Later of:

(i) due date; or

(ii) actual date of payment,

until the end of the tax month in which the repayment order was issued.

[¶1-500] Rates of interest

(FA 2009, s. 101–102; SI 2011/2446)

(Tax Reporter: ¶182-925; ¶182-975)

The following table gives the rates of interest applicable in recent years.

From	Late payment %	Repayment %
29 September 2009	3.00	0.50
24 March 2009	2.50	0.00
27 January 2009	3.50	0.00
6 January 2009	4.50	0.75
6 December 2008	5.50	1.50
6 November 2008	6.50	2.25
6 January 2008	7.50	3.00
6 August 2007	8.50	4.00
6 September 2006	7.50	3.00
6 September 2005	6.50	2.25
6 September 2004	7.50	3.00(1)
6 December 2003	6.50	2.25(1)
6 August 2003	5.50	1.50(1)
6 November 2001	6.50	2.25(1)
6 May 2001	7.50	3.00(1)
6 February 2000	8.50	4.00(1)
6 March 1999	7.50	3.00
6 January 1999	8.50	4.00
6 August 1997	9.50	4.75
31 January 1997	8.50	4.00

Notes

SI 2011/2446 sets the interest rates for the purposes of s. 101 and 102 at the Bank of England base rate plus 2.5% and minus 1% respectively. Changes in interest rates announced in Bank of England Monetary Policy Committee meetings take effect from the 13th working day following the meeting and apply in respect of interest running from before that date as well as interest running from on or after that date.

(1) Rates revised by HMRC (press release 16 September 2009).

[¶1-600] Interest rates on certificates of tax deposit (CTD)

CTDs can be purchased to settle most tax liabilities, except PAYE, VAT and corporation tax falling due under Pay and File, or for subsequent encashment. (No CTDs are available for purchase for use against corporation tax liabilities since the start of the Pay and File regime.) A higher rate of interest is paid if the CTD is used in payment of tax. Interest is allowed/paid gross and is taxable.

Rates of interest vary according to the period for which the deposit is held. The rates in force at issue apply for one year; thereafter, the rate applicable is that on the most recent anniversary of the date of issue.

Details of how to purchase a CTD and use it in payment of tax can be found on the HMRC website at www.hmrc.gov.uk/payinghmrc/cert-tax-deposit.htm.

Rates applicable over recent years have been as follows:

Certificates of Tax Deposit Interest Rates

Deposits on or after	Deposits under £100,000		Deposits of £100,000 or more: Deposits held for under 1 month		Deposits held for 1 to under 3 months		Deposits held for 3 to under 6 months		Deposits held for 6 to under 9 months		Deposits held for 9–12 months	
	Applied in payment of tax %	Cash value %	Applied in payment of tax %	Cash value %	Applied in payment of tax %	Cash value %	Applied in payment of tax %	Cash value %	Applied in payment of tax %	Cash value %	Applied in payment of tax %	Cash value %
7 May 1997	2.75	1.50	2.75	1.50	5.50	2.75	5.25	2.75	5.50	2.75	5.25	2.75
9 June 1997	3.00	1.50	3.00	1.50	5.50	2.75	5.50	2.75	5.50	2.75	5.50	2.75
11 July 1997	3.25	1.75	3.25	1.75	6.00	3.00	5.75	3.00	5.75	3.00	6.00	3.00
8 Aug. 1997	4.50	2.25	4.50	2.25	6.00	3.00	6.00	3.00	6.00	3.00	5.75	3.00
7 Nov. 1997	4.00	2.00	4.00	2.00	6.50	3.25	6.50	3.25	6.25	3.25	6.25	3.25
5 June 1998	4.00	2.00	4.00	2.00	6.50	3.25	6.25	3.25	6.25	3.25	6.00	3.00
9 Oct. 1998	3.75	2.00	3.75	2.00	6.25	3.25	5.75	3.00	5.50	2.75	5.25	2.75
6 Nov. 1998	3.25	1.75	3.25	1.75	5.75	3.00	5.25	2.75	5.00	2.50	4.75	2.50
11 Dec. 1998	3.00	1.50	3.00	1.50	5.25	2.75	4.75	2.50	4.50	2.25	4.25	2.25
8 Jan. 1999	2.50	1.25	2.50	1.25	5.00	2.50	4.50	2.25	4.00	2.00	4.00	2.00
5 Feb. 1999	1.75	1.00	1.75	1.00	4.50	2.25	4.00	2.00	3.75	2.00	3.75	2.00
9 Apr. 1999	1.75	1.00	1.75	1.00	4.25	2.25	4.00	2.00	3.75	2.00	3.75	2.00
11 June 1999	1.50	0.75	1.50	0.75	4.00	2.00	4.00	2.00	4.00	2.00	4.00	2.00
9 Sept. 1999	1.75	1.00	1.75	1.00	4.50	2.25	4.50	2.25	4.50	2.25	4.50	2.25
4 Nov. 1999	2.00	1.00	2.00	1.00	5.00	2.50	4.75	2.50	4.75	2.50	4.75	2.50
14 Jan. 2000	2.25	1.25	2.25	1.25	5.00	2.50	5.00	2.50	5.00	2.50	5.25	2.75
11 Feb. 2000	2.50	1.25	2.50	1.25	5.25	2.75	5.00	2.50	5.25	2.75	5.25	2.75
9 Feb. 2001	2.25	1.25	2.25	1.25	4.75	2.50	4.25	2.25	4.25	2.25	4.00	2.00
6 Apr. 2001	2.00	1.00	2.00	1.00	4.25	2.25	4.00	2.00	3.75	2.00	3.50	1.75
11 May 2001	2.00	1.00	2.00	1.00	4.00	2.00	4.00	2.00	3.75	2.00	3.75	2.00
3 Aug. 2001	1.50	0.75	1.50	0.75	4.00	2.00	3.75	2.00	3.75	2.00	3.75	2.00
19 Sept. 2001	1.25	0.75	1.25	0.75	3.50	1.75	3.25	1.75	3.25	1.75	3.00	1.50
5 Oct. 2001	1.00	0.50	1.00	0.50	3.25	1.75	3.00	1.50	3.00	1.50	3.00	1.50
9 Nov. 2001	0.50	0.25	0.50	0.25	2.75	1.50	2.50	1.25	2.25	1.25	2.25	1.25
7 Feb. 2003	0.25	Nil	0.25	Nil	2.75	1.25	2.25	1.00	2.25	1.00	2.00	1.00
11 July 2003	Nil	Nil	Nil	Nil	2.50	1.25	2.25	1.00	2.00	1.00	2.00	1.00
7 Nov. 2003	0.25	Nil	0.25	Nil	3.00	1.50	3.00	1.50	3.00	1.50	3.00	1.50
6 Feb. 2004	0.50	0.25	0.50	0.25	3.00	1.50	3.00	1.50	3.00	1.50	3.00	1.50

Certificates of Tax Deposit Interest Rates

Deposits on or after	Deposits under £100,000		Deposits of £100,000 or more									
			Deposits held for under 1 month		Deposits held for 1 to under 3 months		Deposits held for 3 to under six months		Deposits held for 6 to under 9 months		Deposits held for 9–12 months	
	Applied in payment of tax %	Cash value %	Applied in payment of tax %	Cash value %	Applied in payment of tax %	Cash value %	Applied in payment of tax %	Cash value %	Applied in payment of tax %	Cash value %	Applied in payment of tax %	Cash value %
7 May 2004	0.75	0.25	0.75	0.25	3.25	1.50	3.25	1.50	3.25	1.50	3.25	1.50
11 June 2004	1.00	0.50	1.00	0.50	3.75	1.75	3.50	1.75	3.75	1.75	3.75	1.75
6 Aug. 2004	1.25	0.50	1.25	0.50	3.75	1.75	3.75	1.75	3.75	1.75	3.75	1.75
5 Aug. 2005	1.00	0.50	1.00	0.50	3.50	1.75	3.25	1.50	3.00	1.50	3.00	1.50
4 Aug. 2006	1.75	0.75	1.75	0.75	4.25	2.00	4.25	2.00	4.00	2.00	4.00	2.00
10 Nov. 2006	1.50	0.75	1.50	0.75	4.00	2.00	4.00	2.00	3.75	1.75	3.75	1.75
12 Jan. 2007	1.50	0.75	1.50	0.75	4.25	2.00	4.00	2.00	4.00	2.00	4.00	2.00
11 May 2007	2.00	1.00	2.00	1.00	4.75	2.25	4.50	2.25	4.50	2.25	4.50	2.25
6 July 2007	2.25	1.10	2.25	1.10	5.00	2.50	4.75	2.25	4.75	2.25	4.75	2.25
7 Dec. 2007	3.00	1.50	3.00	1.50	5.50	2.75	5.00	2.50	4.75	2.25	4.50	2.25
8 Feb. 2008	2.00	1.00	2.00	1.00	4.50	2.25	4.25	2.25	4.00	2.00	3.75	1.50
11 Apr. 2008	2.00	1.00	2.00	1.00	4.75	2.25	4.50	2.25	4.25	2.00	4.25	2.00
9 Oct. 2008	2.50	1.25	2.50	1.25	5.25	2.50	5.00	2.50	5.00	2.50	4.75	2.25
7 Nov. 2008	1.75	0.75	1.75	0.75	4.50	2.25	4.25	2.00	4.25	2.00	4.00	2.00
5 Dec. 2008	0.00	0.00	0.00	0.00	2.50	1.25	2.50	1.25	2.50	1.25	2.25	1.00
9 Jan. 2009	0.00	0.00	0.00	0.00	1.50	0.75	1.25	0.50	1.25	0.50	1.25	0.50
6 Feb. 2009	0.00	0.00	0.00	0.00	1.00	0.50	1.00	0.50	1.00	0.50	0.75	0.25
6 Mar. 2009	0.00	0.00	0.00	0.00	0.75	0.25	0.75	0.25	0.75	0.25	0.75	0.25

[¶1-650] Remission of tax for official error

(ESC A19)

Arrears of income tax and capital gains tax may be given up if they result from HMRC's failure to make proper and timely use of information supplied by the taxpayer, or in certain circumstances by the taxpayer's employer or the Department for Work and Pensions.

The taxpayer must have reasonably believed that his or her affairs were in order. Tax will normally only be given up where there was a gap of 12 months or more between HMRC receiving the information that tax was due, and notifying the taxpayer of the arrears.

TAXATION OF BUSINESS PROFITS

[¶2-000] Relief for fluctuating profits (farming and market gardening; creative artists)

(ITTOIA 2005, s. 221ff.)

(Tax Reporter: ¶272-300ff.; ¶268-300)

Full averaging

Full averaging applies where profits of one of the tax years are less than 70% of profits for the other year or where profits of one (but not both) of the tax years are nil.

Marginal averaging

The amount of the adjustment to the profits of each relevant tax year, where lower profits are between 70 and 75% of higher profits, is computed as follows:

$$(D \times 3) - (P \times 0.75)$$

D is the difference between the relevant profits of the two years; and

P is the relevant profits of the tax year of which those profits are higher.

[¶2-010] Cash basis for small businesses

(ITTOIA 2005, Pt. 2, Ch. 3A)

(Tax Reporter: ¶206-481ff.)

From April 2013 (with effect for the tax year 2013–14 and subsequent tax years), eligible businesses may elect to calculate their profits on the cash basis instead of in accordance with generally accepted accountancy principles. The cash basis is optional but circumstances under which a business can leave the scheme are limited (businesses must continue to use the scheme until their circumstances change so that the cash basis is no longer suitable for them). Under the scheme, businesses will calculate their taxable income by taking business income received in a year and deducting business expenses paid in a year. This will mean they will not need to adjust for debtors, creditors and stock, and will generally not have to distinguish between revenue and capital expenditure. Capital allowances will remain available for expenditure on cars only. Businesses using the cash basis will not have to use the simplified flat rate expenses for their cars.

Eligible barristers will be able to choose either to use the new cash basis and simplified expenses or the current accruals basis. The existing cash basis arrangement for barristers will be withdrawn except for barristers already using it, for the remainder of their qualifying period.

	Relevant max. Joining[2] £	Leaving Threshold[2] £
From April 2014		
Standard	81,000	162,000
Recipients of Universal credit[1]	162,000	
2013–14		
Standard	79,000	158,000
Recipients of Universal credit[1]	158,000	

Notes

[1] Recipients of universal credit must use the cash basis for income assessment for UC purposes.

[2] Joining and leaving thresholds are determined by reference to the VAT registration threshold (in place at the end of the tax year) and twice the VAT registration threshold respectively.

Excluded businesses:

- Companies
- Limited liability partnerships
- Partnerships with a non individual partner during the basis period
- Lloyds underwriters
- Farming businesses with a herd basis election in effect for the tax year
- Farming and creative businesses with a profits averaging election in effect for the tax year
- Businesses that have claimed business premises renovation allowances within the previous seven years (ending immediately before the basis period)
- Businesses that carry on a mineral extraction trade during the basis period for the tax year
- Businesses that still own an asset in respect of which research and development allowances have been claimed (at any time)

[¶2-020] Trade profits: deductions allowable at a fixed rate

(ITTOIA 2005, Pt. 2, Ch. 5A)

(Tax Reporter: ¶208-380)

From April 2013 (with effect for the tax year 2013–14 and subsequent tax years), unincorporated businesses will be entitled to use flat rates to calculate certain types of expenses rather than having to calculate actual amounts.

Expense	From 6 April 2013
Expenditure on vehicles	
Car or goods vehicle	
– first 10,000 miles	£0.45/mile
– above 10,000 miles	£0.25/mile
Motorcycle	£0.24/mile
	Rate per Month £
Use of home for business[1]	
25–50 hours per month	10.00
51–100 hours per month	18.00
101 hours or more per month	26.00
Or claim allowable portion of actual costs	

Expense	From 6 April 2013
Premises used both as home and business premises[(2)]	
Disallowance (for personal element of expenses)	
1 occupant using premises as a home	350.00
2 occupants using premises as a home	500.00
3 or more occupants using premises as a home	650.00
Or identify allowable portion of actual costs	

Notes

[(1)] Deduction is given for each month or part of a month in relation to the number of hours spent wholly and exclusively on work done by the person in their home wholly and exclusively for the purposes of the trade (ITTOIA 2005, s. 94H).

[(2)] Available for premises which are mainly used for the purposes of carrying on the trade but also used by the person as a home. Instead of apportioning expenses between business and personal use, a deduction may be claimed for the full expense minus the relevant flat rate non-business use amount (ITTOIA 2005, s. 94I).

[¶2-030] Limited liability partnerships: salaried members

(ITTOIA 2005, s. 863A–863G)

(Tax Reporter: ¶292-650)

From 6 April 2014, an individual member (M) of an LLP will be treated as an employee for tax purposes (subject to PAYE and to tax on any benefits in kind) if all of the three conditions set out below are met. The rules apply only to LLPs formed under the *Limited Liability Partnership Act* 2000, not to general partnerships or limited partnerships that are formed under the *Partnership Act* 1890 and the *Limited Parternship Act* 1907, respectively.

Condition	Requirements for condition to be satisfied
Condition A: Disguised salary	Arrangements are in place under which: • M is to perform services for the LLP; and • It is reasonable to expect that at least 80% of the total amount payable by the LLP in respect of M's performance of those services will be 'disguised salary' (i.e. fixed, or variable but without reference to the overall amount of the profits or losses of the LLP; or not in practice affected by the overall profits or losses of the LLP).
Condition B: Significant influence	If the mutual rights and duties of the members and the LLP do not give M significant influence over the affairs of the partnership.
Condition C: Capital contribution	M's contribution to the LLP is less than 25% of the disguised salary which it is reasonable to expect will be payable in a relevant tax year in respect of M's performance of services for the partnership.

[¶2-050] Car hire: leases starting from 6 April 2009

(ITTOIA 2005, s. 48ff.)

(Tax Reporter: ¶212-025)

Leased cars, where the lease begins from 6 April 2009 (for income tax purposes), suffer a 15% disallowance of relevant payments if CO_2 emissions exceed the limits set out below, otherwise no disallowance. This applies to all cars (not just those costing more than £12,000).

	CO_2 emissions
From 6 April 2013	Over 130g/km
6 April 2009 to 5 April 2013	Over 160g/km

[¶2-060] Car hire: leases starting before 6 April 2009

(ITTOIA 2005, s. 48ff.)

(Tax Reporter: ¶212-050)

For leased cars where the lease began before 6 April 2009, the restricted deduction for hire charges of motor cars with a retail price greater than £12,000 is calculated as follows:

$$\text{Allowable amount} = \frac{\pounds 12{,}000 + \tfrac{1}{2}\,(\text{retail price} - \pounds 12{,}000)}{\text{retail price}} \times \text{hire charge}$$

[¶2-100] Time limits for elections and claims

(TMA 1970, s. 43(1))

(Tax Reporter: ¶191-635)

In the absence of any provision to the contrary, under self-assessment for the purposes of income tax, the normal rule is that claims are to be made within four years from the end of the tax year to which they relate. Before 1 April 2010, the time limit was generally five years from 31 January following the end of the tax year.

Other specific income tax provisions are as below.

Provision	Time limit	Statutory reference
Averaging of profits of farmers or creative artists	first anniversary of the normal self-assessment filing date for the second tax year	ITTOIA 2005, s. 222
Stock transferred to a connected party on cessation of trade (or, from April 2009, profession or vocation) to be valued at higher of cost or sale price	first anniversary of the normal self-assessment filing date for the tax year of cessation	ITTOIA 2005, s. 178
Post-cessation expenses relieved against income and chargeable gains	first anniversary of the normal self-assessment filing date for the tax year	ITTOIA 2005, s. 257(4); ITA 2007, s. 96
Current and preceding year set-off of trading losses	first anniversary of the normal self-assessment filing date for the loss-making year	ITA 2007, s. 64
Three-year carry-back of trading losses in first four years of trade	first anniversary of the normal self-assessment filing date for the tax year in which the loss is made	ITA 2007, s. 72
Carry-forward of trading losses	normal rules apply (see above)	ITA 2007, s. 83ff.
Carry-back of terminal losses	normal rules apply (see above)	ITA 2007, s. 89

TAXATION OF INVESTMENT INCOME

[¶3-000] Registered pension schemes

(FA 2004, Pt. 4, Ch. 1 to 7 and Sch. 28 to 36; SI 2014/1843)

From 6 April 2006, ('A' day) a new simplified set of rules apply to all forms of pension provision.

Individuals may obtain tax relief on any contributions made to a registered pension scheme, up to 100% of their relevant UK earnings for a tax year, or £3,600 per year if their relevant UK earnings are less than this amount. Employer's contributions do not count towards an individual's contributions. Greater amounts than these limits may be contributed to a registered scheme, without the benefit of tax relief for the individual, but see below for the effects on the scheme and individual. The normal minimum pension age is 55 from 6 April 2010 (previously 50) except for retirement on ill-health grounds and some preserved, lower retirment ages; see below. From 2011–12 onwards, there is no minimum benefit age. Previously benefits had to be taken by the age of 77 at the latest (age 75 before 22 June 2010).

Recent and forthcoming changes

- From April 2015, replacing the existing 55% tax charge on death:
  - beneficiaries of individuals who die under the age of 75 with a joint life or guaranteed term annuity will be able to receive any future payments from such policies tax free. The tax rules will also be changed to allow joint life annuities to be passed on to any beneficiary;

  (Autumn Statement 2014)
  - individuals with a drawdown arrangement or with uncrystallised pension funds will be able to nominate a beneficiary to pass their pension to if they die before the age of 75. The person receiving the pension will pay no tax on the money they withdraw (whether as a lump sum or through drawdown);
  - individuals who die with a drawdown arrangement or with uncrystallised pension funds at or over the age of 75 will also be able to nominate a beneficiary to pass their pension to, who will be able to access the pension funds flexibly, at any age, and pay tax at their marginal rate of income tax. There will be no restrictions on how much the beneficiary can withdraw at any one time and there will also be an option to receive the pension as a lump sum payment, subject to a tax charge of 45%.

  (Chancellor announcement 29 September 2014)
- From April 2015, changes to pension tax rules to give individuals aged 55 and over greater flexibility to access their pension savings. In particular, to:
  - allow all of the funds in a money purchase arrangement to be taken as an authorised taxed lump sum, removing the higher unauthorised payment tax charges;
  - increase the flexibility of the income drawdown rules by removing the maximum 'cap' on withdrawal and minimum income requirements for all new drawdown funds from 6 April 2015;

- enable those with 'capped' drawdown to convert to a new drawdown fund once arranged with their scheme should they wish;
- enable pension schemes to make payments directly from pension savings with 25% taken tax-free (instead of a tax-free lump sum);
- introduce a limited right for scheme trustees and managers to override their scheme's rules to pay flexible pensions from money purchase pension savings;
- remove some restrictions on lifetime annuity payments;
- ensure that individuals do not exploit the new system to gain unintended tax advantages by introducing a reduced annual allowance of £10,000 for money purchase savings where the individual has flexibly accessed their savings;
- increase the maximum value and scope of trivial commutation lump sum death benefits;
- provide new information requirements to ensure that individuals who have flexibly accessed their pension savings are aware of the tax consequences of doing so;
- reduce certain tax charges that apply to death benefits; and
- make changes to the rules for UK individuals who receive UK tax relief for contributions to non-UK pension schemes, so that the flexibilities and restrictions to relief will apply equally to them.

(Draft Taxation of Pensions Bill 2014–15)

- Legislation in Finance Bill 2015 to give equivalent treatment to Qualifying non-UK pension schemes and to UK-registered pension schemes (Budget 2014);
- Legislation in *Finance Act* 2014 gives HMRC powers to tackle pension liberations schemes; and
- From 27 March 2014:
  - the minimum income requirement for accessing flexible drawdown is reduced from £20,000 to £12,000;
  - the capped drawdown limit is increased from 120% to 150% of the amount of an equivalent annuity;
  - the trivial commutation lump sum limit is increased from £18,000 to £30,000; and
  - the small pots limit is increased from £2,000 to £10,000 and the number of small personal pension pots that can be taken as a lump sum is increased from two to three.

Annual and lifetime allowances

(Tax Reporter: ¶386-000 and ¶384-000)

There are annual and lifetime limits on the value of contributions made to a registered scheme. Tax charges will be applied where these limits are exceeded.

Year	Annual allowance(1)(7)	Annual allowance charge(2)	Lifetime allowance(3)(5)(6)(7)	Lifetime allowance charge(4)
2014–15	£40,000	the 'appropriate rate' on any annual increase in pension scheme value in excess of limit	£1.25m	25% on excess if taken as pension; 55% on excess if taken as a lump sum

Year	Annual allowance[1][7]	Annual allowance charge[2]	Lifetime allowance[3][5][6][7]	Lifetime allowance charge[4]
2013–14 and 2012–13	£50,000	the 'appropriate rate' on any annual increase in pension scheme value in excess of limit	£1.5m	25% on excess if taken as pension; 55% on excess if taken as a lump sum
2011–12	£50,000	the 'appropriate rate' on any annual increase in pension scheme value in excess of limit	£1.80m	25% on excess if taken as pension; 55% on excess if taken as a lump sum
2010–11	£255,000	40% on any annual increase in pension scheme value in excess of limit	£1.80m	25% on excess if taken as pension; 55% on excess if taken as a lump sum
2009–10	£245,000	40% on any annual increase in pension scheme value in excess of limit	£1.75m	25% on excess if taken as pension; 55% on excess if taken as a lump sum
2008–09	£235,000	40% on any annual increase in pension scheme value in excess of limit	£1.65m	25% on excess if taken as pension; 55% on excess if taken as a lump sum

Notes

(1) An individual's annual allowance (AA) applies to all of that individual's pension arrangements for a year. It measures the 'pension input amount' for a tax year. That is the increase in the pension savings in that tax year (including contributions made by the individual and employer); and/or the increase in the value of the individual's pension rights (depending on the type of scheme, i.e. money purchase, defined benefit, etc.). If the 'pension input amount' for a year exceeds the AA for that year, the excess is subject to the charge. For future years the AA will be fixed by Treasury Order.

(2) An AA charge is the liability of the individual member of the scheme (or schemes where an individual is a member of more than one scheme), but provisions introduced from 6 April 2011 enable the member to transfer that liability onto the scheme administrator in certain circumstances (Tax Reporter: ¶386-010; FA 2004, s. 227 to 238). From 2011–12 onwards, the rate of tax to be charged on the excess is to be the 'appropriate rate'; that is, the rate or rates which would be charged on the excess if it was to be added to the individual's 'reduced net income' for the tax year concerned. That figure is the sum calculated at Step 3 of the prescribed method of calculating income tax liabilities. Any increase in the basic rate or higher rate bands due to pension contributions made under deduction of tax or gift aid payments is also taken into account for this purpose.

(3) An individual's lifetime allowance (LTA) is a measure of the total value of an individual's pension savings at the time that pension benefits begin to be taken. For future years the LTA will be fixed by Treasury Order.

(4) An LTA charge (55% on any excess over the LTA constituting a lump sum payment; and 25% on any excess over the LTA not used to pay a lump sum but to fund pension payments) is the joint and several liability of the individual and the pension scheme administrator (Tax Reporter: ¶384-050; FA 2004, s. 214 to 226).

(5) *Finance Act* 2013, Sch. 22 provides a transitional protection regime (fixed protection 2014) for individuals with UK tax relieved pension rights of more than £1.25m (or who anticipate rights of £1.25m by the time they take their pension benefits) who notify HMRC by 5 April 2014 (conditions apply). Fixed protection will entitle relevant individuals to a lifetime allowance of the greater of £1.5m and the standard lifetime allowance. Where an individual dies before 6 April 2014 but a relevant lump sum death benefit is paid on or after 6 april 2014, the relevant lump sum death benefit will be tested against the standard lifetime allowance at the time of the individual's death.

(6) *Finance Act* 2014 introduces a new transitional protection regime, individual protection 2014 ('IP14') which entitles individuals who have pension savings on 5 April 2014 of greater than £1.25m and who do not have primary protection to a lifetime allowance equal to the value of those savings, subject to an overall limit of £1.5m. SI 2014/1842 sets out how an individual must give notice to HMRC if they intend to rely on IP14.

(7) Annual allowance and lifetime allowance to remain at £40,000 and £1.25m respectively in 2015–16 (Budget 2014).

Other charges

If unauthorised payments are made out of a registered pension scheme, the person receiving the payment(s) (i.e. the member, the employer or the recipient of any death benefits) is liable to a tax charge equal to 40% of the payment(s). A surcharge of 15%, in addition to the basic 40% charge, may be added to the unauthorised payment charge if a scheme pays out more than 25% of the scheme's fund in unauthorised payments (Tax Reporter: ¶383-500ff.; FA 2004, s. 208 to 213).

Where a registered scheme loses its registered status a 'deregistration charge' of 40% of the aggregate value of the pension scheme's assets is levied on and payable by the scheme administrator (Tax Reporter: ¶388-500; FA 2004, s. 242).

A tax charge arises where a registered pension scheme repays tax-relieved pension contributions to a member who has completed less than two years service ('short service refund lump sums'). The rate is 20% on the first £20,000 and 50% thereafter (Tax Reporter: ¶383-100; FA 2004, s. 205).

A charge also arises where a serious ill-health lump sum is paid on or after 6 April 2011 to a member over the age of 75. Tax is charged at the rate of 55%. Tax is also chargeable under this heading in respect of a lump sum paid to a 'relieved member' or a 'transfer member' of a 'relevant non-UK scheme' (Tax Reporter: ¶383-120; FA 2004, s. 205A).

A special lump sum death benefits charge arises where a pension protection lump sum death benefit, an annuity protection lump sum death benefit or a drawdown (previously, unsecured) pension fund lump sum death benefit is paid by a registered pension scheme. Tax is also chargeable under this heading in respect of a lump sum paid to a relieved member or a transfer member of a 'relevant non-UK scheme'. From 6 April 2011, the charge also applies to a defined benefits lump sum death benefit or an uncrystallised funds lump sum death benefit paid in respect of a member who dies having reached the age of 75. The rate of tax is 55% with effect from 6 April 2011 and was previously 35% (¶383-150; FA 2004, s. 206).

[¶3-150] Early retirement ages: retirement annuity contracts and personal pension schemes

From 6 April 2006

(FA 2004, Sch. 36, para. 23)

(Tax Reporter: ¶390-450)

Under the simplified pensions' rules applying from 6 April 2006 onwards early retirement ages (apart from on ill-health grounds) are eliminated for all new schemes. The 'normal minimum pension age' is 55. Where arrangements for pre-6 April 2006 schemes permit retirement earlier than 55 the 'normal minimum pension age' will be 50, with effect from 6 April 2006; rising to 55, with effect from 6 April 2010.

It is possible for members of pre-6 April 2006 schemes that permit retirement earlier than the 'normal minimum pension age' to preserve their rights to early retirement in some circumstances. Members of retirement annuity contracts or personal pension schemes will be able to protect their right to take pension and lump sum benefits before the 'normal minimum pension age' (i.e. before 50 until 6 April 2010) by establishing their 'unqualified right', as at 6 April 2006, to a protected pension age that is lower than the 'normal minimum pension age'.

In order to exercise the right to a lower than normal pension age the member must:

- be or have been in one of the occupations prescribed in the list at *Registered Pension Schemes (Prescribed Schemes and Occupations) Regulations* 2005 (SI 2005/3451), Sch. 2, prior to 6 April 2006; and
- have had an 'unqualified right' to take a pension before the age of 50, prior to 6 April 2006 (an 'unqualified right' is when the individual needs no other party to consent to their request to take an early pension before it becomes binding upon the scheme or contract holder).

The list below will continue to apply to retirement annuity contract holders and personal pension scheme members who are able to meet the conditions for a protected pension age lower than 50, as at 6 April 2006. All of the professions noted in the list below that have a retirement age of less than 50 are included in the list at SI 2005/3451, Sch. 2.

	Retirement age[1]	
Profession or occupation	**Retirement annuity contracts**	**Personal pension schemes**
Athletes (appearance and prize money)	35	35
Badminton Players	35	35
Boxers	35	35
Cricketers	40	40
Cyclists	35	35
Dancers	35	35
Divers (Saturation, Deep Sea and Free Swimming)	40	40
Footballers	35	35
Golfers (tournament earnings)	40	40
Ice hockey players	35	35
Jockeys – Flat Racing	45	45
– National Hunt	35	35
Members of the Reserve Forces	45	45
Models	35	35
Motorcycle Riders (Motocross or Road Racing)	40	40
Motor Racing Drivers	40	40
Rugby League Players	35	35
Rugby Union Players	35	35
Skiers (Downhill)	–	30
Snooker or billiards players	40	40
Speedway Riders	40	40
Squash Players	35	35
Table Tennis Players	35	35

Profession or occupation	Retirement age[1]	
	Retirement annuity contracts	Personal pension schemes
Tennis Players (including Real Tennis)	35	35
Trapeze Artistes	40	40
Wrestlers	35	35

Note

[1] The pension age shown applies only to pension arrangements funded by contributions paid in respect of the relevant earnings from the occupation or profession carrying that age.

If an individual wishes to make pension provisions in respect of another source of relevant earnings to which the pension age shown above does not apply then a separate arrangement, with a pension age within the normal range, must be made.

In particular, the ages shown above for professional sportsmen apply only to arrangements made in respect of relevant earnings from activities as professional sportsmen, e.g. tournament earnings, appearance and prize money. They do not apply to relevant earnings from sponsorship or coaching.

[¶3-175] Equalisation of and increase in pensionable ages for both men and women

For the purposes of social security legislation, an individual's pensionable age is determined by the following rules and tables. These gradually increase the pensionable age for women from the traditional age of 60 to bring it into line with that for men, while also increasing the ages for both sexes. Dates in the table below are grouped in one-month periods. A person born towards the end of one of these periods would have a slightly younger pension age than someone born at the beginning.

A man born before 6 December 1953 still attains pensionable age at age 65, while a woman born before 6 April 1950 attained pensionable age at age 60. The date the pensionable age is attained by individuals born after those dates is set out in the tables below. Table 1 relates to women born before 6 December 1953, while Table 2 relates to someone of either sex born on or after that date.

Autumn Statement 2013 announced that state pension age will increase to age 68 in the mid 2030s and to age 69 in the late 2040s.

Table 1: Women

Date of birth (by month)	State pension age *y.m*	Pensionable age attained
06/04/50 to 05/05/50	60.1 – 60.0	06/05/2010
06/05/50 to 05/06/50	60.2 – 60.1	06/07/2010
06/06/50 to 05/07/50	60.3 – 60.2	06/09/2010
06/07/50 to 05/08/50	60.4 – 60.3	06/11/2010
06/08/50 to 05/09/50	60.5 – 60.4	06/01/2011
06/09/50 to 05/10/50	60.6 – 60.5	06/03/2011
06/10/50 to 05/11/50	60.7 – 60.6	06/05/2011
06/11/50 to 05/12/50	60.8 – 60.7	06/07/2011
06/12/50 to 05/01/51	60.9 – 60.8	06/09/2011
06/01/51 to 05/02/51	60.10 – 60.9	06/11/2011

Date of birth (by month)	State pension age *y.m*	Pensionable age attained
06/02/51 to 05/03/51	60.11 – 60.10	06/01/2012
06/03/51 to 05/04/51	61.0 – 60.11	06/03/2012
06/04/51 to 05/05/51	61.1 – 61.0	06/05/2012
06/05/51 to 05/06/51	61.2 – 61.1	06/07/2012
06/06/51 to 05/07/51	61.3 – 61.2	06/09/2012
06/07/51 to 05/08/51	61.4 – 61.3	06/11/2012
06/08/51 to 05/09/51	61.5 – 61.4	06/01/2013
06/09/51 to 05/10/51	61.6 – 61.5	06/03/2013
06/10/51 to 05/11/51	61.7 – 61.6	06/05/2013
06/11/51 to 05/12/51	61.8 – 61.7	06/07/2013
06/12/51 to 05/01/52	61.9 – 61.8	06/09/2013
06/01/52 to 05/02/52	61.10 – 61.9	06/11/2013
06/02/52 to 05/03/52	61.11 – 61.10	06/01/2014
06/03/52 to 05/04/52	62.0 – 61.11	06/03/2014
06/04/52 to 05/05/52	62.1 – 62.0	06/05/2014
06/05/52 to 05/06/52	62.2 – 62.1	06/07/2014
06/06/52 to 05/07/52	62.3 – 62.2	06/09/2014
06/07/52 to 05/08/52	62.4 – 62.3	06/11/2014
06/08/52 to 05/09/52	62.5 – 62.4	06/01/2015
06/09/52 to 05/10/52	62.6 – 62.5	06/03/2015
06/10/52 to 05/11/52	62.7 – 62.6	06/05/2015
06/11/52 to 05/12/52	62.8 – 62.7	06/07/2015
06/12/52 to 05/01/53	62.9 – 62.8	06/09/2015
06/01/53 to 05/02/53	62.10 – 62.9	06/11/2015
06/02/53 to 05/03/53	62.11 62.10	06/01/2016
06/03/53 to 05/04/53	63.0 – 62.11	06/03/2016
06/04/53 to 05/05/53	63.3 – 63.2	06/07/2016
06/05/53 to 05/06/53	63.6 – 63.5	06/11/2016
06/06/53 to 05/07/53	63.9 – 63.8	06/03/2017
06/07/53 to 05/08/53	64.0 – 63.11	06/07/2017
06/08/53 to 05/09/53	64.3 – 64.2	06/11/2017
06/09/53 to 05/10/53	64.6 – 64.5	06/03/2018
06/10/53 to 05/11/53	64.9 – 64.8	06/07/2018
06/11/53 to 05/12/53	65.0 – 64.11	06/11/2018

Table 2: Men and Women

Date of birth (by month)	State pension age[(1)] *y.m*	Pensionable age attained[(1)]
06/12/53 to 05/01/54	65.3–65.2	06/03/2019
06/01/54 to 05/02/54	65.4–65.3	06/05/2019
06/02/54 to 05/03/54	65.5–65.4	06/07/2019

Date of birth (by month)	State pension age[(1)] *y.m*	Pensionable age attained[(1)]
06/03/54 to 05/04/54	65.6–65.5	06/09/2019
06/04/54 to 05/05/54	65.7–65.6	06/11/2019
06/05/54 to 05/06/54	65.8–65.7	06/01/2020
06/06/54 to 05/07/54	65.9–65.8	06/03/2020
06/07/54 to 05/08/54	65.10–65.9	06/05/2020
06/08/54 to 05/09/54	65.11–65.10	06/07/2020
06/09/54 to 05/10/54	66.0–65.11	06/09/2020
06/10/54 to 05/04/60	Age 66	[06/10/2020–05/04/2026]
06/04/60 to 05/05/60	Age 66 years and 1 month	[06/05/2026–05/06/2026]
06/05/60 to 05/06/60	Age 66 years and 2 months	[06/07/2026–05/08/2026]
06/06/60 to 05/07/60	Age 66 years and 3 months	[06/09/2026–05/10/2026]
06/07/60[(2)] to 05/08/60	Age 66 years and 4 months	[06/11/2026–05/12/2026]
06/08/60 to 05/09/60	Age 66 years and 5 months	[06/01/2027–05/02/2027]
06/09/60 to 05/10/60	Age 66 years and 6 months	[06/03/2027–05/04/2027]
06/10/60 to 05/11/60	Age 66 years and 7 months	[06/05/2027–05/06/2027]
06/11/60 to 05/12/60	Age 66 years and 8 months	[06/07/2027–05/08/2027]
06/12/60[(3)] to 05/01/61	Age 66 years and 9 months	[06/09/2027–05/10/2027]
06/01/61[(4)] to 05/02/61	Age 66 years and 10 months	[06/11/2027–05/12/2027]
06/02/61 to 05/03/61	Age 66 years and 11 months	[06/01/2028–05/02/2028]
06/03/61 to 06/04/77	Age 67	[06/03/2028–06/04/2044]
06/04/77 to 05/05/77	67.1–67.0	06/05/2044
06/05/77 to 05/06/77	67.2–67.1	06/07/2044
06/06/77 to 05/07/77	67.3–67.2	06/09/2044
06/07/77 to 05/08/77	67.4–67.3	06/11/2044
06/08/77 to 05/09/77	67.5–67.4	06/01/2045
06/09/77 to 05/10/77	67.6–67.5	06/03/2045
06/10/77 to 05/11/77	67.7–67.6	06/05/2045
06/11/77 to 05/12/77	67.8–67.7	06/07/2045
06/12/77 to 05/01/78	67.9–67.8	06/09/2045
06/01/78 to 05/02/78	67.10–67.9	06/11/2045
06/02/78 to 05/03/78	67.11–67.10	06/01/2046
06/03/78 to 05/04/78	68.00–67.11	06/03/2046
On or after 06/04/78	Age 68	[On or after 06/04/2046]

Notes

(1) Individuals born between 06/04/54 and 06/04/77 and those born on or after 06/04/78 attain state pension age at the age shown in column 2 (with figures in square brackets in column 3 being calculated date ranges). Otherwise, individuals attain state pension age at the date shown in column 3.

(2) A person born on 31 July 1960 is to be taken to attain the age of 66 years and four months at the commencement of 30 November 2026.

(3) A person born on 31 December 1960 is to be taken to attain the age of 66 years and nine months at the commencement of 30 September 2027.

(4) A person born on 31 January 1961 is to be taken to attain the age of 66 years and ten months at the commencement of 30 November 2027.

[¶3-200] State retirement pensions

	Weekly rates[1]		
	Single person[2] £	**Married couple wife not a contributor £**	**Age addition (over 80) each £**
From 7/4/14	113.10	180.90	0.25
8/4/13 to 6/4/14	110.15	176.15	0.25
9/4/12 to 7/4/13	107.45	171.85	0.25
11/4/11 to 8/4/12	102.15	163.35	0.25
5/4/10 to 10/4/11	97.65	156.15	0.25
7/4/09 to 4/4/10	95.25	152.30	0.25
7/4/08 to 6/4/09	90.70	145.05	0.25

Note

(1) *Pensions Act* 2014 includes legislation which introduces a new Single Tier Pension from 6 April 2016. Individuals reaching pensionable age after the start date will no longer be entitled to the current two-component state pension (the basic state pension and additional state pension based on amounts of National Insurance contributions paid) but will instead be entitled to a single-component flat-rate pension. Basic conditions of entitlement at the full rate will be having attained pensionable age and having 35 or more 'qualifying years' of National Insurance contributions (based on the individuals earnings factor reaching the qualifying amount for the tax year). Entitlement will be subject to a minimum number of qualifying years (no more than ten) and pro-rated for individuals with fewer than 35 years. Transitional provisions will apply for individuals who have paid, or are treated as having paid, National Insurance contributions in respect of tax years before the introduction of the new state pension; for inheriting entitlement from a late spouse or civil partner who had made contributions prior to the introduction of the new state pension; for women who before 1977 elected to pay a reduced rate of National Insurance contributions, and for sharing a pension with a former spouse or civil partner upon divorce.

(2) From April 2015, the basic state pension will be increased by 2.5%; a cash increase of £2.85 per week for the full basic state pension (Autumn Statement 2014).

[¶3-300] Gilt-edged securities held by non-residents

(ITA 2007, s. 893–897; s. 10204; ITTOIA 2005, s. 713)

(Tax Reporter: ¶120-800)

Interest on all gilt-edged securities is payable gross. Interest may be paid net, if the holder wishes, by notice to the Registrar of Government Stock. Payment gross does not of itself imply that the interest is exempt from tax.

All gilt-edged securities are automatically given FOTRA status (Free Of Tax for Residents Abroad), thereby guaranteeing exemption from tax for holders not resident in the UK. Where income tax has been deducted from such gilts, a repayment claim (on form R43) may be submitted to HM Revenue & Customs, Saxon House, 1 Causeway Lane, Leicester, England, LE1 4AA.

[¶3-350] Individual savings accounts (ISAs)

(ITTOIA 2005, s. 694–701; SI 1998/1870; SI 2004/1450)
(Tax Reporter: ¶315-000)

	2015–16[7][8]	2014–15[8]		2013–14	2012–13	2011–12	2010–11
		1 July 2014 – 5 April 2015	6 April 2014 – 30 June 2014				
	£	£	£	£	£	£	£
'Adult' ISAs							
Maximum subscription limit	15,240	15,000	11,880	11,520	11,280	10,680	10,200
Cash limit	–[4]	–[4]	5,940	5,760	5,640	5,340	5,100
Junior ISAs/Child Trust Funds[5][6]							
Maximum subscription limit	4,080	4,000	3,840	3,720	3,600	3,600[5]	1,200

Notes

[1] To open an ISA an individual has to be aged 18 or over (or over the age of 16 for cash ISAs) and resident in the UK for tax purposes.

[2] All income and gains derived from investments within the account are tax free and withdrawals from the account will not attract any tax charge.

[3] From 6 April 2011, the ISA subscription limits have been increased in line with inflation. From 2012–13 onwards, the index used is the Consumer Prices Index ('CPI') (previously RPI).

[4] From 1 July 2014, the restriction that only 50% of the overall subscription limit may be invested in a cash ISA was removed. SI 1998/1870 was also amended to allow transfers to be made from a stocks and shares account to a cash account (SI 2014/1450).

[5] Children born between 1 September 2002 and 2 January 2011, living in the UK and in receipt of child benefit were eligible for a Child Trust Fund account. Child Trust Funds are now closed to new accounts but subscriptions can still be paid into existing accounts. Withdrawals are not permitted until the child has reached the age of 18, except in cases of terminal illness. The child Trust Fund subscription limit for 2011–12 was £1,200 to 30 October 2011 and increased to equal the Junior ISA subscription limit with effect from 1 November 2011.

[6] Junior ISAs became available form 1 November 2011 to any child under 18, living in the UK, who is not eligible for a Child Trust Fund account. Withdrawals are not permitted until the child has reached the age of 18, except in cases of terminal illness.

[7] Rates per Autumn Statement 2014.

[8] From 3 December 2014, if an ISA saver in a marriage or civil partnership dies, their spouse or civil partner will inherit their ISA tax advantages. From 6 April 2015, surviving spouses will be able to invest as much into their own ISA as their spouse used to have, on top of their usual allowance (Autumn Statement 2014).

[¶3-400] Enterprise investment scheme (EIS)

(ITA 2007, Pt. 5)

(Tax Reporter: ¶323-000ff.; ¶565-400ff.)

EIS relief is available for qualifying individuals who subscribe cash for the issue of qualifying shares issued by non-quoted trading companies (except those carrying on prohibited trades).

Qualifying EIS shares issued:	Maximum individual investment[3]	Rate of IT relief on investment	Disposal of qualifying EIS shares	Carry back of EIS relief to previous tax year[2]
2014–15, 2013–14 and 2012–13	£1,000,000 per annum	30%	Capital gains not chargeable, losses allowable[1]	Entire investment (subject to not exceeding £1,000,000 for the earlier year).
2011–12	£500,000 per annum	30%	Capital gains not chargeable, losses allowable[1]	Entire investment (subject to not exceeding £500,000 for the earlier year).
2009–10 and 2010–11	£500,000 per annum	20%	Capital gains not chargeable, losses allowable[1]	Entire investment (subject to not exceeding £500,000 for the earlier year).
2008–09	£500,000 per annum	20%	Capital gains not chargeable, losses allowable[1]	Lower of: (i) 50% of relief; and (ii) £50,000
2007–08 and 2006–07	£400,000 per annum	20%	Capital gains not chargeable, losses allowable[1]	Lower of: (i) 50% of relief; and (ii) £50,000
2005–06 and 2004–05	£200,000 per annum	20%	Capital gains not chargeable, losses allowable[1]	Lower of: (i) 50% of relief; and (ii) £25,000
1998–99 to 2003–04	£150,000 per annum	20%	Capital gains not chargeable, losses allowable[1]	Lower of: (i) 50% of relief; and (ii) £25,000

Notes

[1] The exemption from capital gains applies where EIS shares are held for more than three years from their issue. Losses are eligible for relief in the normal way but the base cost is treated as reduced by any EIS income tax relief which has been given and not withdrawn. A CGT deferral relief permits the postponement of a capital gain to be claimed where an investor subscribes for EIS shares within the period of one year prior to and three years after the gain accrues.

[2] Carry back of EIS relief was permitted for years to 2008–09, subject to the limits, where qualifying shares are subscribed for between 6 April and 5 October in a tax year. Those limits were removed for 2009–10 onwards.

[3] For an investment to qualify under EIS, the company must have raised no more than £5m (from 6 April 2012) under any or all EIS, VCT, SEIS (from 6 April 2012) or CVS (pre-1 April 2010) schemes in the 12 months ending on the date of the relevant investment. Between 17 July 2007 and 5 April 2012, the limit was £2m and prior to 17 July 2007 there was no limit.

[4] From 6 April 2015, companies benefiting substantially from subsidies for the generation of renewable energy will be excluded from also benefiting from EIS, SEIS and VCTs by legislation to be included in Finance Bill 2015 (Autumn Statement 2014).

[¶3-420] Seed enterprise investment scheme

(ITA 2007, Pt. 5A; TCGA 1992, Sch. 5BB)

(Tax Reporter: ¶319-000ff.; ¶568-500ff.)

SEIS relief is available to qualifying individuals who subscribe cash for the issue of qualifying shares in unquoted trading companies with fewer than 25 employees and assets of up to £200,000, carrying on or preparing to carry on new business.

Qualifying SEIS shares issued[4][5]:	Maximum individual investment[2]	Rate of IT relief on investment	Disposal of qualifying SEIS shares[1]	Carry back of SEIS relief to previous year	Capital gains reinvestment limit[3]
2014–15 and 2013–14	£100,000 per annum	50%	Capital gains not chargeable, losses allowable	Entire investment (subject to not exceeding £100,000 for the earlier year)	50% of qualifying SEIS expenditure
2012–13	£100,000 per annum	50%	Capital gains not chargeable, losses allowable	N/A	100% of qualifying SEIS expenditure

Notes

[1] The exemption from capital gains applies where SEIS shares are held for more than three years from their issue. Losses are eligible for relief in the normal way but the base cost is treated as reduced by any SEIS income tax relief which has been given and not withdrawn.

[2] For an investment to qualify under SEIS, the company must have raised no more than £150,000 and must not have raised any capital under EIS or VCT.

[3] The reinvestment exemption is available in respect of a gain arising on the disposal of any asset with so much of the gain that is matched with the relevant percentage of qualifying SEIS investment expenditure being exempt from CGT (subject to the £100,000 investment limit). The investment exemption was introduced initially for 2012–13 only, but extended by FA 2013 to 2013–14 and was made permanent by *Finance Act* 2014.

[4] *Finance Act* 2013 amended the control and independence requirement so as to prevent a company from being disqualified from SEIS where it is established by a corporate formation agent before sale to its ultimate owners, with effect in relation to shares issued on or after 6 April 2013.

[5] Initially due to end on 5 April 2017, *Finance Act* 2014 made the relief permanent.

[6] From 6 April 2015, companies benefiting substantially from subsidies for the generation of renewable energy will be excluded from also benefiting from EIS, SEIS and VCTs by legislation to be included in Finance Bill 2015 (Autumn Statement 2014).

[¶3-430] Social investment tax relief (SITR)

(ITA 2007, Pt. 5B; TCGA 1992, s. 255A–255E, Sch. 8B)

(Tax Reporter: ¶322-000ff. and ¶569-300ff.)

Social investment tax relief is available to individual investors who invest in cash in new shares or new qualifying debt investments in qualifying social enterprises (an unquoted community interest company, community benefit society or charity with fewer than 500 full-time equivalent employees) or after 6 April 2014. Relief is not available on any investment in respect of which the investor has obtained relief under the Enterprise Investment Scheme, the Seed Enterprise Investment Scheme or the Community Investment Tax Relief Scheme.

Qualifying investment made:	Maximum individual investment[(3)(4)]	Rate of IT on investment	Disposal of qualifying investment[(1)]	Carry back of SI relief to previous tax year
On or after 6 April 2014 and before 6 April 2019	£1,000,000 per annum	30%	Capital gains not chargeable, losses allowable[(2)]	From 2015–16, entire investment (subject to not exceeding £1m for the earlier year)

Notes

(1) The exemption from capital gains applies where an investment on which income tax relief has been received (and not subsequently withdrawn) is disposed of after it has been held for at least three years. If no claim to income tax relief is made, the investment will not qualify for exemption from capital gains tax. Losses are eligible for relief in the normal way but the base cost is treated as reduced by the amount of the SI relief attributable to the asset.

(2) A capital gains tax deferral relief enables a capital gain arising from the disposal of any asset in the period from 6 April 2014 to 5 April 2019 to be deferred where the gain is reinvested (within the period one year before to three years after the gain arising) in shares or debt investments which also qualify for SITR income tax relief. It is not, however, necessary for the investor to have made a claim for SITR income tax relief.

(3) For an investment to qualify under SI, the social enterprise must (including its subsidiaries if a parent company) have no more than £15m in gross assets immediately before the investment and £16m immediately after the investment. Additionally, the social enterprise is restricted as to the amount of money it may raise under SITR, as determined by the formula:

$$\left(\frac{€200{,}000 - M}{RCG + RSI}\right) - T$$

Where: T is the total of any earlier SITR investments made in the previous three years
M is the total of any other de minimis aid received in the previous three years by the social enterprise, or by a qualifying subsidiary
RCG is the highest rate of capital gains tax in the previous three years, and
RSI is the highest rate of SITR income tax relief in the previous three years.

(4) From 6 April 2015 (subject to EU state aids approval), annual investment limit to be increased to £5m per annum up to a total of £15m per organisation, and relief to be extended to small-scale community farms and horticultural activities (Autumn Statement 2014).

[¶3-450] Venture capital trusts (VCTs)

(ITA 2007, Pt. 6; TCGA 1992, s. 151A, 151B; ITTOIA 2005, s. 709)

(Tax Reporter: ¶326-000ff.)

A VCT is a specialised form of investment trust, which has been approved by the Board of HMRC on or since 6 April 1995. Certain tax advantages are obtained by individuals who subscribe for eligible shares issued by a qualifying VCT for the purposes of raising money.

Qualifying VCT Shares issued:	Maximum individual investment	Rate of IT relief on investment	Dividends paid by VCT	Disposal of shares in VCT	Minimum holding period
On or after 6 April 2006	£200,000 per annum	30%	Exempt from IT in hands of investor	Exempt from CGT	5 years
2005–06 and 2004–05	£200,000 per annum	40%	Exempt from IT in hands of investor	Exempt from CGT	3 years

Taxation of Investment Income

Qualifying VCT Shares issued:	Maximum individual investment	Rate of IT relief on investment	Dividends paid by VCT	Disposal of shares in VCT	Minimum holding period
2000–01 to 2003–04	£100,000 per annum	20%	Exempt from IT in hands of investor	Exempt from CGT	3 years

An investment in qualifying VCT shares, issued prior to 6 April 2004, was eligible for a CGT deferral relief that enabled an investor to postpone the incidence of a capital gain arising on the disposal of a chargeable asset.

To obtain and retain HMRC's approval, a VCT must satisfy a number of detailed conditions. The main ones are as follows:

- it must be a non-close company whose shares are quoted on the stock exchange;
- its income must be wholly or mainly derived from investments in shares or securities;
- at least 70% (by value) of its total investments must comprise of 'qualifying holdings' (broadly, shares and securities in unquoted trading companies except those carrying on prohibited trades; from 6 April 2007 cash held will be treated as an 'investment' for the purposes of the percentage limits);
- no holding in any company (other than a VCT or a company that would qualify as a VCT but for the listing condition) can represent more than 15% of the value of the VCT's investments;
- the gross assets of the companies in which the VCT has invested may not exceed £15m immediately before the issue of shares to the VCT and £16m immediately afterwards (from 19 July 2012, previously these limits were £7m and £8m respectively).

For an investment to qualify under VCT, the company must have raised no more than £5m (from 6 April 2012) under any or all EIS, VCT, SEIS (from 6 April 2012) or CVS (pre 1 April 2010) schemes in the 12 months ending on the date of the relevant investment (ITA 2007, s. 292A). Between 6 April 2007 and 5 April 2012, the limit was £2m (other than in respect of 'protected money' (as defined by FA 2007, Sch. 16, para. 6)) and prior to 6 April 2007 there was no limit.

From April 2014, investments that are conditionally linked in any way to a VCT share buy-back, or that have been made within six months of a disposal of shares in the same VCT, will not qualify for new tax relief (ITA 2007, s. 264A). *Finance Act* 2014 also includes legislation to enable investors to subscribe for shares in a VCT via a nominee (with effect from 17 July 2014) (ITA 2007, s. 330A) and to prevent VCTs returning capital subscribed by investors within three years from the end of the accounting period in which the shares were issued (from 6 April 2014) (ITA 2007, s. 281).

From 6 April 2015, companies benefiting substantially from subsidies for the generation of renewable energy will be excluded from also benefiting from EIS, SEIS and VCTs by legislation to be included in Finance Bill 2015 (Autumn Statement 2014).

[¶3-465] Community investment tax relief

(ITA 2007, Pt. 7; CTA 2010, Pt. 7)

(Tax Reporter: ¶325-000ff.)

Tax relief is claimed on an annual basis at the rate of 5% of the 'invested amount' for the tax year (or accounting period for a corporate investor) in which the investment date falls and the four subsequent tax years (or accounting periods). If the investment is by way of a loan, the 'invested amount' is not necessarily the amount of the loan made available at the beginning of the five-year investment period. The tax relief cannot reduce the taxpayer's tax liability below zero for any single tax year (or accounting period).

[¶3-500] Lease premiums

(ITTOIA 2005, s. 277 and CTA 2009, s. 217)

(Tax Reporter: ¶300-110 and ¶711-375)

Where a short-term lease, (i.e. one not exceeding 50 years in duration) is granted, a proportion of any premium charged on the grant is assessable as property business profits. The amount of the premium to be treated as rental income, received at the time of the grant, is given by a formula:

$$P \times \frac{50 - Y}{50} = TP$$

Where:

- 'P' is total premium paid;
- 'Y' is duration of lease in complete years (ignoring the first year). Only whole years are counted, part years are ignored; and
- 'TP' is the amount of the premium taxed on the landlord as if it were rent.

Amount taken into account in calculating a chargeable gain will be the balance of the premium (TCGA 1992, s. 240 and Sch. 8, para. 5 and 7) for which the restriction of allowable expenditure is applicable:

Length of lease in complete years	Premium % chargeable as gain	Premium % chargeable as rent
Over 50	100	0
50	98	2
49	96	4
48	94	6
47	92	8
46	90	10
45	88	12
44	86	14
43	84	16
42	82	18
41	80	20
40	78	22
39	76	24

Length of lease in complete years	Premium % chargeable as gain	Premium % chargeable as rent
38	74	26
37	72	28
36	70	30
35	68	32
34	66	34
33	64	36
32	62	38
31	60	40
30	58	42
29	56	44
28	54	46
27	52	48
26	50	50
25	48	52
24	46	54
23	44	56
22	42	58
21	40	60
20	38	62
19	36	64
18	34	66
17	32	68
16	30	70
15	28	72
14	26	74
13	24	76
12	22	78
11	20	80
10	18	82
9	16	84
8	14	86
7	12	88
6	10	90
5	8	92
4	6	94
3	4	96
2	2	98
1 or less	0	100

The following arrangements relating to short leases may also cause amounts to be treated as rent paid to the landlord:

- the tenant carrying out work on the rented premises;
- the commutation of rent for some other type of payment;
- the payment of a lump sum from the surrender of a lease;
- the payment of a lump sum for the variation or waiver of a lease's terms; and
- the assignment of a lease which has been previously granted at undervalue.

Premiums paid by instalment

Where an amount of a premium is received by instalments any income tax or corporation tax due on the amount may be paid by instalments, at the taxpayer's request and by agreement with HMRC. The tax instalment period may not exceed eight years and must end on or before the time that the final instalment of the premium is due (ITTOIA 2005, s. 299 for income tax; and CTA 2009, s. 236(1)–(3) for corporation tax).

Relief for premiums paid

Where a tenant occupies land, under a short lease, for the purposes of a trade, profession or vocation and has paid a premium in respect of the lease; an amount of lease premium paid is allowed as a deduction in computing the business profits (ITTOIA 2005, s. 60 for income tax; and CTA 2009, s. 62 for corporation tax). The amount of the premium taxed as rent in the hands of the landlord (see above) is treated as if it were daily rent paid by the tenant over the course of the lease. The effective deduction for an accounting or basis period is therefore:

$$\frac{\text{TP}}{\text{Lease duration in days}} \times \text{No. of days in accounting or basis period} = \text{DRP}$$

Where:

- 'TP' is the amount of the premium taxed on the landlord as if it were rent; and
- 'DRP' is the amount of the deemed rent paid by the tenant.

Relief is also available, in respect of premiums paid, for the computation of property business profits where an intermediate landlord has paid a premium to the superior landlord for premises that are in turn sub-let to a tenant.

[¶3-550] Settlements on children

(ITTOIA 2005, s. 629(3))

(Tax Reporter: ¶356-300)

Income paid to or for the benefit of a minor child arising from capital provided by a parent is not treated as parents' income if it does not exceed £100 per tax year.

[¶3-700] Time limits for elections and claims

In the absence of any provision to the contrary, for the purposes of income tax, the normal rule is that claims are to be made within four years from the end of the tax year to which they relate. Before 1 April 2010, the time limit was generally five years from 31 January next following the end of the tax year (TMA 1970, s. 43(1)).

In certain cases, HMRC *may* permit an extension of the strict time limit in relation to certain elections and claims.

Provision	Time limit	Statutory reference
Averaging election for furnished holiday accommodation	12 months from 31 January following year to which claim applies	ITTOIA 2005, s. 326 (Tax Reporter: ¶303-170)
Set-off of property business loss against income of current or next year	12 months from 31 January following year of set-off	ITA 2007, s. 124 (Tax Reporter: ¶300-090)
Property business post-cessation relief	12 months from 31 January following year in which deduction to be made	ITA 2007, s. 125 (Tax Reporter: ¶300-095)
Set-off of loss on disposal of shares in unquoted trading company against income	12 months from 31 January following year in which loss arose	ITA 2007, s. 132 (Tax Reporter: ¶330-000ff.)
EIS, SEIS and SI relief	five years from 31 January following tax year in which shares are issued (or previous tax year in relation to carry back claims)	ITA 2007, s. 202, 257EA and 257P (Tax Reporter: ¶323-120, ¶319-120)

TAXATION OF EARNINGS

Company cars

[¶4-000] Car benefits 2014–15

(ITEPA 2003, s. 139)

(Tax Reporter: ¶415-050ff.)

The benefit is calculated as a percentage of the list price of the car appropriate to the level of the car's CO_2 emissions. The 'appropriate percentage' depends upon whether the car was first registered on or after 1st January 1998 and whether it has a CO_2 emissions figure or is a diesel car. Relevant percentages are set out below:

For cars registered on or after 1 January 1998 (with CO_2 emissions figures)

CO_2 emissions	2013–14 & 2012–13	2014–15	2015–16[3]	2016–17[4]	2017–18[5]	2018–19[5]
50g/km or below[2]	5%[2]	5%[2]	5%	7%	9%	13%
51–75g/km			9%	11%	13%	16%
Above 75g/km up to relevant threshold	10%	11%	13%	15%	17%	19%
Equal to relevant threshold[1]	11%	12%	14%	16%	18%	20%
Above relevant threshold[1]	Increase 1% for each 5g/km[1] above relevant threshold up to 35%	Increase 1% for each 5g/km[1] above relevant threshold up to 35%	Increase 1% for each 5g/km[1] above relevant threshold up to 37%	Increase 1% for each 5g/km[1] above relevant threshold up to 37%	Increase 1% for each 5g/km[1] above relevant threshold up to 37%	Increase 1% for each 5g/km[1] above relevant threshold up to 37%
Diesel supplement[6]	3%	3%	3%	N/A	N/A	N/A

The relevant threshold is as follows:

Year	Relevant threshold
2014–15	95g/km
2013–14	95g/km
2012–13	100g/km

Notes

[1] Where CO_2 emissions are not a multiple of five, round down to the nearest multiple of five.

[2] If a car cannot emit CO_2 by being driven, the appropriate percentage is 0% until 5 April 2015 (when the five year exemption for zero carbon cars ends).

[3] *Finance Act* 2013 introduced two new percentage bands from 2015–16 for cars emitting 50g CO_2 per km or less and for cars emitting between 51–75g CO_2 per km, with the appropriate percentages set at 5% and 9%

respectively. *Finance Act* 2013 also increases the appropriate percentage for cars emitting more than 75g CO_2 per km by two percentage points up to a new maximum of 37%.

[4] In 2016–17, each band within the graduated table of bands will be increased by two percentage points, starting at 7% for cars emitting 0–50g CO_2/km up to a maximum of 37% for cars emitting 200g CO_2/km or more (*Finance Act* 2014).

[5] In 2017–18 and 2018–19, the appropriate percentage will increase by two percentage points for cars emitting more than 75g CO_2/km, to a maximum of 37%. In 2017–18, there will be a four percentage point differential between the 0–50 and 51–75g CO_2/km bands and between the 51–75 and 76–94g CO_2/km bands. In 2018–19, this differential will reduce to three percentage points (Budget 2014).

[6] All diesel cars are currently subject to a 3% addition (but subject to the absolute cap). The 3% diesel supplement is abolished from 2016–17 (*Finance Act* 2014).

Cars registered on or after 1 January 1998 without CO_2 emissions, or cars first registered before 1 January 1998

	2014–15 Registered		2015–16 Registered		2016–17
	on or after 01/01/1998	before 01/01/1998	on or after 01/01/1998	before 01/01/1998	
Cylinder capacity of car with internal combustion engine in cubic centimetres					
• 1,400 or less	15%	15%	15%	15%	16%
• more than 1,400 but not more than 2,000	25%	22%	25%	22%	27%
• more than 2,000	35%	32%	37%	32%	37%
Cars without an internal combustion engine					
• zero-emission cars registered on or after 1 January 1998	0%[1]	–	5%	–	7%
• any other case	35%	32%	37%	32%	37%
Diesel supplement[2]	3%	N/A	3%	N/A	N/A

Notes

[1] If emissions are zero when driven, the appropriate percentage is zero until 5 April 2015.

[2] All diesel cars registered on or after 1 January 1998 are currently subject to a 3% addition (but subject to the absolute cap). The 3% diesel supplement is abolished from 2016–17 (*Finance Act* 2014).

[¶4-002] Car benefits: table of percentages 2012–13 to 2018–19

Table of taxable percentages

(ITEPA 2003, s. 139)

(Tax Reporter: ¶415-720)

From 6 April 2012, new percentages will apply:

	Appropriate percentage						
CO_2 emissions	2012–13[1]	2013–14[1]	2014–15[1]	2015–16[1][2]	2016–17[3]	2017–18[4]	2018–19[4]
0	0	0	0	5	7	9	13
1–50	5	5	5				
51–75				9	11	13	16
76–94	10	10	11	13	15	17	19
95–99		11	12	14	16	18	20
100–104	11	12	13	15	17	19	21
105–109	12	13	14	16	18	20	22
110–114	13	14	15	17	19	21	23
115–119	14	15	16	18	20	22	24
120–124	15	16	17	19	21	23	25
125–129	16	17	18	20	22	24	26
130–134	17	18	19	21	23	25	27
135–139	18	19	20	22	24	26	28
140–144	19	20	21	23	25	27	29
145–149	20	21	22	24	26	28	30
150–154	21	22	23	25	27	29	31
155–159	22	23	24	26	28	30	32
160–164	23	24	25	27	29	31	33
165–169	24	25	26	28	30	32	34
170–174	25	26	27	29	31	33	35
175–179	26	27	28	30	32	34	36
180–184	27	28	29	31	33	35	37
185–189	28	29	30	32	34	36	
190–194	29	30	31	33	35	37	
195–199	30	31	32	34	36		
200–204	31	32	33	35	37		
205–209	32	33	34	36			
210–214	33	34	35	37			
215–219	34	35					
220+	35						

Notes

[1] All diesel cars are subject to a 3% loading, but not to take the maximum figure above 35% for years up to including 2014–15 and 37% for 2015–16. This addition is abolished from 2016–17 (*Finance Act* 2014).

[2] For 2015–16 and 2016–17 there will be an increase of two percentage points to a new absolute cap of 37%.

[3] In 2017–18 and 2018–19, the appropriate percentage will increase by two percentage points for cars emitting more than 75g CO_2/km to a maximum of 37% (Budget 2014).

[4] The differential between each of the bottom three CCT bands is set at four percentage points for 2015–16 to 2017–18. In 2018–19, this differential will reduce to three percentage points and in 2019–20 the differential will reduce further to two percentage points in line with the Budget 2013 announcement (Budget 2014).

[¶4-010] Car benefits: lower thresholds to 5 April 2012

(ITEPA 2003, s. 139)

(Tax Reporter: ¶415-050ff.)

The benefit is calculated on a percentage of the list price of the car appropriate to the level of the car's CO_2 emissions, as follows:

- 15% of the list price of cars emitting up to the lower threshold of emissions of carbon dioxide in grams per kilometre;
- increased by 1% per 5g/km over the lower threshold; but
- capped at 35% of the list price.

The lower thresholds are as follows:

Tax year	Lower threshold (in g/km)
2011–12	125
2010–11	130
2009–10	135
2008–09	135

If the exact CO_2 emissions figure does not end in 0 or 5, it should be rounded *down* to the nearest 5g/km before applying the above figures.

3% addition to the above percentages may apply for diesel cars: see ¶4-015.

From 6 April 2012, a new set of thresholds will apply: see ¶4-002.

[¶4-012] Car benefits: table of percentages to 5 April 2012

(ITEPA 2003, s. 139)

(Tax Reporter: ¶415-720ff.)

This table provides the 'appropriate percentage' figures for calculating the taxable benefit of a company car, based on CO_2 emissions figures for petrol cars, for periods to 5 April 2012. See ¶4-002 for later years.

CO_2 emissions[1]	2011–12 %	2010–11 %	2008–09 to 2009–10 %	2005–06 to 2007–08 %
120	[2]	[2]	[2]	
125	15	15	15	15
130	16	15	15	15
135	17	16	15	15
140	18	17	16	15
145	19	18	17	16
150	20	19	18	17
155	21	20	19	18
160	22	21	20	19
165	23	22	21	20

CO_2 emissions[(1)]	2011–12 %	2010–11 %	2008–09 to 2009–10 %	2005–06 to 2007–08 %
170	24	23	22	21
175	25	24	23	22
180	26	25	24	23
185	27	26	25	24
190	28	27	26	25
195	29	28	27	26
200	30	29	28	27
205	31	30	29	28
210	32	31	30	29
215	33	32	31	30
220	34	33	32	31
225	35	34	33	32
230	35	35	34	33
235	35	35	35	34
240	35	35	35	35
245	35	35	35	35
250	35	35	35	35
255	35	35	35	35

Notes

(1) The actual CO_2 emissions figure, if it is not a multiple of five, should be rounded down to the nearest multiple of five before applying this table, except that rounding does not apply to emissions of between 121 and 124g/km.

(2) Special rules apply to:

- diesel cars: see ¶4-015;
- qualifying low emissions cars (QUALECs): see ¶4-020;
- ultra-low emission cars: see ¶4-025; and
- cars using alternative fuels and technologies: see ¶4-030.

(3) From 6 April 2012, a new table applies: see ¶4-002.

[¶4-015] Diesel cars: loading of appropriate percentage

(ITEPA 2003, s. 141)

(Tax Reporter: ¶415-740)

Most diesel cars have an appropriate percentage that is three points higher than an equivalent petrol car (but still subject to a 35% overall cap). See ¶4-000ff. for details of the petrol figures.

The 3% diesel supplement is abolished from 6 April 2016.

Cars that do not meet the Euro IV emissions standard

These cars are subject to the three-point loading in all cases.

Cars that do meet the Euro IV emissions standard

The following table shows whether or not a 3% loading is needed for diesel cars meeting the Euro IV emissions standard:

Tax year	Car first registered by 31 December 2005	Car first registered from 1 January 2006
2011–12 to 5 April 2016	3% loading applies	3% loading applies
2006–07 to 2010–11	No loading	3% loading applies

[¶4-020] Qualifying low emissions cars

(Tax Reporter: ¶415-750)

The concept of a 'qualifying low emissions car' no longer applies after 5 April 2012.

From 6 April 2008 to 5 April 2012, a lower tax charge was made if the vehicle was a 'qualifying low emissions car' ('QUALEC') for the tax year in which it is provided as a company car.

A car is a QUALEC if its CO_2 emissions figure did not exceed 120g/km.

In such a case, the appropriate percentage will be 10% for petrol cars (but with a 3% penalty loading, so a figure of 13%, for most diesel cars).

A lower percentage applies to ultra-low emission cars from 6 April 2010 to 5 April 2015: see ¶4-025.

[¶4-025] Ultra-low emission cars

(ITEPA 2003, s. 139)

(Tax Reporter: ¶415-750)

A reduced appropriate percentage of 5% applies, from 6 April 2010 for five years, for company cars with an approved CO_2 emissions figure not exceeding 75g per kilometre. Diesel cars are still subject to the appropriate 3% loading until 5 April 2016: see ¶4-015.

From April 2015, the first-year exemption for ultra-low emission cars will come to an end and two new bands will be introduced for cars emitting 0–50g/km and 51–75g/km. The appropriate percentages will be 5% for cars emitting 0–50g/km in 2015–16, rising to 7% in 2016–17 and for cars emitting 51–75g/km, the rate will be 9% for 2015–16 and 11% for 2016–17.

[¶4-030] Zero emission cars

(ITEPA 2003, s. 140)

(Tax Reporter: ¶415-760ff.)

From 6 April 2010 to 5 April 2015, there is a zero tax charge for cars producing no emissions when driven (e.g. electric cars).

From 6 April 2015, the percentage for cars producing no emissions when driven (e.g. electric cars) will be 5%, rising to 7% for 2016–17.

Battery electric cars had an appropriate percentage of 9% from 6 April 2006 to 5 April 2010.

[¶4-035] Alternative fuel cars

(Tax Reporter: ¶415-760ff.)

The following discounts applied until 5 April 2011 but were then withdrawn.

Type of car	*Discounted charge*
Bi-fuel gas and petrol cars manufactured or converted before type approval	Appropriate percentage of list price, less 2% discount
Hybrid electric and petrol cars	Appropriate percentage of list price, less 3% discount
Cars capable of running on E85 fuel	Appropriate percentage of list price, less 2% discount. (But NB discount applies only from 6 April 2008)

Notes

The cost of conversion is ignored for bi-fuel gas and petrol cars converted after type approval, but no additional percentage discount is given.

These discounts are not available for QUALEC cars (see ¶4-020).

[¶4-040] Alternative fuel cars: periods to 5 April 2006

(Tax Reporter: ¶415-760ff.)

Type of car	*Discounted charge*
Battery electric cars	15% of list price, less 6% discount – i.e. 9% of list price.
Hybrid electric cars	Appropriate percentage of list price, less 2% discount and a further 1% discount for each full 20g/km that the CO_2 emissions figure is below the lower threshold.
Cars using liquid petroleum gas (LPG) or compressed natural gas (CNG)	
• Cars running on road fuel gas alone • Bi-fuel cars (both gas and petrol)	Appropriate percentage of list price, less 1% discount and a further 1% discount for each full 20g/km that the CO_2 emissions figure is below the lower threshold.
Cars first registered on or after 1 January 2000, and approved for running on both petrol and gas:	Appropriate percentage of list price applying to gas CO_2 emissions, less 1% discount and a further 1% discount for each full 20g/km that the CO_2 emissions figure is below the lower threshold.
Cars first registered before 1 January 2000, and petrol cars that are retro-fitted:	Appropriate percentage of list price applying to petrol CO_2 emissions, less 1% discount.

Fuel for company cars

[¶4-140] Fuel benefit charges

(ITEPA 2003, s. 150)

(Tax Reporter: ¶416-000ff.)

The additional taxable benefit of free fuel provided for a company car is calculated using the same CO_2 percentages as are used for calculating the company car charge.

The CO_2 percentage figure is applied to a fixed amount in accordance with the following table:

Tax year	£
2015–16	22,100[1]
2014–15	21,700
2013–14	21,100
2012–13	20,200
2011–12	18,800

Note

(1) Rate per Autumn Statement 2014.

The fuel benefit is reduced to nil if the employee is required to make good the full cost of all fuel provided for private use, and does so.

A proportionate reduction is made where the company car is only available for part of the year, where car fuel ceases to be provided part-way through the year, or where the benefit of the company car is shared.

[¶4-160] Fuel types from 6 April 2011

Employers must notify HMRC of the type of fuel (or other power) used by an employer provided car by entering the appropriate 'key letter' on the forms P11D and P46(Car). The key letters in use for P11D reporting and form P46(Car) in respect of periods post 6 April 2011 are as follows:

Key letter	Fuel or power type description
A	All other cars
D	Diesel (all Euro standards)
E	Zero emission cars (including electric cars)

[¶4-180] Advisory fuel rates for company cars: recent rates

(Tax Reporter: ¶416-040)

HMRC publish rates that can be used by employers wishing to pay their employees the cost of fuel for business journeys in company cars (or, where the employer initially pays for all fuel, for reimbursement of private mileage by company car drivers to their employers). Passenger payments may be made for company cars as for private cars (see ¶4-220). Petrol hybrid cars are treated as petrol cars for this purpose.

In a change of policy announced in May 2011, HMRC now review the rates four times a year – on 1 March, 1 June, 1 September and 1 December. For one month from the date of change, employers may use either the previous or new current rates, as they choose.

Engine size	Cost per mile		
	Petrol	**Diesel**	**LPG**
Rates applying from 1 December 2014			
1400cc or less	13p	–	9p
1600cc or less	–	11p	–
1401cc to 2000cc	16p	–	11p
1601cc to 2000cc	–	13p	–
Over 2000cc	23p	16p	16p
Rates applying from 1 September 2014			
1400cc or less	14p	–	9p
1600cc or less	–	11p	–
1401cc to 2000cc	16p	–	11p
1601cc to 2000cc	–	13p	–
Over 2000cc	24p	17p	16p
Rates applying from 1 June 2014			
1400cc or less	14p	–	9p
1600cc or less	–	12p	–
1401cc to 2000cc	16p	–	11p
1601cc to 2000cc	–	14p	–
Over 2000cc	24p	17p	16p
Rates applying from 1 March 2014			
1400cc or less	14p	–	9p
1600cc or less	–	12p	–
1401cc to 2000cc	16p	–	11p
1601cc to 2000cc	–	14p	–
Over 2000cc	24p	17p	17p
Rates applying from 1 December 2013			
1400cc or less	14p	–	9p
1600cc or less	–	12p	–
1401cc to 2000cc	16p	–	11p
1601cc to 2000cc	–	14p	–
Over 2000cc	24p	17p	16p
Rates applying from 1 September 2013			
1400cc or less	15p	–	10p
1600cc or less	–	12p	–
1401cc to 2000cc	18p	–	11p
1601cc to 2000cc	–	15p	–
Over 2000cc	26p	18p	16p

Engine size	Cost per mile		
	Petrol	Diesel	LPG
Rates applying from 1 June 2013			
1400cc or less	15p	–	10p
1600cc or less	–	12p	–
1401cc to 2000cc	17p	–	12p
1601cc to 2000cc	–	14p	–
Over 2000cc	25p	18p	18p
Rates applying from 1 March 2013			
1400cc or less	15p	–	10p
1600cc or less	–	13p	–
1401cc to 2000cc	18p	–	12p
1601cc to 2000cc	–	15p	–
Over 2000cc	26p	18p	18p
Rates applying from 1 December 2012			
1400cc or less	15p	–	11p
1600cc or less	–	12p	–
1401cc to 2000cc	18p	–	13p
1601cc to 2000cc	–	15p	–
Over 2000cc	26p	18p	18p
Rates applying from 1 September 2012			
1400cc or less	15p	–	10p
1600cc or less	–	12p	–
1401cc to 2000cc	18p	–	13p
1601cc to 2000cc	–	15p	–
Over 2000cc	26p	18p	17p

Private vehicles

[¶4-200] Mileage allowance payments

(ITEPA 2003, s. 230)

(Tax Reporter: ¶432-100ff.)

Statutory rates are set for mileage allowance payments. An employer may, of course, reimburse business mileage driven in a privately-owned car at more or less than the statutory rates but any excess is taxable. Any shortfall is tax deductible and the employee may claim relief accordingly. The rates were last amended from 6 April 2011.

Kind of vehicle	Rate per mile from 6 April 2011	Rate per mile from 6 April 2002 to 5 April 2011
Car or van	45p for the first 10,000 miles 25p after that	40p for the first 10,000 miles 25p after that
Motorcycle	24p	24p
Cycle	20p	20p

[¶4-220] Passenger payments

(ITEPA 2003, s. 233)

(Tax Reporter: ¶432-150)

No liability to income tax arises in respect of an approved passenger payment made to an employee for a car or a van, whether the vehicle is privately owned or provided by the employer. The approved amount is 5p per passenger mile. This was extended in the March 2011 Budget to cover volunteer workers as well as employees.

Company vans

[¶4-300] Rules applying from April 2007

(ITEPA 2003, s. 114, 154–164)

(Tax Reporter: ¶416-200ff.)

	£
2015–16	3,150[1]
2014–15	3,090
2013–14 (from April 2007)	3,000

Note

(1) Rate per Autumn Statement 2014.

But nil if:

(1) the restricted private use conditions are met (available and used only for ordinary commuting and business travel);

(2) private use in the tax year is insignificant; or

(3) (for tax years 2010–11 to 2014–15) the van cannot produce any CO_2 emissions under any circumstances by being driven (e.g. an electric van).

Budget 2014 announced legislation will be introduced in Finance Bill 2015 to extend VBC support for zero-emission vans to 5 April 2020 on a tapered basis. In 2015–16, the VBC rate paid by zero-emission vans will be 20% of the rate paid by conventionally fuelled vans, followed by 40% in 2016–17, 60% in 2017–18, 80% in 2018–19 and 90% in 2019–20, with the rates equalised in 2020–21.

[¶4-345] Fuel for company vans

(ITEPA 2003, s. 160ff.)

(Tax Reporter: ¶416-200ff.)

Tax Year	£
2015–16	594[1]
2014–15	581
2013–14	564
2012–13	550

Tax Year	£
2011–12	550
2010–11	550
2009–10	500
2008–09	500
2007-08	500

Note
[1] Rate per Autumn Statement 2014.

But nil if:

(1) the restricted private use conditions are met (available and used only for ordinary commuting and business travel);

(2) private use in the tax year is insignificant; or

(3) (for tax years 2010–11 to 2014–15) the van cannot produce any CO_2 emissions by being driven.

There was no taxable benefit on the provision of fuel for private journeys in a company van before 6 April 2007.

Buses

[¶4-360] Bus services

(ITEPA 2003, s. 242 and 243)

(Tax Reporter: ¶432-600ff.)

An exemption applies to:

(1) works transport services, which must be a bus or minibus:
  (a) available to employees generally;
  (b) used mainly for qualifying journeys; and
  (c) used substantially by employees or their children;

(2) support for public bus services:
  (a) available to employees generally;
  (b) used for qualifying journeys by employees of one or more employers; and
  (c) either:
    (i) a local bus service; or
    (ii) the bus must be provided to other passengers on terms that are as favourable as the terms on which the bus is provided to employees.

Used cycles

[¶4-380] Used cycles: valuation table

(Tax Reporter: ¶419-090)

HMRC allow used cycles to be transferred to employees using disposal values as follows:

Age of cycle	Original price less than £500	Original price £500+
1 year	18%	25%
18 months	16%	21%
2 years	13%	17%
3 years	8%	12%
4 years	3%	7%
5 years	Negligible	2%
6 years & over	Negligible	Negligible

Beneficial loans

[¶4-390] Beneficial loans threshold

(ITEPA 2003, Pt. 3, Ch. 7; s. 180)

(Tax Reporter: ¶417-000ff.)

A taxable benefit may arise where an employee (or a relative of an employee) is provided with a loan either interest-free or at a favourable rate of interest. A tax charge does not arise where the amount outstanding on the loan does not exceed the threshold at all times during the year. Current and announced forthcoming thresholds are as follows:

Period	Threshold £
2014–15 and subsequent years	10,000
2013–14 and earlier years (post 6 April 1994)	5,000

Official rates of interest

[¶4-400] Official rate of interest

(ITEPA 2003, s. 181)

(Tax Reporter: ¶417-100)

The official rate of interest is used to calculate the cash equivalent of the benefit of an employment-related loan which is a taxable cheap loan. HMRC review the level of the official rate of interest on a quarterly basis but normally set a single rate in advance for the whole tax year in line with a commitment given in January 2000, that (following announcement of the rate for any given tax year) the official rate may be reduced but will not be increased in the light of interest rate changes generally.

Date	Rate %	SI No.
From 6 April 2014	3.25	SI 2014/496
From 6 April 2010 to 5 April 2014	4.00	SI 2010/415
From 1 March 2009 to 5 April 2010	4.75	SI 2009/199
From 6 April 2007 to 28 February 2009	6.25	SI 2007/684

The average official rates of interest are given at ¶4-405.

[¶4-405] Official rate of interest: average rates

(ITEPA 2003, s. 181)

(Tax Reporter: ¶417-100)

Official rates of interest are given at ¶4-400. Average official rates of interest, given below, should be used if the loan was outstanding throughout the tax year and the normal averaging method of calculation is being used.

Year	Average official rate %
2014–15	3.25
2013–14	4.00
2012–13	4.00
2011–12	4.00
2010–11	4.00
2009–10	4.75
2008–09	6.10

[¶4-420] Official rate of interest: foreign currency loans

(ITEPA 2003, s. 181)

(Tax Reporter: ¶418-100)

The official rate of interest for certain employer-provided loans in Japanese yen or Swiss francs has been set as follows since 6 July 1994:

- Loans in Swiss francs: 5.5%.
- Loans in Japanese yen: 3.9%.

Travel and subsistence

[¶4-500] Day subsistence rates

(Tax Reporter: ¶457-560)

The following 'day subsistence' rates may be used when applying for a dispensation for payments to employees away from home for work purposes:

Rate	Detail	£
Breakfast rate	Irregular early starters	5
One meal rate	Away for at least five hours	5
Two meal rate	Away for at least ten hours	10
Late evening meal rate	Irregular late finishers	15

[¶4-520] Accommodation and subsistence – overseas rates

(Tax Reporter: ¶457-570)

In March 2008, HMRC published for the first time benchmark scale rates that employers were to be allowed to use when paying for accommodation and subsistence costs for employees working abroad. Payments up to these rates did not require receipts and did not need to be shown on form P11D.

Recent rates (as at the dates shown) are available as follows:.

From October 2014: www.gov.uk/government/uploads/system/uploads/attachment_data/file/359797/2014_Worldwide_subsistence_rates.pdf

From October 2013: www.gov.uk/government/uploads/system/uploads/attachment_data/file/348024/wwsr-bench-2013.pdf

[¶4-540] Incidental overnight expenses and benefits

(ITEPA 2003, s. 240)

(Tax Reporter: ¶432-900)

Benefits, reimbursements and expenses provided by an employer for employees' minor, personal expenditure whilst on business-related activities requiring overnight accommodation away from home are not taxable provided that the total amount reimbursed, etc. does not exceed the relevant maximum amount(s) per night, multiplied by the number of nights' absence. If the limit is exceeded, the whole amount provided remains taxable.

	Authorised maximum per night	
From	In UK £	Overseas £
6 April 1995	5	10

[¶4-550] Lorry drivers subsistence allowances

(ITEPA 2003, s. 337 and 338)

(Tax Reporter: ¶455-020 and ¶455-040)

A subsistence allowance paid to long distance lorry drivers will not be taxed provided the following two conditions are satisfied:

(1) there is documentary evidence available to show that the employee has spent the night away from home and away from his or her permanent workplace (if any) as a necessary result of a business journey and has incurred expenses in so doing;

(2) the amounts paid are no more than a reasonable reimbursement to cover the cost of accommodation and subsistence incurred as a result of the business journey.

HMRC accept the following amounts as reasonable for nights in the UK:

	Payment per night	
Year ended	Drivers with non-sleeper cabs £	Drivers with sleeper cabs[1] £
31 December 2014[2]	34.90	26.20
31 December 2013	34.90	26.20

Notes

[1] The mere fact that a lorry has a sleeper cab does not prevent the employer paying an amount tax free up to the limit shown for drivers with non-sleeper cabs (or locally agreed limits) provided that the employer is satisfied that the driver did incur expenses on overnight accommodation (for example by staying in a hotel) and meals. HMRC accept that a payment of 75% of the figure shown for drivers with non-sleeper cabs does no more than reimburse the expense incurred when the driver uses the sleeper cab overnight.

[2] In April 2014, HMRC announced that the overnight subsistence allowance rate would remain unchanged at £26.20 for drivers with sleeper cabs and £34.90 for drivers with non-sleeper cabs.

Shares and share incentives

[¶4-600] Share incentive plans

(ITEPA 2003, s. 488ff., Sch. 2; TCGA 1992, s. 236A, 238A, Sch. 7C, 7D, Pt. 1)

(Tax Reporter: ¶468-000ff.)

	Free shares	**Partnership shares**	**Matching shares**	**Dividend shares**
Employment before eligibility[(1)]	Up to 18 months employment	Up to 18 months employment[(4)] where no accumulation period, up to six months with accumulation period	Only awarded to employees who buy partnership shares	Must be acquired with dividends from plan shares
Limits	Up to £3,600 per tax year from 6 April 2014 (previously £3,000 per tax year)	Up to £1,800 per tax year from 6 April 2014 (previously £1,500 per tax year) or 10% of salary, if less.	Up to two matching shares for each partnership share bought	Dividends from shares in the plan reinvested: – no limit from 2013–14 (previously £1,500 per tax year)[(6)]
Minimum amount if stated[(1)]	–	£10 per month	–	–
Performance measures[(1)]	Yes	No	No	No
Holding period	At least three years from award[(2)]	None	At least three years from award[(2)]	three years from acquisition
Forfeiture on cessation of employment[(1)]	Yes[(5)]	No	Yes[(5)]	No
Tax on award	None	None – tax relief for salary used to buy shares	None	None

	Free shares	Partnership shares	Matching shares	Dividend shares
Tax on removal of shares from plan within three years of award[3]	On market value when taken out	On market value when taken out	On market value when taken out	Original dividend taxable but in year when shares taken out of plan.
Tax on removal between three and five years of award[2]	On lower of: – value at award; and – value on removal	On lower of: – salary used to buy shares; and – value on removal	On lower of: – value at award; and – value on removal	None
Tax on removal after five years	None	None	None	None
CGT on removal – any time	None	None	None	None

Notes

(1) These conditions can be included at the option of the company.

(2) The holding period may be up to five years at the option of the company.

(3) PAYE and NICs will be operated in relation to any income tax charge where the shares are readily convertible assets.

(4) Maximum accumulation period for partnership shares is 12 months.

(5) Restrictions apply to provisions for forfeiture that may be applied including a maximum forfeiture period of up to three years from award, that forfeiture provisions cannot relate to cesation of employment through injury, disability, redundancy, TUPE transfers, changes of control, retirement (at normal age), death, or be linked to the performence of any person.

(6) *Finance Act* 2013 removes the £1,500 per annum limit on reinvestment of cash dividends paid on SIP shares in 'dividend shares' held under SIP from 2013–14 onwards. Additionally, the requirement that reinvestment of dividends must take place within three years is also abolished with effect in relation to amounts held by trustees on or after 6 April 2013 (including amounts originally retained before that date).

(7) *Finance Act* 2013 includes provisions to simplify employee share scheme rules with effect from 17 July 2013. Main SIP changes are as follows:

- removal of requirement for a SIP scheme to include a 'specified retirement age';
- no income tax liability where shares are withdrawn from a SIP on certain cash takeovers of companies;
- present rules for SIPs that prevent participation by employees holding a 'material interest' in the company are abolished;
- removal of present prohibitions under SIP on the use of certain restricted shares;
- amending rules on allocation of SIP Partnership shares where employees purchase shares by deduction from salary over an 'accumulation period'; and
- repealing the provision in SIP legislation concerning the acquisition by SIP trustees of shares from qualifying employee share ownership trusts.

(8) From 6 April 2014, SIPs are self-certified by employers rather than approved by HMRC (*Finance Act* 2014).

[¶4-610] Company share option plan

(ITEPA 2003, s. 521–526, Sch. 4; TCGA 1992, s. 238A, Sch. 7D, Pt. 3)

(Tax Reporter: ¶467-000ff.)

Maximum options(1)(2)	£30,000

Notes

(1) This includes options granted under the scheme, or under any other approved CSOP scheme established by the scheme organiser or an associated company of the scheme organiser.

(2) The 'market value' of shares is calculated at the date of grant, or of each relevant option grant (if more than one grant); or if any agreement relating to any such shares has been made under ITEPA 2003, Sch. 4, para. 22, the earlier time or times stated in the agreement.

(3) *Finance Act* 2013 simplifies employee shares scheme rules with effect from 17 July 2013. Main CSOP changes are as follows:

- removal of requirement for a CSOP scheme to specify a retirement age in the scheme rules, where the rules provide for exercise of CSOP options on retirement;
- extension of circumstances in which favourable tax treatment is available where CSOP options are exercised before the third anniversary of the date of grant (to include TUPE transfers and group schemes were employer company ceases to be controlled by company organising the scheme);
- no income tax liability where CSOP option is exercised before third anniversary of grant on certain cash takeovers of constituent companies;
- where certain conditions are met a CSOP may allow for the exercise of share options in a company subject to a cash takeover under a general offer, within six months of the general offer;
- increase in limit for determining whether an individual has a material interest to 30% (from 25%); and
- removal of present prohibitions under CSOP on the use of certain restricted shares.

(4) From 6 April 2014, CSOP schemes are self-certified by the scheme organiser rather than approved by HMRC (*Finance Act* 2014).

[¶4-620] Enterprise management incentives (EMI)

(ITEPA 2003, s. 527–541, Sch. 5; TCGA 1992, s. 238A, Sch. 7D, Pt. 4)

(Tax Reporter: ¶466-000ff.)

Qualifying company	• Gross assets not exceeding £30m. • Fewer than 250 employees (full-time or equivalent), in relation to options granted from 21 July 2008.
Maximum options	£250,000 from 16 June 2012 (£120,000 between 6 April 2008 and 15 June 2012 and £100,000 prior to 6 April 2008).

Notes

(1) The above rule is qualified as follows:

(a) options held by the employee under a (HMRC-approved) Company Share Ownership Plan (CSOP), that are unexercised at the date of grant of an EMI option, are taken into account in applying the maximum figure above;

(b) by the 'three-year restriction period' rule; the grant of an option to an employee within three years from the most recent EMI option grant to him, cannot itself qualify as an EMI option if the value of the shares which were the subject of all previous EMI option grants, down to and including the most recent grant, amounted to £250,000 (or other applicable threshold figure in earlier periods). This applies whether or not any of such previously granted options have been exercised; and

(c) there is an overriding company limit; the total value (as defined) of shares in the company that are the subject of unexercised EMI options cannot exceed £3,000,000.

For purposes of (a) and (b) above, one takes into account all options granted by reason of the same employment, or employment by any member of the same group of companies.

(2) *Finance Act* 2013 simplifies employee share scheme rules with effect from 17 July 2013. The main EMI change is the extension to 90 days (from 40 days) of the time available for exercise of EMI options with favourable tax treatment following a disqualifying event.

[¶4-635] SAYE

(ITEPA 2003, s. 516–520, Sch. 3; TCGA 1992, s. 238A, Sch. 7D, Pt. 2)

(Tax Reporter: ¶470-000ff.)

Limits	Savings periods	Monthly contributions
Minimum	36 months	£5–10[1]
Maximum[2]	60 months	£500 (£250 before 6 April 2014)

Notes

[1] Company may impose a minimum monthly payment of up to £10 per month; otherwise the minimum is £5 per month.

[2] Seven-year savings feature abolished with effect from 23 July 2013.

[3] *Finance Act* 2013 simplifies employee share scheme rules with effect from 17 July 2013. Main SAYE changes are as follows:

- removal of requirement for an SAYE scheme to include a 'specified age' for retirement in the scheme rules, and repeal of the current provision allowing exercise of options by those who reach the 'specified age' without retiring;
- no income tax liability where an SAYE option is exercised before the third anniversary of grant on certain cash takeovers of companies;
- scheme rules to allow for exercise of SAYE options when employment ceases in relation to a TUPE transfer and in certain cases of companies ceasing to be associated with the company organising the scheme on a change of control;
- scheme rules may allow for the exercise of share options relating to shares in a company subject to a cash takeover under general offer, within six months of the general offer;
- removal of material interest requirement for determining whether an employee is eligible to participate in an SAYE option scheme; and
- removal of the present prohibition under SAYE on the use of certain restricted shares.

[4] From 6 April 2014, SAYE schemes are self-certified by the scheme organiser rather than approved by HMRC (*Finance Act* 2014).

[¶4-640] SAYE bonus rates: multiple of monthly payments

(ITEPA 2003, Sch. 3)

(Tax Reporter: ¶470-000ff.)

The bonus rate applicable to a scheme is set at the time the savings contract is entered into and is unaffected by any subsequent change to the rates. Current and historical rates are shown below. See ¶4-660 for details of the 'early leaver rate' applying for those who withdraw their funds after 12 monthly contributions, but before the three-year anniversary.

From	3-year	5-year	7-year[1]
28 July 2014	0.0	0.6	–
1 August 2012	0.0	0.0	0.0
23 September 2011	0.0	0.0	1.6
12 August 2011	0.0	0.9	3.5
27 February 2011	0.1	1.7	4.8
12 September 2010	0.0	0.9	3.2
14 May 2010	0.0	1.8	4.9

From	3-year	5-year	7-year[1]
29 May 2009	0.3	2.2	5.2
17 February 2009	0.6	2.6	5.6
27 December 2008	1.5	4.8	9.3
1 September 2008	2.4	7.0	12.7
4 April 2008	1.6	5.1	9.8
1 September 2007	2.4	7.2	13.3

Note

(1) The seven-year savings period of Save As You Earn (SAYE) Share Option Schemes was withdrawn with effect from 23 July 2013. Employees already saving under existing SAYE contracts before that date were not affected by the change.

[¶4-660] SAYE 'early leaver rates'

(ITEPA 2003, Sch. 3)

(Tax Reporter: ¶470-000ff.)

The following 'early leaver rates' have applied for employees whose SAYE contracts are cancelled after 12 monthly contributions but before the maturity date:

Dates	Rates %
28 July 2014	0.00
1 August 2012	0.00
23 September 2011	0.00
12 August 2011	0.00
27 February 2011	0.12
12 September 2010	0.00
14 May 2010	0.00
29 May 2009	0.36
17 February 2009	0.50
27 December 2008	2.00
1 September 2008	3.00
4 April 2008	2.00
1 September 2007	3.00

Note

The relevant date is that on which the employee starts saving under the contract, not the date on which the contract is cancelled.

[¶4-680] SAYE effective interest rates

(ITEPA 2003, Sch. 3)

(Tax Reporter: ¶470-000ff.)

From	3-year	5-year	7-year[1]
28 July 2014	0.00	0.39	–
1 August 2012	0.00	0.00	0.00

From	3-year	5-year	7-year[1]
23 September 2011	0.00	0.00	0.58
12 August 2011	0.00	0.59	1.25
27 February 2011	0.18	1.10	1.70
12 September 2010	0.00	0.59	1.15
14 May 2010	0.00	1.16	1.74
29 May 2009	0.54	1.42	1.84
17 February 2009	1.08	1.67	1.98
27 December 2008	2.67	3.04	3.20
1 September 2008	4.23	4.36	4.28
4 April 2008	2.84	3.22	3.36
1 September 2007	4.23	4.48	4.46

Note

[1] The seven-year savings period of Save As You Earn (SAYE) Share Option Schemes was withdrawn with effect from 23 July 2013. Employees already saving under existing SAYE contracts before that date were not affected by the change.

[¶4-690] Employee shareholder status

(ITEPA 2003, s. 226A–226D; TCGA 1992, s. 236B–236G)

(Tax Reporter: ¶471-500ff.; ¶565-050)

Employee shareholder is a new employment status, available from 1 September 2013 to new hire or existing employees. Employees accepting a position under an employee shareholder employment contract must be awarded at least £2,000 (market value) of fully paid up shares in their employer or parent company, at no cost to the employee. Employee shareholders retain the majority of employment rights (such as SSP, SMP, SPP, SAP, certain automatic unfair dismissal rights, TUPE rights, time off rights, NMW entitlement, etc.) but will give up unfair dismissal rights (apart from the exception), rights to statutory redundancy pay, the statutory right to request flexible working except in the two-week period after a return from parental leave and certain statutory rights to request time off to train. Additionally, an employee shareholder will have to give 16 weeks' notice to their employer if they intend to return early from maternity, additional paternity or adoption leave. The employer can, however, choose to offer contractual rights that are more generous than those provided for in statute.

	From 1 September 2013 £
Minimum value of share award (market value on acquisition)	2,000
Income tax and NIC exemption[1] (market value on acquisition)	2,000

	From 1 September 2013 £
Capital gains tax exemption[(2)] (market value on acquisition)	50,000

Notes

(1) Employee is treated as having made a payment of £2,000 for the acquisition of shares and accordingly; any excess (of market value) over £2,000 is treated as earnings from the employment subject to income tax (and NIC as applicable).

(2) Gains on the disposal of up to £50,000 worth of shares (based on acquisition value) are exempt from capital gains tax. Where a particular acquisition of shares causes the £50,000 limit to be breached, the remainder of the £50,000 limit is applied against the total value of the particular share acquisition and only that portion of the total number of shares acquired by the particular acquisition will be exempt from capital gains tax. The capital gains tax exemption is not available if the shareholder or connected person has a material interest (25% or more) in the company or parent undertaking. Normal share pooling and share identification rules do not apply to exempt employee shareholder shares.

[¶4-695] Employee ownership trusts

(ITEPA 2003, s. 312A–312I)

Finance Act 2014 introduced provisions that provide an exemption from income tax for any relevant bonus payment made in a tax year to an employee by a qualifying indirectly employee-owned company that meets the relevant conditions (a trading company in which a controlling interest is held by an employee-ownership settlement). A relevant bonus will be a cash award other than regular salary or wages that is paid to all employees on equal terms, although bonuses can be set by an employer by reference to a percentage of salary or length of service or hours worked. The exemption is available from 1 October 2014 and subject to an annual cap per employee for each qualifying company as set out below.

Period	£
From 1 October 2014	3,600

National minimum wage

[¶4-700] National minimum wage: from 1 October 2010

	Workers aged 21 plus £	Workers aged at least 18 but under 21 £	Workers aged under 18 £	Apprentices aged under 19 or in the first year of apprenticeship £
From 01.10.14	6.50	5.13	3.79	2.73
01.10.13–30.09.14	6.31	5.03	3.72	2.68

	Workers aged 21 plus £	Workers aged at least 18 but under 21 £	Workers aged under 18 £	Apprentices aged under 19 or in the first year of apprenticeship £
01.10.12–30.09.13	6.19	4.98	3.68	2.65
01.10.11–30.09.12	6.08	4.98	3.68	2.60
01.10.10–30.09.11	5.93	4.92	3.64	2.50

[¶4-720] National minimum wage: accommodation offset

The maximum permitted daily and weekly rates of accommodation offset in relation to the national minimum wage are as follows:

Period	Daily offset £	Weekly offset £
From 01.10.14	5.08	35.56
01.10.13–30.09.14	4.91	34.37
01.10.12–30.09.13	4.82	33.74
01.10.11–30.09.12	4.73	33.11
01.10.10–30.09.11	4.61	32.27
01.10.09–30.09.10	4.51	31.57
01.10.08–30.09.09	4.46	31.22
01.10.07–30.09.08	4.30	30.10

Flat-rate expenses

[¶4-750] Fixed sum deductions for repairing and maintaining equipment

(ITEPA 2003, s. 367)

(Tax Reporter: ¶457-500)

A tax deduction is given for certain amounts 'representing the average annual expenses incurred by employees of the class to which the employee belongs in respect of the repair and maintenance of work equipment'. The term 'flat-rate expenses' is often used for these figures. The following table is from EIM 32712:

Manual and certain other employees: flat-rate expenses deduction for tools and special clothing

Industry	Occupation	Deduction for 2008–09 onwards £	Deduction for 2004–05 to 2007–08 £
Agriculture	All workers	100	70
Aluminium	a. Continual casting operators, process operators, de-dimplers, driers, drill punchers, dross unloaders, firemen, furnace operators and their helpers, leaders, mouldmen, pourers, remelt department labourers, roll flatteners	140	130
	b. Cable hands, case makers, labourers, mates, truck drivers and measurers, storekeepers	80	60
	c. Apprentices	60	45
	d. All other workers	120	100
Banks and Building Societies	Uniformed doormen and messengers	60	45
Brass and copper	Braziers, coppersmiths, finishers, fitters, moulders, turners and all other workers.	120	100
Building	a. Joiners and carpenters	140	105
	b. Cement works, roofing felt and asphalt labourers	80	55
	c. Labourers and navvies	60	45
	d. All other workers	120	85
Building materials	a. Stone-masons	120	85
	b. Tilemakers and labourers	60	45
	c. All other workers	80	55
Clothing	a. Lacemakers, hosiery bleachers, dyers, scourers and knitters, knitwear bleachers and dyers	60	45
	b. All other workers	60	45
Constructional Engineering	a. Blacksmiths and their strikers, burners, caulkers, chippers, drillers, erectors, fitters, holders up, markers off, platers, riggers, riveters, rivet heaters, scaffolders, sheeters, template workers, turners, welders	140	115
	b. Banksmen labourers, shop-helpers, slewers, straighteners	80	60

Industry	Occupation		Deduction for 2008–09 onwards £	Deduction for 2004–05 to 2007–08 £
	c.	Apprentices and storekeepers	60	45
	d.	All other workers	100	75
Electrical and Electricity supply	a.	Those workers incurring laundry costs only (generally CEGB employees)	60	45
	b.	All other workers	120	90
Engineering	a.	Pattern makers	140	120
	b.	Labourers, supervisory and unskilled workers	80	60
	c.	Apprentices and storekeepers	60	45
	d.	Motor mechanics in garage repair shops	120	100
	e.	All other workers	120	100
Fire service	Uniformed fire fighters & fire officers		80	60
Food	All workers		60	45
Forestry	All workers		100	70
Glass	All workers		80	60
Healthcare staff in the National Health Service, private hospitals and nursing homes	a.	Ambulance staff on active service (i.e. excluding staff who take telephone calls or provide clerical support)	140	110
	b.	Nurses, midwives, chiropodists, dental nurses, occupational, speech, physiotherapists and other therapists, healthcare assistancs, phlebotomists and radiographers	100	70
	c.	Plaster room orderlies, hospital porters, ward clerks, sterile supply workers, hospital domestics, hospital catering staff	100	60
	d.	Laboratory staff, pharmacists, pharmacy assistants	60	45
	e.	Uniformed ancillary staff – maintenance workers, grounds staff, drivers, parking attendants and security guards, receptionists and other uniformed staff	60	45
Heating	a.	Pipe fitters and plumbers	120	100
	b.	Coverers, laggers, domestic glaziers, heating engineers and their mates	120	90

Industry	Occupation	Deduction for 2008–09 onwards £	Deduction for 2004–05 to 2007–08 £
	c. All gas workers, all other workers	100	70
Iron Mining	a. Fillers, miners and underground workers	120	100
	b. All other workers	100	75
Iron and Steel	a. Day labourers, general labourers, stockmen, time-keepers, warehouse staff and weighmen	80	60
	b. Apprentices	60	45
	c. All other workers	140	120
Leather	a. Curriers (wet workers), fellmongering workers, tanning operatives (wet)	80	55
	b. All other workers	60	45
Particular	a. Pattern makers	140	120
Engineering	b. All chainmakers; cleaners, galvanisers, tinners and wire drawers in the wire drawing industry; tool-makers in the lock making industry	120	100
	c. Apprentices and storekeepers	60	45
	d. All other workers	80	60
Police Force	Police officers (ranks up to and including Chief Inspector)	140	55 (but £110 for 2007–08)
Precious Metals	All workers	100	70
Printing	a. *Letterpress Section*: Electrical engineers (rotary presses), electrotypers, ink and roller makers, machine minders (rotary), maintenance engineers (rotary presses) and stereotypers	140	105
	b. Bench hands (periodical and bookbinding section), compositors (letterpress section), readers (letterpress section) telecommunications and electronic section wire room operators, warehousemen (paper box making section)	60	45
	c. All other workers	100	70

Industry	Occupation	Deduction for 2008–09 onwards £	Deduction for 2004–05 to 2007–08 £
Prisons	Uniformed prison officers	80	55
Public Service	a. *Dock and inland waterways* – Dockers, dredger drivers, hopper steerers	80	55
	– All other workers	60	45
	b. *Public transport* – Garage hands (including cleaners)	80	55
	– Conductors and drivers	60	45
Quarrying	All workers	100	70
Railways	(See the appropriate category for craftsmen, e.g. engineers, vehicle, etc.)		
	All other workers	100	70
Seamen	a. Carpenters (Seamen) Passenger liners	165	165
	b. Carpenters (Seamen) Cargo vessels, tankers, coasters and ferries	140	130
Shipyards	a. Blacksmiths and their strikers, boilermakers, burners, carpenters, caulkers, drillers, furnacemen (platers), holders up, fitters, platers, plumbers, riveters, sheet iron workers, shipwrights, tubers, welders	140	115
	b. Labourers	80	60
	c. Apprentices and storekeepers	60	45
	d. All other workers	100	75
Textiles and Textile Printing	a. Carders, carding engineers, overlookers and technicians in spinning mills	120	85
	b. All other workers	80	60
Vehicles	a. Builders, railway vehicle repairers and railway wagon lifters	140	105
	b. Railway vehicle painters, letterers, and builders' and repairers' assistants	80	60
	c. All other workers	60	45

Industry		Occupation	Deduction for 2008–09 onwards £	Deduction for 2004–05 to 2007–08 £
Wood & Furniture (formerly Wood)	a.	Carpenters, cabinet makers, joiners, wood carvers and woodcutting machinists	140	115
	b.	Artificial limb makers (other than in wood), organ builders and packaging case makers	120	90
	c.	Coopers not providing own tools, labourers, polishers and upholsterers	60	45
	d.	All other workers	100	75

Notes
'Workers' and 'all other workers' are references to manual workers or to workers who have to pay for the upkeep of tools and special clothing.
'Firemen' means persons engaged to light and maintain furnaces.
'Constructional engineering' means engineering undertaken on a construction site, including buildings, shipyards, bridges, roads and other similar operations.
'Particular engineering' means engineering undertaken on a commercial basis in a factory or workshop for the purposes of producing components such as wire, springs, nails and locks.

Miscellaneous

[¶4-800] Mobile phones

(ITEPA 2003, s. 319)

(Tax Reporter: ¶437-700)

No tax charge on employer-provided mobile phones but exemption restricted to one phone per employee, with no exemption for phones provided for family members. Limited exemption for vouchers supplied for mobile phone use. The right of the employee to surrender the phone for additional pay does not trigger a tax charge.

[¶4-805] Recommended medical treatment

(ITEPA 2003, s. 320C)

(Tax Reporter: ¶437-900)

With effect from a date to be appointed by Treasury order, an exemption from income tax will be available where an employer meets the cost of recommended medical treatment provided to an employee to assist them to return to work after a period of absence due to ill-health or injury, subject to an annual cap of £500.

[¶4-810] Childcare vouchers

(ITEPA 2003, s. 270A)

(Tax Reporter: ¶434-500ff.)

Year	Weekly limit	Monthly limit
2014–15	£55	£243
2013–14	£55	£243
2012–13	£55	£243
2011–12	£55	£243
2010–11	£55	£243
2009–10	£55	£243

Note

(1) At Budget 2013, it was announced that a new tax free childcare scheme will be phased in from Autumn 2015 and existing schemes for childcare vouchers and employer provided childcare will be closed to new applicants. The Childcare Payments Bill 2014–15 provides the statutory framework for the new scheme under which parents will need to open an online account with the scheme's account provider, National Savings and Investments (NS&I) and parents will then receive a Government contribution towards their childcare costs of £2 for every £8 that families pay into the account, up to £2,000 per child per year.

[¶4-815] Childcare: cap on relief from April 2011

(ITEPA 2003, s. 270A(6ZA), 318A(6A))

(Tax Reporter: ¶434-500ff.)

The amount of childcare relief is restricted to the following figures for those joining a scheme from 6 April 2011:

	Basic rate £	Higher rate £	Additional rate £
From 6 April 2013			
Weekly	55	28	25
Monthly	243	124	111
Annual	2,915	1,484	1,325
From 6 April 2011			
Weekly	55	28	22
Monthly	243	124	97
Annual	2,915	1,484	1,166

Note

(1) At Budget 2013, it was announced that a new tax free childcare scheme will be phased in from Autumn 2015 and existing schemes for childcare vouchers and employer provided childcare will be closed to new applicants. The Childcare Payments Bill 2014–15 provides the statutory framework for the new scheme, under which parents will need to open an online account with the scheme's account provider, National Savings and Investments (NS&I) and parents will then receive a Government contribution towards their childcare costs of £2 for every £8 that families pay into the account, up to £2,000 per child per year.

[¶4-820] Computer equipment

(ITEPA 2003, s. 316, former s. 320)

(Tax Reporter: ¶437-715ff.)

No special treatment so private use of a computer triggers a tax charge on normal principles. HMRC have indicated, though, that no tax charge will normally arise in practice if the computer is provided for work purposes.

Additionally, no tax charge will arise in relation to computers first made available before 6 April 2006 (e.g. under home computing initiative (HCI) scheme arrangements).

[¶4-830] Relocation allowance

(ITEPA 2003, s. 271–289)

(Tax Reporter: ¶433-850)

Tax exemption for the provision by employers of removal benefits, or payment or reimbursement of removal expenses in connection with an employee's change of residence where the employee's job or place of work is changed is generally subject to a statutory maximum of £8,000. No tax relief is available for the employee where expenses are not reimbursed by the employer.

[¶4-840] Payments and benefits on termination of employment

(ITEPA 2003, s. 401–416)

(Tax Reporter: ¶437-000ff.)

Period	Relief
From 1998–99	£30,000 exempt

Notes

The exemption is not available for any payment or other benefit chargeable to income tax under other legislation (ITEPA 2003, s. 401(3)).

There is therefore no exemption for any amounts already taxable as earnings (e.g. payments made under a contract of employment).

[¶4-850] Scholarships and sandwich courses

(SP 4/86)

(Tax Reporter: ¶419-200)

Subject to conditions, employers may make tax-free payments up to a specified figure to employees who are attending certain educational courses. The specified amount for recent years has been as follows:

Period	Specified amount
From 01.09.07	£15,480
01.09.05 to 31.08.07	£15,000
Before 01.09.05	£7,000 but different principles also then applied

PAYE

[¶4-900] PAYE thresholds

(SI 2003/2682)

(Tax Reporter: ¶493-240ff.)

	Amount	
	Weekly	Monthly
Tax year	£	£
2014–15	192.00	833.00
2013–14	182.00	787.00
2012–13	156.00	675.00
2011–12	144.00	623.00
2010–11	125.00	540.00
2009–10	125.00	540.00

Notes

Under normal circumstances, employers need not deduct tax from employees who earn less than the above amounts. The PAYE monthly and weekly thresholds are calculated arithmetically from the personal allowance (SI 2003/2682, reg. 9(8)).

[¶4-920] PAYE codes

The PAYE code enables an employer or payer of pension to give the employee or pensioner the approved amount of tax-free pay.

L	For people born after 5 April 1948 and eligible for the basic personal allowance – 1000L for the 2014–15 tax year. Also used for 'emergency' codes
P	For people born between 6 April 1938 and 5 April 1948 and eligible for the full personal allowance
Y	For people born before 6 April 1938 and eligible for the full personal allowance
T	Used where HMRC are reviewing other items in tax code (i.e. income-related reduction to the personal allowance)
K	Total allowances are less than total 'deductions'
BR	All income is taxed at the basic rate, currently 20%, most commonly used for a second job or pension
D0	All income taxed at the higher rate, currently 40%, most commonly used for a second job or pension
D1	All income taxed at the additional rate, currently 45%, most commonly used for a second job or pension
NT	No tax to be deducted from income or pension
0T	Allowances fully used up or reduced to nil and income is taxed at the relevant rates, may also be used for a new job where the employee does not have a P45 or hasn't completed a P46 before the first pay day

Other codes

Code FT is used for certain farmers employed under a hiring contract.

An emergency code may be used on a Week One basis. The emergency code for 2014–15 is 1000L. This is also the code used for employees eligible for the basic personal allowance (and who have no other coded out income, benefits or expenses deductions).

V codes have been obsolete since 6 April 2009 (as all individuals born before 6 April 1935 and qualifying for married couple's allowance (MCA) will be aged 75 and over during the tax year ended 5 April 2010. MCA will then be due at the higher rate.)

[¶4-925] PAYE coding out limits

Debts

(ITEPA 2003, s. 684; SI 2003/2682, reg. 14A–14C)

(Tax Reporter: ¶493-340)

HMRC may collect specified relevant debts up to the permitted limit through the PAYE system. The table below sets out the maximum amount that may be collected in this way (but see also the 'overall limit' and the 'overriding limit' below):

Tax year in which deduction made	Maximum deduction £
2015–16	17,000
2012–13 to 2014–15[1]	3,000

Note

[1] SI 2003/2682, reg. 14A which provides for determination of a tax code to recover a 'relevant debt' within the meaning of ITEPA 2003, s. 684 was introduced with effect from 6 April 2012.

To the extent that the payee does not object, HMRC may also determine a code to collect or repay income tax payable or overpaid in respect of the high income child benefit charge and, from 2015–16, to collect child or working tax credit debt.

Self-assessment balancing payments

(SI 2003/2682, reg.186)

(Tax Reporter: ¶493-330)

Payments due on or after	Maximum deduction £
6 April 2012[1]	3,000

Note

[1] Prior to 6 April 2012, in relation to amounts due under self-assessment and coded out under SI 2003/2682, reg. 186, the maximum deductible amount was £2,000.

Overall limit

(SI 2003/2682, reg. 14D)

With effect for tax codes issued for the tax year 2015–16 onwards, and to coincide with the increase in the coding out limit above from £3,000 to £17,000, an overall limit on the total amount of 'relevant debt' (under SI 2003/2682, reg. 14A) and 'tax credit debt' (under SI 2003/2682, reg. 14C) that may be recovered from an employee in a tax year via their tax code will be introduced, based on the expected amount of the individual's PAYE income for the tax year and as set out in the table below (subject to the 'overriding limit' below):

Expected amount of PAYE income in the tax year for which the code is determined	Total amount of debt recoverable in that tax year
Less than £30,000	No more than £3,000
£30,000 or more but less than £40,000	No more than £5,000
£40,000 or more but less than £50,000	No more than £7,000
£50,000 or more but less than £60,000	No more than £9,000
£60,000 or more but less than £70,000	No more than £11,000
£70,000 or more but less than £80,000	No more than £13,000
£80,000 or more but less than £90,000	No more than £15,000
£90,000 or more	No more than £17,000

Overriding limit

(SI 2003/2682, reg. 2)

The 'overriding limit' is the limit on the amount of tax that may be deducted from a relevant payment and is an amount equal to 50% of the amount of the relevant payment. A relevant payment is defined as a payment of net PAYE income, except PAYE social security income, UK social security pensions, excluded relocation expenses, excluded business expenses, excluded pecuniary liabilities, and excluded notional payments (SI 2003/2682, reg. 4).

Additionally, HMRC will further not code out debts which result in the individual's liability for the year doubling, even though the debt might otherwise fall within the limits set out above (i.e. only debts that equate to less than the individual's expected liability for the tax year will be coded out) (see HMRC Manuals: PAYE12070).

[¶4-930] PAYE real time information returns

(SI 2012/822; SI 2003/2682)

(Tax Reporter: ¶493-015)

From 6 April 2013, reporting PAYE information in real time is mandatory unless HMRC have notified otherwise. Each time an employee is paid after 6 April 2013 the employer must submit details about the employees' pay and deductions to HMRC using payroll software. However, until 5 April 2014, this PAYE reporting deadline was temporarily relaxed for businesses with 50 or less employees (who may pay employees weekly, or more frequently, but only process their payroll monthly). Such businesses could instead send information to HMRC by the date of their regular payroll run but no later than the end of the tax month (5th). Key RTI requirements are as follows:

Submissions	Deadlines	Details
Full Payment Submission (FPS)	On or before the day employees are paid (until 5 April 2014 only, by the end of tax month (5th) for small businesses) Final submission by 19 April (cannot file an FPS after this date)	• Include all employees that are paid (including those earning below the NIC lower earnings limit (e.g. students); • information to be submitted includes; amounts paid, deductions (tax and national insurance), starter and leaver dates (if applicable)
Employer Payment Submission (EPS)	19 April following tax year (by 19 May following tax year to avoid a penalty)	• to report a reduction in the amount you pay to HMRC or if you haven't paid any employees in a pay period
Earlier Year Update (EYU)	Up to six years after original FPS or EPS filed (by 19 May following tax year to avoid a penalty)	• to correct, after 19 April, any of the year to date totals submitted in your final FPS for the previous tax year. This only applies to years after you started to send information in real time
National Insurance verification request (NVR)	–	• to verify or obtain an National Insurance number for new employees
Employer Alignment Submission (EAS)	Notified by HMRC	• to align employee records with HMRC records before submission of other information, • only required for larger PAYE schemes with over 250 employees, or payroll administered by two or more payroll systems, including those operated by different payroll providers

[¶4-932] PAYE RTI: forms no longer needed

Reporting PAYE pre-RTI	Reporting in real time
Forms P14 and P35 end of year returns – do not use after you have submitted your 2012–13 return	FPS each time you pay employees EPS each month for any adjustments to what you owe Earlier Year Update (EYU) to amend details for earlier years
P45 – don't send any parts to HMRC – only use for the employees own records after 6 April 2013	Include starters and leavers information on your FPS

Reporting PAYE pre-RTI	Reporting in real time
P46, P46(Pen) or P46(Expat) – do not use these forms after 6 April 2013	Include starters and leavers on your FPS.
Form CA6855 to trace or check a National Insurance number – do not use after 6 April 2013	Use payroll software to issue a National Insurance number verification request (NVR) to trace or check a National Insurance number
Form P38(S) – do not use after 6 April 2013	Include on your payroll and in your FPS

[¶4-935] PAYE RTI: procedures unchanged

- **PAYE** – remains the same, only reporting that changes,
- **Coding notices** – employers will still be able to choose how they receive coding notices as previously,
- **Reporting a change to HMRC,** e.g. updating employee's new name or address for HMRC records – a real time submission will not update HMRC records. It remains the responsibility of the individual employee to notify HMRC of changes to name, address, etc.
- **HMRC messages to employers** – HMRC will continue to use the Data Provisioning Services (DPS) and EDI outbound message services,
- **Payment dates** – remain unchanged,
- **Forms P60** – P60s will remain the same,
- **Expenses and benefits** – real time reporting is not changing how expenses and benefits are reported. Employers will continue to complete and file any forms P9D, P11D and P11D(b) due under existing arrangements,
- **The Construction Industry Scheme (CIS) payment and reporting process** – real time reporting is not changing the existing CIS process. Employers will continue to complete and file monthly returns (CIS300) due under the existing CIS arrangements. But where a limited company acting as a subcontractor has suffered CIS deductions they will report these amounts to HMRC on an EPS and, as existing practice, subtract these from the amounts of PAYE due to be paid to HMRC.

[¶4-938] PAYE RTI: correcting errors

Error in a Full Payment Submission (FPS) or EPS in the current tax year

Submit an additional FPS or EPS in the week or month of discovery or include correction in the next FPS or EPS for the next payroll run.

Error in FPS or EPS for previous tax year

Errors can be corrected before 20 April by submitting an additional FPS or EPS.

After 20 April it is not possible to submit an additional FPS and instead the correction must be made on an EYU, however, errors on an EPS may be corrected by submitting an additional EPS for the tax year even after 20 April.

[¶4-940] PAYE returns up to 2012–13

(Tax Reporter: ¶494-700)

PAYE returns: deadlines

Forms	Date	Provision	Penalty provisions
P14, P35, P38 and P38A	19 May following tax year	*Income Tax (Pay As You Earn) Regulations* 2003 (SI 2003/2682), reg. 73 and 74	TMA 1970, s. 98A
P60 (to employee)	31 May following tax year	*Income Tax (Pay As You Earn) Regulations* 2003 (SI 2003/2682), reg. 67	TMA 1970, s. 98A
P9D and P11D	6 July following tax year	*Income Tax (Pay As You Earn) Regulations* 2003 (SI 2003/2682), reg. 85	TMA 1970, s. 98
P46 (Car)	3 May, 2 August, 2 November, 2 February	*Income Tax (Pay As You Earn) Regulations* 2003 (SI 2003/2682), reg. 90	TMA 1970, s. 98

[¶4-942] PAYE Late filing penalties

(FA 2009, Sch. 55)

RTI: From 2014–15

New late filing penalties will apply to returns due from employers for the tax year 2014–15 onwards but starting from 6 October 2014 (rather than 6 April 2014) for large employers (with 50 or more employees) and from 6 March 2015 for small employers (with no more than 49 employees at 6 October 2014) and new employers (who become employers after 6 October 2014). Where payment information is not received as expected on an FPS, or HMRC have not been notified that no employees have been paid in a tax period by submission of an EPS, late filing penalties will apply. The rules apply to each PAYE scheme, rather than each employer.

Late filing penalties will apply on a monthly basis, however, no penalty will apply for the first month in each tax year that returns are filed late.

New employers will not be penalised if their first FPS is received within 30 days of making their first payment to an employee.

Initial penalties

Number of employees[1]	Monthly Penalty[2] £
1 to 9	100
10 to 49	200
50 to 249	300
250 or more	400

Notes
[1] HMRC will use the latest information available to determine the number of employees, and the size of the filing penalty for each period where a return is late.
[2] Filing penalty notices will be issued quarterly in July, October, January and April, if appropriate, showing the amount of the filing penalty for each tax month identified in that quarter.

Additional penalties for returns over three months late

	Penalty
3 months late	5%[1]

Note
[1] Calculated as a percentage of the tax/NICs that should have been shown on the late return.

RTI: 2012–13 and 2013–14

There is no change to the penalties for late filing of returns for the tax years 2012–13 and 2013–14. The current penalty regime (see below) continues to apply at the year-end.

HMRC have confirmed that they want employers to file on time, rather than issue penalties, and employers won't be charged penalties for sending FPS late unless, it's the final one for the tax year. This means for these two tax years, employers operating PAYE in real time will be in a similar position to employers who were still operating traditional PAYE.

Key deadlines	Penalty
Final FPS submitted by 19 April (last date for submission of an FPS)	None
EYU submitted after 19 April but by 19 May	None
Final payments unreported at 19 May	£100 per 50 employees for each month return outstanding[1]

Note
[1] Penalty notices will be issued after 19 September (once return outstanding for four months) and again, the following January and May.

Penalties (fixed, but see ESC B46) imposed for delays (TMA 1970, s. 98A)

Forms	First 12 months	Thereafter
P14, P35, P38 and P38A	£100 per 50 employees per month	Additional penalty not exceeding 100% of the tax and NIC payable for the year but remaining unpaid by 19 April following end of tax year

Penalties (mitigable) that may be imposed for delays (TMA 1970, s. 98)

Forms	Initial	Continuing
P9D and P11D	£300 per return	£60 per day

[¶4-945] PAYE penalties for incorrect returns

(FA 2007, Sch. 24)

(Tax Reporter: ¶184-850)

HMRC use a risk based approach to identify employers they think may be submitting incorrect returns. Where HMRC discover careless or deliberate errors, the penalties that could apply will be based on the behaviour that led to the error and the amount of potential lost revenue for that return. Errors that arise despite taking reasonable care attract no penalty at all and penalties for errors due to failure to take reasonable care can be reduced to zero with full and unprompted disclosure to HMRC.

RTI: 2013–14

HMRC have confirmed that for the tax year 2013–14, an inaccuracy in any FPS submitted could attract a penalty. It will be based on the potential lost revenue for the FPS which contained the inaccuracy. HMRC may issue one penalty notice for inaccuracy penalties for multiple tax periods in a year.

RTI: 2012–13

HMRC confirmed that employers who operated PAYE in real time in 2012–13 will not be charged a penalty in-year for inaccuracies on FPS returns submitted each payday, but penalties may be charged after the end of the tax year if there is an error on the final FPS for the year, or a failure to correct earlier errors by the year-end. This is so as to ensure employers who joined the RTI pilot are treated in line with employers who did not start sending real time information until April 2013.

Penalties from 1 April 2009

(FA 2007, Sch. 24, para. 1 and 4)

The maximum penalty for an incorrect return is 100% of the potential lost revenue (deliberate and concealed action), 70% (deliberate but not concealed) or 30% (careless action).

Penalties for earlier periods

Penalties that may be imposed for incorrect returns (returns due before 1 April 2009)

Forms	Provision TMA 1970	Penalty
P14, P35, P38 and P38A	s. 98A(4)	Maximum of 100% of tax underpaid
P9D and P11D	s. 98(2)	Maximum penalty £3,000

[¶4-946] PAYE: late payment penalties

(FA 2009, s. 107 and Sch. 56)

(Tax Reporter: ¶184-975)

From April 2015, late payment penalties will be charged in-year on a late payment for the tax year 2015–16 onwards. Late payment penalty notices will be issued quarterly in July, October, January and April showing the amount of the penalty due for each tax month. The total penalty charged can be made up of:

- a default penalty, for failure to pay monthly/quarterly payments on time and in full; and
- penalties for amounts still unpaid after six and 12 months.

From April 2014, HMRC will continue to issue late payment penalties on a risk-assessed basis for 2014–15 as in previous years. Penalties will only be charged in respect of the most serious and persistent failures.

Penalties for late monthly or quarterly PAYE payments

No penalty if only one PAYE amount is late in a tax year, unless that payment is over six months late.

<table>
<tr><th>No. defaults in a tax year</th><th>Penalty percentage</th><th>Amount to which penalty percentages apply</th></tr>
<tr><td>1–3[(1)]</td><td>1%</td><td rowspan="4">Total amount that is late in the tax year (ignoring the first late payment in that tax year)
From April 2014: the total amount that is late in the relevant tax month (ignoring the first late payment in the tax year)</td></tr>
<tr><td>4–6</td><td>2%</td></tr>
<tr><td>7–9</td><td>3%</td></tr>
<tr><td>10 or more</td><td>4%</td></tr>
</table>

Note

(1) The first failure to pay on time does not count as a default.

Additional penalties	Amount
6 months late	5%
12 months late	Further 5%

Amounts due annually or occasionally (Class 1A and 1B NIC)

Penalty date	5%
5 months after initial penalty date	further 5%
11 months after initial penalty date	further 5%

Penalty dates

The penalty date varies according to the type of payment. For payments such as Class 1A and Class 1B NICs, HMRC determinations, assessments and amendments, or corrections to returns the 'penalty date' is 30 days after the due date. In most other cases, the penalty date is the day after the due date.

[¶4-948] Interest on certain PAYE paid late

(FA 2009, s. 101 and 102)

(Tax Reporter: ¶494-900; ¶494-910)

2014–15

For the tax year 2014–15 onwards, HMRC charge in-year, rather than annual, interest on all unpaid:

- PAYE tax, Class 1 National Insurance contributions (NICs) and student loan deductions, including specified charges (estimates HMRC make in the absence of a PAYE submission);
- Construction Industry Scheme charges;
- In-year late filing penalties (which start from October 2014); and
- In-year late payment penalties (which will be charged automatically from April 2015).

Interest will also be charged on underpayments that arise because of adjustments reported on Earlier Year Updates submitted in respect of tax year 2014 to 2015 onwards.

For annual payments such as Class 1A and Class 1B NICs, HMRC will continue to charge interest on any amount which remains unpaid after the due date.

Interest is charged daily, from the date a payment is due and payable to the date it is paid in full.

Repayment interest will apply where a payment is made and the charge is then reduced resulting in an overpayment which is either reallocated to a later charge or repaid.

Years to 2013–14

(SI 2003/2682, former reg. 82, 83)

Where an employer has not paid the net tax deductible by him under PAYE to the collector within 14 days of the end of the tax year, the unpaid tax carries interest at the prescribed rate from the reckonable date until the date of payment. Certain repayments of tax also attract interest.

[¶4-962] PAYE electronic communications penalty: form P45 (Part 1 or Part 3), P46 or P46 (Pen)

(SI 2003/2682, reg. 210B, 210BA)

(Tax Reporter ¶498-745; ¶498-750)

2013–14 and subsequent years Table 9AA		2011–12 and 2012–13 Table 9A		2009–10 and 2010–11 Former Table 9A	
Number of items	Penalty	Number of items	Penalty	Number of items	Penalty
		1–2	nil	1–5	nil
1–49	£100	3–49	£100	6–49	£100
50–149	£300	50–149	£300	50–149	£300
150–299	£600	150–299	£600	150–299	£600
300–399	£900	300–399	£900	300–399	£900
400–499	£1,200	400–499	£1,200	400–499	£1,200
500–599	£1,500	500–599	£1,500	500–599	£1,500
600–699	£1,800	600–699	£1,800	600–699	£1,800
700–799	£2,100	700–799	£2,100	700–799	£2,100
800–899	£2,400	800–899	£2,400	800–899	£2,400
900–999	£2,700	900–999	£2,700	900–999	£2,700
1000+	£3,000	1000+	£3,000	1000+	£3,000

Note

(1) Number of items of specified information the employer has failed to deliver in the tax year. (Each item mentioned in reg. 207(1) para. (a) to (d) counts as a separate item of specified information.) An item of specified information counts even if it relates to the same employee as one or more other items.

[¶4-965] PAYE electronic communications penalty: forms P35 and P14

(SI 2003/2682, reg. 210AA, former 210A)

(Tax Reporter: ¶498-755; ¶498-760; ¶498-765)

2010–11 and subsequent years Table 9ZA		2009–10 Former Table 9		2004–05 to 2008–09 Former Table 9	
Number of employees	Penalty	Number of employees	Penalty	Number of employees	Penalty
1–5	£100	1–5	nil		
6–49	£300	6–49	£100	1–49	nil

2010–11 and subsequent years Table 9ZA		2009–10 Former Table 9		2004–05 to 2008–09 Former Table 9	
50–249	£600	50–249	£600	50–249	£600
250–399	£900	250–399	£900	250–399	£900
400–499	£1,200	400–499	£1,200	400–499	£1,200
500–599	£1,500	500–599	£1,500	500–599	£1,500
600–699	£1,800	600–699	£1,800	600–699	£1,800
700–799	£2,100	700–799	£2,100	700–799	£2,100
800–899	£2,400	800–899	£2,400	800–899	£2,400
900–999	£2,700	900–999	£2,700	900–999	£2,700
1000+	£3,000	1000+	£3,000	1000+	£3,000

Notes

(1) Number of employees for whom particulars should have been included with the specified information.

(2) But nil for tax year 2004–05 only (50–249 employees).

[¶4-970] PAYE surcharges (to 5 April 2010)

(SI 2003/2682, former reg. 203)

(Tax Reporter: ¶498-510)

Specified percentage for each default in a surcharge period	
Default number (within the surcharge period)	**Specified percentage %**
1	0.00
2	0.00
3	0.17
4	0.17
5	0.17
6	0.33
7	0.33
8	0.33
9	0.58
10	0.58
11	0.58
12 and more defaults	0.83

[¶4-975] PAYE monthly accounting periods

(SI 2003/2682, reg. 69)

(Tax Reporter: ¶494-510)

Period	Month no.	Payment due (electronic)	Payment due (other)
6 Apr to 5 May	1	22 May	19 May
6 May to 5 June	2	22 June	19 June
6 June to 5 July	3	22 July	19 July
6 July to 5 Aug	4	22 August	19 August
6 Aug to 5 Sept	5	22 September	19 September
6 Sept to 5 Oct	6	22 October	19 October
6 Oct to 5 Nov	7	22 November	19 November
6 Nov to 5 Dec	8	22 December	19 December
6 Dec to 5 Jan	9	22 January	19 January
6 Jan to 5 Feb	10	22 February	19 February
6 Feb to 5 Mar	11	22 March	19 March
6 Mar to 5 Apr	12	22 April	19 April

[¶4-976] PAYE quarterly accounting periods

(SI 2003/2682, reg. 70)

(Tax Reporter: ¶494-570)

Period	Month no.	Payment due (electronic)	Payment due (other)
6 Apr to 5 July	1–3	22 July	19 July
6 July to 5 Oct	4–6	22 October	19 October
6 Oct to 5 Jan	7–9	22 January	19 January
6 Jan to 5 Apr	10–12	22 April	19 April

[¶4-980] Payroll giving scheme

(ITEPA 2003, s. 713)

(Tax Reporter: ¶457-500)

Employees whose remuneration is subject to deduction of tax at source under PAYE can make unlimited tax-deductible donations to charity by requesting that their employers deduct the donations from their pay.

[¶4-985] Student loan deductions

(SI 2009/470, reg. 29; SI 2011/784, reg. 6; SI 2012/1309)

New repayment conditions apply in relation to loans taken out by new students starting new courses on or after 1 September 2012. Borrowers of post-2012 loans are not required to repay any part of the post-2012 student loan before 6 April 2016. The repayment threshold for post-2012 student loans is £21,000. The existing repayment threshold (which is increased annually in line with the retail prices index until 6 April 2016) continues to apply in relation to non-2012 loans only.

Post-2012 Student loans

Year	Percentage	Threshold
2016–17	9%	£21,000

Pre-2012 Student loans

Year	Percentage	Threshold
2014–15	9%	£16,910
2013–14	9%	£16,365
2012–13	9%	£15,795
2011–12	9%	£15,000
2010–11	9%	£15,000
2009–10	9%	£15,000

TAXATION OF CAPITAL GAINS

[¶5-000] Rates, annual exemption, chattel exemption

(TCGA 1992, s. 3, 4 and 262)

(Tax Reporter: ¶500-220, ¶509-050, ¶535-100)

Tax year	Annual exempt amount[1]		Chattel exemption (max sale proceeds)[4] £	Rates		
	Individuals, PRs[2], trusts for mentally disabled £	Other trusts[3] £		Gains eligible for entrepreneurs' relief %	Individuals[6] %	Trustees and PRs %
2014–15	11,000	5,500	6,000	10	18/28	28
2013–14	10,900	5,450	6,000	10	18/28	28
2012–13	10,600	5,300	6,000	10	18/28	28
2011–12	10,600	5,300	6,000	10	18/28	28
2010–11	10,100	5,050	6,000	10/18[5]	18/28	18/28[7]
2009–10	10,100	5,050	6,000	18[5]	18	18

Notes

[1] The annual exempt amount is increased annually, unless Parliament determines otherwise, by reference to the increase in CPI. 2013–14 is the first year that the AEA has been increased by reference to CPI rather than RPI. *Finance Act* 2014 sets the annual exemption for 2015–16 at £11,100.

[2] For year of death and next two years in the case of personal representatives (PRs) of deceased persons.

[3] Multiple trusts created by the same settlor; each attracts relief equal to the annual amount divided by the number of such trusts (subject to a minimum of 10% of the full amount).

[4] Where disposal proceeds exceed the exemption limit, marginal relief restricts any chargeable gain to 5/3 of the excess. Where there is a loss and the proceeds are less than £6,000 the proceeds are deemed to be £6,000.

[5] Chargeable gains arising on disposals eligible for entrepreneurs' relief in the period from 6 April 2008 to 22 June 2010 are to be reduced by 4/9ths before being charged to tax at the flat-rate of 18%. Eligible gains arising on or after 23 June 2010 are charged to tax at 10%.

[6] For gains arising on disposals occurring on or before 22 June 2010, the rate is 18%. Where disposals occur on or after 23 June 2010, the chargeable gains arising from those disposals are aggregated with the individual's taxable income and to the extent that the aggregate falls above the threshold of the income tax basic rate, capital gains tax is charged at 28% (taking the chargeable gains as being the highest part of that aggregate). If the aggregate falls below the threshold, the capital gains tax rate remains at 18%.

[7] For gains arising on disposals occurring on or before 22 June 2010, the rate is 18%. Where disposals occur on or after 23 June 2010, the rate is 28%.

Capital gains tax: Non-residents and UK residential property

From April 2015, capital gains tax will apply to gains made by non-residents disposing of UK residential property (Autumn Statement 2013).

[¶5-020] ATED-related capital gains on high value residential property

(TCGA 1992, s. 2B, Sch. 4ZZA)

(Tax Reporter: ¶808-015)

From 6 April 2013, capital gains tax applies to companies and other corporate bodies on disposals of UK residential property valued at over £2m (due to be reduced from 6 April 2015 to £1m and from 6 April 2016 to £500,000 by legislation to be included in Finance Bill 2015 (Budget 2014)). If a residential property which has been subject to Annual Tax on Enveloped Dwellings (ATED) is disposed of some or all of the gains or losses will be 'ATED-related' and will be charged to capital gains tax at the rate of 28%.

The charge applies to any of the following that own an interest in residential property that is subject to the Annual Tax on Enveloped Dwellings:

- companies that are resident in the UK for tax purposes;
- companies that are not UK resident;
- companies (both UK resident and non UK resident) which are a partner in a partnership; and
- some collective investment schemes, depending on the terms and nature of the scheme.

The charge arises in respect of ATED-related gains only, which, normally, will be gains attributable to periods after 5 April 2013. However, it is possible to elect out of the rules of apportionment between pre and post April 2013 periods, and calculate the ATED-related gain by reference to the entire period of ownership. In most cases such an election will only be beneficial where the market value at 5 April 2013 is greater than the value at the time of disposal.

Gains and losses that are ATED-related are ring-fenced from non ATED-related gains and losses, and a general computational feature of the rules is that indexation allowance is available only against non ATED-related gains.

[¶5-050] Other exemptions and reliefs

Entrepreneurs' relief (from 6 April 2008 onwards)

(TCGA 1992, s. 169H–169S)

(Tax Reporter: ¶572-500ff.)

Chargeable gains arising on disposals of qualifying business assets on or after 23 June 2010 are charged to tax at a rate of 10%. Eligible gains arising in the period from 6 April 2008 to 22 June 2010 were reduced by 4/9ths before being charged to tax at the flat-rate of 18%.

Period	Limit £
From 06.04.11	10 million
23.06.10 to 05.04.11	5 million
06.04.10 to 22.06.10	2 million
06.04.08 to 05.04.10	1 million

The above limits are lifetime limits applying to disposals on or after 6 April 2008. Transitional provisions allow relief to be claimed in certain circumstances where gains deferred from disposals made on or before 5 April 2008 subsequently become chargeable (FA 2008, Sch. 3, para. 7 and 8).

With effect for transfers on or after 3 December 2014, individuals will be prevented from claiming entrepreneurs' relief on disposals of the reputation and customer relationships associated with a business ('goodwill') when they transfer the business to a related close company, by legislation to be included in Finance Bill 2015 (Autumn Statement 2014).

EMI shares

(TCGA 1992, s. 169I(7A)–(7R))

(Tax Reporter: ¶572-950)

With effect in relation to disposals on or after 6 April 2013 of shares acquired pursuant to the exercise of a qualifying EMI option, entrepreneur's relief will be available in respect of the disposal notwithstanding that the 'personal company' requirement (>5% holding) may not be satisfied. To qualify, the shares must be:

- acquired since 6 April 2012;
- disposed of at least one year after the grant of the option; and
- the individual must have been an employee of the company, or a company in the same trading group, throughout the one year period ending with the disposal.

Employee shareholder status

(TCGA 1992, s. 236B–236G)

(Tax Reporter: ¶565-050)

Capital gains tax exemption[1]	From 1 September 2013 £
Market value on acquisition	50,000

Note

[1] Gains on the disposal of up to £50,000 worth of shares (based on acquisition value) are exempt from capital gains tax. Where a particular acquisition of shares causes the £50,000 limit to be breached, the remainder of the £50,000 limit is applied against the total value of the particular share acquisition and only that portion of the total number of shares acquired by the particular acquisition will be exempt from capital gains tax. The capital gains tax exemption is not available if the shareholder or connected person has a material interest (25% or more) in the company or parent undertaking. Normal share pooling and share identification rules do not apply to exempt employee shareholder shares.

See ¶4-690 for further details on employee shareholder status and income tax reliefs.

Employee-ownership trusts

(TCGA 1992, s. 236H–236U)

(Tax Reporter: ¶361-400ff.)

From 6 April 2014, disposals of shares to a trust with specific characteristics which benefits all employees of a company (or a group) may be wholly relieved from capital gains tax if certain criteria are met. The relief requirements are:

- the trading requirement: the company whose shares are disposed of must be a trading company, or the parent company of a trading group;
- the all-employee benefit requirement: the trust which acquires the shares must operate for the benefit all employees;
- the controlling interest requirement: the trust must have a controlling interest in the company at the end of the tax year, which it did not have at the start of that year;

- the limited participation requirement: certain participators must be excluded from being beneficiaries of the trust; and
- neither the claimant (nor anyone connected with him) has previously received relief on the same company's (or any group company's) shares.

The relief operates by disapplying TCGA 1992, s. 17(1) (market value disposals) and treats the disposal (and acquisition by the trustees) as a no gain, no loss disposal. The relief is available on disposals which take place in a single tax year; disposals may be made by more than one person and can be of any number of shares. Where a disqualifying event (broadly, the relief requirements cease to be met) occurs in the following tax year, any relief given is withdrawn and where a disqualifying event occurs in any later tax year, this triggers a deemed disposal and reacquisition at market value by the trustees.

Indexation allowance

(TCGA 1992, s. 53 and 54)

(Tax Reporter: ¶523-250)

Indexation allowance in respect of changes shown by the retail prices indices for months after April 1998 is allowed only for the purposes of corporation tax. For disposals made by individuals, trustees and personal representatives after April 1998 and before 6 April 2008, indexation allowance up to 5 April 1998 and taper relief could be obtained.

The table at ¶11-020 sets out the figure that is determined by the formula of (RD – RI)/RI where RD is the Retail Prices Index for April 1998 and RI is the Retail Prices Index for the later of March 1982 and the date that the item of relevant allowable expenditure was incurred. The indexation allowance is the aggregate of the indexed rise in each item of relevant allowable expenditure. In relation to each item of expenditure, the indexed rise is a sum produced by multiplying the amount of that item of expenditure by the appropriate figure in that table (for a fuller table applying for corporation tax purposes, see ¶11-000ff).

Rollover relief

(TCGA 1992, s. 152)

(Tax Reporter: ¶570-100)

To qualify for rollover relief, an asset must fall within one of the 'relevant classes of assets' and the reinvestment must generally take place within the period from 12 months before to three years after the disposal of the old asset. Classes of assets qualifying for relief are as follows, but see TCGA 1992, s. 156ZB for the interaction of this section with the corporation tax rules for gains and losses on intangible fixed assets:

- land and buildings occupied and used exclusively for the purposes of a trade;
- fixed plant or machinery (not forming part of a building);
- ships, aircraft, hovercraft;
- satellites, space stations and spacecraft (including launch vehicles);
- goodwill;
- milk quotas and potato quotas, ewe and suckler cow premium quotas, fish quotas;
- entitlements under the single farm payments scheme;
- entitlements under the basic payment scheme (with effect in relation to disposals of old assets or acquisitions of new assets on or after 20 December 2013); and
- Lloyd's members' syndicate rights and assets treated as acquired by members.

Private residence relief

(TCGA 1992, s. 222)

(Tax Reporter: ¶540-000)

Relief is given on gains arising on the disposal of a dwelling house and on land enjoyed with the residence as its garden or grounds (up to the permitted area of half a hectare, or more if required for the reasonable enjoyment of the property).

Gains are apportioned across the period of ownership between periods of occupation (including deemed occupation) and other periods, with relief available for the portion of the gain attributable to periods of occupation. The final period of ownership is always eligible for relief provided the property was at some time the only or main residence. For disposals on or after 6 April 2014, the final period exemption applies to the last 18 months of ownership (previously, 36 months) except for individuals who are disabled or in a care home and with no other property who continue to get a 36 month final period exemption.

Where a residence is let during a period of non occupation, relief is available on the portion of the gain attributable to the let period up to £40,000.

Enterprise investment scheme

(TCGA 1992, s. 150A and Sch. 5B)

(Tax Reporter: ¶564-400ff. and ¶568-000)

A disposal of shares on which income tax relief has not been withdrawn is exempt from capital gains tax; losses arising are eligible for relief in the normal way, but the base cost is treated as reduced by any EIS income tax relief which has been given and not withdrawn.

Reinvestment relief is available for gains on assets where the disposal proceeds are reinvested in new EIS shares.

See ¶3-400 for EIS income tax relief.

Gains that are eligible for entrepreneurs' relief and deferred into investment under the enterprise investment scheme on or after 3 December 2014 will benefit from entrepreneurs' relief when the gain is realised, by legislation to be included in Finance Bill 2015 (Autumn Statement 2014).

Seed enterprise investment scheme

(TCGA 1992, Sch. 5BB)

(Tax Reporter: ¶568-500)

The exemption from capital gains applies where SEIS shares are held for more than three years from their issue. Losses are eligible for relief in the normal way but the base cost is treated as reduced by any SEIS income tax relief which has been given and not withdrawn.

For 2012–13 initially a re-investment exemption is available in respect of a gain arising on the disposal of any asset to the extent that the individual makes a qualifying investment under SEIS in the 2012–13 tax year, with so much of the gain that is matched with SEIS expenditure being exempt from CGT (subject to a £100,000 investment limit). *Finance Act* 2013 extended this relief in relation to gains accruing in 2013–14 that are matched with investment in 2013–14 but with a limit on the amount that is treated as not being a chargeable gain of 50% of the qualifying SEIS expenditure. *Finance Act* 2014 makes permanent the relief for 2014–15 and subsequent years at the 50% rate.

Investment in social enterprises

(TCGA 1992, s. 255A–255E, Sch. 8B)

(Tax Reporter: ¶569-300ff.)

The disposal relief provides an exemption from capital gains tax in respect of the disposal of an investment where the investor has received income tax relief (which has not subsequently been withdrawn) on the cost of the investment, and the investment is disposed of after it has been held for at least three years. However, if no claim to income tax relief is made, then any subsequent disposal of the investment will not qualify for exemption from capital gains tax.

The deferral relief enables the payment of tax on a capital gain to be deferred where the gain is reinvested in shares or debt investments which also qualify for SITR income tax relief. It is not, however, necessary for the investor to have made a claim for SITR income tax relief. The gain can arise from the disposal of any kind of asset, but must arise in the period from 6 April 2014 to 5 April 2019. The SITR qualifying investment must be made in the period one year before or three years after the gain arose. There is no minimum period for which the investment must be held; the deferred capital gain is brought back into charge whenever the investment is disposed of or the social enterprise ceases to meet the requirements of the scheme, but if an amount equal to the gain is once more invested in shares or debt investments which also qualify for SITR income tax relief then the gain may be held over again.

Gains that are eligible for entrepreneurs' relief and deferred into investment under the enterprise investment scheme on or after 3 December 2014 will benefit from entrepreneurs' relief when the gain is realised, by legislation to be included in Finance Bill 2015 (Autumn Statement 2014).

Charities

(CTA 2010, s. 466ff.; TCGA 1992, s. 256, 257; ITA 2007, s. 518ff.)

(Tax Reporter: ¶815-440)

The gains of charities are not taxable provided they are applicable, and applied, for charitable purposes only. The legislation is designed to charge charities to tax on the amount of their income and gains that has not been invested, lent or spent in an approved way.

A charge to capital gains tax arises if a charity ceases to be a charity, when there is a deemed sale and reacquisition of the trust property by the trustees at market value.

Gifts to the nation

(TCGA 1992, s. 258; FA 2012, Sch. 14)

(Tax Reporter: ¶535-620)

Gains arising on gifts of pre-eminent property to be held for the benefit of the public or the nation are not chargeable to capital gains tax.

For the tax year 2012–13 and subsequent tax years, a reduction in income tax and/or capital gains tax is available where an individual makes a gift of pre-eminent property to be held for the benefit of the public or the nation. The tax reduction is 30% of the value of the gift. A gift offer must be made and registered in accordance with the scheme and relief is available against the individual's liability for the year in which the gift offer is registered and/or any of the succeeding four tax years.

Pre-eminent property includes any picture, print, book, manuscript, work of art, scientific object or other thing that is pre-eminent for its national, scientific, historic or artistic interest, collections of such items and any object kept in a significant building where it is desirable that it remain associated with the building.

Disincorporation relief

(FA 2013, s. 58–60; TCGA 1992, s. 162B and 162C; CTA 2009, s. 849A)

Disincorporation relief is a form of rollover or deferral relief which allows a company to transfer certain assets to its shareholders who continue the business in an unincorporated form. The assets are deemed to be transferred at below market value so that no corporation tax charge arises to the company, although shareholders may still be liable to income tax or capital gains tax on the transfer of assets to them by the company. Shareholders will be liable to capital gains tax, as usual, on a future sale of the assets, for which purpose the assets are treated as having been acquired at the reduced transfer value.

The relief applies in relation to a 'qualifying transfer' of a business with a disposal date falling within the period of five years beginning 1 April 2013. A qualifying transfer is one which meets the following conditions:

- the business must be transferred as a going concern;
- the business must be transferred together with all the assets of the business or together with all the assets of the business apart from cash;
- the total market value of the 'qualifying assets' at the time of the transfer must not be more than £100,000;
- the shareholders that the business is transferred to must be individuals; and
- those shareholders must have held shares in the company throughout the 12 months before the transfer.

Qualifying assets are interests in land (other than land held as trading stock) and goodwill. Special rules apply to determine the transfer value of any post-FA 2002 goodwill.

A claim for Disincorporation Relief must be made jointly by the company and all the shareholders to whom the business is transferred. The claim must be made within two years of the business transfer date.

[¶5-100] Leases which are wasting assets

Restrictions of allowable expenditure

(TCGA 1992, s. 240 and Sch. 8, para. 1)

(Tax Reporter: ¶509-600ff.)

Fraction equal to $\frac{P(1) - P(3)}{P(1)}$ excluded from expenditure under TCGA 1992, s. 38(1)(a),

and fraction equal to $\frac{P(2) - P(3)}{P(2)}$ excluded from expenditure under TCGA 1992, s. 38(1)(b), where:

P(1) = table percentage for duration of lease at time of acquisition (or 31 March 1982 where applicable);

P(2) = table percentage for duration of lease at time expenditure incurred; and

P(3) = table percentage for duration of lease at time of disposal.

Years	%	Monthly(1) increment
50 or more	100	–
49	99.657	0.029
48	99.289	0.031
47	98.902	0.032
46	98.490	0.034

Years	%	Monthly[(1)] increment
45	98.059	0.036
44	97.595	0.039
43	97.107	0.041
42	96.593	0.043
41	96.041	0.046
40	95.457	0.049
39	94.842	0.051
38	94.189	0.054
37	93.497	0.058
36	92.761	0.061
35	91.981	0.065
34	91.156	0.069
33	90.280	0.073
32	89.354	0.077
31	88.371	0.082
30	87.330	0.087
29	86.226	0.092
28	85.053	0.098
27	83.816	0.103
26	82.496	0.110
25	81.100	0.116
24	79.622	0.123
23	78.055	0.131
22	76.399	0.138
21	74.635	0.147
20	72.770	0.155
19	70.791	0.165
18	68.697	0.175
17	66.470	0.186
16	64.116	0.196
15	61.617	0.208
14	58.971	0.221
13	56.167	0.234
12	53.191	0.248
11	50.038	0.263
10	46.695	0.279
9	43.154	0.295
8	39.399	0.313
7	35.414	0.332

Years	%	Monthly[(1)] increment
6	31.195	0.352
5	26.722	0.373
4	21.983	0.395
3	16.959	0.419
2	11.629	0.444
1	5.983	0.470
0	0	0.499

Note

[(1)] Where duration is *not* an *exact* number of years, the table percentage for the whole number of years is increased by 1/12 of the difference between that and the next highest percentage for each odd month. Fourteen odd days or more are rounded up and treated as a month; less than 14 odd days are ignored.

[¶5-150] Premiums for short leases: CGT/IT charge

(ITTOIA 2005, s. 277)

(Tax Reporter: ¶509-950)

The chart at ¶3-500 shows the proportion of any premium received in respect of a lease of less than 50 years which is chargeable to capital gains tax and that which is chargeable to income tax as property business profits.

[¶5-200] CGT exempt gilt-edged securities

(TCGA 1992, s. 16(2) and 115(1) and Sch. 9)

(Tax Reporter: ¶559-000)

Gains on the following securities are not chargeable gains and any losses are not allowable losses.

Stocks and bonds charged on the National Loans Funds	
2½%	Annuities 1905 or after
2¾%	Annuities 1905 or after
2½%	Consolidated Stock 1923 or after
3½%	War Loan 1952 or after
4%	Consolidated Loan 1957 or after
3½%	Conversion Loan 1961 or after
3%	Treasury Stock 1966 or after
2½%	Treasury Stock 1975 or after
12¾%	Treasury Loan 1992
8%	Treasury Loan 1992
10%	Treasury Stock 1992
3%	Treasury Stock 1992
12¼%	Exchequer Stock 1992

Stocks and bonds charged on the National Loans Funds – cont'd	
13½%	Exchequer Stock 1992
10½%	Treasury Convertible Stock 1992
2%	Index-Linked Treasury Stock 1992
12½%	Treasury Loan 1993
6%	Funding Loan 1993
13¾%	Treasury Loan 1993
10%	Treasury Loan 1993
8¼%	Treasury Stock 1993
14½%	Treasury Loan 1994
12½%	Exchequer Stock 1994
9%	Treasury Loan 1994
10%	Treasury Loan 1994
13½%	Exchequer Stock 1994
8½%	Treasury Stock 1994
8½%	Treasury Stock 1994 'A'
2%	Index-Linked Treasury Stock 1994
3%	Exchequer Gas Stock 1990–95
12%	Treasury Stock 1995
10¼%	Exchequer Stock 1995
12¾%	Treasury Loan 1995
9%	Treasury Loan 1992–96
15¼%	Treasury Loan 1996
13¼%	Exchequer Loan 1996
14%	Treasury Stock 1996
2%	Index-Linked Treasury Stock 1996
10%	Conversion Stock 1996
10%	Conversion Stock 1996 'A'
10%	Conversion Stock 1996 'B'
13¼%	Treasury Loan 1997
10½%	Exchequer Stock 1997
8¾%	Treasury Loan 1997
8¾%	Treasury Loan 1997 'B'
8¾%	Treasury Loan 1997 'C'
8¾%	Treasury Loan 1997 'D'
8¾%	Treasury Loan 1997 'E'
15%	Exchequer Stock 1997
7%	Treasury Convertible Stock 1997
6¾%	Treasury Loan 1995–98

Stocks and bonds charged on the National Loans Funds – cont'd	
15½%	Treasury Loan 1998
12%	Exchequer Stock 1998
12%	Exchequer Stock 1998 'A'
9¾%	Exchequer Stock 1998
9¾%	Exchequer Stock 1998 'A'
7¼%	Treasury Stock 1998 'A'
7¼%	Treasury Stock 1998 'B'
12%	Exchequer Stock 1998 'B'
4⅝%	Index-Linked Treasury Stock 1998
7¼%	Treasury Stock 1998
9½%	Treasury Loan 1999
10½%	Treasury Stock 1999
12¼%	Exchequer Stock 1999
12¼%	Exchequer Stock 1999 'A'
12¼%	Exchequer Stock 1999 'B'
2½%	Index-Linked Treasury Convertible Stock 1999
10¼%	Conversion Stock 1999
6%	Treasury Stock 1999
	Floating Rate Treasury Stock 1999
9%	Conversion Stock 2000
9%	Conversion Stock 2000 'A'
9%	Conversion Stock 2000 'B'
9%	Conversion Stock 2000 'C'
8½%	Treasury Loan 2000
8%	Treasury Stock 2000
8%	Treasury Stock 2000 'A'
13%	Treasury Stock 2000
13%	Treasury Stock 2000 'A'
7%	Treasury Stock 2001
7%	Treasury Stock 2001 'A'
14%	Treasury Stock 1998–2001
2½%	Index-Linked Treasury Stock 2001
9¾%	Conversion Stock 2001
10%	Treasury Stock 2001
9½%	Conversion Loan 2001
10%	Treasury Stock 2001 'A'
10%	Treasury Stock 2001 'B'
	Floating Rate Treasury Stock 2001

Stocks and bonds charged on the National Loans Funds – cont'd	
12%	Exchequer Stock 1999–2002
12%	Exchequer Stock 1999–2002 'A'
9½%	Conversion Stock 2002
10%	Conversion Stock 2002
9%	Exchequer Stock 2002
7%	Treasury Stock 2002
9¾%	Treasury Stock 2002
9¾%	Treasury Stock 2002 'A'
9¾%	Treasury Stock 2002 'B'
9¾%	Treasury Stock 2002 'C'
13¾%	Treasury Stock 2000–2003
13¾%	Treasury Stock 2000–2003 'A'
2½%	Index-Linked Treasury Stock 2003
9¾%	Conversion Loan 2003
6½%	Treasury Stock 2003
8%	Treasury Stock 2003
8%	Treasury Stock 2003 'A'
10%	Treasury Stock 2003
10%	Treasury Stock 2003 'A'
10%	Treasury Stock 2003 'B'
3½%	Funding Stock 1999–2004
11½%	Treasury Stock 2001–2004
9½%	Conversion Stock 2004
10%	Treasury Stock 2004
6¾%	Treasury Stock 2004
5%	Treasury Stock 2004
6¾%	Treasury Stock 2004 'A'
4⅜%	Index-Linked Treasury Stock 2004
9½%	Conversion Stock 2004 'A'
12½%	Treasury Stock 2003–2005
12½%	Treasury Stock 2003–2005 'A'
10½%	Exchequer Stock 2005
9½%	Conversion Stock 2005
9½%	Conversion Stock 2005 'A'
8½%	Treasury Stock 2005
8%	Treasury Loan 2002–2006
8%	Treasury Loan 2002–2006 'A'
2%	Index-Linked Treasury Stock 2006

Stocks and bonds charged on the National Loans Funds – cont'd	
9¾%	Conversion Stock 2006
7½%	Treasury Stock 2006
7¾%	Treasury Stock 2006
11¾%	Treasury Stock 2003–2007
11¾%	Treasury Stock 2003–2007 'A'
7¼%	Treasury Stock 2007
4½%	Treasury Stock 2007
8½%	Treasury Loan 2007
8½%	Treasury Loan 2007 'A'
8½%	Treasury Loan 2007 'B'
8½%	Treasury Loan 2007 'C'
13½%	Treasury Stock 2004–2008
9%	Treasury Loan 2008
9%	Treasury Loan 2008 'A'
9%	Treasury Loan 2008 'B'
9%	Treasury Loan 2008 'C'
9%	Treasury Loan 2008 'D'
5%	Treasury Stock 2008
2½%	Index-Linked Treasury Stock 2009
5¾%	Treasury Stock 2009
8%	Treasury Stock 2009
4%	Treasury Stock 2009
8%	Treasury Stock 2009 'A'
6¼%	Treasury Stock 2010
4¾%	Treasury Stock 2010
4¼%	Treasury Gilt 2011
3¼%	Treasury Gilt 2011
2½%	Index-Linked Treasury Stock 2011
9%	Conversion Loan 2011
9%	Conversion Loan 2011 'A'
9%	Conversion Loan 2011 'B'
9%	Conversion Loan 2011 'C'
9%	Conversion Loan 2011 'D'
5½%	Treasury Stock 2008–2012
9%	Treasury Stock 2012
9%	Treasury Stock 2012 'A'
5%	Treasury Stock 2012
5¼%	Treasury Gilt 2012

Stocks and bonds charged on the National Loans Funds – cont'd	
2½%	Index-Linked Treasury Stock 2013
8%	Treasury Stock 2013
4½%	Treasury Gilt 2013
5%	Treasury Stock 2014
2¼%	Treasury Gilt 2014
7¾%	Treasury Loan 2012–2015
4¾%	Treasury Stock 2015
2¾%	Treasury Gilt 2015
8%	Treasury Stock 2015
8%	Treasury Stock 2015 'A'
2½%	Treasury Stock 1986–2016
2½%	Index-Linked Treasury Stock 2016
2½%	Index-Linked Treasury Stock 2016 'A'
4%	Treasury Gilt 2016
2%	Treasury Gilt 2016
12%	Exchequer Stock 2013–2017
1%	Treasury Gilt 2017
1¼%	Index-Linked Treasury Gilt 2017
1¾%	Treasury Gilt 2017
8¾%	Treasury Stock 2017
8¾%	Treasury Stock 2017 'A'
1¼%	Treasury Gilt 2018
5%	Treasury Gilt 2018
0⅛%	Index-linked Treasury Gilt 2019
1¾%	Treasury Gilt 2019
4½%	Treasury Gilt 2019
3¾%	Treasury Gilt 2019
2½%	Index-Linked Treasury Stock 2020
3¾%	Treasury Gilt 2020
4¾%	Treasury Stock 2020
3¾%	Treasury Gilt 2021
8%	Treasury Stock 2021
1¾%	Treasury Gilt 2022
4%	Treasury Gilt 2022
1⅞%	Index-Linked Treasury Gilt 2022
2¼%	Treasury Gilt 2023
0⅛%	Index-Linked Treasury Gilt 2024
2½%	Index-Linked Treasury Stock 2024
2¾%	Treasury Gilt 2024

Stocks and bonds charged on the National Loans Funds – cont'd	
5%	Treasury Stock 2025
1¼%	Index-Linked Treasury Gilt 2027
4¼%	Treasury Gilt 2027
6%	Treasury Stock 2028
0⅛%	Index-Linked Treasury Gilt 2029
4⅛%	Index-Linked Treasury Stock 2030
4¾%	Treasury Gilt 2030
4¼%	Treasury Stock 2032
1¼%	Index-linked Treasury Gilt 2032
0¾%	Index-linked Treasury Gilt 2034
4½%	Treasury Gilt 2034
2%	Index-Linked Treasury Stock 2035
4¼%	Treasury Stock 2036
1⅛%	Index-Linked Treasury Gilt 2037
4¾%	Treasury Stock 2038
4¼%	Treasury Gilt 2039
0⅝%	Index-linked Treasury Gilt 2040
4¼%	Treasury Gilt 2040
4½%	Treasury Gilt 2042
0⅝%	Index-linked Treasury Gilt 2042
0⅛%	Index-linked Treasury Gilt 2044
4¼%	Treasury Gilt 2046
3¼%	Treasury Gilt 2044
0¾%	Index-Linked Treasury Gilt 2047
4¼%	Treasury Gilt 2049
0½%	Index-linked Treasury Gilt 2050
0¼%	Index-linked Treasury Gilt 2052
3¾%	Treasury Gilt 2052
1¼%	Indexed-linked Treasury Gilt 2055
4¼%	Treasury Gilt 2055
4%	Treasury Gilt 2060
0½%	Index-linked Treasury Gilt 2060
0⅜%	Index-linked Treasury Gilt 2062
0⅛%	Index-linked Treasury Gilt 2068
3½%	Treasury Gilt 2068

Securities issued by certain public corporations and guaranteed by the Treasury

3%	North of Scotland Electricity Stock 1989–92

[¶5-250] Securities of negligible value

(TCGA 1992, s. 24(2))

(Tax Reporter: ¶515-150)

The HMRC website contains a list, constantly updated, of shares or securities formerly quoted (largely) on the London Stock Exchange which have been officially declared of negligible value for the purposes of a claim under s. 24(2). A summary of principles, together with a link to the current list, may be found at www.hmrc.gov.uk/cgt/negvalist.htm.

The time limit for a claim is two years from the end of the tax year (or accounting period of a company) in which the deemed disposal and reacquisition take place.

[¶5-300] Identification of securities

(TCGA 1992, s. 104–109)

(Tax Reporter: ¶556-525ff.)

Disposals by individuals and trustees: 2008–09 onwards

Disposals on or after 6 April 2008 are to be identified with acquisitions in the following order:

(1) same-day acquisitions, but subject to an election under s. 105A (see below);

(2) acquisitions within the following 30 days on the basis of earlier acquisitions in that period, rather than later ones (a FIFO basis); and

(3) securities within the expanded s. 104 holding, which specifically does not include acquisitions under (1) and (2) above.

Where the number of securities which comprise the disposal exceed those identified under the above rules, that excess is identified with subsequent acquisitions beyond the 30-day period referred to above.

Where an individual acquires shares of the same class on the same day and some of those shares are acquired pursuant to the exercise of approved scheme share options, a s. 105A election may be made. The election treats the option scheme shares as a separate holding from the other shares acquired and as being disposed of after the remainder of the other shares.

Disposals by companies

The order of identification is:

(1) any acquisition on the same day;

(2) acquisitions within the previous nine days;

(3) acquisitions since 1 April 1982, ‘the s. 104 holding’, previously termed ‘the new holding’;

(4) acquisitions in the period 6 April 1965 to 31 March 1982, ‘the 1982 holding’; and

(5) those held on 6 April 1965, in respect of which no election has been made to include them in the pre-1982 pool; these will be identified on a last-in, first-out (LIFO) basis

In respect of disposals before 5 December 2005, where a company or group of companies held at least 2% of the shares or securities of that class, acquisitions and disposals within one month (for most quoted shares or securities) or six months (for most other shares or securities) could be matched.

[¶5-350] Expenses incurred by personal representatives

(SP 2/04)

(Tax Reporter: ¶367-575)

In respect of deaths after 5 April 2004, the scale of expenses allowable in computing the gains or losses of personal representatives on the sale of assets in a deceased person's estate is as follows:

Gross value of estate	Allowable expenditure
Up to £50,000	1.8% of probate value of assets sold by personal representatives
£50,001–£90,000	£900, divided among all assets in the estate in proportion to their probate values and allowed in those proportions on assets sold by personal representatives
£90,001–£400,000	1% of probate value of assets sold
£400,001–£500,000	£4,000, divided as above
£500,001–£1,000,000	0.8% of probate value of assets sold
£1,000,001–£5,000,000	£8,000, divided as above
Over £5,000,000	0.16% of the probate value of the assets sold, subject to a maximum of £10,000

Note

Computations based either on the above scale or on actual expenditure incurred are accepted.

[¶5-500] Compliance and administration

(TMA 1970, s. 8ff.)

(Tax Reporter: ¶180-000ff.)

For summary of the main provisions which relate both to capital gains tax and income tax, see ¶1-250ff.

[¶5-950] Time limits for elections and claims

In the absence of any specific provision to the contrary, under self-assessment the normal rule is that claims by individuals, trustees and companies are to be made within four years from the end of the tax year or chargeable period to which they relate. Before 1 April 2010, these limits were five years from 31 January next following the end of the tax year for individuals and six years from the end of the relevant chargeable period for companies (TMA 1970, s. 43(1) and FA 1998, Sch. 18, para. 55).

In certain cases HMRC *may* permit an extension of the strict time limit in relation to certain elections and claims.

Provision	Time limit	References
Post-cessation expenses relieved against gains	12 months from 31 January next following the tax year in which expenses paid	TCGA 1992, s. 261D(6) (Tax Reporter: ¶524 125)
Trading losses relieved against gains	12 months from 31 January next following the tax year loss arose	TCGA 1992, s. 261B(8) (Tax Reporter: ¶524-100)
Value of asset negligible	Two years from end of tax year (or accounting period if a company) in which deemed disposal/ reacquisition takes place	TCGA 1992, s. 24(2) (Tax Reporter: ¶515-150)

Provision	Time limit	References
Re-basing of all assets to 31 March 1982 values (pre-06/04/08 disposals for individuals)	Two years from end of accounting period of disposal for company (12 months from 31 January next following the tax year of disposal for individuals)	TCGA 1992, s. 35(6) (Tax Reporter: ¶520-350)
50% relief if deferred charge on gains before 31 March 1982 (pre-06/04/08 disposals for individuals)	Two years from end of accounting period of disposal for company (12 months from 31 January next following the tax year of disposal for individuals)	TCGA 1992, s. 36 and Sch. 4, para. 9(1) (Tax Reporter: ¶520-600)
Variation within two years of death not to have CGT effect	Six months from date of variation (election not necessary for variations on or after 1 August 2002)	TCGA 1992, s. 62 (Tax Reporter: ¶367-825)
Specifying which 'same day' share acquisitions (through employee share schemes) should be treated as disposed of first	Within 12 months from 31 January next following the tax year of disposal	TCGA 1992, s. 105A (Tax Reporter: ¶556-650)
Replacement of business assets (rollover relief)	Four years from the end of the tax year/accounting period (before 1 April 2010, five years from 31 January next following the tax year for individuals or six years from the end of the accounting period for companies) Replacement asset to be purchased between 12 months before and three years after disposal of old asset	TCGA 1992, s. 152(1) (Tax Reporter: ¶570-250)
Disapplication of incorporation relief under TCGA 1992, s. 162	Two years from 31 January following the end of the year of assessment in which the business is transferred	TCGA 1992, s. 162A (Tax Reporter: ¶574-125)
Holdover of gain on gift of business asset	Four years from the end of the tax year (before 1 April 2010, five years from 31 January next following the tax year)	TCGA 1992, s. 165(1) (Tax Reporter: ¶574-550)
Determination of main residence	Two years from acquisition of second property (see ESC D21)	TCGA 1992, s. 222(5) (Tax Reporter: ¶545-950)
Irrecoverable loan to a trader	Four years from the end of the tax year/accounting period (before 1 April 2010, five years from 31 January next following the tax year for individuals or six years from the end of the accounting period for companies)	TCGA 1992, s. 253(4A) (Tax Reporter: ¶511-150)
Deemed disposal/reacquisition on expiry of mineral lease	Four years from the date of the relevant event (before 1 April 2010, six years)	TCGA 1992, s. 203(2) (Tax Reporter: ¶799-475)
Delayed remittances of foreign gains	Four years from the end of the tax year/accounting period (before 1 April 2010, five years from 31 January next following the tax year for individuals or six years from the end of the accounting period for companies)	TCGA 1992, s. 279(5) (Tax Reporter: ¶591-150)

Provision	Time limit	References
Deferred unascertainable consideration: election for treatment of loss	12 months from 31 January next following the tax year loss arose	TCGA 1992, s. 279A and 279D (Tax Reporter: ¶524-250)
Earn out right treated as a security	Within 12 months from 31 January next following the tax year in which the right is received for individuals or two years from the end of the accounting period for companies	TCGA 1992, s. 138A (Tax Reporter: ¶561-600)
Appropriations of assets to trading stock; no deemed disposal at market value on transfer to stock but subsequent trading profits adjusted by gain or loss that would have arisen	Within 12 months from 31 January next following tax year of assessment for the period of account in which the appropriation is made for capital gains tax purposes, or within two years from the end of the accounting period in which the appropriation is made for corporation tax	TCGA 1992, s. 161 (Tax Reporter: ¶573-800)
Entrepreneurs' relief	Within 12 months from 31 January next following tax year in which qualifying disposal is made	TCGA 1992, s. 169M (Tax Reporter: ¶572-550)
Small part disposals of land; no disposal but base cost on subsequent disposal reduce by consideration received	Within 12 months from 31 January next following tax year in which part disposal is made for individuals, or two years from end of accounting period in which part disposal is made for companies	TCGA 1992, s. 242 (Tax Reporter: ¶510-350)
Holdover relief on gifts chargeable to Inheritance tax	Four years from end of the tax year of gift (before 1 April 2010, five years from 31 January next following the tax year)	TCGA 1992, s. 260 (Tax Reporter: ¶548-700)
Disincorporation relief	Within two years beginning with the business transfer date	FA 2013, s. 60
EIS/SEIS/SI deferral relief	Five years from 31 January following tax year in which shares are issued/ investment is made	TCGA 1992, Sch. 5B, para. 6; Sch. 5BB, para. 3; Sch. 8B, para. 8 (Tax Reporter: ¶565-600; ¶569-200; ¶569-800)

INHERITANCE TAX

[¶6-000] Rates of tax

(IHTA 1984, s. 7 and Sch. 1)

(Tax Reporter: ¶607-000; ¶624-000)

From 15 March 1988

	Gross rate of tax
Lifetime transfers	
Gross transfers up to cumulative limit	Nil
Gross transfers over cumulative limit	20%
Grossing-up fraction	$^{1}/_{4}$
Death transfers	
Gross transfers up to cumulative limit	Nil
Gross transfers over cumulative limit	40%
Grossing-up fraction	$^{2}/_{3}$
Reduced rate[1]	36%

Note

[1] For deaths occurring on or after 6 April 2012, a reduced rate of inheritance tax of 36% applies where 10% or more of a deceased person's net estate (after deducting IHT exemptions, reliefs and the nil-rate band) is left to charity. To determine whether the lower rate will apply, the estate is broken down into three components (with the nil-rate band apportioned): the survivorship component (property passing automatically to the survivor), the settled property component (settled property in which the deceased held an interest in possession) and the general component (all other property excluding gifts with reservation of benefit to which the lower rate cannot apply). The 10% test is applied to each component separately and the lower rate applied to those components which satisfy the 10% test. An election to merge components of the estate and apply the 10% test in aggregate is possible, as is an election to opt out of the lower rate for one or more components of the estate. Both elections must be made within two years of the date of death and may be withdrawn within two years and one month of the date of death.

[¶6-050] Cumulative chargeable transfers limit

(IHTA 1984, s. 7 and Sch. 1)

Transfers from 15 March 1988

Period	Cumulative chargeable transfers limit[1] £
2014–15[2]	325,000
2009–10 to 2013–14	325,000
2008–09	312,000
2007–08	300,000

Period	Cumulative chargeable transfers limit[1] £
2006–07	285,000
2005–06	275,000
2004–05	263,000
2003–04	255,000
2002–03	250,000
2001–02	242,000
2000–01	234,000
1999–00	231,000
1998–99	223,000
1997–98	215,000
1996–97	200,000
1995–96	154,000
10/03/92 to 05/04/95	150,000
06/04/91 to 09/03/92	140,000
1990–91	128,000
1989–90	118,000
15/03/88 to 05/04/89	110,000

Notes

(1) FA 2008, s. 10 and Sch. 4 allow a claim to be made to transfer any unused nil-rate band of the first deceased spouse or civil partner to the estate of their surviving spouse or civil partner who dies on or after 9 October 2007.

(2) FA 2010, s. 8 froze the inheritance tax nil-rate band at £325,000 for tax years 2012–13 to 2014–15. FA 2014, Sch. 25, para. 2 extends the freeze for a further three years from 2015–16 until 2017–18.

[¶6-200] Annual and small gift exemption

(IHTA 1984, s. 19 and 20)

(Tax Reporter: ¶643-200 and ¶643-700)

	On or after 6 April 1981 £	6 April 1980 to 5 April 1981 £	6 April 1976 to 5 April 1980 £
Annual	3,000	2,000	2,000
Small gift (to the same person)	250	250	100

[¶6-250] Gifts in consideration of marriage/civil partnership

(IHTA 1984, s. 22)

(Tax Reporter: ¶644-450)

Donor	Exemption limit £
Parent of party to the marriage/civil partnership	5,000
Remote ancestor of party to the marriage/ civil partnership	2,500
Party to the marriage/civil partnership	2,500
Any other person	1,000

[¶6-300] Transfers by UK-domiciled spouse/civil partner to non-UK domiciled spouse/civil partner

(IHTA 1984, s. 18)

(Tax Reporter: ¶644-900)

Transfer on or after	Exemption limit £
6 April 2013	325,000[(1)]
9 March 1982	55,000

Note

[(1)] *Finance Act* 2013 increased the lifetime limit on the amount that can be transferred exempt from IHT to a spouse or civil partner domiciled outside the UK to the exemption limit at the time of the transfer per IHTA 1984, Sch. 1 (the nil-rate band).

[¶6-325] Election to be treated as domiciled in UK

(IHTA 1984, s. 267ZA–267ZB)

(Tax Reporter: ¶684-575)

A person who is not domiciled in the UK but who is, or has been married to, or in a civil partnership with, someone who is domiciled in the UK can elect to be treated as domiciled in the UK for the purposes of inheritance tax. There are two types of elections:

1. A lifetime election by the non-domiciled individual who is at any time on or after 6 April 2013 and during the period of seven years ending with the date of the election married to or in a civil partnership with a UK domiciled individual.
2. A death election by the personal representatives of a deceased person who was at any time on or after 6 April 2013, and during the period of seven years ending with the date of death themselves domiciled in the UK and married to or in a civil partnership with a non domiciled person who is, by virtue of the election, to be treated as domiciled in the UK.

The election is irrevocable but ceases to have effect if the individual is not resident in the UK for income tax purposes for four successive tax years. The election must be in writing and in the case of a death election made within two years of the date of death. The election cannot relate back to before 6 April 2013, or more than seven years before either the election is made or the date of death and any date the election relates back to must be a date when the individual was married, or in a civil partnership, and either the individual or their spouse (as the case may be) was UK domiciled on that date.

[¶6-350] Gifts to the nation

(IHTA 1984, s. 25; FA 2012, Sch. 14)

(Tax Reporter: ¶646-050)

Gifts of pre-eminent property to be held for the benefit of the public or the nation are exempt from inheritance tax. Pre-eminent property includes any picture, print, book, manuscript, work of art, scientific object or other thing that is pre-eminent for its national, scientific, historic or artistic interest, collections of such items and any object kept in a significant building where it is desirable that it remain associated with the building.

[¶6-360] Employee ownership trusts

(IHTA 1984, s. 13A; 28A; 72(3A); 75A; 86)

(Tax Reporter: ¶646-750; ¶363-770; ¶364-750)

Finance Act 2014 introduces an exemption from inheritance tax for transfers on or after 6 April 2014 by individuals of shares in a company to an employee ownership trust and for transfers of cash and other assets by a close company to the employee ownership trust (such transfers are not transfers of value for IHT purposes). Employee-ownership trusts are also excluded from the definition of 'relevant property' and, therefore, not subject to the ten-year charge or the exit charge under the relevant property regime (from 6 April 2014).

[¶6-400] Agricultural and business property relief

(IHTA 1984, s. 103ff. and 115ff.)

(Tax Reporter: ¶664-000 and ¶658-000)

	Rate of relief for disposals			
Type of relief	**on or after 6/4/96 %**	**1/9/95–5/4/96 %**	**10/3/92–31/8/95 %**	**before 10/3/92 %**
Agricultural property[(1)(2)]				
Vacant possession or right to obtain it within 12 months	100	100	100	50
Tenanted land with vacant a possession value	100	100	100	50
Entitled to 50% relief at 9 March 1981 and not since able to obtain vacant possession	100	100	100	50

Type of relief	Rate of relief for disposals on or after 6/4/96 %	1/9/95–5/4/96 %	10/3/92–31/8/95 %	before 10/3/92 %
Agricultural land let on or after 1 September 1995	100	100	N/A	N/A
Other circumstances	50	50	50	30
Business property				
Nature of property				
Business or interest in business	100	100	100	50
Controlling shareholding in quoted company	50	50	50	50
Controlling shareholding in unquoted[(3)] company	100	100	100	50
Settled property used in life tenant's business	100/50[(4)]	100/50[(4)]	100/50[(4)]	50/30[(4)]
Shareholding in unquoted[(3)] company: more than 25% interest	100	100	100	50[(5)]
Minority shareholding in unquoted[(3)] company: 25% or less	100	50	50	30[(6)]
Land, buildings, machinery or plant used by transferor's company or partnership	50	50	50	30

Notes

[(1)] FA 2009, s. 122 extends agricultural property relief to property in the European Economic Area. IHT due or paid on or after 23 April 2003 in relation to agricultural property located in a qualifying EEA state at the time of the chargeable event will become eligible for relief.

[(2)] From 6 April 1995, short rotation coppice is regarded as agricultural property.

[(3)] With effect from 10 March 1992, 'unquoted' means shares not quoted on a recognised stock exchange and therefore includes shares dealt in on the Unlisted Securities Market (USM) or Alternative Investment Market (AIM).

[(4)] The higher rate applies if the settled property is transferred along with business itself.

[(5)] 30% if a minority interest transferred before 17 March 1987, or if transferor had not held at least 25% interest throughout preceding two years.

[(6)] The relief was 20% for transfers after 26 October 1977 but before 15 March 1983.

[¶6-450] Quick succession relief

(IHTA 1984, s. 141)

(Tax Reporter: ¶627-400)

Years between transfers: More than	Not more than	Percentage applied to formula below
0	1	100
1	2	80
2	3	60
3	4	40
4	5	20

Formula

$$\text{Tax charge on earlier transfer} \times \frac{\text{Increase in transferee's estate}}{\text{Diminution in transferor's estate}}$$

Inheritance Tax

[¶6-475] Intestate rules

Note: See ¶26-500 for succession and intestacy rules applicable in Scotland

<table>
<tr><th rowspan="2">Surviving family</th><th colspan="2">Beneficiaries</th></tr>
<tr><th>Deaths
before 1 October 2014[1]</th><th>Deaths
on or after 1 October 2014[2]</th></tr>
<tr><td>Spouse or civil partner but no issue
Spouse or civil partner only (no issue, parents, brothers or sisters of the whole blood (or their issue)).</td><td>Spouse or civil partner takes everything, absolutely.</td><td>Spouse or civil partner takes everything, absolutely.</td></tr>
<tr><td>Spouse or civil partner (no issue) and parent or whole blood brother or sister, or issue of whole blood brother or sister.</td><td>Spouse or civil partner takes:
• personal chattels;
• £450,000 absolutely (or the entire estate where this is less);
• one-half share of residue (if any) absolutely.</td><td>Spouse or civil partner takes everything, absolutely.</td></tr>
<tr><td></td><td>Remainder distributable to:
• parent(s);
• failing a parent then on trust for the deceased's whole blood brothers and sisters, (nephews and nieces step into their parent's shoes if the latter is dead).</td><td>Parents/siblings receive nothing</td></tr>
<tr><td>Spouse or civil partner and issue</td><td>Spouse or civil partner takes:
• personal chattels (e.g. furniture, pictures, clothing, jewellery, etc.), absolutely;
• £250,000 absolutely (or the entire estate where this is less);
• life interest in one-half of the residue (if any).

Issue receive:
• one half of residue (if any) on statutory trusts;
• the other half of residue on statutory trusts upon the death of the spouse or civil partner.</td><td>Spouse or civil partner takes:
• personal chattels (e.g. furniture, pictures, clothing, jewellery, etc.), absolutely;
• £250,000[3] absolutely (or the entire estate where this is less);
• one half of the residue (if any) absolutely.

Issue receive:
• one half of residue (if any) on statutory trusts.</td></tr>
<tr><td>No spouse or civil partner</td><td colspan="2">Everything is taken by:
• Issue, but if none;
• Parent(s), but if none;
• Brothers and sisters of the whole blood (nephews and nieces step into their parent's shoes), but if none;</td></tr>
</table>

Surviving family	Beneficiaries	
	Deaths before 1 October 2014[1]	Deaths on or after 1 October 2014[2]
	• Brothers and sisters of the half blood (nephews and nieces step into their parent's shoes), but if none; • Grandparents, but if none; • Uncles and aunts of the whole blood and the issue of any deceased uncle or aunt, but if none; • Uncles and aunts of the half blood and the issue of any deceased uncle or aunt, but if none; • The Crown.	

Notes

[1] For deaths on or after 1 February 2009 under the *Administration of Estates Act* 1925, s. 46(1); not applicable in Scotland.

[2] For deaths after 1 October 2014 (2014/2039) under the *Administration of Estates Act* 1925, s. 46(1) (as amended by the *Inheritance and Trustees' Powers Act* 2014); not applicable in Scotland.

[3] The fixed sum statutory legacy is to be index-linked using the consumer prices index and amended by statutory instrument (*Administration of Estates Act* 1925, Sch. 1A (as inserted by the *Inheritance and Trustees' Powers Act* 2014)).

[¶6-500] Instalment option

(IHTA 1984, s. 227)

(Tax Reporter: ¶183-215)

Interest-free:

- Controlling shareholdings;
- Holdings of 10% or more of unquoted shares with value over £20,000;
- Certain other death transfers of unquoted shares;
- Business or interest in business;
- Agricultural value of agricultural property; and
- Woodlands.

Not interest-free:

- Land, wherever situated, other than within categories above; and
- Shareholdings in certain land investment and security dealing companies, or market makers or discount houses.

[¶6-550] Fall in value relief

(IHTA 1984, s. 179; s. 191 and 197A)

(Tax Reporter: ¶627-900)

Type of property	Period after death
Quoted securities sold	One year
Qualifying investments[1]	One year
Interests in land – deaths after 15 March 1990	Four years

Note

[1] Qualifying investments mean shares or securities which are quoted at the date of death in question, holdings in a unit trust which at that date is an authorised unit trust, shares in an open-ended investment company and shares in any common investment fund established under s. 42 of the *Administration of Justice Act* 1982.

[¶6-600] Taper relief

(IHTA 1984, s. 7(4))

(Tax Reporter: ¶611-400)

Years between gift and death		Percentage of full tax charge at death – rates actually due
More than	Not more than	%
3	4	80
4	5	60
5	6	40
6	7	20

[¶6-650] Pre-owned assets

(FA 2004, s. 84 and Sch. 15)

(Tax Reporter: ¶614-800)

A freestanding income tax charge where individuals continue to enjoy property previously owned by them with effect from 6 April 2005. The charge to tax arises under three main heads, relating to:

- land;
- chattels; and
- intangible property in settlor interested trusts.

In determining whether charges arise in respect of land or chattels, certain transactions are excluded and there are a number of exemptions.

Limited reliefs prevent double charges to tax. Special rules apply to individuals not resident or not domiciled in the UK. Provisions allow for opting out of the pre-owned assets charge arising in respect of any property, with inheritance tax consequences.

Land

The chargeable amount in the case of land or any interest in land is the 'appropriate rental value' less an amount paid under any legal obligation in respect of the occupation of the land. The appropriate rental value is:

$$R \times \frac{DV}{V}$$

Where:

R is the 'rental value' of the relevant land for the 'taxable period';

DV is the value at the 'valuation date' of the interest in the relevant land that was disposed of by the chargeable person or, where the disposal was a non-exempt sale, the appropriate proportion of that value; and

V is the value of the relevant land at the valuation date.

The 'taxable period' is the year of assessment, or part of the year of assessment, during which the relevant conditions are met.

The 'rental value' is based on the assumption of a letting from year-to-year where the tenant pays the taxes, rates and charges and the landlord is responsible for repair and insurance. Land may be valued on a five-yearly rather than an annual valuation (SI 2005/724).

Chattels

In respect of chattels, the chargeable amount is the 'appropriate amount' less an amount paid under a legal obligation to the owner of the chattel. The 'appropriate amount' is:

$$N \times \frac{DV}{V}$$

Where:

N is the notional interest for the taxable period, at the prescribed rate, on the value of the chattel at the valuation date;

DV is the value at the valuation date of the interest in the relevant chattel that was disposed of by the chargeable person or, where the disposal was a non-exempt sale, the appropriate proportion of that asset; and

V is the value of the chattel at the valuation date.

Intangible property in settlor interested trusts

The chargeable amount in relation to the relevant property is:

$$N - T$$

Where:

N is the notional amount of interest for the taxable period, at the prescribed rate, on the value of the property at the valuation date; and

T is the amount of income tax or capital gains tax payable by the chargeable person in the taxable period on gains from contracts of life assurance, income where settlor retains an interest, transfer of assets abroad, charge on settlor with interest in settlement and attribution of gains to settlors with interest in non-resident or dual resident settlements.

Where the aggregate amount attributable to a chargeable person in respect of land, chattels and intangibles does not exceed £5,000, there is no income tax payable. If benefits exceed £5,000, the charge is on the full amount including the first £5,000.

[¶6-700] Delivery of accounts

(IHTA 1984, s. 216)

(Tax Reporter: ¶180-725)

Nature of transfer	Due Date
Chargeable lifetime transfer	Later of: – 12 months after end of month in which transfer occurred – three months after person became liable
Potentially exempt transfers which have become chargeable	12 months after end of month in which death of transferor occurred

Nature of transfer	Due Date
Transfers on death	Later of: – 12 months after end of month in which death occurred – three months after personal representatives first act or have reason to believe an account is required
Gifts subject to reservation included in donor's estate at death	12 months after end of month in which death occurred
National heritage property	Six months after end of month in which chargeable event occurred
Relevant property settlements: ten-year anniversary and exit charges	Six months from end of month in which the occasion occurs[1]

Note

[1] Chargeable transfers on or after 6 April 2014 (previously 12 months from the end of the month in which the transfer is made or if later, three months from the date when the trustee first becomes liable for the tax).

Values below which no account required

(SI 2008/605)

(Tax Reporter: ¶180-775)

Excepted lifetime chargeable transfers on or after 6 April 2007	**£**
Where the property given away, or in which the interest subsists, is wholly attributable to cash or quoted stocks and securities, the cumulative total of all chargeable transfers made by the transfer in the seven years before the transfer must not exceed the nil-rate band.	
Where the property given away, or in which the interest subsists, is wholly or partly attributable to property other than cash or quoted stocks and securities: (1) the value transferred by the chargeable transfer together with the cumulative total of all chargeable transfers made by the transferor in the seven years before the transfer must not exceed 80% of the relevant IHT nil-rate band; (2) the value transferred must not exceed the nil-rate band that is available to the transferor at the time the disposal takes place.	
Excepted lifetime chargeable transfers from 1 April 1981 to 5 April 2007	
Transfer in question, together with all other chargeable transfers in same 12-month period ending on 5 April	10,000
Transfer in question, together with all previous chargeable transfers during preceding ten years	40,000

Excepted settlements

(SI 2008/606)

(Tax Reporter: ¶180-905)

Excepted settlements: chargeable events on or after 6 April 2007

No qualifying interest in possession subsists and:

Either:

- Cash is and has always been the only property comprised in the settlement;
- No further property has been added to the settlement (since it was made);
- The trustees are and have always been UK resident;
- Gross value of settled property less than **£1,000** throughout; and
- No related settlements.

Or:

- UK domiciled settlor (when settlement made until earlier of the chargeable event or death of settlor);
- Trustees are and have always been UK resident;
- No related settlements; and
- One of following conditions satisfied:

Chargeable event:

1) ***Ten-year anniversary*** (IHTA 1984, s. 64)
Value transferred does not exceed 80% of IHT threshold
2) ***Exit charge before first ten-year anniversary*** (IHTA 1984, s. 65)
Value transferred does not exceed 80% of IHT threshold
3) ***Exit charge after one or more ten-year anniversaries*** (IHTA 1984, s. 65)
Value transferred (under IHTA 1984, s. 66(3), taking into account s. 69) does not exceed 80% of IHT threshold
4) ***Exit charge age 18–25 trusts*** (IHTA 1984, s. 71E)
Value transferred (under IHTA 1984, s. 71F) does not exceed 80% of IHT threshold

Excepted estates

(SI 2004/2543)

(Tax Reporter: ¶180-855)

Domiciled in the United Kingdom

Deaths on and after	But on or before	Total gross value(1)(2)(3)(4)(5) £	Total gross value of property outside UK £	Total value of settled property £	Aggregate value of 'specified transfers' £
06 April 2014	05 April 2015	325,000	100,000	150,000	150,000
06 April 2009	05 April 2014	325,000	100,000	150,000	150,000
06 April 2008	05 April 2009	312,000	100,000	150,000	150,000

Deaths on and after	But on or before	Total gross value[(1)(2)(3)(4)(5)] £	Total gross value of property outside UK £	Total value of settled property £	Aggregate value of 'specified transfers' £
06 April 2007	05 April 2008	300,000	100,000	150,000	150,000
01 Sept 2006	05 April 2007	285,000	100,000	150,000	150,000
06 April 2006	31 Aug 2006	285,000	75,000	100,000	100,000
06 April 2005	05 April 2006	275,000	75,000	100,000	100,000
06 April 2004	05 April 2005	263,000	75,000	100,000	100,000
06 April 2003	05 April 2004	240,000	75,000	100,000	100,000
06 April 2002	05 April 2003	220,000	75,000	100,000	100,000
06 April 2000	05 April 2002	210,000	50,000	–	75,000
06 April 1998	05 April 2000	200,000	50,000	–	75,000
06 April 1996	05 April 1998	180,000	30,000	–	50,000
06 April 1995	05 April 1996	145,000	15,000	–	–
01 April 1991	05 April 1995	125,000	15,000	–	–
01 April 1990	31 March 1991	115,000	15,000	–	–
01 April 1989	31 March 1990	100,000	15,000	–	–
01 April 1987	31 March 1989	70,000	10,000	–	–

Notes

(1) The aggregate of the gross value of that person's estate, the value transferred by any specified transfers made by that person, and the value transferred by any specified exempt transfers made by that person, must not exceed the IHT threshold. (Where the deceased dies after 5 April and before 6 August and application for probate or confirmation is made before 6 August in the same year as death, the inheritance tax threshold used is that for the preceding tax year.)

(2) An estate will qualify as an excepted estate where the gross value of the estate, plus the chargeable value of any transfers in the seven years to death, does not exceed £1,000,000 and the net chargeable estate after deduction of spouse or civil partner and/or charity exemption only is less than the IHT threshold, and the total value transferred on that person's death by a spouse, civil partner or charity transfer must be greater than nil (SI 2004/2543).

(3) For deaths on or after 6 April 2002, the limit applies to the aggregate of the gross value of the estate *plus* the value of 'specified transfers' which is extended and includes chargeable transfers, within seven years prior to death, of cash, quoted shares or securities, or an interest in land and furnishings and chattels disposed of at the same time to the same person (excluding property transferred subject to a reservation or property which becomes settled property).

For deaths on or after 6 April 1996 but before 6 April 2002, this limit applies to the total gross value of the estate *plus* the value of any transfers of cash or of quoted shares or securities made within seven years before death.

(4) For deaths after 5 April 2010, the IHT threshold for these purposes is increased by 100% where (SI 2004/2543):

(a) the deceased is a surviving spouse or civil partner;
(b) a claim has been made for the transfer of the unused nil-rate band of their deceased spouse or civil partner;
(c) all of the first deceased spouse's or civil partner's nil-rate band was unused; and
(d) the first deceased met similar criteria to those listed above for excepted estates.

(5) For deaths after 28 February 2011, where, in any tax year in the seven years prior to death, a person has transferred over £3,000 that is considered to be exempt as part of normal expenditure out of income, the amount will be included in the value of a person's estate for the purposes of determining whether the estate is an excepted estate, even though the transfer itself may qualify for the exemption (SI 2004/2543).

For deaths occurring before 6 April 2011, an estate does not qualify as an excepted estate where the deceased was a person by reason of whose death one of the alternatively secured pension fund provisions applied. These provisions were repealed in relation to deaths on or after 6 April 2011 by FA 2011, Sch. 16, para. 48.

[¶6-750] Due dates for payment

(IHTA 1984, s. 226)

(Tax Reporter: ¶183-205)

Transfer	Due Date
Chargeable lifetime transfers between 6 April and 30 September	30 April in following year
Chargeable lifetime transfers between 1 October and 5 April	Six months after end of month in which transfer made
Potentially exempt transfers which become chargeable	Six months after end of month in which death occurred
Transfers on death; extra tax payable on chargeable lifetime transfers within seven years before death	Six months after end of month in which death occurred or on delivery of accounts by personal representatives, if earlier
Relevant property settlements: ten-year anniversary and exit charges	Six months after end of month in which the occasion occurs[(1)]

Note

(1) Chargeable transfers on or after 6 April 2014 (previously 30 April in the following year for chargeable events before 1 October (in any tax year), otherwise six months after the end of the month in which the event occurs).

[¶6-800] Penalties for failure in relation to obligations falling due after 22 July 2004

(IHTA 1984, s. 245–253; FA 2007, Sch. 24; FA 2008, Sch. 36).

(Tax Reporter: ¶181-550)

Failure to deliver an IHT account (IHTA 1984, s. 245)	Account outstanding at end of statutory period	Fixed penalty of £100 (but not exceeding tax due)[(1)]
	Daily penalty after failure declared by a court or the tribunal	Up to £60 a day
	Penalty after six months from end of statutory period, if proceedings for declaring the failure not started before then	Fixed penalty of further £100 (but not exceeding tax due)[(1)]
	Penalty after 12 months from end of statutory period where tax is payable	Up to £3,000[(2)]

Failure by professional person to deliver a return of a settlement by a UK-domiciled person but with non-resident trustees (IHTA 1984, s. 245A)	Account outstanding at end of statutory period (three months from making of settlement)	Up to £300
	Daily penalty after failure declared by a court or the tribunal	Up to £60 a day
Failure to report a deed of variation which increases the IHT liability (IHTA 1984, s. 245A)	Penalty for failure to report within 18 months of deed of variation being executed	Up to £3,000[(3)]
	Penalty	Up to £100
	Daily penalty after failure declared by a court or the tribunal	Up to £60 a day
Failure to comply with a notice requiring information (FA 2008, Sch. 36)	Penalty	Up to £300
	Daily penalty	Up to £60 a day
	Penalty where continued failure and significant tax at stake, determined by tribunal	Tax related
Incorrect information or document provided in compliance with information notice (FA 2008, Sch. 36)	Penalty	Up to £3,000 per inaccuracy
Incorrect information provided by any person (IHTA 1984, s. 247(3))	Fraud or negligence	Up to £3,000[(4)]
Before 1 April 2013: Person assisting in providing incorrect information, etc. (IHTA 1984, s. 247(4))	Penalty	Up to £3,000
Error in taxpayers's document (careless or deliberate) (FA 2007, Sch. 24, para. 1)[(5)]	standard amount (careless behaviour) where the inaccuracy is deliberate but not concealed where the inaccuracy is deliberate and concealed	30% of potential revenue lost 70% of potential lost revenue 100% of the potential lost revenue

Error in taxpayer's document attributable to another person (FA 2007, Sch. 24, para. 1A)[6]	Penalty	Tax geared

Notes

[1] The change took effect on 23 January 2005.

[2] The change applies where the due date for delivery of an account expires after 22 July 2004. Where the due date has expired before 22 July 2004, the penalty does not apply until 23 July 2005. The penalty is subject to the defence of reasonable excuse.

[3] The change applies where the due date for notification expires after 22 July 2004. Where the due date has expired before 22 July 2004, the penalty does not apply until 23 July 2005.

[4] These changes take effect for accounts, information and documents delivered after 22 July 2004.

[5] FA 2008, Sch. 40 extended the new penalty regime in FA 2007, Sch. 24 to inheritance tax from 1 April 2009 where documents are due to be filed on or after 1 April 2010.

There are certain maximum reductions from the fixed penalties available which vary according to the level of the fixed penalty and whether a disclosure was prompted or unprompted (FA 2007, Sch. 24, para. 10).

[6] FA 2007, Sch. 24, para. 1A as added by FA 2008, Sch. 40 allows a penalty to be charged where an inaccuracy in the liable person's document was attributable to another person. Where it can be shown that the other person deliberately withheld information or supplied false information to the liable person, with the intention that the account or return would contain an inaccuracy, a penalty may be charged on that other person. But that will not necessarily mean that the personal representative themselves may not also be chargeable to a penalty. If the withheld or false information gave rise to inconsistencies in the information they had received about the estate and they did not question those inconsistencies; the liable person may still be charged a penalty for failing to take reasonable care as well.

[¶6-850] Prescribed rates of interest

(IHTA 1984, s. 233 and 235)

Interest is charged at the following rates on late payments or repayments of inheritance tax or capital transfer tax.

Interest period	Interest rate %	Repayment interest rate %	Days
From 29 Sept. 2009	3	0.5	–
24 Mar. 2009 to 28 Sept. 2009	0	0	189
27 Jan. 2009 to 23 Mar. 2009	1	1	56
6 Jan. 2009 to 26 Jan. 2009	2	2	21
6 Nov. 2008 to 5 Jan. 2009	3	3	61
6 Jan. 2008 to 5 Nov. 2008	4	4	304
6 Aug. 2007 to 5 Jan. 2008	5	5	153
6 Sept. 2006 to 5 Aug. 2007	4	4	334
6 Sept. 2005 to 5 Sept. 2006	3	3	365
6 Sept. 2004 to 5 Sept. 2005	4	4	365
6 Dec. 2003 to 5 Sept. 2004	3	3	275
6 Aug. 2003 to 5 Dec. 2003	2	2	122
6 Nov. 2001 to 5 Aug. 2003	3	3	638

Interest period	Interest rate %	Repayment interest rate %	Days
6 May 2001 to 5 Nov. 2001	4	4	184
6 Feb. 2000 to 5 May 2001	5	5	455
6 Mar. 1999 to 5 Feb. 2000	4	4	337

Note

(1) Fixed by Treasury order under SI 1989/1297. From September 2009, interest charged on late payments of tax will be the Bank of England base rate plus 2.5% and the interest rate on overpayments is the Bank of England rate minus 1, subject to a minimum rate of 0.5% on repayment.

TAXATION OF COMPANIES

[¶7-000] Rates of corporation tax

(Tax Reporter: ¶704-000ff.)

Financial year[1]	Main rate %[2][3]	Small profits rate %[2][3]	Limit for small profits rate (lower limit) £[2][4]	Limit for marginal relief (upper limit) £[2][4]	Standard fraction for marginal relief[2][3]	Special IP rate %[5]
2014	21	20	300,000	1,500,000	1/400	10
2013	23	20	300,000	1,500,000	3/400	10
2012	24	20	300,000	1,500,000	1/100	–
2011	26	20	300,000	1,500,000	3/200	–
2010	28	21	300,000	1,500,000	7/400	–
2009	28	21	300,000	1,500,000	7/400	–
2008	28	21	300,000	1,500,000	7/400	–
2007	30	20	300,000	1,500,000	1/40	–

Notes

[1] A financial year begins on 1 April and ends on 31 March. The financial year 2014 began on 1 April 2014 and will end on 31 March 2015.

[2] The main rate for financial year 2015 will be unified with the small profits rate at 20% (*Finance Act* 2013). The small profits rate for non-ring fence profits is abolished with effect for the financial year 2015 and subsequent financial years (*Finance Act* 2014).

[3] 'Close investment holding companies' do not receive the benefit of the small profits rate or of marginal relief and so are taxable entirely at the main rate regardless of the level of their profits (CTA 2010, s. 18).

For companies with ring fence profits, the rates are as above except that:

- the small profits rate of tax is 19% and the standard fraction is 11/400; and
- for financial years 2008 to 2015 the main rate is 30%.

Special rules also apply to companies in liquidation and administration (CTA 2010, s. 628 and 630) and to open-ended investment companies and authorised unit trusts (CTA 2010, s. 614 and 618).

[4] The lower and upper limits for the small profits rate and marginal relief are reduced proportionally:

- for accounting periods of less than 12 months; and
- in the case of associated companies, by dividing the limits by the total number of associated companies (CTA 2010, s. 24).

[5] For accounting periods beginning on or after 1 April 2013, qualifying companies may elect that relevant intellectual property profits of a trade are chargeable at a lower rate of corporation tax (CTA 2010, s. 357A) (see ¶7-050).

[6] Autumn Statement 2014 announced:

- the introduction of a new diverted profits tax from 1 April 2015 at a rate of 25% where multinational companies use artificial arrangements to divert profits overseas in order to avoid UK tax (Finance Bill 2015);
- a restriction on the amount of banks' profits than can be offset by carried-forward losses to 50% from 1 April 2015 (to ensure banks continue to contribute through corporation tax payments notwithstanding having large accumulated losses). The restriction will apply to losses accruing up to 1 April 2015 and will include an exemption for losses incurred in the first five years of a bank's authorisation (Finance Bill 2015);
- a restriction on corporation tax relief for the acquisition of the reputation and customer relationships associated with a business ('goodwill') when the business is acquired from a related individual or partnership, with effect for acquisitions on or after 3 December 2014 (Finance Bill 2015).

Effective marginal rates

For marginal relief and marginal starting rate relief, there is an effective rate of tax in the margin, i.e. between the lower and upper limits given for each in the preceding table, which *exceeds* the main rate. These marginal rates are not prescribed by statute, but are derived from the appropriate corporation tax rates and fractions. The applicable rates are as follows.

Financial year	Marginal rate %
2014	21.25
2013	23.75
2012	25.00
2011	27.50
2010	29.75
2009	29.75
2008	29.75
2007	32.50

Marginal relief

(CTA 2010, s. 19)

(Tax Reporter: ¶704-200)

$$\text{Deduction} = (\text{Upper Limit} - \text{Augmented Profits}) \times \frac{\text{Taxable Total Profits}}{\text{Augmented Profits}} \times \text{Standard Fraction}$$

'Augmented Profits' (formerly 'Profits') means a company's taxable total profits *plus* franked investment income *excluding* franked investment income received from companies in the same group (CTA 2010, s. 32). Distributions are treated as coming from within the group if they are received from a company which is either a 51% subsidiary or a consortium company (the recipient being a member of the consortium).

'Franked investment income' means a distribution in respect of which the company is entitled to a tax credit (CTA 2010, s. 1126). This includes a distribution which is exempt for the purposes of CTA 2009, Pt. 9A (CTA 2010, s. 1109).

'Taxable Total Profits' (formerly 'Basic Profits') means profits as finally computed for corporation tax purposes (CTA 2010, s. 4(2)).

Charge on loan to participators

(CTA 2010, s. 455)

(Tax Reporter: ¶776-900ff.)

The rate of charge is fixed at 25% of the amount of the loan or advance until further notice.

The charge itself is separate from other liabilities, being treated as if it were an amount of corporation tax chargeable on the company.

[¶7-050] Patent profits election

(CTA 2010, Pt. 8A)

(Tax Reporter: ¶705-000ff.)

The Patent Box enables companies to apply a lower rate of corporation tax to profits earned after 1 April 2013 from its patented inventions and certain other innovations. The lower rate of corporation tax to be applied is 10%. The relief is subject to a number of conditions.

A company must elect into the regime, the election must be in writing, and specify the first accounting period for which the election will apply. The election will apply for all subsequent accounting periods until the election is revoked by notice in writing.

Any revocation must be in writing, specifying the accounting period for which it is to take effect. Any new election will have no effect for any accounting period which begins less than five years after the last day of the accounting period following the period identified in the revocation notice.

In order to avoid complications where losses and other reliefs are claimed, the reduced 10% rate is applied by subtracting an additional trading deduction from corporation tax profits as calculated below.

Additional deduction

The amount of the deduction is–

$$RP \times FY\% \times \left(\frac{MR - IPR}{MR}\right)$$

where–

RP is the relevant IP (patent box) profits of the trade of the company;

FY% is the appropriate percentage for each financial year;

MR is the main rate of corporation tax; and

IPR is the special IP rate of corporation tax.

Financial year	Appropriate percentage
2013	60%
2014	70%
2015	80%
2016	90%
2017 and subsequent years	100%

[¶7-100] Additional relief for research and development

(CTA 2009, Pt. 13)

(Tax Reporter: ¶715-000ff.)

Additional relief is available for companies incurring expenditure on qualifying research and development (R&D). The relief is subject to a number of conditions. SMEs with losses can claim a payable tax credit.

	Expenditure incurred on or after				
	1 April 2014	**1 April 2013**	**1 April 2012**	**1 April 2011**	**1 August 2008**[2]
Additional deduction where SME qualifies for main or pre-trading relief	125%[3]	125%	125%	100%	75%
Rate of payable tax credit (SMEs only)	14.5%	11%	11%	12.5%	14%
Additional deduction where R&D subcontracted to SME	30%	30%	30%	30%	30%
Additional deduction where expenditure of SME is subsidised or capped	30%	30%	30%	30%	30%
Additional deduction for non-SME	30%	30%	30%	30%	30%
R&D expenditure credit[1]	10%[3]	10%	–	–	–

Notes

[1] With effect for expenditure incurred on or after 1 April 2013, large companies and some SMEs may claim a new R&D expenditure credit ('above-the-line credit') as an alternative to (not in addition to) the traditional enhanced deduction scheme of R&D relief. The ATL credit scheme is optional but once a company has started claiming ATL credits, it may not revert back to the enhanced deduction scheme. Companies that do not opt to claim the ATL credit will be able to continue claiming R&D relief under the current large company scheme until 31 March 2016, when the ATL credit becomes mandatory. The credit is taxable but paid net of tax to companies with no corporation tax liability.

[2] For the rates of relief applying before 1 August 2008, see BTR ¶715-000ff.

[3] From 1 April 2015, the rate of the ATL credit will be increased to 11% (from 10%) and the rate of the additional SME deduction to 130% (from 125%), by legislation to be included in Finance Bill 2015 (Autumn Statement 2014).

Limits applying for SMEs (expenditure incurred on or after 1 August 2008):

A company must pass the headcount test and either the turnover test or the Balance Sheet total test.

Staff headcount less than	500
Turnover not exceeding	€100m
Balance Sheet total not exceeding	€86m

[¶7-125] Creative industry tax reliefs

(CTA 2009, Pt. 15, 15A and 15B)

(Tax Reporter: ¶714-000ff.)

Creative industry tax reliefs are a group of four corporation tax reliefs that allow qualifying companies to claim a larger deduction, or in some circumstances, claim a payable tax credit when calculating their taxable profits. The reliefs work by increasing the amount of allowable expenditure, which may be surrendered in exchange for a payable tax credit if the company makes a loss.

Additional relief is available for companies incurring expenditure on (i) qualifying film production, (ii) animation and high-end television production, (iii) video-games development and (iv) theatrical productions. Autumn Statement 2014 announced a further new tax relief for children's television programmes from 1 April 2015 at a rate of 25% on qualifying production expenditure, and a formal consultation in early 2015 on the introduction of a new tax relief for orchestras from 1 April 2016.

The creative industry tax reliefs are all subject to a number of conditions (in particular, that the film, animation, high-end television programme or game must be certified as culturally British to qualify).

	Rates from 1 April 2014	**Rates pre-1 April 2014**
Minimum expenditure (% of core expenditure)		
Film (UK expenditure)	10%	25%
Animation/television (UK expenditure)	25%	25%
Video games development/theatrical productions (EEA expenditure)	25%	25%
Additional deduction (% of qualifying core expenditure)		
Film: limited budget	100%	100%
Film: any other	80%	80%
Animation/television/video games development/ theatrical productions[2]	100%	100%
Maximum qualifying core expenditure (% of total core expenditure)	80%	80%
Tax credits (% of surrendered loss)		
Film: first £20m	25%	
Film: remainder	20%	–
Film: limited budget[1]	–	25%
Film: any other	–	20%
Animation/television/video games development/ theatrical productions[2]	25%	25%

Notes

[1] Limited-budget films are those with a total core expenditure of £20m or less.

[2] Film production relief has been available since 1 January 2007. Animation and Television reliefs were introduced from 1 April 2013, Video games development relief from 1 April 2014 and Theatrical productions relief from 1 September 2014.

[¶7-150] Gifts to the nation

(FA 2012, Sch. 14)

(Tax Reporter: ¶716-685ff.)

For accounting periods beginning on or after 1 April 2012, a reduction in corporation tax is available where a company makes a gift of pre-eminent property to be held for the benefit of the public or the nation. The tax reduction is 20% of the value of the gift. A gift offer must be made and registered in accordance with the scheme and relief is available against the company's liability for the accounting period in which the gift offer is registered.

Pre-eminent property includes any picture, print, book, manuscript, work of art, scientific object or other thing that is pre-eminent for its national, scientific, historic or artistic interest, collections of such items and any object kept in a significant building where it is desirable that it remain associated with the building.

[¶7-200] Car hire

(CTA 2009, s. 56ff.)

(Tax Reporter: ¶707-860ff.)

Leased cars, where the lease begins from 1 April 2009, suffer a 15% disallowance of relevant payments if CO_2 emissions exceed the limits set out below, otherwise no disallowance. This applies to all cars (not just those costing more than £12,000).

	CO_2 emissions
From 1 April 2013	Over 130g/km
1 April 2009 to 31 March 2013	Over 160g/km

For leased cars where the lease began before 1 April 2009, the restricted deduction for hire charges of motor cars with a retail price greater than £12,000 is calculated as follows:

$$\text{Allowable amount} = \frac{\text{£12,000} + \tfrac{1}{2}\,(\text{retail price} - \text{£12,000})}{\text{retail price}} \times \text{hire charge}$$

[¶7-300] Bank levy

(FA 2011, Sch. 19)

(Tax Reporter: ¶807-000)

The rates of charge are as follows:

Period	Chargeable equity and long-term chargeable liabilities %	Short-term chargeable liabilities %
1 Jan. 2014 onwards	0.078[(1)]	0.156[(1)]
1 Jan. 2013–31 Dec. 2013	0.065	0.130
1 Jan. 2012–31 Dec. 2012	0.044	0.088
1 May 2011–31 Dec. 2011	0.0375	0.075
1 Mar. 2011–30 Apr. 2011	0.05	0.1
1 Jan. 2011–28 Feb. 2011	0.025	0.05

Note

[(1)] Rates per *Finance Act* 2014 supersede rates announced previously.

[¶7-350] Annual tax on enveloped dwellings (ATED)

(FA 2013, Pt. 3; SI 2014/854)

(Tax Reporter: ¶807-800ff.)

From 1 April 2013, annual tax on enveloped dwellings (ATED) is a tax payable by companies and other corporate bodies (partnerships with corporate partners or other collective investment vehicle) that own UK residential property valued at over £2m.

The tax is charged for the chargeable period concerned. Chargeable periods are the period beginning 1 April 2013 and ending with 31 March 2014, and each subsequent 12-month period beginning with 1 April.

Property value		Annual charge[1]		
More than £	Less than £	2015–16 £	2014–15 £	2013–14 £
–[2]	1,000,000	0	0	0
1,000,000	2,000,000	7,000[2]	0	0
2,000,000	5,000,000	23,350[3]	15,400	15,000
5,000,000	10,000,000	54,450[3]	35,900	35,000
10,000,000	20,000,000	109,050[3]	71,850	70,000
20,000,000		218,200[3]	143,750	140,000

Note

[1] The annual charge will be increased by consumer prices index inflation each year.

[2] *Finance Act* 2014 introduces a new band from 1 April 2015 for properties with a value greater than £1m but not more than £2m with an annual charge of £7,000 (returns for persons falling within this band for the chargeable period 1 April 2015 to 31 March 2016 must be filed by 1 October 2015 and payment made by 31 October 2015) and a further new band from 1 April 2016 for properties with a value greater than £500,000 but not more than £1m with an annual charge of £3,500.

[3] Rates per Autumn Statement 2014.

Reliefs	References
Property rental businesses	FA 2013, s. 133 (Tax Reporter: ¶807-922)
Rental property: preparation for sale, etc.	FA 2013, s. 134
Dwellings opened to the public	FA 2013, s. 137 (Tax Reporter: ¶807-923)
Property developers	FA 2013, s. 138
Property developers: exchange of dwellings	FA 2013, s. 139
Property traders	FA 2013, s. 141
Financial institutions acquiring dwellings in the course of lending	FA 2013, s. 143
Occupation by certain employees or partners	FA 2013, s. 145 (Tax Reporter: ¶807-924)
Farmhouses	FA 2013, s. 148 (Tax Reporter: ¶807-925)
Providers of social housing	FA 2013, s. 150

Exemptions	References
Charitable companies	FA 2013, s. 151 (Tax Reporter: ¶807-927)
Public bodies	FA 2013, s. 153 (Tax Reporter: ¶807-928)
Bodies established for national purpose	FA 2013, s. 154 (Tax Reporter: ¶807-929)
Dwelling conditionally exempt from inheritance tax	FA 2013, s. 155 (Tax Reporter: ¶807-930)

Administration

[¶7-400] Filing deadlines

(FA 1998, Sch. 18, para. 14)

(Tax Reporter: ¶181-075ff.)

The filing date for a return of profits (CT600) is generally the **later** of the dates outlined below:

- 12 months from the end of the return period;
- where the period of account is 18 months or less, 12 months from the end of the period of account;
- where the period of account is greater than 18 months, 30 months from the start of the period of account; and
- three months after the issue of a notice to deliver a corporation tax return.

Notes

Obligation to file a return is not automatic but is imposed by notice.

Every company which is chargeable to corporation tax in respect of any accounting period, and which has not made a return of its profits for that period, nor received a notice to make such a return, is under a duty to give notice to the inspector that it is so chargeable. The notice must be given not later than 12 months after the end of that accounting period.

A company must notify HMRC that its first accounting period has begun within three months of the accounting period beginning. This also applies to dormant companies which cease to be dormant.

An amended return under self-assessment may not be made later than 12 months after the filing date stipulated above.

[¶7-450] Due and payable dates

(TMA 1970, s. 59D–59FA; SI 1998/3175; ITA 2007, Pt. 15)

(Tax Reporter: ¶183-410ff.; ¶117-000ff.)

Liability	Due date
Corporation tax	Nine months and one day after end of an accounting period[1]
Corporation tax in instalments[2]:	The 14th day of the 7th, 10th, 13th and 16th months after start of a 12-month accounting period.
Income tax on interest, annual payments, etc.	14 days after end of return period.[3]

Notes

[1] TMA 1970, s. 59G provides for companies to enter into voluntary payment plans with HMRC under which corporation tax liabilities can be paid in instalments spread equally before and after the due date. It should be noted that only corporation tax payable in accordance with TMA 1970, s. 59D (i.e. tax payable nine months and one day after the end of the accounting period) can be the subject of a managed payment plan. This excludes corporation tax payable by large companies in accordance with the quarterly instalment payment scheme. In addition, companies which have entered into a group payment arrangement can not enter into a managed payment plan.

[2] TMA 1970, s. 59E and SI 1998/3175 provide for the payment of corporation tax by 'large' companies (defined in accordance with the small profits marginal relief upper limit) in instalments.

Companies which are 'large' because of the number of associated companies or because of substantial dividend income will not have to pay by instalments if their corporation tax liabilities are less than £10,000. Companies which become 'large' in an accounting period, having previously had profits below the upper limit, may be exempt from instalment arrangements in certain circumstances. Groups containing 'large' companies are able to pay corporation tax on a group-wide basis.

For accounting periods ending after 30 June 2005, corporation tax and the supplementary charge payable by oil companies on ring fence profits are payable in three equal instalments. Corporation tax due on other profits (i.e. non-ring fence) continues to be payable in quarterly instalments as above.

The payment dates for the three instalments once the transitional period (see below) has passed are as follows:

(1) one-third payable six months and 13 days from the start of the accounting period (unless the date for instalment (3) is earlier);

(2) one-third payable three months from the first instalment due date (unless (3) is earlier); and

(3) the balance payable 14 days from the end of the accounting period (regardless of the length of the period).

Transitional arrangements apply for the first accounting period affected. These arrangements leave the first two quarterly instalments unchanged (at one-quarter each of the estimated liability for the period) but then require payment of the remainder of the estimated liability on ring fence profits for that accounting period to be paid on the new third instalment date.

[3] Return periods end on 31 March, 30 June, 30 September, 31 December and at the end of an accounting period.

The requirement for companies to deduct and account for income tax on certain payments is removed with effect for payments after 31 March 2001 of:

- interest, royalties, annuities and other annual payments made to companies within the charge to UK corporation tax on that income; and
- interest on quoted Eurobonds paid to non-residents.

[¶7-500] Penalties

(Tax Reporter: ¶181-350ff.)

Infringement penalised	Maximum penalty	Provision
Failure to notify chargeability[1] • deliberate and concealed act or failure • deliberate but not concealed act or failure • any other case	*Standard amount* 100% of potential lost revenue 70% of potential lost revenue 30% of potential lost revenue	FA 2008, Sch. 41, para. 1, 6
Failure to make return[2] • up to three months after filing date • more than three months after filing date	*Fixed rate penalty*[3] £100 (persistent failure, £500) £200 (persistent failure, £1,000)	FA 1998, Sch. 18, para. 17(2), (3)
• at least 18 months but less than 24 months after end of return period • 24 months or more after end of return period	*Tax-geared penalty*[4] 10% of tax unpaid at 18 months after end of return period 20% of tax unpaid at 18 months after end of return period	FA 1998, Sch. 18, para. 18
Error in a return (careless or deliberate) • standard amount • where the inaccuracy is deliberate but not concealed • where the inaccuracy is deliberate and concealed	30% of potential lost revenue 70% of potential lost revenue 100% of potential lost revenue	FA 2007, Sch. 24, para. 4
Failure to keep and preserve records (subject to specific exceptions)	Up to £3,000	FA 1998, Sch. 18, para. 23
Failure to produce document required in connection with an enquiry[5] • standard amount • continued failure	£300 daily penalty of £60	FA 2008, Sch. 36, para. 39 and 40

Notes

[1] FA 2008, Sch. 41 applies with effect from 1 April 2010. Prior to that date, a penalty was provided for by FA 1998, Sch. 18, para. 2(3) and (4). The standard penalty imposed by FA 2008, Sch. 41 can be reduced where disclosure is made or where there are special circumstances.

[2] From a date yet to be announced, *Finance Act* 2009 introduced a new flat-rate and tax-geared penalty regime for the late filing of corporation tax returns (FA 2009, Sch. 55).

[3] Fixed rate penalty does not apply if return filed by date allowed by Registrar of Companies.

[4] Tax geared penalty is charged in addition to fixed penalty. Where more than one tax-geared penalty is incurred the total penalty shall not exceed the largest individual penalty on that part.

[5] An additional tax-related penalty can be imposed under FA 2008, Sch. 36, para. 50.

[6] Prior to 1 April 2010, a penalty was chargeable in accordance with TMA 1970, s. 98 where a company failed to notify HMRC of the start of an accounting period under the obligation at FA 2004, s. 55.

[7] From a date yet to be announced, *Finance Act* 2009 introduced a new penalty regime for late payment of corporation tax (FA 2009, Sch. 56).

[8] For financial years beginning on or after 21 July 2009, the senior accounting officer of a qualifying company is obliged to ensure that the company establishes and maintains appropriate tax accounting arrangements, and to provide a certificate to HMRC indicating whether or not this was the case for each financial year (FA 2009, Sch. 46; see Tax Reporter ¶191-660ff.). Qualifying companies are obliged to provide details of their senior accounting officer to HMRC. Failure to comply with these requirements will make the senior accounting officer and/or the company liable to a penalty.

[¶7-550] Interest on overdue tax

(Tax Reporter: ¶183-430ff.)

Interest on	Interest runs from	Provision in TMA 1970
Overdue corporation tax	Date tax due and payable (nine months and one day after end of accounting period)[1]	s. 87A
Corporation tax payable in instalments	Date instalment is due to be paid	s. 87A[2]
Overdue income tax deducted from certain payments	14 days after end of return period	s. 87
Overdue tax due on loans to participators	Date tax due and payable	s. 109

Notes

[1] Where one group company is liable to interest and another group company with the same accounting period is due a repayment of corporation tax an election may be made for the overpayment to be surrendered so as to reduce the interest liability of the first company which will be treated as having paid tax at the same time as the surrendering company (CTA 2010, s. 963).

[2] As modified by SI 1998/3175, reg. 7.

[3] *Finance (No. 3) Act* 2010 contains provisions to apply the harmonised interest regime introduced by *Finance Act* 2009 to corporation tax and PRT. The provisions will be brought into force by Treasury Order.

[¶7-650] Interest on tax repayments

(ICTA 1988, s. 826; SI 1998/3175, reg. 8)

(Tax Reporter: ¶183-430ff.)

Repayment interest on corporation tax runs from later of:

(1) due and payable date (nine months after end of accounting period); and

(2) date of actual payment; except for

   (a) overpayments of instalments of corporation tax, when interest runs from the first instalment date on which the excess amount would have been due and payable or, if later, the date on which that excess arises; and

(b) for companies outside the instalments regime, if tax was paid earlier than the normal due date, then interest on repayments in advance of agreement of liability runs from the first instalment date on which the excess amount would have been due and payable had the instalments regime applied or, the date on which the amount repayable was originally paid, whichever is later.

Interest on repayments of income tax deducted at source from income will run from the day after the end of the accounting period in which the income was received for accounting periods under self-assessment.

Finance (No. 3) Act 2010 contains provisions to apply the harmonised interest regime introduced by *Finance Act* 2009 to corporation tax and PRT. The provisions will be brought into force by Treasury Order.

[¶7-700] Rates of interest

With effect for **interest** periods commencing on 6 February 1997, the rates of interest for the purposes of corporation tax are different from those for other taxes. The rate of interest on corporation tax will depend on the accounting period for which the tax is due and, under self-assessment, the nature of the tax due or repayable.

Self-assessment

For accounting periods within the self-assessment regime (CTSA), i.e. APs on or after 1 July 1999, the rates of interest are distinct from those for pre-CTSA periods, because the interest is taxable and tax deductible (see below).

In addition, there are separate provisions for:

- overpaid instalments of corporation tax; and
- payments of corporation tax made after the normal due date.

Pre-self-assessment

For accounting periods before the start of self-assessment, there are two rates of interest applicable depending on whether the accounting period is within the Pay and File regime (APs ending after 30 September 1993) or not (i.e. periods ending before 1 October 1993).

CTSA

1. CT (other than instalments and CT not due by instalments)

From	Late payment %	Repayment %
29 September 2009	3.00	0.50
24 March 2009	2.50	0.00
27 January 2009	3.50	0.00
6 January 2009	4.50	1.00
6 December 2008	5.50	2.00

From	Late payment %	Repayment %
6 November 2008	6.50	3.00
6 January 2008	7.50	4.00
6 August 2007	8.50	5.00
6 September 2006	7.50	4.00
6 September 2005	6.50	3.00
6 September 2004	7.50	4.00
6 December 2003	6.50	3.00
6 August 2003	5.50	2.00
6 November 2001	6.50	3.00
6 May 2001	7.50	4.00
6 February 2000	8.50	5.00

2. Instalments and CT not due by instalments

From	Late payment %	Repayment %
21 September 2009	1.50	0.50
16 March 2009	1.50	0.25
16 February 2009	2.00	0.75
19 January 2009	2.50	1.25
15 December 2008	3.00	1.75
17 November 2008	4.00	2.75
20 October 2008	5.50	4.25
21 April 2008	6.00	4.75
18 February 2008	6.25	5.00
17 December 2007	6.50	5.25
16 July 2007	6.75	5.50
21 May 2007	6.50	5.25
22 January 2007	6.25	5.00
20 November 2006	6.00	4.75
14 August 2006	5.75	4.50
15 August 2005	5.50	4.25
16 August 2004	5.75	4.50

From	Late payment %	Repayment %
21 June 2004	5.50	4.25
17 May 2004	5.25	4.00
16 February 2004	5.00	3.75
17 November 2003	4.75	3.50
21 July 2003	4.50	3.25
17 February 2003	4.75	3.50
19 November 2001	5.00	3.75
15 October 2001	5.50	4.25
1 October 2001	5.75	4.50
13 August 2001	6.00	4.75
21 May 2001	6.25	5.00
16 April 2001	6.50	5.25
19 February 2001	6.75	5.50
20 April 2000	7.00	5.75
21 February 2000	8.00	5.75
24 January 2000	7.75	5.50
15 November 1999	7.50	5.25
20 September 1999	7.25	5.00
21 June 1999	7.00	4.75
19 April 1999	7.25	5.00
15 February 1999	7.50	5.25
18 January 1999	8.00	5.75
1 January 1999	8.25	6.00

Pre CTSA

From	Late payment		Repayment	
	Pre Pay and File %	Pay and File %	Pre Pay and File %	Pay and File %
29 September 2009	3.00	3.00	0.50	0.50
24 March 2009	2.00	1.75	2.00	0.00
27 January 2009	2.75	2.75	2.75	0.00
6 January 2009	3.50	3.50	3.50	0.50

From	Late payment		Repayment	
	Pre Pay and File %	Pay and File %	Pre Pay and File %	Pay and File %
6 December 2008	4.25	4.25	4.25	1.25
6 November 2008	5.00	5.00	5.00	2.00
6 January 2008	5.75	6.00	5.75	2.75
6 August 2007	6.50	6.75	6.50	3.50
6 September 2006	5.75	6.00	5.75	2.75
6 September 2005	5.00	5.25	5.00	2.00
6 September 2004	5.75	6.00	5.75	2.75
6 December 2003	5.00	5.25	5.00	2.00
6 August 2003	4.25	4.25	4.25	1.25
6 November 2001	5.00	5.00	5.00	2.00
6 May 2001	5.75	6.00	5.75	2.75
6 February 2000	6.50	6.75	6.50	3.50

[¶7-900] Time limits for elections and claims

(Tax Reporter: ¶191-835)

In the absence of any provision to the contrary (some of which are considered below), the normal rule is that a claim must be made within four years of the end of the accounting period to which it relates (six years prior to 1 April 2010) (FA 1998, Sch. 18, para. 55).

In certain cases, HMRC *may* permit an extension of the strict time limit in relation to certain elections and claims.

Provision	Time limit	References
Stock transferred to a connected party on cessation of trade to be valued at higher cost or sale price	Two years from end of accounting period in which trade ceased	CTA 2009, s. 167(4)
Carry-forward of trading losses	Relief is given automatically	CTA 2010, s. 45
Set-off of trading losses against profits of the same, or an earlier, accounting period[1]	Two years from end of accounting period in which loss incurred	CTA 2010, s. 37(7)

Provision	Time limit	References
Group relief	Claims to group relief must be made (or withdrawn) by the later of: (1) 12 months after the claimant company's filing date for the return for the accounting period covered by the claim; (2) 30 days after a closure notice is issued on the completion of an enquiry[2]; (3) 30 days after HMRC issue a notice of amendment to a return following the completion of an enquiry (issued where the company fails to amend the return itself); or (4) 30 days after the determination of any appeal against an HMRC amendment (as in (3) above).	FA 1998, Sch. 18, para. 74
Set-off of loss on disposal of shares in unquoted trading company against income of investment company	Two years from end of accounting period	CTA 2010, s. 70(4)
Surrender of company tax refund within group	Before refund made to surrendering company	CTA 2010, s. 963(3)
Election to reallocate a chargeable gain or an allowable loss within a group[3]	Two years from end of transferring company's accounting period during which the gain or loss accrues	TCGA 1992, s. 171A
Relief for a non-trading deficit on loan relationships (including any non-trading exchange losses) – set off against profits of deficit or earlier periods – carry forward to later periods	 – two years from end of period in which deficit arises – two years from end of the accounting period following the deficit period, or such further period as an officer of Revenue & Customs allows	CTA 2009, s. 458(2) and 460(1)
Appropriation of asset to trading stock: election to adjust trading profit by the amount of the gain or loss on the deemed disposal at market value	Two years from the end of the accounting period in which the asset is appropriated as trading stock	TCGA 1992, s. 161(3)
Terminal loss relief on cessation of trade	Two years from end of the loss making accounting period	CTA 2010, s. 39
Intangible fixed assets: election to write down cost for tax purposes at fixed rate	Two years from end of accounting period in which company creates or acquires the asset	CTA 2009, s. 730
Election by recipient that company distribution should not be exempt	Second anniversary of end of accounting period in which distribution received	CTA 2009, s. 931R

Provision	Time limit	References
Claims included in a company tax return, including research and development tax relief claim, land remediation tax credits and life assurance company tax credits, and film tax credits	One year from filing date for return or a later date if an officer of Revenue & Customs allows it	FA 1998, Sch. 18, para. 83E, 83K, 83W
Election for special treatment of profits from patents, etc. (Patent box)	Two years from end of first accounting period to which it relates	CTA 2010, s. 357G

(1) The carry-back period is extended to three years for accounting periods ending in the period 23 November 2008 to 24 November 2010 (FA 2009, s. 23, Sch. 6).
(2) 'Enquiry' in the above does not include a restricted enquiry into an amendment to a return (restricted because the time limit for making an enquiry into the return itself has expired), where the amendment consists of a group relief claim or withdrawal of claim.
These time limits have priority over any other general time limits for amending returns and are subject to HMRC permitting an extension to the time limits.
(3) Following the enactment of *Finance Act* 2009, it is now possible for chargeable gains and allowable losses to be transferred within a group. For gains and losses made before 21 July 2009, this result could only be achieved by electing for the notional transfer of an asset before its disposal to a third party (TCGA 1992, s. 171A prior to the changes made by FA 2009, s. 31, Sch. 12). The election had to be made jointly on or before the second anniversary of the end of the actual vendor group company's accounting period in which it made the disposal.

CAPITAL ALLOWANCES

[¶8-000] Plant and machinery: overview of allowances

(CAA 2001)

(Tax Reporter: ¶235-000ff.)

Plant and machinery allowances are normally given by way of:

- annual investment allowances: see ¶8-100;
- first-year allowances: see ¶8-200; or
- writing-down allowances: see ¶8-300.

In specified circumstances, balancing allowances may be due or balancing charges may be made.

[¶8-100] Plant and machinery: annual investment allowances

(CAA 2001, s. 51A)

(Tax Reporter: ¶236-400ff.)

	Maximum (£)
1/6 April 2014 to 31 December 2015	500,000[1]
1 January 2013 to 31 March/5 April 2014	250,000[1]
1/6 April 2012 to 31 December 2012	25,000
1/6 April 2010 to 31 March/5 April 2012	100,000
1/6 April 2008 to 31 March/5 April 2010	50,000
Before 1/6 April 2008	–

Note

[1] Temporary increase in the annual invesment allowance initially for the period of two years beginning with 1 January 2013 (FA 2013, s. 7 and Sch. 1), was extended to 31 December 2015 (and increased to £500,000) by FA 2014, s. 10 and Sch. 2, after which the allowance will return to £25,000.

This figure is adjusted pro rata for chargeable periods shorter or longer than one year.

Where a chargeable period spans the above dates of change (i.e. 1/6 April 2014, or 1 January 2016) the maximum AIA is calculated by splitting the chargeable period into separate periods falling before and after each of the dates of change. Transitional rules are then applied to determine the maximum AIA available in respect of the total chargeable period and the maximum AIA that may be allocated against qualifying expenditure incurred in each of the separate periods (FA 2014, Sch. 2; FA 2013, Sch. 1; FA 2011, s. 11).

Groups of companies, companies and qualifying activities carried on by individuals or partnerships, under common control which share premises and carry on similar activities are entitled to a single annual investment allowance only.

[¶8-200] Plant and machinery: first-year allowances – overview

Most first-year allowances are permanently available, and give immediate relief for the whole of the qualifying expenditure: see ¶8-210.

Other allowances are given on a temporary basis only, and at a lower level of relief: see below.

General exclusions

See ¶8-220 re general exclusions from first-year allowances (but see also Tax Reporter: ¶237-075 re leasing restriction for fixtures owned by landlords).

Temporary first-year allowances

(FA 2009, s. 24)

(Tax Reporter: ¶237-075)

Temporary first-year allowances at 40% were given for general expenditure on plant or machinery incurred by businesses of any size in the year ended 31 March or 5 April 2010 (for corporation tax and income tax respectively).

Older first-year allowances

(CAA 2001, s. 52)

(Tax Reporter: ¶237-000ff.)

Until April 2008, entitlement to some first-year allowances depended on the size of the business.

Medium-sized enterprises were entitled to a 40% FYA on most plant and machinery.

Small enterprises were similarly entitled to first-year allowances on most plant and machinery. The first-year allowance rate of 40% was increased to 50% for the years 2004–05, 2006–07 (but not 2005–06) and 2007–08 (and for financial years 2004, 2006 and 2007 (but not 2005)).

[¶8-210] Plant and machinery: 100% first-year allowances

(CAA 2001, s. 52)

(Tax Reporter: ¶237-000ff.)

Subject to the general exclusions listed at ¶8-220, full 100% allowances are available for the following types of expenditure incurred by a business of any size. If full FYAs are not claimed, WDA is normally available on a reducing balance basis (see ¶8-300).

Nature of expenditure	Authority (CAA 2001)	Notes
Energy-saving plant or machinery	s. 45A–45C	Loss-making companies may claim tax rebate[(1)(2)] (CAA 2001, Sch. A1).
Cars with low CO_2 emissions	s. 45D	Initially due to end on 31 March 2013, but extended to 31 March 2015 (except for leased cars), with a reduction in the qualifying threshold to 95g/km of CO_2 from 1 April 2013 (previously 110g/km). See also ¶8-500.

Nature of expenditure	Authority (CAA 2001)	Notes
Zero-emission goods vehicles	s. 45DA	On expenditure incurred before 1 April 2015 (corporation tax) or 6 April 2015 (income tax). [Budget 2014 announced legislation to be included in Finance Bill 2015 to extend to March/April 2018.]
Plant or machinery for certain refuelling stations	s. 45E	Initially due to end on 31 March 2013, but extended to 31 March 2015.
Plant or machinery (other than a long life asset) for use by a company wholly in a ring fence trade	s. 45F	
Environmentally beneficial plant or machinery	s. 45H–45J	Loss-making companies may claim tax rebate[(2)]
Expenditure on plant and machinery for use in designated assisted areas	s. 45K	Initially due to end on 31 March 2017 but extended to 31 March 2020.

Notes

[(1)] FYAs are not available on expenditure incurred on or after 1 April 2012 (corporation tax) or 6 April 2012 (income tax) on plant or machinery to generate renewable electricity or heat where tariff payments are received under the Feed-in Tariff or Renewable Heat Incentive schemes. In the case of expenditure incurred on a combined heat and power system, this restriction applies from 1 April 2014 (corporation tax) or 6 April 2014 (income tax). FYAs granted in respect of expenditure incurred from April 2012 (or April 2014 for CHP installations) will be withdrawn if FIT or RHI tariffs are paid subsequently (CAA 2001, s. 45AA).

[(2)] First-year tax credits, for companies surrendering losses attributable to their expenditure on designated energy-saving or environmentally beneficial plant or machinery has been extended for a further five years until 31 March 2018 (SI 2013/464).

[¶8-220] Plant and machinery: first-year allowances – general exclusions

(CAA 2001, s. 46(2))

(Tax Reporter: ¶237-150)

No first-year allowances are available for:

- expenditure incurred in the final chargeable period;
- cars (other than those with very low CO_2 emissions);
- [certain ships and railway assets (pre-1 April 2013)][(1)];
- items excluded from the long-life asset treatment only by virtue of the transitional provisions in CAA 2001, Sch. 3, para. 20;
- plant or machinery for leasing;
- in certain anti-avoidance cases where the obtaining of a FYA is linked to a change in the nature or conduct of a trade;

- where an asset was initially acquired for purposes other than those of the qualifying activity;
- where an asset was acquired by way of a gift; and
- where plant or machinery that was provided for long funding leasing starts to be used for other purposes.

Note

(1) Exclusion from first-year allowances for expenditure incurred on either ships or railway assets omitted with effect for qualifying expenditure incurred on or after 1 April 2013.

[¶8-300] Plant and machinery: writing-down allowances

(CAA 2001, s. 56)

(Tax Reporter: ¶238-050ff.)

	Standard rate (%)	Special rate (%)
From April 2012	18	8
April 2008 to April 2012	20	10
Before April 2008	25	n/a

Notes

Before April 2008, long-life assets attracted allowances at 6%.

Different rules apply for certain: cars see ¶8-500.

WDA for small pools

Main pool or special rate pool only where tax written down value brought forward plus expenditure added to the pool during the period minus disposal receipts deducted from the pool during the period totals less than or equal to £1,000 (apportioned for periods of more or less than one year), an allowance may be claimed for the former amount in place of the standard rates above (CAA 2001, s. 56A).

Pooling

Expenditure is allocated to the main pool unless it is allocated to either a single asset pool or single class pool. Single asset and single class pools are as follows:

Single asset pools

- short life asset (CAA 2001, s. 86);
- ship (CAA 2001, s. 127);
- assets with partial non qualifying use (CAA 2001, s. 206);
- expenditure in relation to which a partial depreciation subsidy is received (CAA 2001, s. 211); and
- contribution allowances: plant and machinery (CAA 2001, s. 538).

Single class pools

- special rate expenditure (see below) (CAA 2001, s. 104A); and
- overseas leasing (CAA 2001, s. 107).

Special rate expenditure

Expenditure	Incurred on or after	Provision
Thermal insulation of buildings	1 April 2008 (corporation tax) or 6 April 2008 (income tax)	CAA 2001, s. 28
Integral features	1 April 2008 (corporation tax) or 6 April 2008 (income tax)	CAA 2001, s. 33A
Long life asset expenditure	26 November 1996, or 1st January 2001 in pursuance of a contract entered into before 26 November 1996 or incurred before 26 November 1996 but allocated to a pool in a chargeable period beginning on or after that date	CAA 2001, Ch. 10
Cars (excluding main rate cars (first registered before 1 March 2001, cars with low CO_2 emissions, electrically propelled cars))	1 April 2009 (corporation tax) or 6 April 2009 (income tax)	CAA 2001, s. 104AA
Provision of cushion gas	1 April 2010	CAA 2001, s. 70J(7)
Solar panels	1 April 2012 (corporation tax) or 6 April 2012 (income tax)	CAA 2001, s. 104A(1)(g)

[¶8-400] Plant and machinery: integral features

(CAA 2001, s. 33A)

(Tax Reporter: ¶243-400ff.)

The following assets are designated as integral features:

- electrical systems (including lighting systems);
- cold water systems;
- space or water heating systems, powered systems of ventilation, air cooling or air purification, and any floor or ceiling comprised in such systems;
- lifts, escalators and moving walkways; and
- external solar shading.

[¶8-410] Plant and machinery: expenditure unaffected by statutory restrictions re buildings

(CAA 2001, s. 23)

(Tax Reporter: ¶245-550)

The restrictions in CAA 2001, s. 21 and 22 (buildings, structures and other assets) do not apply to the following categories of expenditure:

- Thermal insulation of buildings (CAA 2001, s. 28);
- Personal security (CAA 2001, s. 33);
- Integral features (CAA 2001, s. 33A); and
- Software and rights to software (CAA 2001, s. 71).

Note

Before 1 April 2013, expenditure on safety at designated sports grounds, safety at regulated stands at sports grounds and safety at other sports grounds was also included in the list of exclusions.

The restrictions in CAA 2001, s. 21 and 22 (buildings, structures and other assets) also do not apply to expenditure in List C at CAA 2001, s. 23. List C, as amended, is as follows:

(1) Machinery (including devices for providing motive power) not within any other item in this list.

(2) Gas and sewerage systems provided mainly:

(a) to meet the particular requirements of the qualifying activity;

(b) to serve particular plant or machinery used for the purposes of the qualifying activity.

(3) [omitted by *Finance Act* 2008].

(4) Manufacturing or processing equipment; storage equipment (including cold rooms); display equipment; and counters, checkouts and similar equipment.

(5) Cookers, washing machines, dishwashers, refrigerators and similar equipment; washbasins, sinks, baths, showers, sanitary ware and similar equipment; and furniture and furnishings.

(6) Hoists.

(7) Sound insulation provided mainly to meet the particular requirements of the qualifying activity.

(8) Computer, telecommunication and surveillance systems (including their wiring or other links).

(9) Refrigeration or cooling equipment.

(10) Fire alarm systems; sprinkler and other equipment for extinguishing or containing fires.

(11) Burglar alarm systems.

(12) Strong rooms in bank or building society premises; safes.

(13) Partition walls, where moveable and intended to be moved in the course of the qualifying activity.

(14) Decorative assets provided for the enjoyment of the public in hotel, restaurant or similar trades.

(15) Advertising hoardings; signs, displays and similar assets.

(16) Swimming-pools (including diving boards, slides and structures on which such boards or slides are mounted).

(17) Any glasshouse constructed so that the required environment (namely, air, heat, light, irrigation and temperature) for the growing of plants is provided automatically by means of devices forming an integral part of its structure.

(18) Cold stores.

(19) Caravans provided mainly for holiday lettings.

(20) Buildings provided for testing aircraft engines run within the buildings.

(21) Moveable buildings intended to be moved in the course of the qualifying activity.

(22) The alteration of land for the purpose only of installing plant or machinery.

(23) The provision of dry docks.

(24) The provision of any jetty or similar structure provided mainly to carry plant or machinery.

(25) The provision of pipelines or underground ducts or tunnels with a primary purpose of carrying utility conduits.

(26) The provision of towers to support floodlights.

(27) The provision of:

  (a) any reservoir incorporated into a water treatment works; or

  (b) any service reservoir of treated water for supply within any housing estate or other particular locality.

(28) The provision of:

  (a) silos provided for temporary storage; or

  (b) storage tanks.

(29) The provision of slurry pits or silage clamps.

(30) The provision of fish tanks or fish ponds.

(31) The provision of rails, sleepers and ballast for a railway or tramway.

(32) The provision of structures and other assets for providing the setting for any ride at an amusement park or exhibition.

(33) The provision of fixed zoo cages.

Items 1–16 of the above list do not, however, include any asset with the principal purpose of insulating or enclosing the interior of a building or of providing an interior wall, floor or ceiling that is intended to remain permanently in place (CAA 2001, s. 33A).

[¶8-420] Assets treated as buildings

(CAA 2001, s. 21)

(Tax Reporter: ¶245-550)

Plant and machinery allowances are not available on expenditure on the provision of a building, including its construction or acquisition. Building includes:

- an asset incorporated in the building;
- although not incorporated in the building (whether because the asset is moveable or for any other reason), is in the building and is of a kind normally incorporated in a building; or
- is in, or connected with the building and is in list A as follows:
  - walls, floors, ceilings, doors, gates, shutters, windows and stairs.
  - mains services, and systems, for water, electricity and gas.
  - waste disposal systems.
  - sewerage and drainage systems.
  - shafts or other structures in which lifts, hoists, escalators and moving walkways are installed.
  - fire safety systems.

[¶8-430] Excluded structures and other assets

(CAA 2001, s. 22)

Plant and machinery does not include expenditure on the provision of a structure or other asset within list B, or any works involving the alteration of land. List B is as follows:

1. A tunnel, bridge, viaduct, aqueduct, embankment or cutting.
2. A way, hard standing (such as a pavement), road, railway, tramway, a park for vehicles or containers, or an airstrip or runway.
3. An inland navigation, including a canal or basin or a navigable river.
4. A dam, reservoir or barrage, including any sluices, gates, generators and other equipment associated with the dam, reservoir or barrage.
5. A dock, harbour, wharf, pier, marina or jetty or any other structure in or at which vessels may be kept, or merchandise or passengers may be shipped or unshipped.
6. A dike, sea wall, weir or drainage ditch.
7. Any structure not within items 1 to 6 other than–
   (a) a structure (but not a building) within the meaning of 'industrial building',
   (b) a structure in use for the purposes of an undertaking for the extraction, production, processing or distribution of gas, and
   (c) a structure in use for the purposes of a trade which consists in the provision of telecommunication, television or radio services.

Note

Structure means a fixed structure of any kind, other than a building (as defined by s. 21(3) (see ¶8-420 above)). Land does not include buildings or other structures.

[¶8-450] Fixtures

(CAA 2001, s. 187A)

From April 2012, purchasers of buildings which include fixtures on which capital allowances have previously been claimed will only be able to claim capital allowances on the fixtures if either:

1. the fixed value requirement is met whereby the value of the fixtures transferred is agreed within two years of the transfer either;

- between the seller and purchaser by joint election under CAA 2001, s. 198–199; or
- by determination of the First-tier Tribunal;

or,

2. the purchaser obtains a written statement from the seller that the fixed value requirement has not been met and is no longer capable of being met and the purchaser obtains from a past owner a written statement of the disposal value brought into account by that owner (this will apply in cases where the seller is an intermediate owner or lessee not entitled to claim allowances but who acquired the fixtures from a past owner who was entitled to claim allowances).

From April 2014, it will also be necessary to show that historic expenditure has been pooled, or that the past owner claimed a first year allowance on the expenditure (or any part of it) before a subsequent transfer to another person.

[¶8-500] Plant and machinery: allowances for cars

(CAA 2001, s. 104A and 104AA)

From April 2009

(Tax Reporter: ¶238-500ff.)

CO_2 emissions		
From 2009–10 to 2012–13	**From 2013–14 to 2014–15**	**Capital allowances**
Up to 110g/km	Up to 95g/km	100% FYA (see also ¶8-210), (CAA 2001, s. 45D)
Up to 160g/km	Up to 130g/km	Main rate pool applies
Over 160g/km	Over 130g/km	Special rate pool applies

Cars with private use go to a single asset pool but still with WDA as above, but then adjusted for private use percentage.

Before April 2009

(CAA 2001, s. 74ff.)

(Tax Reporter: ¶238-900ff.)

Bought cars attract allowances at standard 20% (previously 25%) rate, but cars costing more than £12,000 have annual WDA restricted to £3,000. No restriction on balancing allowances.

Cars with emissions that do not exceed 110g/km (previously 120g/km) attract first-year allowances at 100%.

Permanent disallowance of a proportion of the hire cost of cars where the retail price when new exceeds £12,000.

[¶8-550] Enterprise zones: 100% capital allowances

Legislation included in *Finance Act* 2012 provides that expenditure incurred by companies (not unincorporated businesses) between 1 April 2012 and 31 March 2017 on new and unsued plant and machinery for use primarily in designated assisted areas in Enterprise Zones will qualify for 100% allowances. Expenditure must be incurred for the purposes of a new or expanding business carried on by the company, must not be replacement expenditure and is limited to €125m per single investment project (as defined) (CAA 2001, s. 45K–45N). A full list of current zones and designated assisted areas is available at:

- http://enterprisezones.communities.gov.uk
- http://business.wales.gov.uk/enterprisezones/enhanced-capital-allowances
- www.scotland.gov.uk/Topics/Economy/EconomicStrategy/Enterprise-Areas/Incentives/Capital-Allowances

[¶8-600] Industrial buildings, hotels and sports pavilions; agricultural buildings and structures

(Former CAA 2001, s. 271ff.)

(Tax Reporter: ¶246-750ff.)

No IBAs or ABAs are given for any chargeable period beginning after 1 or 6 April 2011.

Between 2007 and 2011, these allowances were being phased out. To achieve this, the following percentages were applied to the writing-down allowances that would otherwise have been available for industrial buildings, hotels and sports pavilions and agricultural buildings and structures.

Financial year beginning	Tax year	Percentage
1 April 2011 and later	2011–12 and later	0% (i.e. no further allowances given)
1 April 2010	2010–11	25%
1 April 2009	2009–10	50%
1 April 2008	2008–09	75%
1 April 2007 and earlier	2007–08 and earlier	100%

Where a chargeable period straddles the financial or tax year, the WDA is to be apportioned on a strict time basis.

The restriction applies both to the standard 4% WDA and to the higher WDA available to some used buildings.

No initial allowances are available.

[¶8-650] Enterprise zones: industrial buildings, hotels, commercial buildings or structures

(Former CAA 2001, s. 271ff.; FA 2008, Sch. 27, para. 31)

(Tax Reporter: ¶250-950ff.)

No IBAs are given for any chargeable period beginning after 1 or 6 April 2011. For enterprise zone expenditure only, a balancing charge can still be incurred up to 5 April 2018.

Initial allowances (at 100%) or writing-down allowances (at 25%) were formerly available for certain buildings in enterprise zones (industrial buildings; hotels and commercial buildings or structures).

Enterprise zones can be valid for up to a maximum of 20 years in total. Those that still fall within that 20-year period are as follows:

Statutory instrument	Area	Start date
1995/2624	Dearne Valley (Barnsley, Doncaster, Rotherham)	3 November 1995
1995/2625	Holmewood (North East Derbyshire)	3 November 1995
1995/2738	Bassetlaw	16 November 1995
1995/2758	Ashfield	21 November 1995
1995/2812	East Durham (No. 1 to No. 6)	29 November 1995
1996/106	Tyne Riverside (North Tyneside)	19 February 1996
1996/1981	Tyne Riverside (Silverlink North Scheme)	26 August 1996
1996/1981	Tyne Riverside (Silverlink Business Park Scheme)	26 August 1996
1996/1981	Tyne Riverside (Middle Engine Lane Scheme)	26 August 1996
1996/1981	Tyne Riverside (New York Industrial Park Scheme)	26 August 1996
1996/1981	Tyne Riverside (Balliol Business Park West Scheme)	26 August 1996
1996/2435	Tyne Riverside (Baltic Enterprise Park Scheme)	21 October 1996
1996/2435	Tyne Riverside (Viking Industrial Park – Wagonway West Scheme)	21 October 1996
1996/2435	Tyne Riverside (Viking Industrial Park – Blackett Street Scheme)	21 October 1996
1996/2435	Tyne Riverside (Viking Industrial Park – Western Road Scheme)	21 October 1996

[¶8-800] Other allowances

Allowance	Date expenditure incurred (from)	Initial allowance (%)	WDA (%)	CAA 2001	Tax Reporter
Business premises renovation[3]	11 April 2007 (to 31 March or 5 April 2017)	100	25	s. 360A	¶252-500
[*Flat conversion*[1]]	[*11 May 2001 (to 31 March or 5 April 2013)*]	[*100*]	[25]	[*former s. 393A*]	¶254-000
Mineral extraction[4]	1 April 1986	–	25	s. 394	¶255-500
Research and development	6 November 1962	100	–	s. 437	¶256-000
Know-how[2]	1 April 1986	–	25	s. 452	¶257-000
Patents[2]	1 April 1986	–	25	s. 464	¶257-500
Dredging	6 November 1962	–	4	s. 484	¶258-000
Assured tenancy	10 March 1982 (to 31 March 1992)	–	4	s. 490	¶258-500

Notes

[1] Flat conversion allowances are abolished in respect of expenditure incurred on or after 1 April 2013 for corporation tax purposes and 6 April 2013 for income tax purposes (FA 2012, s. 227 and Sch. 39, para. 36 and 37). The entitlement to claim writing-down allowances on any residual expenditure is also withdrawn from that date.

[2] Capital allowances for know-how and patents still apply for income tax but were replaced for most corporation tax purposes by the intangible assets regime with effect from 1 April 2002.

[3] With effect from 1/6 April 2014, *Finance Act* 2014 amended CAA 2001, Pt. 3A to: specify qualifying expenditure for BPRA; prevent claims where another form of State aid has or will be received on the same investment project; introduce a time limit for works to be completed after expenditure has been incurred (and relief claimed) of 36 months (otherwise relief is withdrawn and the expenditure is treated as incurred when the works are provided); and reduce the period in which balancing adjustments must be made if certain events occur from seven years to five years.

[4] With effect in relation to claims made on or after 1 April 2014 (corporation tax) or 6 April 2014 (income tax), the treatment of MEAs is aligned with the existing principles for plant and machinery allowances and a mineral extraction trade for the purposes of MEAs must consist of activity within the charge to UK tax. *Finance Act* 2014 also amends the legislation to confirm that activity of an exempt foreign permanent establishment (FPE) is treated as a separate mineral extraction trade for the purposes of MEAs and to confirm that notional allowances will be given automatically in calculating the profits or losses of the exempt FPE as if the exempt FPE were within the charge to UK tax (with effect in relation to elections under CTA 2009, s. 18A which start to have effect on or after 1 April 2014). With effect from 17 July 2014, expenditure incurred on seeking planning permission qualifies as expenditure on mineral exploration and access, whether the planning permission is successful or not. Previously, where planning permission was granted, the expenditure was treated as acquiring a mineral asset and eligible for relief at the lower rate of 10%.

[¶8-950] Time limits for elections and claims

(CAA 2001, s. 3; TMA 1970, s. 43; FA 1998, Sch. 18, para. 54–60)

(Tax Reporter: ¶235-050)

Capital allowances must be claimed in a tax return. However, the rules for claims outside a return for income tax (TMA 1970, s. 42) and corporation tax (FA 1998, Sch. 18, para. 54–60) apply in certain instances:

- special leasing plant and machinery allowance claims;
- claims for patent allowances on non-trading expenditure (in income tax cases).

Provision	Time limit	Statutory reference
General claim to capital allowances under corporation tax self-assessment	Claims to capital allowances must be made (or amended or withdrawn) by the later of: (1) 12 months after the claimant company's filing date for the return for the accounting period covered by the claim; (2) 30 days after a closure notice is issued on the completion of an enquiry; (3) 30 days after HMRC issue a notice of amendment to a return following the completion of an enquiry (issued where the company fails to amend the return itself); or (4) 30 days after the determination of any appeal against an HMRC amendment (as in (3) above). 'Enquiry' in the above does not include a restricted enquiry into an amendment to a return (restricted because the time limit for making an enquiry into the return itself has expired), where the amendment consists of making, amending or withdrawing a claim for capital allowances. These time limits have priority over any other general time limits for amending returns to the extent that an amendment makes, amends or withdraws a claim for capital allowances. A claim for capital allowances may be made, amended or withdrawn at a later time if an officer of Revenue & Customs allows it.	FA 1998, Sch. 18, para. 82
Certain plant and machinery treated as 'short life' assets (income tax elections)	12 months from 31 January next following the tax year in which ends the chargeable period in which the qualifying expenditure was incurred	CAA 2001, s. 85

Provision	Time limit	Statutory reference
Certain plant and machinery treated as 'short life' assets (corporation tax elections)	Two years from end of the chargeable period in which the qualifying expenditure was incurred	CAA 2001, s. 85
Set-off of capital allowances on special leasing (corporation tax)	Two years from end of accounting period	CAA 2001, s. 260(3), (6)
Business successions: election between connected parties to transfer plant and machinery at tax written down value	Two years from date on which succession takes effect	CAA 2001, s. 266(4)
Transfer between connected parties of certain assets treated as being at market value; election for sale to be treated as being for an alternative amount value	Two years from date of sale	CAA 2001, s. 570(5)
Purchase of interest in land that includes a fixture – election to fix apportionment of disposal proceeds	Two years from the date of purchase	CAA 2001, s. 198, 201
Lease of interest in land that includes a fixture – election to fix apportionment of disposal proceeds	Two years from the date the lease is granted	CAA 2001, s. 199, 201

NATIONAL INSURANCE CONTRIBUTIONS

[¶9-000] NIC rates: general

There are six classes of National Insurance contributions payable according to the individual circumstances of the payer.

Class 1 contributions

Class 1 contributions are earnings-related and payable by employer and employee on earnings above the earnings thresholds. The primary threshold (PT) applies for employees and the secondary threshold (ST) for employers. Employees pay at the main rate up to the upper earnings limit (UEL) and the additional rate above the limit.

Where the employee is a member of the employer's contracted-out pension scheme, a contracted-out rebate reduces the contributions due from both on any earnings between the lower earnings limit (LEL) and the upper accruals point (UAP). Earnings between the LEL and the PT/ST attract the rebate despite there being no contributions due at that level.

The *Pensions Act* 2014 contains legislation to abolish the contracting-out for salary-related occupational pensions schemes (from 6 April 2016) and to introduce a new single-component state pension to replace the existing state pension comprising basic state pension and additional state pension (from 6 April 2016).

The current value of the contracting-out rebate is 3.4% for employers and 1.4% for employees on earnings between the LEL and UAP.

Contracting out for money purchase schemes (COMPS), mixed benefit schemes (COMB) contracted-out on a defined contribution basis, appropriate personal pension schemes (APP) and APP stakeholder schemes was abolished on 5 April 2012.

The reduced rate applies to married women or widows with a valid certificate of election and affects only primary contributions.

Individuals over state pension age pay no primary contributions, though employers still pay the secondary contribution, at the not contracted-out rate, regardless of the previous category of contribution liability. Children under 16 and their employers pay no contributions.

Employer NIC for the under 21s and apprentices under 25

(SSCBA 1992, s. 9A, prospectively inserted by NICA 2014; Autumn Statement 2014)

From 6 April 2015, every employer with employees under the age of 21 will no longer be required to pay Class 1 secondary National Insurance contributions on earnings up to the upper earning limit (UEL), for those employees.

Autumn Statement 2014 further announced that from April 2016, employer's National Insurance contributions will be abolished for apprentices aged under 25 or earnings up to the UEL.

[¶9-020] Class 1 NIC: 2015–16

(Autumn Statement 2014)

Class 1 contributions

Class 1 primary (employee) contributions 2015–16	
Lower earnings limit (LEL)[(4)]	£112 weekly £486[(2)] monthly £5,824[(2)] yearly
Primary threshold (PT)[(4)]	£155 weekly £672[(3)] monthly £8,060[(3)] yearly
Upper earnings limit (UEL)	£815 weekly £3,532[(3)] monthly £42,385[(3)] yearly
Upper accruals point (UAP)	£770 weekly £3,337[(2)] monthly £40,040[(2)] yearly
Rate on earnings up to PT[(1)]	0%
Not contracted-out rate	12% on £155.01 to £815 weekly 2% on excess over £815 weekly
Contracted-out rate	10.6% on £155.01 to £770 weekly 12% on £770.01 to £815 weekly 2% on excess over £815 weekly
Reduced rate	5.85% on £155.01 to £815 weekly 2% on excess over £815 (no rebate even if contracted out)

Notes

(1) Earnings from the LEL, up to and including the PT, count towards the employee's basic state pension, even though no contributions are paid on those earnings. Similarly, earnings between the LEL and the PT count towards the employee's entitlement to certain benefits including the second state pension (S2P). Employees in contracted-out employment earn no S2P rights and receive a rebate of contributions of 1.4%. This applies from the LEL to the UAP, so earnings from LEL to PT attract a 'negative' contribution of 1.4 per cent and the rate for earnings from PT to UAP becomes 10.6%. Earnings from UAP to UEL are subject to the main not contracted-out rate.

(2) Monthly and annual LEL and UAP figures are calculated as per SI 2001/1004, reg. 11.

(3) Monthly and annual PT and UEL figures are prescribed by SI 2001/1004, reg. 11 and amended by Statutory Instrument. Rates for 2015–16 figures have yet to be specified and the amounts shown are calculated amounts (by reference to prior year equivalents) and may be subject to change.

(4) These thresholds are uprated by CPI.

Class 1 secondary (employer) contributions 2015–16	
Secondary earnings threshold (ST)[(4)]	£156 weekly £676[(2)] monthly £8,112[(2)] yearly
Upper secondary threshold (UST) for U21's[(3)]	£815 weekly
Not contracted-out rate	13.8% on earnings above ST
Contracted-out rate[(1)]	10.4% for salary related (COSR) on earnings from ST to UAP (plus 3.4% rebate for earnings from LEL to ST), then 13.8% above UAP
Employment allowance[(5)]	£2,000 per year, per employee

Notes

(1) Although employer contributions do not per se give any benefit entitlements, earnings between the LEL and ST are those classed as relevant for S2P. Employers with contracted-out occupational pension schemes receive a rebate of contributions for scheme members of 3.4% (COSR). This applies from the LEL to the UAP, so earnings from LEL to ST attract a 'negative' contribution and the rate for earnings from ST to UAP is reduced as shown.

(2) Monthly and annual ST figures are prescribed by SI 2001/1004, reg. 11 and amended by Statutory Instrument. Rates for 2015–16 figures have yet to be specified and the amounts shown are calculated amounts (by reference to prior year equivalents) and may be subject to change.

(3) Upper secondary threshold (UST) introduced from April 2015 for employees under the age of 21. The rate of secondary NICs for employees under the age of 21 on earnings between the ST and UST will be 0%.

(4) The weekly secondary threshold is uprated by RPI.

(5) From April 2015, the allowance is extended to care and support workers (Autumn Statement 2014).

[¶9-025] Class 1 NIC: 2014–15

Class 1 contributions

Class 1 primary (employee) contributions 2014–15	
Lower earnings limit (LEL)	£111 weekly £481[2] monthly £5,772[2] yearly
Primary threshold (PT)	£153 weekly £663[3] monthly £7,956[3] yearly
Upper earnings limit (UEL)	£805 weekly £3,489[3] monthly £41,865[3] yearly
Upper accruals point (UAP)	£770 weekly £3,337[2] monthly £40,040[2] yearly
Rate on earnings up to PT[1]	0%
Not contracted-out rate	12% on £153.01 to £805 weekly 2% on excess over £805 weekly
Contracted-out rate	10.6% on £153.01 to £770 weekly 12% on £770.01 to £805 weekly 2% on excess over £805 weekly
Reduced rate	5.85% on £153.01 to £805 weekly 2% on excess over £805 (no rebate even if contracted-out)

Notes

(1) Earnings from the LEL, up to and including the PT, count towards the employee's basic state pension, even though no contributions are paid on those earnings. Similarly, earnings between the LEL and the PT count towards the employee's entitlement to certain benefits including the second state pension (S2P). Employees in contracted-out employment earn no S2P rights and receive a rebate of contributions of 1.4%. This applies from the LEL to the UAP, so earnings from LEL to PT attract a 'negative' contribution of 1.4% and the rate for earnings from PT to UAP becomes 10.6%. Earnings from UAP to UEL are subject to the main not contracted-out rate.

(2) Monthly and annual LEL and UAP figures are calculated as per SI 2001/1004, reg. 11.

(3) Monthly and annual PT and UEL figures are prescribed by SI 2001/1004, reg. 11 and amended by Statutory Instrument.

Class 1 secondary (employer) contributions 2014–15	
Secondary earnings threshold (ST)	£153 weekly £663[2] monthly £7,956[2] yearly
Not contracted-out rate	13.8% on earnings above ST
Contracted-out rate[1]	10.4% for salary related (COSR) on earnings from ST to UAP (plus 3.4% rebate for earnings from LEL to ST), then 13.8% above UAP
Employment allowance	£2,000 (per year, per employer)

Notes

[1] Although employer contributions do not per se give any benefit entitlements, earnings between the LEL and ST are those classed as relevant for S2P. Employers with contracted-out occupational pension schemes receive a rebate of contributions for scheme members of 3.4% (COSR). This applies from the LEL to the UAP, so earnings from LEL to ST attract a 'negative' contribution and the rate for earnings from ST to UAP is reduced as shown.

[2] Monthly and annual ST figures are prescribed by SI 2001/1004, reg. 11 and amended by Statutory Instrument.

[¶9-030] Class 1 NIC: 2013–14

Class 1 contributions

Class 1 primary (employee) contributions 2013–14	
Lower earnings limit (LEL)	£109 weekly £473[2] monthly £5,668[2] yearly
Primary threshold (PT)	£149 weekly £646 monthly £7,755 yearly
Upper earnings limit (UEL)	£797 weekly £3,454 monthly £41,450 yearly
Upper accruals point (UAP)	£770 weekly £3,337[2] monthly £40,040[2] yearly
Rate on earnings up to PT[1]	0%
Not contracted-out rate	12% on £149.01 to £797 weekly 2% on excess over £797 weekly
Contracted-out rate	10.6% on £149.01 to £770 weekly 12% on £770.01 to £797 weekly 2% on excess over £797 weekly

Class 1 primary (employee) contributions 2013–14	
Reduced rate	5.85% on £149.01 to £797 weekly 2% on excess over £797 (no rebate even if contracted-out)

Notes

(1) Earnings from the LEL, up to and including the PT, count towards the employee's basic state pension, even though no contributions are paid on those earnings. Similarly, earnings between the LEL and the PT count towards the employee's entitlement to certain benefits including the second state pension (S2P). Employees in contracted-out employment earn no S2P rights and receive a rebate of contributions of 1.4%. This applies from the LEL to the UAP, so earnings from LEL to PT attract a 'negative' contribution of 1.4% and the rate for earnings from PT to UAP becomes 10.6%. Earnings from UAP to UEL are subject to the main not contracted-out rate.

(2) Monthly and annual LEL and UAP figures are calculated as per SI 2001/1004, reg. 11.

Class 1 secondary (employer) contributions 2013–14(2)	
Secondary earnings threshold (ST)	£148 weekly £641 monthly £7,696 yearly
Not contracted-out rate	13.8% on earnings above ST
Contracted-out rate(1)	10.4% for salary related (COSR) on earnings from ST to UAP (plus 3.4% rebate for earnings from LEL to ST), then 13.8% above UAP

Notes

(1) Although employer contributions do not per se give any benefit entitlements, earnings between the LEL and ST are those classed as relevant for S2P. Employers with contracted-out occupational pension schemes receive a rebate of contributions for scheme members of 3.4% (COSR). This applies from the LEL to the UAP, so earnings from LEL to ST attract a 'negative' contribution and the rate for earnings from ST to UAP is reduced as shown.

(2) From 22 June 2010 until 5 September 2013, qualifying businesses will be exempt (when a claim is made and accepted) from the first £5,000 of Class 1 NICs due in respect of the first ten qualifying employees hired in the first year of business (*National Insurance Contributions Act* 2011, s. 4).

[¶9-035] Class 1 NIC: 2012–13

Class 1 contributions

Class 1 primary (employee) contributions 2012–13	
Lower earnings limit (LEL)(1)	£107 weekly £464(2) monthly £5,564(2) yearly
Primary threshold (PT)	£146 weekly £634 monthly £7,605 yearly
Upper earnings limit (UEL)	£817 weekly £3,540 monthly £42,475 yearly
Upper accrual point (UAP)	£770 weekly £3,337(2) monthly £40,040(2) yearly

Class 1 primary (employee) contributions 2012–13	
Rate on earnings up to PT[1]	0%
Not contracted-out rate	12% on £146.01 to £817 weekly 2% on excess over £817 weekly
Contracted-out rate	10.6% on £146.01 to £770 weekly 12% on £770.01 to £817 weekly 2% on excess over £817 weekly
Reduced rate	5.85% on £146.01 to £817 weekly 2% on excess over £817 (no rebate even if contracted-out)

Notes

[1] Earnings from the LEL, up to and including the PT, count towards the employee's basic state pension, even though no contributions are paid on those earnings. Similarly, earnings between the LEL and the PT count towards the employee's entitlement to certain benefits including the second state pension (S2P). Employees in contracted-out employment earn no S2P rights and receive a rebate of contributions of 1.4%. This applies from the LEL to the UAP, so earnings from LEL to PT attract a 'negative' contribution of 1.4% and the rate for earnings from PT to UAP becomes 10.6%. Earnings from UAP to UEL are subject to the main not contracted-out rate.

[2] Monthly and annual LEL and UAP figures are calculated as per SI 2001/1004, reg. 11.

Class 1 secondary (employer) contributions 2012–13[2]	
Secondary earnings threshold (ST)	£144 weekly £624 monthly £7,488 yearly
Not contracted-out rate	13.8% on earnings above the ST
Contracted-out rate[1]	10.4% for salary-related (COSR) on earnings from ST to UAP (plus 3.4% rebate for earnings from LEL to ST), then 13.8% above UAP

Notes

[1] Although employer contributions do not *per se* give any benefit entitlements, earnings between the LEL and ST are those classed as relevant for S2P. Employers with contracted-out occupational pension schemes receive a rebate of contributions for scheme members of 3.4% (COSR). This applies from the LEL to the UAP, so earnings from LEL to ST attract a 'negative' contribution and the rate for earnings from ST to UAP is reduced as shown.

[2] From 22 June 2010 until 5 September 2013, qualifying businesses will be exempt (when a claim is made and accepted) from the first £5,000 of Class 1 NICs due in respect of the first ten qualifying employees hired in the first year of business (*National Insurance Contributions Act* 2011, s. 4).

[¶9-040] Class 1 NIC: 2011–12

Class 1 contributions

Class 1 primary (employee) contributions 2011–12	
Lower earnings limit (LEL)[1]	£102 weekly £442[2] monthly £5,304[2] yearly
Primary threshold (PT)	£139 weekly £602 monthly £7,225 yearly

Class 1 primary (employee) contributions 2011–12	
Upper earnings limit (UEL)	£817 weekly £3,540 monthly £42,475 yearly
Upper accrual point (UAP)	£770 weekly £3,337[2] monthly £40,040[2] yearly
Rate on earnings up to PT[1]	0%
Not contracted-out rate	12% on £139.01 to £817 weekly 2% on excess over £817
Contracted-out rate	10.4% on £139.01 to £770 weekly 12% on £770.01 to £817 weekly 2% on excess over £817
Reduced rate	5.85% on £139.01 to £817 weekly 2% on excess over £817 (no rebate even if contracted-out)

Notes

[1] Earnings from the LEL, up to and including the PT, count towards the employee's basic state pension, even though no contributions are paid on those earnings. Similarly, earnings between the LEL and the PT count towards the employee's entitlement to certain benefits including the second state pension (S2P). Employees in contracted-out employment earn no S2P rights and receive a rebate of contributions of 1.6%. This applies from the LEL to the UAP, so earnings from LEL to PT attract a 'negative' contribution of 1.6% and the rate for earnings from PT to UAP becomes 10.4%. Earnings from UAP to UEL are subject to the main not contracted-out rate.

[2] Monthly and annual LEL and UAP figures are calculated as per SI 2001/1004, reg. 11.

Class 1 secondary (employer) contributions 2011–12[2]	
Secondary earnings threshold (ST)	£136 weekly £589 monthly £7,072 yearly
Not contracted-out rate	13.8% on earnings above the ST
Contracted-out rate[1]	10.1% for salary-related (COSR) and 12.4% for money-purchase (COMP) schemes on earnings from ST to UAP (plus 3.7% and 1.4% rebates for earnings from LEL to ST), then 13.8% above UAP.

Notes

[1] Although employer contributions do not *per se* give any benefit entitlements, earnings between the LEL and ST are those classed as relevant for S2P. Employers with contracted-out occupational pension schemes receive a rebate of contributions for scheme members of 3.7% (COSR) or 1.4% (COMP). This applies from the LEL to the UAP, so earnings from LEL to ST attract a 'negative' contribution and the rate for earnings from ST to UAP is reduced as shown.

[2] From 22 June 2010 until 5 September 2013, qualifying businesses will be exempt (when a claim is made and accepted) from the first £5,000 of Class 1 NICs due in respect of the first ten qualifying employees hired in the first year of business (*National Insurance Contributions Act* 2011, s. 4).

[¶9-045] Class 1 NIC: 2010–11

Class 1 contributions

Class 1 primary (employee) contributions 2010–11	
Lower earnings limit (LEL)[1]	£97 weekly £421[2] monthly £5,044[2] yearly
Primary threshold (PT)	£110 weekly £476 monthly £5,715 yearly
Upper earnings limit (UEL)	£844 weekly £3,656 monthly £43,875 yearly
Upper accrual point (UAP)	£770 weekly £3,337[2] monthly £40,040[2] yearly
Rate on earnings up to PT[1]	0%
Not contracted-out rate	11% on £110.01 to £844 weekly 1% on excess over £844
Contracted-out rate	9.4% on £110.01 to £770 weekly 11% on £770.01 to £844 weekly 1% on excess over £844
Reduced rate	4.85% on £110.01 to £844 weekly 1% on excess over £844 (no rebate even if contracted-out)

Notes

[1] Earnings from the LEL, up to and including the PT, count towards the employee's basic state pension, even though no contributions are paid on those earnings. Similarly, earnings between the LEL and the PT count towards the employee's entitlement to certain benefits including the second state pension (S2P). Employees in contracted-out employment earn no S2P rights and receive a rebate of contributions of 1.6%. This applies from the LEL to the UAP, so earnings from LEL to PT attract a 'negative' contribution of 1.6% and the rate for earnings from PT to UAP becomes 9.4%. Earnings from UAP to UEL are subject to the main not contracted-out rate.

[2] Monthly and annual LEL and UAP figures are calculated as per SI 2001/1004, reg. 11.

Class 1 secondary (employer) contributions 2010–11[2]	
Secondary earnings threshold (ST)	£110 weekly £476 monthly £5,715 yearly
Not contracted-out rate	12.8% on earnings above the ST
Contracted-out rate[1]	9.1% for salary-related (COSR) and 11.4% for money-purchase (COMP) schemes on earnings from ST to UAP (plus 3.7% and 1.4% rebates for earnings from LEL to ST), then 12.8% above UAP.

Notes

(1) Although employer contributions do not *per se* give any benefit entitlements, earnings between the LEL and ST are those classed as relevant for S2P. Employers with contracted-out occupational pension schemes receive a rebate of contributions for scheme members of 3.7% (COSR) or 1.4% (COMP). This applies from the LEL to the UAP, so earnings from LEL to ST attract a 'negative' contribution and the rate for earnings from ST to UAP is reduced as shown.

(2) From 22 June 2010 until 5 September 2013, qualifying businesses will be exempt (when a claim is made and accepted) from the first £5,000 of Class 1 NICs due in respect of the first ten qualifying employees hired in the first year of business (*National Insurance Contributions Act* 2011, s. 4).

[¶9-050] Class 1 NIC: 2009–10

Class 1 contributions

Class 1 primary (employee) contributions 2009–10	
Lower earnings limit (LEL)[1]	£95 weekly £412[2] monthly £4,940[2] yearly
Primary threshold (PT)	£110 weekly £476 monthly £5,715 yearly
Upper earnings limit (UEL)	£844 weekly £3,656 monthly £43,875 yearly
Upper accrual point (UAP)	£770 weekly £3,337[2] monthly £40,040[2] yearly
Rate on earnings up to PT[1]	0%
Not contracted-out rate	11% on £110.01 to £844 weekly 1% on excess over £844
Contracted-out rate	9.4% on £110.01 to £770 weekly 11% on £770.01 to £844 weekly 1% on excess over £844
Reduced rate	4.85% on £110.01 to £844 weekly 1% on excess over £844 (no rebate even if contracted-out)

Notes

(1) Earnings from the LEL, up to and including the PT, count towards the employee's basic state pension, even though no contributions are paid on those earnings. Similarly, earnings between the LEL and the PT count towards the employee's entitlement to certain benefits including the second state pension (S2P). Employees in contracted-out employment earn no S2P rights and receive a rebate of contributions of 1.6%. This applies from the LEL to the UAP, so earnings from LEL to PT attract a 'negative' contribution of 1.6% and the rate for earnings from PT to UAP becomes 9.4%. Earnings from UAP to UEL are subject to the main not contracted-out rate.

(2) Monthly and annual LEL and UAP figures are calculated as per SI 2001/1004, reg. 11.

Class 1 secondary (employer) contributions 2009–10	
Secondary earnings threshold (ST)	£110 weekly £476 monthly £5,715 yearly
Not contracted-out rate	12.8% on earnings above the ST
Contracted-out rate[1]	9.1% for salary-related (COSR) and 11.4% for money-purchase (COMP) schemes on earnings from ST to UAP (plus 3.7% and 1.4% rebates for earnings from LEL to ST), then 12.8% above UAP.

Note

[1] Although employer contributions do not *per se* give any benefit entitlements, earnings between the LEL and ST are those classed as relevant for S2P. Employers with contracted-out occupational pension schemes receive a rebate of contributions for scheme members of 3.7% (COSR) or 1.4% (COMP). This applies from the LEL to the UAP, so earnings from LEL to ST attract a 'negative' contribution and the rate for earnings from ST to UAP is reduced as shown.

[¶9-350] Class 1A contributions

Since 6 April 2000, employers (but not employees) have paid NICs on an annual basis on benefits in kind provided to employees earning at the rate of £8,500 p.a. or more or to directors (SSCBA 1992, s. 10). Contributions for the year are due by 19 July following the end of the tax year to which they relate (22 July for electronic payment). Rates applying are always the full Class 1 secondary (employer) rate for each year, with no rebate for contracted-out employees. They have been as follows:

Period	%
2011–12 to 2014–15	13.8
2003–04 to 2010–11	12.8

For rates of interest on late paid Class 1A contributions, see ¶9-650.

[¶9-400] Return deadlines for Class 1 and 1A contributions

Forms	Date	Penalty provision
See ¶4-930 RTI reporting (former end of year returns P14, P35, P38 and P38A)	See ¶4-930 for RTI deadlines (previously 19 May following tax year)	FA 2009, Sch. 55 (TMA 1970, s. 98A)
P11D(b)	6 July following year of assessment	SI 2001/1004, reg. 81(2)

Note

In cases of PAYE and NIC default, there are provisions to prevent double charging. Class 1A contributions are recorded annually in arrears. Penalties will only be imposed if there is a delay in the submission of the relevant year's PAYE return or P11Ds and P11D(b).

[¶9-450] Class 1B contributions

Class 1B contributions are payable by employers on the amount of earnings in a PAYE settlement agreement (PSA) that are chargeable to Class 1 or Class 1A NICs, together with the total amount of income tax payable under the agreement (SSCBA 1992, s. 10A). Class 1B contributions are charged at the same rate as Class 1A contributions (see above) and are payable by 19 October after the end of the tax year to which the PSA applies (22 October for electronic payment).

[¶9-500] Class 2 contributions

Class 2 contributions are paid at a flat rate by a self-employed person unless he has applied for and been granted exception because his earnings are below the small earnings exception (SEE) limit for Class 2 contributions. If a person is excepted, he may still pay the contributions voluntarily to keep up his right to the benefits they provide.

Draft National Insurance Contributions Bill 2014–15 includes provisions to give effect to the collection of Class 2 NICs through self-assessment alongside income tax and Class 4 NICs, with effect for the tax year 2015–16.

Rates and SEE limit

Tax year	Weekly contribution rate[1]			Small earnings exception limit[2] £
	Rate £	Share fishermen £	Volunteer development workers £	
2015–16[3]	2.80	3.45	5.60	5,965
2014–15	2.75	3.40	5.55	5,885
2013–14	2.70	3.35	5.45	5,725
2012–13	2.65	3.30	5.35	5,595
2011–12	2.50	3.15	5.10	5,315
2010–11	2.40	3.05	4.85	5,075
2009–10	2.40	3.05	4.75	5,075

Notes

(1) These rates are uprated by CPI.

(2) The 'small profits threshold' replaces the 'small earnings exception' from 6 April 2015. This threshold is uprated by CPI.

(3) Rates per Autumn Statement 2014.

[¶9-550] Class 3 contributions

Class 3 contributions are paid voluntarily by persons not liable for contributions, or who have been excepted from Class 2 contributions, or whose contribution record is insufficient to qualify for benefits (i.e. Class 3 contributions allow people to fill gaps in their contributions record for basic state pension purposes). They are paid at a flat-rate. Class 3 contributions may not be paid where an individuals earnings factor (earnings on which primary Class 1 or Class 2 contributions have been paid) equals or exceeds the qualifying limit for the year.

Rate and earnings factor

Tax year	Weekly contribution rate[1] £	Earnings factor for each contribution in col. 2 £
2015–16[2]	14.10	112.00
2014–15	13.90	111.00
2013–14	13.55	109.00
2012–13	13.25	107.00
2011–12	12.60	102.00
2010–11	12.05	97.00
2009–10	12.05	95.00

Notes

(1) Rate is uprated by CPI.

(2) Rates per Autumn Statement 2014.

[¶9-570] Class 3A contributions

(SSCBA 1992, s. 14A–14C)

Autumn Statement 2013 announced the introduction, from October 2015, of a new class of voluntary National Insurance contribution to be known as the State Pension top up. Primary legislation for the measure was introduced by the *Pensions Act* 2014.

Existing pensioners and those reaching state pension age before 6 April 2016 will have the opportunity to gain additional state pension by paying Class 3A voluntary National Insurance contributions. There are two conditions:

- contributors must have entitlement to a UK state pension; and
- contributors must reach state pension age before 6 April 2016.

The new measure is in addition to Class 3 voluntary contributions (see above).

The amount of a Class 3A contribution needed to obtain a unit of additional pension is to be determined in accordance with Treasury regulations. Secondary legislation will also define the following features:

- £25 per week as the maximum amount that contributions can provide;
- Class 3A VNICs will be available for 18 months from October 2015; and
- A cooling off period of 90 elapsed days.

Rates published 5 December 2013

Age at payment date (October 2015 to April 2017)	Rate for each additional pension unit of £1 per week £	Age at payment date (October 2015 to April 2017)	Rate for each additional pension unit of £1 per week £
63 (women only)	934	82	484
64 (women only)	913	83	454
65	890	84	424

Age at payment date (October 2015 to April 2017)	Rate for each additional pension unit of £1 per week £	Age at payment date (October 2015 to April 2017)	Rate for each additional pension unit of £1 per week £
66	871	85	394
67	847	86	366
68	827	87	339
69	801	88	314
70	779	89	291
71	761	90	270
72	738	91	251
73	719	92	232
74	694	93	216
75	674	94	200
76	646	95	185
77	625	96	172
78	596	97	159
79	574	98	148
80	544	99	137
81	514	100	127

[¶9-600] Class 4 contributions

Self-employed people whose profits or gains are over a certain amount have to pay Class 4 contributions as well as Class 2 contributions. These contributions are earnings-related and paid at a main rate on trading profits (earnings) between the lower and upper annual limits (which are the same as the Class 1 earnings threshold and upper earnings limit), with an additional 2% on profits above the upper limit since 6 April 2011.

Tax year	Rate on profits between upper and lower limits %	Annual lower profits limit[(2)] £	Annual upper profits limit £	Rate on profits in excess of upper limit %	Maximum contribution £
2015–16[(3)]	9	8,060	42,385	2	unlimited
2014–15	9	7,956	41,865	2	unlimited
2013–14	9	7,755	41,450	2	unlimited
2012–13	9	7,605	42,475	2	unlimited

Tax year	Rate on profits between upper and lower limits %	Annual lower profits limit[2] £	Annual upper profits limit £	Rate on profits in excess of upper limit %	Maximum contribution £
2011–12	9	7,225	42,475	2	unlimited
2010–11	8	5,715	43,875	1	unlimited
2009–10	8	5,715	43,875	1	unlimited

Note

[1] The maximum Class 4 contribution is now based on 9% of profits above the lower annual limit up to the upper profits limit, plus 2% of any excess, and 53 weeks of Class 2 contributions. Until April 2003, the value was fixed, as the Class 4 liability was capped, but the introduction of the 1% contribution on trading profits above the annual limit (2% from 6 April 2011) means that the annual maximum has become variable, since the 2% is without limit.

[2] This threshold is uprated by CPI.

[3] Rates per Autumn Statement 2014

[¶9-650] Rates of interest on National Insurance contributions

(SSCBA 1992, Sch. 1, para. 6(2))

The same rates of interest apply in relation to overdue and overpaid National Insurance as apply in relation to overdue and overpaid income tax (see ¶1-500).

Interest on **overdue** National Insurance contributions is payable from the due date of payment:

- **Class 1:** from 2014–15, see ¶4-948: interest on certain PAYE paid late (previously 19 April, or 22 April (electronic payments) following end of the tax year in respect of which the NIC was due (SI 2001/1004, Sch. 4, para. 17(3))).
- **Class 1A:** 19 July, or 22 July (where payment is made electronically) following the end of the tax year in respect of which the NIC was due to the date of payment (SI 2004/1004, reg. 76(3)).
- **Class 1B:** 19 October, or 22 October (where payment is made electronically) following the end of the tax year in respect of which the NIC was due to the date of payment (SI 2004/1004, Sch. 4, para. 17(3)).

The qualifying period for repayment interest on **overpaid** National Insurance contributions is as set out below:

- **Class 1:** from 2014–15, see ¶4-948: interest on certain PAYE paid late (previously from 19 April following the end of the tax year in respect of which the NIC was paid to the date on which the order for the repayment is issued. Contributions paid late, i.e. after 19 April, and later repaid carry interest from the actual date of payment (SI 2001/1004, Sch. 4, para. 18(3))).
- **Class 1A:** from 19 April following the end of the tax year in respect of which the NIC was paid, or if the contribution was paid later, from the date of actual payment – usually 19 July in practice – to the date on which the order for the repayment is issued (SI 2001/1004, reg. 77(2)).
- **Class 1B:** from 19 October following the end of the tax year in respect of which the NIC was paid to the date on which the order for the repayment is issued. Contributions paid late, i.e. after 19 October, and later repaid carry interest from the actual date of payment (SI 2001/1004, Sch. 4, para. 18(3)).

TAX CREDITS

[¶10-000] Working tax credits

(SI 2002/2005)

Maximum rates 2010–11 to 2015–16

Element	2014–15[1][2] £	2014–15[1] £	2013–14 £	2012–13 £	2011–12 £	2010–11 £
Basic element	1,960	1,940	1,920	1,920	1,920	1,920
Disabled worker element	2,970	2,935	2,855	2,790	2,650	2,570
Severe disability element	1,275	1,255	1,220	1,190	1,130	1,095
30-hour element	810	800	790	790	790	790
Couple and lone parent element	2,010	1,990	1,970	1,950	1,950	1,890
50-plus element:						
(a) working at least 16 hours but less than 30 hours per week		–	–	–	1,365	1,320
(b) working at least 30 hours per week		–	–	–	2,030	1,965
Childcare element:						
percentage of eligible costs covered	70%	70%	70%	70%	70%	80%
• maximum eligible cost for one child (per week)	175	175	175	175	175	175
• maximum eligible cost of two or more children (per week)	300	300	300	300	300	300

Note

(1) All rates of benefits and tax credits (except basic state pension, disability benefits, carers benefits, premia and the additional state pension) are being increased by 1% in 2014–15 and 2015–16 (Autumn Statement 2012).

(2) Rates per Autumn Statement 2014.

[¶10-100] Child tax credits

(SI 2002/2007)

Maximum rates 2010–11 to 2015–16

Element	Circumstance	2015–16[2][3]	Maximum annual rate 2014–15[2] £	Maximum annual rate 2013–14 £	Maximum annual rate 2012–13 £	Maximum annual rate 2011–12 £	Maximum annual rate 2010–11 £
Family	Normal case	545	545	545	545	545	545
	Where there is a child under the age of one	–[1]	–[1]	–[1]	–[1]	–[1]	1,090
Individual	Each child or young person	2,780	2,750	2,720	2,690	2,555	2,300
	Each disabled child or young person	5,920	5,850	5,735	5,640	5,355	5,015
	Each severely disabled child or young person	7,195	7,105	6,955	6,830	6,485	6,110

Notes

(1) The 'baby element' of the child tax credit (i.e. where there is a child under the age of one) was abolished from April 2011.

(2) All rates of benefits and tax credits (except basic state pension, disability benefits, carers benefits, premia and the additional state pension) are being increased by 1% in 2014–15 and 2015–16 (Autumn Statement 2012).

(3) Rates per Autumn Statement 2014.

Income thresholds and withdrawal rates 2010–11 to 2015–16

	2015–16[3][4]	2014–15[3]	2013–14	2012–13	2011–12	2010–11
First income threshold	£6,420	£6,420	£6,420	£6,420	£6,420	£6,420
First withdrawal rate	41%	41%	41%	41%	41%	39%
Second income threshold	[1]	[1]	[1]	[1]	£40,000	£50,000
Second withdrawal rate	[1]	[1]	[1]	[1]	41.0%	6.67%
First threshold for those entitled to child tax credit only	£16,105	£16,010	£15,910	£15,860	£15,860	£16,190
Income rise disregard	£5,000	£5,000	£5,000	£10,000	£10,000	£25,000
Income fall disregard	£2,500	£2,500	£2,500	£2,500	[2]	[2]

Notes

[1] The second income threshold was withdrawn from 1 April 2012.

[2] The income fall disregard was introduced from April 2012.

[3] All rates of benefits and tax credits (except basic state pension, disability benefits, carers benefits, premia and the additional state pension) are being increased by 1% in 2014–15 and 2015–16 (Autumn Statement 2012).

[4] Rates per Autumn Statement 2014.

STATE BENEFITS AND STATUTORY PAYMENTS

[¶10-500] Taxable state benefits

(ITEPA 2003, s. 577, 660)

(Tax Reporter: ¶490-000ff.)

The following benefits are liable to income tax.

Rates were most recently updated by SI 2014/516.

Benefit	Weekly rate from				
	April 2014 £	April 2013 £	April 2012 £	April 2011 £	April 2010 £
Bereavement					
Bereavement allowance[3]	111.20	108.30	105.95	100.70	97.65
Widowed parent's allowance[4]	111.20	108.30	105.95	100.70	97.65
Carer's allowance	61.35	59.75	58.45	55.55	53.90
Dependent adults					
with retirement pension[1]	64.90	63.20	61.85	58.80	57.05
with carer's allowance[1]	36.10	35.15	34.40	32.70	31.70
with long-term incapacity	60.45	58.85	57.60	54.75	53.10
with short-term incapacity (under pensionable age)	47.10	45.85	44.85	42.65	41.35
with short-term incapacity (over pensionable age)	58.20	56.65	55.45	52.70	51.10
Employment & Support Allowance					
Age 25+ contributions-based ESA	72.40	71.70	71.00	67.50	65.45
Industrial death benefit:					
Widow's pension					
Permanent rate:					
higher	113.10	110.15	107.45	102.15	97.65
lower	33.93	33.05	32.24	30.65	29.30
Widower's pension	113.10	110.15	107.45	102.15	97.65
Incapacity benefit (long-term)					
Rate	104.10	101.35	99.15	94.25	91.40
Increase for age:					
higher rate	11.00	10.70	11.70	13.80	15.00
lower rate	6.15	6.00	5.90	5.60	5.80
Jobseeker's allowance					
See ¶10-600.					

Benefit	Weekly rate from April 2014 £	April 2013 £	April 2012 £	April 2011 £	April 2010 £
Incapacity benefit (short-term)					
Higher rate:					
under pensionable age[2]	92.95	90.50	88.55	84.15	81.60
over pensionable age[2]	104.10	101.35	99.15	94.25	91.40
Non-contributory retirement pension					
Standard rate	67.80	66.00	64.40	61.20	58.50
Age addition (at age 80)	0.25	0.25	0.25	0.25	0.25
Retirement pension					
Standard rate[5]	113.10	110.15	107.45	102.15	97.65
Age addition (at age 80)	0.25	0.25	0.25	0.25	0.25
SSP, SMP, SPP and SAP					
See ¶10-650ff.					
Widow's pension[3]	111.20	108.30	105.95	100.70	97.65
Widowed mother's allowance[4]	111.20	108.30	105.95	100.70	97.65

Notes

[1] No new claims for adult dependency increases payable with the state retirement pension or the carer's allowance may be made on or after 6 April 2010. Adult dependency increases already in payment immediately before 6 April 2010 will be phased out between 2010 and 2020.

[2] A man born before 6 December 1953 still attains pensionable age at age 65, whilst a woman born before 6 April 1950 attained pensionable age at age 60. The date the pensionable age is attained by individuals born after those dates is set out in the tables at ¶3-175.

[3] Bereavement allowance replaced widow's pension from 9 April 2001 for all new claims by widows and widowers.

[4] Widowed parent's allowance replaced widowed mother's allowance from 9 April 2001 for all new claims.

[5] From April 2015, the basic state pension will be increased by 2.5%; a cash increase of 2.85% per week for the full basic state pension (Autumn Statement 2014).

From April 2011, the consumer price index is used for the indexation of benefits. From April 2014, benefits for disabled people and pensioners will increase in line with CPI inflation while benefits and tax credits for working age people are being increased by 1% for 2014–15 and 2015–16 (Autumn Statements 2013 and 2012).

[¶10-550] Non-taxable state benefits

(ITEPA 2003, s. 677(1): see also EIM 76100)

(Tax Reporter: ¶490-000ff.)

The following UK social security benefits are wholly exempt from tax, except where indicated otherwise.

- Attendance allowance
- Back to work bonus (see EIM 76223)
- Bereavement payment (see EIM 76171)
- Child benefit
- Child's special allowance
- Child tax credit
- Constant attendance allowance: see industrial disablement benefit

- Council tax benefit
- Disability living allowance
- Income related employment and support allowance (see EIM 76186)
- Exceptionally severe disablement allowance: see industrial disablement benefit
- Guardian's allowance
- Housing benefit
- Incapacity benefit for first 28 weeks of entitlement, taxable thereafter (see EIM 76180)
- Income support, certain payments (see EIM 76190)
- Industrial injuries benefit, a general term covering industrial injuries pension, reduced earnings allowance, retirement allowance, constant attendance allowance and exceptionally severe disablement allowance
- Invalidity benefit, replaced by incapacity benefit from April 1995 but still payable where invalidity commenced before April 1995
- In-work credit, In-work emergency discretion fund payment, In-work emergency fund payment
- Maternity allowance (see EIM 76361)
- Pensioner's Christmas bonus
- Personal independence payment
- State pension credit
- Reduced earnings allowance: see industrial disablement benefit
- Retirement allowance: see industrial injuries benefit
- Return to work credit and self-employment credit
- Severe disablement allowance
- Social fund payments – help with maternity expenses, funeral costs, financial crisis, community care grants and interest free loans.
- Universal credit
- War widow's pension (see EIM 76103)
- Winter fuel payment (or 'cold weather payment')
- Working tax credit

With regard to wounds and disability pensions for service with the forces see EIM 74302 and for allowances payable to civilians in respect of war injuries see EIM 74700.

Certain foreign social security payments are exempt from UK tax (see EIM 76009).

The new bereavement support payment, which is due to replace three current benefits paid in respect of bereavement from April 2017 (*Pensions Act* 2014) will be exempt from income tax (Autumn Statement 2014).

Benefit rates

	Weekly rate from				
Benefit	**April 2014 £**	**April 2013 £**	**April 2012 £**	**April 2011 £**	**April 2010 £**
Attendance allowance					
Higher rate	81.30	79.15	77.45	73.60	71.40
Lower rate	54.45	53.00	51.85	49.30	47.80
Child benefit(1)(2)(7)					
For the eldest qualifying child	20.50	20.30	20.30	20.30	20.30
For each other child	13.55	13.40	13.40	13.40	13.40

Benefit	Weekly rate from				
	April 2014 £	April 2013 £	April 2012 £	April 2011 £	April 2010 £
Guardian's allowance[7]	16.35	15.90	15.55	14.75	14.30
Child dependency addition					
Payable with: state pension; widowed mothers/parents allowance; short-term incapacity benefit – higher rate or over state pension age; long-term incapacity benefit; carer's allowance; severe disablement allowance; industrial death benefit (higher rate).	11.35	11.35	11.35	11.35	11.35
Reduced rate[3]	8.05	8.10	8.10	8.10	8.10
Constant attendance allowance					
Exceptional rate	132.80	129.40	126.60	120.40	116.80
Intermediate rate	99.60	97.05	94.95	90.30	87.60
Normal maximum rate	66.40	64.70	63.30	60.20	58.40
Part-time rate	33.20	32.35	31.65	30.10	29.20
Exceptionally severe disablement allowance	66.40	64.70	63.30	60.20	58.40
Employment & support allowance – income-related based (ESA(IR))					
Involves over 30 potential components					
Maternity allowances					
(where SMP not available)					
Standard rate	138.18	136.78	135.45	128.73	124.88
MA threshold	30.00	30.00	30.00	30.00	30.00
Disability living allowance (care component)[6]					
Higher rate	81.30	79.15	77.45	73.60	71.40
Middle rate	54.45	53.00	51.85	49.30	47.80
Lower rate	21.55	21.00	20.55	19.55	18.95
Disability living allowance (mobility component)[6]					
Higher rate	56.75	55.25	54.05	51.40	49.85
Lower rate	21.55	21.00	20.55	19.55	18.95
Incapacity benefit (short-term)[4]					
Lower rate:					
under pensionable age[5]	78.50	76.45	74.80	71.10	68.95
over pensionable age[5]	99.90	97.25	95.15	90.45	87.75

Benefit	Weekly rate from				
	April 2014 £	April 2013 £	April 2012 £	April 2011 £	April 2010 £
Severe disablement allowance					
Basic rate	73.75	71.80	69.00	62.95	59.45
Age addition (from Dec 90)					
• Higher rate	11.00	10.70	11.70	13.80	15.00
• Middle rate	6.15	6.00	5.90	7.10	8.40
• Lower rate	6.15	6.00	5.90	5.60	5.45
Adult dependency increase	36.30	35.35	34.60	32.90	31.90
Pensions credit[(8)]					
Standard					
Single	148.35	145.40	142.70	137.35	132.60
Couple	226.50	222.05	217.90	209.70	202.40
Additional amount for severe disability					
Single	61.10	59.50	58.20	55.30	53.65
Couple (one qualifies)	61.10	59.50	58.20	55.30	53.65
Couple (both qualify)	122.20	119.00	116.40	110.60	107.30
Additional amount for carers	34.20	33.30	32.60	31.00	30.05
Savings credit[(8)]					
Threshold – single	120.35	115.30	111.80	103.15	98.40
Threshold – couple	192.00	183.90	178.35	164.55	157.25
Maximum award – single	16.80	18.06	18.54	20.52	20.52
Maximum award – couple	20.70	22.89	23.73	27.09	27.09
Polygamous marriage amounts					
Claimant and first spouse	226.50	222.05	217.90	209.70	202.40
Additional amount for additional spouse	78.15	76.65	75.20	72.35	69.80
Personal independence payment[(6)]					
Daily living component					
Standard rate	54.45	53.00	–	–	–
Enhanced rate	81.30	79.15	–	–	–
Mobility component					
Standard rate	21.55	21.00	–	–	–
Enhanced rate	56.75	55.25	–	–	–

Notes

(1) High income child benefit charge applies from 7 January 2013 (see ¶1-110).

(2) Child benefit rates increase by 1% in 2014–15 and 2015–16 (Autumn Statement 2012).

(3) The rate of child dependency increase is adjusted where it is payable for the eldest child for whom child benefit is also paid. The weekly rate in such cases is reduced by the difference between ChB rates for the eldest and subsequent children.

(4) Incapacity benefit and contributory employment & support allowance (ESA(C)) are taxable, under the *Income Tax (Earnings and Pensions) Act* 2003, Pt. 10, Ch. 3, except for short-term benefit payable at the lower rate. It is not taxable, however, if the recipient started receiving invalidity benefit or sickness benefit before 6 April 1995 and has continued receiving long-term incapacity benefit since then.

[5] A man born before 6 December 1953 still attains pensionable age at age 65, whilst a woman born before 6 April 1950 attained pensionable age at age 60. The date the pensionable age is attained by individuals born after those dates is set out in the tables at ¶3-175.
[6] Personal independence payment (PIP) is being introduced from April 2013 to replace disability living allowance for claimants aged 16 to 64 (but not children under 16 or people aged 65 and over already in receipt of disability living allowance). PIP is being phased in with effect from April 2013 in relation to new claims in Merseyside, North West England, Cumbria, Cheshire and North East England, from June 2013 for new claims from all parts of the country and from 2015 for existing recipients of disability living allowance.
[7] Rates of child benefit for 2015–16 will be £20.70 for the first child and £13.70 for each other child; and the rate of guardian's allowance for 2015–16 will be £16.55 (Autumn Statement 2014).
[8] From April 2015, the standard minimum income guarantee in pension credit will rise by the same amount as the cash increase in the basic state pension (£2.85 per week) and the savings credit threshold will rise by 5.1% (Autumn Statement 2014).

From April 2011, the consumer price index is used for the indexation of benefits. From April 2014, benefits for disabled people and pensioners will increase in line with CPI inflation while benefits and tax credits for working age people are being increased by 1% for 2014–15 and 2015–16 (Autumn Statements 2013 and 2012).

[¶10-600] Income support and jobseeker's allowance

(Tax Reporter: ¶490-250)

	Weekly rate from				
Benefit: Income support	**April 2014 £**	**April 2013 £**	**April 2012 £**	**April 2011 £**	**April 2010 £**
Single					
Under 25	57.35	56.80	56.25	53.45	51.85
25 or over	72.40	71.70	71.00	67.50	65.45
Lone parent					
Under 18	57.35	56.80	56.25	53.45	51.85
18 or over	72.40	71.70	71.00	67.50	65.45
Couple					
Both under 18	57.35	56.80	56.25	53.45	51.85
Both under 18 – higher rate	86.65	85.80	84.95	80.75	78.30
One under 18, one under 25	57.35	56.80	56.25	53.45	51.85
One under 18, one 25 and over	72.40	71.70	71.00	67.50	65.45
Both 18 or over	113.70	112.55	111.45	105.95	102.75
Dependent children	66.33	65.62	64.99	62.33	57.57

	Weekly rate from				
Benefit: Jobseeker's allowance	**April 2014 £**	**April 2013 £**	**April 2012 £**	**April 2011 £**	**April 2010 £**
Contributions based JSA – personal rates					
under 25	57.35	56.80	56.25	53.45	51.85
25 or over	72.40	71.70	71.00	67.50	65.45

			Weekly rate from		
			April 2012 £	**April 2011 £**	**April 2010 £**
Income based JSA – personal allowances					
under 25	57.35	56.80	56.25	53.45	51.85
25 or over	72.40	71.70	71.00	67.50	65.45
Lone parent					
Under 18	57.35	56.80	56.25	53.45	51.85
18 or over	72.40	71.70	71.00	67.50	65.45
Couple					
Both under 18	57.35	56.80	56.25	53.45	51.85
Both under 18 – higher rate	86.65	85.80	84.95	80.75	78.30
One under 18, one under 25	57.35	56.80	56.25	53.45	51.85
One under 18, one 25 and over	72.40	71.70	71.00	67.50	65.45
Both 18 or over	113.70	112.55	111.45	105.95	102.75
Dependent children	66.33	65.62	64.99	62.33	57.57

	Weekly rate from				
Premium: Income support and Jobseeker's allowance	**April 2014 £**	**April 2013 £**	**April 2012 £**	**April 2011 £**	**April 2010 £**
Family/lone parent	17.45	17.40	17.40	17.40	17.40
Pensioner					
Single (JSA only)	75.95	73.70	71.70	69.85	67.15
Couple	112.80	109.50	106.45	103.75	99.65
Disability					
Single	31.85	31.00	30.35	28.85	28.00
Couple	45.40	44.20	43.25	41.10	39.85
Enhanced disability					
Single	15.55	15.15	14.80	14.05	13.65
Disabled child	24.08	23.45	22.89	21.63	21.00
Couple	22.35	21.75	21.30	20.25	19.65
Severe disability					
Single	61.10	59.50	58.20	55.30	53.65
couple (lower rate)	61.10	59.50	58.20	55.30	53.65
couple (higher rate)	122.20	119.00	116.40	110.60	107.30
Disabled child	59.50	57.89	56.63	53.62	52.08
Carer	34.20	33.30	32.60	31.00	30.05

Notes

From April 2011, the consumer price index is used for the indexation of benefits.

Benefits and tax credits for working age people are being increased by 1% for 2014–15 and 2015–16 (Autumn Statement 2012).

[¶10-625] Benefits cap

(*Welfare Reform Act* 2012; SI 2012/2994)

The benefits cap limits the total amount of benefit that working age people can receive.

	Rates from	
	April 2014 £	**April 2013 £**
Housing Benefit (weekly rate)		
Couples and lone parents	500	500
Single adults	350	350
Universal Credit (monthly rate)		
Joint claimants and single claimants with children	2,167	2,167
Single claimants with no dependent children	1,517	1,517

Benefits to which cap is applicable

The cap will apply to household income from the following:

- Bereavement Allowance
- Carer's Allowance
- Child Benefit
- Child Tax Credit
- Employment and Support Allowance (except where paid with support component)
- Guardian's Allowance
- Housing Benefit
- Incapacity Benefit
- Income Support
- Jobseeker's Allowance
- Maternity Allowance
- Severe Disablement Allowance
- Widowed Parent's Allowance (or widowed mother's allowance or widow's pension)

Households not affected by the cap

A partner or any dependant child qualifies for Working Tax Credit, or in receipt of any of the following:

- Disability Living Allowance
- Personal Independence Payment
- Attendance Allowance
- Industrial Injuries Benefits
- Employment Support Allowance (if paid with the support component)
- Armed Forces Compensation Scheme payments

- Armed Forces Independence Payment
- War pensions (incl. War Widow's/Widower's Pension)

[¶10-650] Statutory sick pay (SSP)

Employers are liable to pay SSP in any period of incapacity for work to a maximum of 28 weeks at the SSP rate in force. Statutory sick pay is treated as wages and is subject to PAYE income tax and to National Insurance contributions. Statutory sick pay is not payable for certain periods in which statutory maternity pay is being paid.

The amount of SSP payable to an employee depends on the earnings band into which he or she falls. The earnings bands and the associated SSP payments are as follows:

Period (from)	Average gross weekly earnings £	Weekly SSP rate[(1)] £
6 April 2014	111.00 or more	87.55
6 April 2013	109.00 or more	86.70
6 April 2012	107.00 or more	85.85
6 April 2011	102.00 or more	81.60
6 April 2010	97.00 or more	79.15
6 April 2009	95.00 or more	79.15

Notes

(1) The daily rate of SSP is ascertained by dividing the weekly rate by the number of qualifying days in the week (beginning on Sunday), then multiplying by the number of qualifying days of incapacity in the week, rounded up to the nearest penny.

From April 2011, the consumer price index is used for the indexation of benefits. Benefits and tax credits for working age people are being increased by 1% for 2014–15 and 2015–16 (Autumn Statement 2012).

Maximum entitlement

An employee reaches his maximum entitlement to SSP in one spell of incapacity when he has been paid 28 times the appropriate rate, i.e. £87.55 × 28 = £2,451.40.

[¶10-700] Statutory maternity pay (SMP)

Women expecting a baby who satisfy the qualifying conditions are entitled to a maximum of 39 weeks' SMP (26 weeks up to April 2007). These include having 'average weekly earnings' of:

- £111 if their baby is due between 20 July 2014 and 18 July 2015;
- £109 if their baby is due between 14 July 2013 and 19 July 2014;
- £107 if their baby is due between 15 July 2012 and 13 July 2013; and
- £102 if their baby is due between 17 July 2011 and 14 July 2012.

In other words, 'average weekly earnings' must reach or exceed the then-current NIC LEL in the eight weeks leading up to the fifteenth week before the expected week of childbirth (or placement of an adopted child).

Period (from)	First 6 weeks	Remaining weeks
6 April 2014	90% average weekly earnings	Lower of 90% average weekly earnings and £138.18
6 April 2013	90% average weekly earnings	Lower of 90% of weekly earnings and £136.78
6 April 2012	90% average weekly earnings	Lower of 90% of weekly earnings and £135.45
6 April 2011	90% average weekly earnings	Lower of 90% of weekly earnings and £128.73
6 April 2010	90% average weekly earnings	Lower of 90% of weekly earnings and £124.88
6 April 2009	90% average weekly earnings	Lower of 90% of weekly earnings and £123.06

Note

From April 2011, the consumer price index is used for the indexation of benefits. Benefits and tax credits for working age people are being increased by 1% for 2014–15 and 2015–16 (Autumn Statement 2012).

[¶10-750] Statutory paternity pay (SPP)

SPP was introduced from 6 April 2003 and is payable for a maximum of two weeks (ordinary statutory paternity pay). For babies born due to be born on or after 3 April 2011, a mother may return to work early and pass her entitlement to leave and lower rate benefit to the father, for up to 26 weeks (additional statutory paternity pay). Weekly rates of statutory paternity pay (standard rate and additional rate) are the same as the standard rate of statutory maternity pay (see ¶10-700).

[¶10-800] Statutory adoption pay (SAP)

SAP was introduced, like SPP, in April 2003.

Employees who are adopting a child and are notified that they have been matched with a child or received official notification that they are eligible to adopt a child from abroad who satisfy the qualifying conditions are entitled to a maximum of 39 weeks' SAP. These include having average weekly earnings of:

Eligible to adopt on or after	Average weekly earnings
6 April 2014	£111.00
31 March 2013	£109.00
1 April 2012	£107.00
3 April 2011	£102.00
4 April 2010	£97.00
5 April 2009	£95.00

The weekly rate of statutory adoption pay is the same as the standard rate of statutory maternity pay (see ¶10-700). The adoptive parents are treated in effect as if they have had a baby and qualified for SMP.

[¶10-900] Universal credit

(SI 2013/376)
(Tax Reporter: ¶490-760)

Universal credit is a new benefit that has started to replace six existing benefits with a single monthly payment. Universal credit will eventually replace all of the following tax credits and benefits:

- tax credits – both Child Tax Credit and Working Tax Credit;
- income-based Jobseeker's Allowance;
- income-related Employment and Support Allowance;
- Income Support; and
- Housing Benefit.

Universal credit will not replace Child Benefit.

Universal credit started to be introduced in stages from April 2013. Existing claimants of the above benefits will be moved to Universal Credit during 2016 and 2017. Universal credit is exempt from income tax.

Universal credit	**Per month**	
	2014 £	**2013 £**
Universal credit amounts		
Standard allowance		
– single under 25	249.28	246.81
– single over 25	314.67	311.55
– joint claimants, both under 25	391.29	387.42
– joint claimants, one or both over 25	493.95	489.06
Child element		
– first child	274.58	272.08
– second/subsequent child	229.17	226.67
Disabled child additions		
– lower rate	124.86	123.62
– higher rate	362.92	352.92
LCW and WRA elements		
– limited capability for work	124.86	123.62
– limited capability for work and work related activity	311.86	303.66
Carer element	148.61	144.70
Childcare costs element		
– max for one child	532.29	532.29
– max for two or more children	912.50	912.50
Non-dependants' housing cost contributions	68.68	68.00
Work allowances		
Higher work allowance (no housing element)		
– single claimant, no dependent children	111.00	111.00
– single claimant, one or more children	734.00	734.00
– single claimant, limited capability for work	647.00	647.00
– joint claimant, no dependent children	111.00	111.00
– joint claimant, one or more children	536.00	536.00
– joint claimant, limited capability for work	647.00	647.00

Universal credit	Per month	
	2014 £	2013 £
Lower work allowance		
– single claimant, no dependent children	111.00	111.00
– single claimant, one or more children	263.00	263.00
– single claimant, limited capability for work	192.00	192.00
– joint claimant, no dependent children	111.00	111.00
– joint claimant, one or more children	222.00	222.00
– joint claimant, limited capability for work	192.00	192.00
Assumed income from capital	4.35	4.35

GENERAL

Retail prices index

[¶11-000] Retail prices index: general

The Retail Prices Index (RPI), issued by the Office for National Statistics, is used to calculate the indexation allowance for the purposes of calculating capital gains on corporation tax. (Since April 1998, the indexation allowance has ceased to be available when calculating gains liable to capital gains tax.) Certain personal and other reliefs are also linked to RPI subject to Parliament determining otherwise, although since April 2011, the Consumer Price Index (CPI) has been used for the indexation of benefits, tax credits and public service pensions. Historically, the RPI was used for indexation of pensions and state benefits.

With effect from February 1987, the reference date to which the price level in each subsequent month is related was changed from 'January 1974 = 100' to 'January 1987 = 100'.

Movements in the RPI in the months after January 1987 are calculated with reference to January 1987 = 100. (With a base of January 1974 = 100, January 1987's RPI was 394.5). A new formula was provided by the then Department of Employment for calculating movements in the index over periods which span January 1987:

> 'The index for the later month (January 1987 = 100) is multiplied by the index for January 1987 (January 1974 = 100) and divided by the index for the earlier month (January 1974 = 100). 100 is subtracted to give the percentage change between the two months.'

CCH has prepared the following table in accordance with this formula:

	1982	1983	1984	1985	1986	1987	1988	1989	1990	1991
Jan.		82.61	86.84	91.20	96.25	100.0	103.3	111.0	119.5	130.2
Feb.		82.97	87.20	91.94	96.60	100.4	103.7	111.8	120.2	130.9
March	79.44	83.12	87.48	92.80	96.73	100.6	104.1	112.3	121.4	131.4
April	81.04	84.28	88.64	94.78	97.67	101.8	105.8	114.3	125.1	133.1
May	81.62	84.64	88.97	95.21	97.85	101.9	106.2	115.0	126.2	133.5
June	81.85	84.84	89.20	95.41	97.79	101.9	106.6	115.4	126.7	134.1
July	81.88	85.30	89.10	95.23	97.52	101.8	106.7	115.5	126.8	133.8
Aug.	81.90	85.68	89.94	95.49	97.82	102.1	107.9	115.8	128.1	134.1
Sept.	81.85	86.06	90.11	95.44	98.30	102.4	108.4	116.6	129.3	134.6
Oct.	82.26	86.36	90.67	95.59	98.45	102.9	109.5	117.5	130.3	135.1
Nov.	82.66	86.67	90.95	95.92	99.29	103.4	110.0	118.5	130.0	135.6
Dec.	82.51	86.89	90.87	96.05	99.62	103.3	110.3	118.8	129.9	135.7
	1992	**1993**	**1994**	**1995**	**1996**	**1997**	**1998**	**1999**	**2000**	**2001**
Jan.	135.6	137.9	141.3	146.0	150.2	154.4	159.5	163.4	166.6	171.1
Feb.	136.3	138.8	142.1	146.9	150.9	155.0	160.3	163.7	167.5	172.0
March	136.7	139.3	142.5	147.5	151.5	155.4	160.8	164.1	168.4	172.2
April	138.8	140.6	144.2	149.0	152.6	156.3	162.6	165.2	170.1	173.1
May	139.3	141.1	144.7	149.6	152.9	156.9	163.5	165.6	170.7	174.2
June	139.3	141.0	144.7	149.8	153.0	157.5	163.4	165.6	171.1	174.4
July	138.8	140.7	144.0	149.1	152.4	157.5	163.0	165.1	170.5	173.3

	1992	1993	1994	1995	1996	1997	1998	1999	2000	2001
Aug.	138.9	141.3	144.7	149.9	153.1	158.5	163.7	165.5	170.5	174.0
Sept.	139.4	141.9	145.0	150.6	153.8	159.3	164.4	166.2	171.7	174.6
Oct.	139.9	141.8	145.2	149.8	153.8	159.5	164.5	166.5	171.6	174.3
Nov.	139.7	141.6	145.3	149.8	153.9	159.6	164.4	166.7	172.1	173.6
Dec.	139.2	141.9	146.0	150.7	154.4	160.0	164.4	167.3	172.2	173.4

	2002	2003	2004	2005	2006	2007	2008	2009	2010	2011
Jan.	173.3	178.4	183.1	188.9	193.4	201.6	209.8	210.1	217.9	229.0
Feb.	173.8	179.3	183.8	189.6	194.2	203.1	211.4	211.4	219.2	231.3
March	174.5	179.9	184.6	190.5	195.0	204.4	212.1	211.3	220.7	232.5
April	175.7	181.2	185.7	191.6	196.5	205.4	214.0	211.5	222.8	234.4
May	176.2	181.5	186.5	192.0	197.7	206.2	215.1	212.8	223.6	235.2
June	176.2	181.3	186.8	192.2	198.5	207.3	216.8	213.4	224.1	235.2
July	175.9	181.3	186.8	192.2	198.5	206.1	216.5	213.4	223.6	234.7
Aug.	176.4	181.6	187.4	192.6	199.2	207.3	217.2	214.4	224.5	236.1
Sept.	177.6	182.5	188.1	193.1	200.1	208.0	218.4	215.3	225.3	237.9
Oct.	177.9	182.6	188.6	193.3	200.4	208.9	217.7	216.0	225.8	238.0
Nov.	178.2	182.7	189.0	193.6	201.1	209.7	216.0	216.6	226.8	238.5
Dec.	178.5	183.5	189.9	194.1	202.7	210.9	212.9	218.0	228.4	239.4

	2012	2013	2014	2015	2016	2017	2018	2019	2020	2021
Jan.	238.0	245.8	252.6							
Feb.	239.9	247.6	254.2							
March	240.8	248.7	254.8							
April	242.5	249.5	255.7							
May	242.4	250.0	255.9							
June	241.8	249.7	255.9							
July	242.1	249.7	256.0							
Aug.	243.0	251.0	257.0							
Sept.	244.2	251.9	257.6							
Oct.	245.6	251.9	257.7							
Nov.	245.6	252.1								
Dec.	246.8	253.4								

[¶11-020] Indexation allowance up to 5 April 1998

(TCGA 1992, s. 53 and 54)

Indexation allowance in respect of changes shown by the retail prices indices for months after April 1998 shall be allowed only for the purposes of corporation tax. For disposals made by individuals, trustees and personal representatives after April 1998 and before 6 April 2008, indexation allowance up to 5 April 1998 and taper relief could be obtained.

The table below sets out the figure that is determined by the formula of (RD – RI)/RI where RD is the Retail Prices Index for April 1998 and RI is the Retail Prices Index for the later of March 1982 and the date that the item of relevant allowable expenditure was incurred. The indexation allowance is the aggregate of the indexed rise in each item of relevant allowable expenditure. In relation to each item of expenditure, the indexed rise is a sum produced by multiplying the amount of that item of expenditure by the appropriate figure in the table below.

	Jan.	Feb.	Mar.	Apr.	May	Jun.	Jul.	Aug.	Sep.	Oct.	Nov.	Dec.
1982	–	–	1.047	1.006	0.992	0.987	0.986	0.985	0.987	0.977	0.967	0.971
1983	0.968	0.960	0.956	0.929	0.921	0.917	0.906	0.898	0.889	0.883	0.876	0.871
1984	0.872	0.865	0.859	0.834	0.828	0.823	0.825	0.808	0.804	0.793	0.788	0.789
1985	0.783	0.769	0.752	0.716	0.708	0.704	0.707	0.703	0.704	0.701	0.695	0.693
1986	0.689	0.683	0.681	0.665	0.662	0.663	0.667	0.662	0.654	0.652	0.638	0.632
1987	0.626	0.620	0.616	0.597	0.596	0.596	0.597	0.593	0.588	0.580	0.573	0.574
1988	0.574	0.568	0.562	0.537	0.531	0.525	0.524	0.507	0.500	0.485	0.478	0.474
1989	0.465	0.454	0.448	0.423	0.414	0.409	0.408	0.404	0.395	0.384	0.372	0.369
1990	0.361	0.353	0.339	0.300	0.288	0.283	0.282	0.269	0.258	0.248	0.251	0.252
1991	0.249	0.242	0.237	0.222	0.218	0.213	0.215	0.213	0.208	0.204	0.199	0.198
1992	0.199	0.193	0.189	0.171	0.167	0.167	0.171	0.171	0.166	0.162	0.164	0.168
1993	0.179	0.171	0.167	0.156	0.152	0.153	0.156	0.151	0.146	0.147	0.148	0.146
1994	0.151	0.144	0.141	0.128	0.124	0.124	0.129	0.124	0.121	0.120	0.119	0.114
1995	0.114	0.107	0.102	0.091	0.087	0.085	0.091	0.085	0.080	0.085	0.085	0.079
1996	0.083	0.078	0.073	0.066	0.063	0.063	0.067	0.062	0.057	0.057	0.057	0.053
1997	0.053	0.049	0.046	0.040	0.036	0.032	0.032	0.026	0.021	0.019	0.019	0.016
1998	0.019	0.014	0.011	–	–	–	–	–	–	–	–	–

[¶11-450] RPI: January 2014 to October 2014

Tables follow showing the indexed rise to be used for disposals between January and October 2014. The amount of indexation allowances is restricted where the indexation allowance gives rise to a loss.

RD Month (January 2014 to October 2014) January 1987 = 100

RI Month		2014									
		Jan.	**Feb.**	**Mar.**	**Apr.**	**May**	**Jun.**	**Jul.**	**Aug.**	**Sept.**	**Oct.**
1982	*Mar.*	2.180	2.200	2.207	2.219	2.221	2.226	2.222	2.235	2.243	2.244
	April	2.117	2.137	2.144	2.155	2.158	2.163	2.159	2.171	2.179	2.180
	May	2.095	2.114	2.122	2.133	2.135	2.140	2.136	2.149	2.156	2.157
	June	2.086	2.106	2.113	2.124	2.126	2.131	2.128	2.140	2.147	2.148
	July	2.085	2.105	2.112	2.123	2.125	2.130	2.127	2.139	2.146	2.147
	Aug.	2.084	2.104	2.111	2.122	2.124	2.129	2.126	2.138	2.145	2.146
	Sept.	2.086	2.106	2.113	2.124	2.126	2.131	2.128	2.140	2.147	2.148
	Oct.	2.071	2.090	2.098	2.109	2.111	2.116	2.112	2.124	2.132	2.133
	Nov.	2.056	2.075	2.082	2.093	2.096	2.101	2.097	2.109	2.116	2.118
	Dec.	2.061	2.081	2.088	2.099	2.101	2.106	2.103	2.115	2.122	2.123
1983	*Jan.*	2.058	2.077	2.084	2.095	2.098	2.102	2.099	2.111	2.118	2.119
	Feb.	2.045	2.064	2.071	2.082	2.084	2.089	2.086	2.098	2.105	2.106
	Mar.	2.039	2.058	2.066	2.076	2.079	2.084	2.080	2.092	2.099	2.100
	April	1.997	2.016	2.023	2.034	2.036	2.041	2.037	2.049	2.056	2.058
	May	1.984	2.003	2.010	2.021	2.023	2.028	2.025	2.036	2.044	2.045
	June	1.977	1.996	2.003	2.014	2.016	2.021	2.017	2.029	2.036	2.037
	July	1.961	1.980	1.987	1.998	2.000	2.005	2.001	2.013	2.020	2.021
	Aug.	1.948	1.967	1.974	1.984	1.987	1.991	1.988	2.000	2.007	2.008
	Sept.	1.935	1.954	1.961	1.971	1.974	1.978	1.975	1.986	1.993	1.994
	Oct.	1.925	1.943	1.950	1.961	1.963	1.968	1.964	1.976	1.983	1.984
	Nov.	1.915	1.933	1.940	1.950	1.953	1.957	1.954	1.965	1.972	1.973
	Dec.	1.907	1.925	1.932	1.943	1.945	1.950	1.946	1.958	1.965	1.966
1984	*Jan.*	1.909	1.927	1.934	1.944	1.947	1.951	1.948	1.959	1.966	1.967
	Feb.	1.897	1.915	1.922	1.932	1.935	1.939	1.936	1.947	1.954	1.955
	Mar.	1.888	1.906	1.913	1.923	1.925	1.930	1.926	1.938	1.945	1.946
	April	1.850	1.868	1.874	1.885	1.887	1.891	1.888	1.899	1.906	1.907
	May	1.839	1.857	1.864	1.874	1.876	1.881	1.877	1.889	1.895	1.896
	June	1.832	1.850	1.856	1.867	1.869	1.873	1.870	1.881	1.888	1.889
	July	1.835	1.853	1.860	1.870	1.872	1.877	1.873	1.884	1.891	1.892

RI Month		2014									
		Jan.	Feb.	Mar.	Apr.	May	Jun.	Jul.	Aug.	Sept.	Oct.
	Aug.	1.809	1.826	1.833	1.843	1.845	1.850	1.846	1.858	1.864	1.865
	Sept.	1.803	1.821	1.828	1.838	1.840	1.844	1.841	1.852	1.859	1.860
	Oct.	1.786	1.804	1.810	1.820	1.822	1.827	1.823	1.834	1.841	1.842
	Nov.	1.777	1.795	1.802	1.811	1.814	1.818	1.815	1.826	1.832	1.833
	Dec.	1.780	1.797	1.804	1.814	1.816	1.820	1.817	1.828	1.835	1.836
1985	*Jan.*	1.770	1.787	1.794	1.804	1.806	1.810	1.807	1.818	1.824	1.826
	Feb.	1.747	1.765	1.771	1.781	1.783	1.788	1.784	1.795	1.802	1.803
	Mar.	1.722	1.739	1.746	1.755	1.758	1.762	1.759	1.769	1.776	1.777
	April	1.665	1.682	1.688	1.698	1.700	1.704	1.701	1.712	1.718	1.719
	May	1.653	1.670	1.676	1.686	1.688	1.692	1.689	1.699	1.706	1.707
	June	1.647	1.664	1.671	1.680	1.682	1.686	1.683	1.694	1.700	1.701
	July	1.652	1.669	1.676	1.685	1.687	1.691	1.688	1.699	1.705	1.706
	Aug.	1.645	1.662	1.668	1.678	1.680	1.684	1.681	1.691	1.698	1.699
	Sept.	1.647	1.664	1.670	1.679	1.681	1.686	1.682	1.693	1.699	1.700
	Oct.	1.643	1.659	1.666	1.675	1.677	1.681	1.678	1.689	1.695	1.696
	Nov.	1.633	1.650	1.656	1.666	1.668	1.672	1.669	1.679	1.686	1.687
	Dec.	1.630	1.647	1.653	1.662	1.664	1.669	1.665	1.676	1.682	1.683
1986	*Jan.*	1.624	1.641	1.647	1.657	1.659	1.663	1.660	1.670	1.676	1.677
	Feb.	1.615	1.631	1.638	1.647	1.649	1.653	1.650	1.660	1.667	1.668
	Mar.	1.611	1.628	1.634	1.643	1.646	1.650	1.647	1.657	1.663	1.664
	April	1.586	1.603	1.609	1.618	1.620	1.624	1.621	1.631	1.638	1.639
	May	1.582	1.598	1.604	1.613	1.615	1.619	1.616	1.627	1.633	1.634
	June	1.583	1.599	1.605	1.615	1.617	1.621	1.618	1.628	1.634	1.635
	July	1.590	1.607	1.613	1.622	1.624	1.628	1.625	1.635	1.642	1.643
	Aug.	1.582	1.599	1.605	1.614	1.616	1.620	1.617	1.627	1.633	1.634
	Sept.	1.570	1.586	1.592	1.601	1.603	1.607	1.604	1.614	1.621	1.622
	Oct.	1.566	1.582	1.588	1.597	1.599	1.603	1.600	1.610	1.616	1.617
	Nov.	1.544	1.560	1.566	1.575	1.577	1.581	1.578	1.588	1.594	1.595
	Dec.	1.536	1.552	1.558	1.567	1.569	1.573	1.570	1.580	1.586	1.587
1987	*Jan.*	1.526	1.542	1.548	1.557	1.559	1.563	1.560	1.570	1.576	1.577
	Feb.	1.516	1.532	1.538	1.547	1.549	1.553	1.550	1.560	1.566	1.567
	Mar.	1.511	1.527	1.533	1.542	1.544	1.548	1.545	1.555	1.561	1.562
	April	1.481	1.497	1.503	1.512	1.514	1.518	1.515	1.525	1.530	1.531
	May	1.479	1.495	1.500	1.509	1.511	1.515	1.512	1.522	1.528	1.529
	June	1.479	1.495	1.500	1.509	1.511	1.515	1.512	1.522	1.528	1.529

RI Month		2014									
		Jan.	Feb.	Mar.	Apr.	May	Jun.	Jul.	Aug.	Sept.	Oct.
	July	1.481	1.497	1.503	1.512	1.514	1.518	1.515	1.525	1.530	1.531
	Aug.	1.474	1.490	1.496	1.504	1.506	1.510	1.507	1.517	1.523	1.524
	Sept.	1.467	1.482	1.488	1.497	1.499	1.503	1.500	1.510	1.516	1.517
	Oct.	1.455	1.470	1.476	1.485	1.487	1.491	1.488	1.498	1.503	1.504
	Nov.	1.443	1.458	1.464	1.473	1.475	1.479	1.476	1.485	1.491	1.492
	Dec.	1.445	1.461	1.467	1.475	1.477	1.481	1.478	1.488	1.494	1.495
1988	*Jan.*	1.445	1.461	1.467	1.475	1.477	1.481	1.478	1.488	1.494	1.495
	Feb.	1.436	1.451	1.457	1.466	1.468	1.472	1.469	1.478	1.484	1.485
	Mar.	1.427	1.442	1.448	1.456	1.458	1.462	1.459	1.469	1.475	1.476
	April	1.388	1.403	1.408	1.417	1.419	1.422	1.420	1.429	1.435	1.436
	May	1.379	1.394	1.399	1.408	1.410	1.413	1.411	1.420	1.426	1.427
	June	1.370	1.385	1.390	1.399	1.401	1.404	1.402	1.411	1.417	1.417
	July	1.367	1.382	1.388	1.396	1.398	1.402	1.399	1.409	1.414	1.415
	Aug.	1.341	1.356	1.361	1.370	1.372	1.375	1.373	1.382	1.387	1.388
	Sept.	1.330	1.345	1.351	1.359	1.361	1.364	1.362	1.371	1.376	1.377
	Oct.	1.307	1.321	1.327	1.335	1.337	1.341	1.338	1.347	1.353	1.353
	Nov.	1.296	1.311	1.316	1.325	1.326	1.330	1.327	1.336	1.342	1.343
	Dec.	1.290	1.305	1.310	1.318	1.320	1.324	1.321	1.330	1.335	1.336
1989	*Jan.*	1.276	1.290	1.295	1.304	1.305	1.309	1.306	1.315	1.321	1.322
	Feb.	1.259	1.274	1.279	1.287	1.289	1.292	1.290	1.299	1.304	1.305
	Mar.	1.249	1.264	1.269	1.277	1.279	1.282	1.280	1.289	1.294	1.295
	April	1.210	1.224	1.229	1.237	1.239	1.242	1.240	1.248	1.254	1.255
	May	1.197	1.210	1.216	1.223	1.225	1.229	1.226	1.235	1.240	1.241
	June	1.189	1.203	1.208	1.216	1.218	1.221	1.218	1.227	1.232	1.233
	July	1.187	1.201	1.206	1.214	1.216	1.219	1.216	1.225	1.230	1.231
	Aug.	1.181	1.195	1.200	1.208	1.210	1.213	1.211	1.219	1.225	1.225
	Sept.	1.166	1.180	1.185	1.193	1.195	1.198	1.196	1.204	1.209	1.210
	Oct.	1.150	1.163	1.169	1.176	1.178	1.181	1.179	1.187	1.192	1.193
	Nov.	1.132	1.145	1.150	1.158	1.159	1.163	1.160	1.169	1.174	1.175
	Dec.	1.126	1.140	1.145	1.152	1.154	1.157	1.155	1.163	1.168	1.169
1990	*Jan.*	1.114	1.127	1.132	1.140	1.141	1.145	1.142	1.151	1.156	1.156
	Feb.	1.101	1.115	1.120	1.127	1.129	1.132	1.130	1.138	1.143	1.144
	Mar.	1.081	1.094	1.099	1.106	1.108	1.111	1.109	1.117	1.122	1.123
	April	1.019	1.032	1.037	1.044	1.046	1.049	1.046	1.054	1.059	1.060
	May	1.002	1.014	1.019	1.026	1.028	1.031	1.029	1.036	1.041	1.042

RI Month		2014									
		Jan.	**Feb.**	**Mar.**	**Apr.**	**May**	**Jun.**	**Jul.**	**Aug.**	**Sept.**	**Oct.**
	June	0.994	1.006	1.011	1.018	1.020	1.023	1.021	1.028	1.033	1.034
	July	0.992	1.005	1.009	1.017	1.018	1.021	1.019	1.027	1.032	1.032
	Aug.	0.972	0.984	0.989	0.996	0.998	1.001	0.998	1.006	1.011	1.012
	Sept.	0.954	0.966	0.971	0.978	0.979	0.982	0.980	0.988	0.992	0.993
	Oct.	0.939	0.951	0.955	0.962	0.967	0.967	0.965	0.972	0.977	0.978
	Nov.	0.943	0.955	0.960	0.967	0.968	0.972	0.969	0.977	0.982	0.982
	Dec.	0.945	0.957	0.962	0.968	0.970	0.973	0.971	0.978	0.983	0.984
1991	*Jan.*	0.940	0.952	0.957	0.964	0.965	0.969	0.966	0.974	0.978	0.979
	Feb.	0.930	0.942	0.947	0.953	0.955	0.958	0.956	0.963	0.968	0.969
	Mar.	0.922	0.935	0.939	0.946	0.947	0.951	0.948	0.956	0.960	0.961
	April	0.898	0.910	0.914	0.921	0.923	0.926	0.923	0.931	0.935	0.936
	May	0.892	0.904	0.909	0.915	0.917	0.920	0.918	0.925	0.930	0.930
	June	0.884	0.896	0.900	0.907	0.908	0.911	0.909	0.916	0.921	0.922
	July	0.888	0.900	0.904	0.911	0.913	0.916	0.913	0.921	0.925	0.926
	Aug.	0.884	0.896	0.900	0.907	0.908	0.911	0.909	0.916	0.921	0.922
	Sept.	0.877	0.889	0.893	0.900	0.901	0.904	0.902	0.909	0.914	0.915
	Oct.	0.870	0.882	0.886	0.893	0.894	0.897	0.895	0.902	0.907	0.907
	Nov.	0.863	0.875	0.879	0.886	0.887	0.890	0.888	0.895	0.900	0.900
	Dec.	0.861	0.873	0.878	0.884	0.886	0.889	0.887	0.894	0.898	0.899
1992	*Jan.*	0.863	0.875	0.879	0.886	0.887	0.890	0.888	0.895	0.900	0.900
	Feb.	0.853	0.865	0.869	0.876	0.877	0.880	0.878	0.886	0.890	0.891
	Mar.	0.848	0.860	0.864	0.871	0.872	0.875	0.873	0.880	0.884	0.885
	April	0.820	0.831	0.836	0.842	0.844	0.847	0.844	0.852	0.856	0.857
	May	0.813	0.825	0.829	0.836	0.837	0.840	0.838	0.845	0.849	0.850
	June	0.813	0.825	0.829	0.836	0.837	0.840	0.838	0.845	0.849	0.850
	July	0.820	0.831	0.836	0.842	0.844	0.847	0.844	0.852	0.856	0.857
	Aug.	0.819	0.830	0.834	0.841	0.842	0.845	0.843	0.850	0.855	0.855
	Sept.	0.812	0.824	0.828	0.834	0.836	0.839	0.836	0.844	0.848	0.849
	Oct.	0.806	0.817	0.821	0.828	0.829	0.832	0.830	0.837	0.841	0.842
	Nov.	0.808	0.820	0.824	0.830	0.832	0.835	0.832	0.840	0.844	0.845
	Dec.	0.815	0.826	0.830	0.837	0.838	0.841	0.839	0.846	0.851	0.851
1993	*Jan.*	0.832	0.843	0.848	0.854	0.856	0.859	0.856	0.864	0.868	0.869
	Feb.	0.820	0.831	0.836	0.842	0.844	0.847	0.844	0.852	0.856	0.857
	Mar.	0.813	0.825	0.829	0.836	0.837	0.840	0.838	0.845	0.849	0.850
	April	0.797	0.808	0.812	0.819	0.820	0.823	0.821	0.828	0.832	0.833

RI Month		2014									
		Jan.	Feb.	Mar.	Apr.	May	Jun.	Jul.	Aug.	Sept.	Oct.
	May	0.790	0.802	0.806	0.812	0.814	0.816	0.814	0.821	0.826	0.826
	June	0.791	0.803	0.807	0.813	0.815	0.818	0.816	0.823	0.827	0.828
	July	0.795	0.807	0.811	0.817	0.819	0.822	0.819	0.827	0.831	0.832
	Aug.	0.788	0.799	0.803	0.810	0.811	0.814	0.812	0.819	0.823	0.824
	Sept.	0.780	0.791	0.796	0.802	0.803	0.806	0.804	0.811	0.815	0.816
	Oct.	0.781	0.793	0.797	0.803	0.805	0.807	0.805	0.812	0.817	0.817
	Nov.	0.784	0.795	0.799	0.806	0.807	0.810	0.808	0.815	0.819	0.820
	Dec.	0.780	0.791	0.796	0.802	0.803	0.806	0.804	0.811	0.815	0.816
1994	*Jan.*	0.788	0.799	0.803	0.810	0.811	0.814	0.812	0.819	0.823	0.824
	Feb.	0.778	0.789	0.793	0.799	0.801	0.804	0.802	0.809	0.813	0.814
	Mar.	0.773	0.784	0.788	0.794	0.796	0.799	0.796	0.804	0.808	0.808
	April	0.752	0.763	0.767	0.773	0.775	0.777	0.775	0.782	0.786	0.787
	May	0.746	0.757	0.761	0.767	0.768	0.771	0.769	0.776	0.780	0.781
	June	0.746	0.757	0.761	0.767	0.768	0.771	0.769	0.776	0.780	0.781
	July	0.754	0.765	0.769	0.776	0.777	0.780	0.778	0.785	0.789	0.790
	Aug.	0.746	0.757	0.761	0.767	0.768	0.771	0.769	0.776	0.780	0.781
	Sept.	0.742	0.753	0.757	0.763	0.765	0.768	0.766	0.772	0.777	0.777
	Oct.	0.740	0.751	0.755	0.761	0.762	0.765	0.763	0.770	0.774	0.775
	Nov.	0.738	0.749	0.754	0.760	0.761	0.764	0.762	0.769	0.773	0.774
	Dec.	0.730	0.741	0.745	0.751	0.753	0.755	0.753	0.760	0.764	0.765
1995	*Jan.*	0.730	0.741	0.745	0.751	0.753	0.755	0.753	0.760	0.764	0.765
	Feb.	0.720	0.730	0.735	0.741	0.742	0.745	0.743	0.749	0.754	0.754
	Mar.	0.713	0.723	0.727	0.734	0.735	0.738	0.736	0.742	0.746	0.747
	April	0.695	0.706	0.710	0.716	0.717	0.720	0.718	0.725	0.729	0.730
	May	0.689	0.699	0.703	0.709	0.711	0.713	0.711	0.718	0.722	0.723
	June	0.686	0.697	0.701	0.707	0.708	0.711	0.709	0.716	0.720	0.720
	July	0.694	0.705	0.709	0.715	0.716	0.719	0.717	0.724	0.728	0.728
	Aug.	0.685	0.696	0.700	0.706	0.707	0.710	0.708	0.714	0.718	0.719
	Sept.	0.677	0.688	0.692	0.698	0.699	0.702	0.700	0.707	0.710	0.711
	Oct.	0.686	0.697	0.701	0.707	0.708	0.711	0.709	0.716	0.720	0.720
	Nov.	0.686	0.697	0.701	0.707	0.708	0.711	0.709	0.716	0.720	0.720
	Dec.	0.676	0.687	0.691	0.697	0.698	0.701	0.699	0.705	0.709	0.710
1996	*Jan.*	0.682	0.692	0.696	0.702	0.704	0.706	0.704	0.711	0.715	0.716
	Feb.	0.674	0.685	0.689	0.694	0.696	0.698	0.696	0.703	0.707	0.708
	Mar.	0.667	0.678	0.682	0.688	0.689	0.692	0.690	0.696	0.700	0.701

RI Month		2014									
		Jan.	**Feb.**	**Mar.**	**Apr.**	**May**	**Jun.**	**Jul.**	**Aug.**	**Sept.**	**Oct.**
	April	0.655	0.666	0.670	0.676	0.677	0.680	0.678	0.684	0.688	0.689
	May	0.652	0.663	0.666	0.672	0.674	0.676	0.674	0.681	0.685	0.685
	June	0.651	0.661	0.665	0.671	0.673	0.675	0.673	0.680	0.684	0.684
	July	0.657	0.668	0.672	0.678	0.679	0.682	0.680	0.686	0.690	0.691
	Aug.	0.650	0.660	0.664	0.670	0.671	0.674	0.672	0.679	0.683	0.683
	Sept.	0.642	0.653	0.657	0.663	0.664	0.666	0.664	0.671	0.675	0.676
	Oct.	0.642	0.653	0.657	0.663	0.664	0.666	0.664	0.671	0.675	0.676
	Nov.	0.641	0.652	0.656	0.661	0.663	0.665	0.663	0.670	0.674	0.674
	Dec.	0.636	0.646	0.650	0.656	0.657	0.660	0.658	0.665	0.668	0.669
1997	*Jan.*	0.636	0.646	0.650	0.656	0.657	0.660	0.658	0.665	0.668	0.669
	Feb.	0.630	0.640	0.644	0.650	0.651	0.654	0.652	0.658	0.662	0.663
	Mar.	0.625	0.636	0.640	0.645	0.647	0.649	0.647	0.654	0.658	0.658
	April	0.616	0.626	0.630	0.636	0.637	0.640	0.638	0.644	0.648	0.649
	May	0.610	0.620	0.624	0.630	0.631	0.634	0.632	0.638	0.642	0.642
	June	0.604	0.614	0.618	0.623	0.625	0.627	0.625	0.632	0.636	0.636
	July	0.604	0.614	0.618	0.623	0.625	0.627	0.625	0.632	0.636	0.636
	Aug.	0.594	0.604	0.608	0.613	0.615	0.617	0.615	0.621	0.625	0.626
	Sept.	0.586	0.596	0.599	0.605	0.606	0.609	0.607	0.613	0.617	0.618
	Oct.	0.584	0.594	0.597	0.603	0.604	0.607	0.605	0.611	0.615	0.616
	Nov.	0.583	0.593	0.596	0.602	0.603	0.606	0.604	0.610	0.614	0.615
	Dec.	0.579	0.589	0.593	0.598	0.599	0.602	0.600	0.606	0.610	0.611
1998	*Jan.*	0.584	0.594	0.597	0.603	0.604	0.607	0.605	0.611	0.615	0.616
	Feb.	0.576	0.586	0.590	0.595	0.596	0.599	0.597	0.603	0.607	0.608
	Mar.	0.571	0.581	0.585	0.590	0.591	0.594	0.592	0.598	0.602	0.603
	April	0.554	0.563	0.567	0.573	0.574	0.576	0.574	0.581	0.584	0.585
	May	0.545	0.555	0.558	0.564	0.565	0.568	0.566	0.572	0.576	0.576
	June	0.546	0.556	0.559	0.565	0.566	0.569	0.567	0.573	0.576	0.577
	July	0.550	0.560	0.563	0.569	0.570	0.572	0.571	0.577	0.580	0.581
	Aug.	0.543	0.553	0.557	0.562	0.563	0.566	0.564	0.570	0.574	0.574
	Sept.	0.536	0.546	0.550	0.555	0.557	0.559	0.557	0.563	0.567	0.568
	Oct.	0.536	0.545	0.549	0.554	0.556	0.558	0.556	0.562	0.566	0.567
	Nov.	0.536	0.546	0.550	0.555	0.557	0.559	0.557	0.563	0.567	0.568
	Dec.	0.536	0.546	0.550	0.555	0.557	0.559	0.557	0.563	0.567	0.568
1999	*Jan.*	0.546	0.556	0.559	0.565	0.566	0.569	0.567	0.573	0.576	0.577
	Feb.	0.543	0.553	0.557	0.562	0.563	0.566	0.564	0.570	0.574	0.574
	Mar.	0.539	0.549	0.553	0.558	0.559	0.562	0.560	0.566	0.570	0.570

RI Month		2014									
		Jan.	Feb.	Mar.	Apr.	May	Jun.	Jul.	Aug.	Sept.	Oct.
	April	0.529	0.539	0.542	0.548	0.549	0.551	0.550	0.556	0.559	0.560
	May	0.525	0.535	0.539	0.544	0.545	0.548	0.546	0.552	0.556	0.556
	June	0.525	0.535	0.539	0.544	0.545	0.548	0.546	0.552	0.556	0.556
	July	0.530	0.540	0.543	0.549	0.550	0.552	0.551	0.557	0.560	0.561
	Aug.	0.526	0.536	0.540	0.545	0.546	0.549	0.547	0.553	0.556	0.557
	Sept.	0.520	0.529	0.533	0.539	0.540	0.542	0.540	0.546	0.550	0.551
	Oct.	0.517	0.527	0.530	0.536	0.537	0.539	0.538	0.544	0.547	0.548
	Nov.	0.515	0.525	0.528	0.534	0.535	0.537	0.536	0.542	0.545	0.546
	Dec.	0.510	0.519	0.523	0.528	0.530	0.532	0.530	0.536	0.540	0.540
2000	*Jan.*	0.516	0.526	0.529	0.535	0.536	0.538	0.537	0.543	0.546	0.547
	Feb.	0.508	0.518	0.521	0.527	0.528	0.530	0.528	0.534	0.538	0.539
	Mar.	0.500	0.510	0.513	0.518	0.520	0.522	0.520	0.526	0.530	0.530
	April	0.485	0.494	0.498	0.503	0.504	0.507	0.505	0.511	0.514	0.515
	May	0.480	0.489	0.493	0.498	0.499	0.501	0.500	0.506	0.509	0.510
	June	0.476	0.486	0.489	0.494	0.496	0.498	0.496	0.502	0.506	0.506
	July	0.482	0.491	0.494	0.500	0.501	0.503	0.501	0.507	0.511	0.511
	Aug.	0.482	0.491	0.494	0.500	0.501	0.503	0.501	0.507	0.511	0.511
	Sept.	0.471	0.480	0.484	0.489	0.490	0.493	0.491	0.497	0.500	0.501
	Oct.	0.472	0.481	0.485	0.490	0.491	0.494	0.492	0.498	0.501	0.502
	Nov.	0.468	0.477	0.481	0.486	0.487	0.489	0.488	0.493	0.497	0.497
	Dec.	0.467	0.476	0.480	0.485	0.486	0.488	0.487	0.492	0.496	0.497
2001	*Jan.*	0.476	0.486	0.489	0.494	0.496	0.498	0.496	0.502	0.506	0.506
	Feb.	0.469	0.478	0.481	0.487	0.488	0.490	0.488	0.494	0.498	0.498
	Mar.	0.467	0.476	0.480	0.485	0.486	0.488	0.487	0.492	0.496	0.497
	April	0.459	0.469	0.472	0.477	0.478	0.481	0.479	0.485	0.488	0.489
	May	0.450	0.459	0.463	0.468	0.469	0.471	0.470	0.475	0.479	0.479
	June	0.448	0.458	0.461	0.466	0.467	0.470	0.468	0.474	0.477	0.478
	July	0.458	0.467	0.470	0.475	0.477	0.479	0.477	0.483	0.486	0.487
	Aug.	0.452	0.461	0.464	0.470	0.471	0.473	0.471	0.477	0.480	0.481
	Sept.	0.447	0.456	0.459	0.464	0.466	0.468	0.466	0.472	0.475	0.476
	Oct.	0.449	0.458	0.462	0.467	0.468	0.470	0.469	0.474	0.478	0.478
	Nov.	0.455	0.464	0.468	0.473	0.474	0.476	0.475	0.480	0.484	0.484
	Dec.	0.457	0.466	0.469	0.475	0.476	0.478	0.476	0.482	0.486	0.486
2002	*Jan.*	0.458	0.467	0.470	0.475	0.477	0.479	0.477	0.483	0.486	0.487
	Feb.	0.453	0.463	0.466	0.471	0.472	0.475	0.473	0.479	0.482	0.483
	Mar.	0.448	0.457	0.460	0.465	0.466	0.469	0.467	0.473	0.476	0.477
	April	0.438	0.447	0.450	0.455	0.456	0.459	0.457	0.463	0.466	0.467

RI Month		2014 Jan.	Feb.	Mar.	Apr.	May	Jun.	Jul.	Aug.	Sept.	Oct.
	May	0.434	0.443	0.446	0.451	0.452	0.455	0.453	0.459	0.462	0.463
	June	0.434	0.443	0.446	0.451	0.452	0.455	0.453	0.459	0.462	0.463
	July	0.436	0.445	0.449	0.454	0.455	0.457	0.455	0.461	0.464	0.465
	Aug.	0.432	0.441	0.444	0.450	0.451	0.453	0.451	0.457	0.460	0.461
	Sept.	0.422	0.431	0.435	0.440	0.441	0.443	0.441	0.447	0.450	0.451
	Oct.	0.420	0.429	0.432	0.437	0.438	0.441	0.439	0.445	0.448	0.449
	Nov.	0.418	0.426	0.430	0.435	0.436	0.438	0.437	0.442	0.446	0.446
	Dec.	0.415	0.424	0.427	0.432	0.434	0.436	0.434	0.440	0.443	0.444
2003	*Jan.*	0.416	0.425	0.428	0.433	0.434	0.437	0.435	0.441	0.444	0.445
	Feb.	0.409	0.418	0.421	0.426	0.427	0.429	0.428	0.433	0.437	0.437
	Mar.	0.404	0.413	0.416	0.421	0.422	0.425	0.423	0.429	0.432	0.432
	April	0.394	0.403	0.406	0.411	0.412	0.414	0.413	0.418	0.422	0.422
	May	0.392	0.401	0.404	0.409	0.410	0.412	0.410	0.416	0.419	0.420
	June	0.393	0.402	0.405	0.410	0.411	0.414	0.412	0.418	0.421	0.421
	July	0.393	0.402	0.405	0.410	0.411	0.414	0.412	0.418	0.421	0.421
	Aug.	0.391	0.400	0.403	0.408	0.409	0.411	0.410	0.415	0.419	0.419
	Sept.	0.384	0.393	0.396	0.401	0.402	0.404	0.403	0.408	0.412	0.412
	Oct.	0.383	0.392	0.395	0.400	0.401	0.404	0.402	0.407	0.411	0.411
	Nov.	0.383	0.391	0.395	0.400	0.401	0.403	0.401	0.407	0.410	0.411
	Dec.	0.377	0.385	0.389	0.393	0.395	0.397	0.395	0.401	0.404	0.404
2004	*Jan.*	0.380	0.388	0.392	0.397	0.398	0.400	0.398	0.404	0.407	0.407
	Feb.	0.374	0.383	0.386	0.391	0.392	0.394	0.393	0.398	0.402	0.402
	Mar.	0.368	0.377	0.380	0.385	0.386	0.388	0.387	0.392	0.395	0.396
	April	0.360	0.369	0.372	0.377	0.378	0.380	0.379	0.384	0.387	0.388
	May	0.354	0.363	0.366	0.371	0.372	0.374	0.373	0.378	0.381	0.382
	June	0.352	0.361	0.364	0.369	0.370	0.372	0.370	0.376	0.379	0.380
	July	0.352	0.361	0.364	0.369	0.370	0.372	0.370	0.376	0.379	0.380
	Aug.	0.348	0.356	0.360	0.364	0.366	0.368	0.366	0.371	0.375	0.375
	Sept.	0.343	0.351	0.355	0.359	0.360	0.363	0.361	0.366	0.369	0.370
	Oct.	0.339	0.348	0.351	0.356	0.357	0.359	0.357	0.363	0.366	0.366
	Nov.	0.337	0.345	0.348	0.353	0.354	0.356	0.354	0.360	0.363	0.363
	Dec.	0.330	0.339	0.342	0.346	0.348	0.350	0.348	0.353	0.357	0.357
2005	*Jan.*	0.337	0.346	0.349	0.354	0.355	0.357	0.355	0.361	0.364	0.364
	Feb.	0.332	0.341	0.344	0.349	0.350	0.352	0.350	0.355	0.359	0.359
	Mar.	0.326	0.334	0.338	0.342	0.343	0.345	0.344	0.349	0.352	0.353
	April	0.318	0.327	0.330	0.335	0.336	0.338	0.336	0.341	0.344	0.345

RI Month		2014									
		Jan.	Feb.	Mar.	Apr.	May	Jun.	Jul.	Aug.	Sept.	Oct.
	May	0.316	0.324	0.327	0.332	0.333	0.335	0.333	0.339	0.342	0.342
	June	0.314	0.323	0.326	0.330	0.331	0.334	0.332	0.337	0.340	0.341
	July	0.314	0.323	0.326	0.330	0.331	0.334	0.332	0.337	0.340	0.341
	Aug.	0.312	0.320	0.323	0.328	0.329	0.331	0.329	0.334	0.337	0.338
	Sept.	0.308	0.316	0.320	0.324	0.325	0.327	0.326	0.331	0.334	0.335
	Oct.	0.307	0.315	0.318	0.323	0.324	0.326	0.324	0.330	0.333	0.333
	Nov.	0.305	0.313	0.316	0.321	0.322	0.324	0.322	0.327	0.331	0.331
	Dec.	0.301	0.310	0.313	0.317	0.318	0.320	0.319	0.324	0.327	0.328
2006	*Jan.*	0.306	0.314	0.317	0.322	0.323	0.325	0.324	0.329	0.332	0.332
	Feb.	0.301	0.309	0.312	0.317	0.318	0.320	0.318	0.323	0.326	0.327
	Mar.	0.295	0.304	0.307	0.311	0.312	0.314	0.313	0.318	0.321	0.322
	April	0.285	0.294	0.297	0.301	0.302	0.304	0.303	0.308	0.311	0.311
	May	0.278	0.286	0.289	0.293	0.294	0.296	0.295	0.300	0.303	0.303
	June	0.273	0.281	0.284	0.288	0.289	0.291	0.290	0.295	0.298	0.298
	July	0.273	0.281	0.284	0.288	0.289	0.291	0.290	0.295	0.298	0.298
	Aug.	0.268	0.276	0.279	0.284	0.285	0.287	0.285	0.290	0.293	0.294
	Sept.	0.262	0.270	0.273	0.278	0.279	0.281	0.279	0.284	0.287	0.288
	Oct.	0.260	0.268	0.271	0.276	0.277	0.279	0.277	0.282	0.285	0.286
	Nov.	0.256	0.264	0.267	0.272	0.273	0.274	0.273	0.278	0.281	0.281
	Dec.	0.246	0.254	0.257	0.261	0.262	0.264	0.263	0.268	0.271	0.271
2007	*Jan.*	0.253	0.261	0.264	0.268	0.269	0.271	0.270	0.275	0.278	0.278
	Feb.	0.244	0.252	0.255	0.259	0.260	0.262	0.260	0.265	0.268	0.269
	Mar.	0.236	0.244	0.247	0.251	0.252	0.254	0.252	0.257	0.260	0.261
	April	0.230	0.238	0.241	0.245	0.246	0.248	0.246	0.251	0.254	0.255
	May	0.225	0.233	0.236	0.240	0.241	0.243	0.242	0.246	0.249	0.250
	June	0.219	0.226	0.229	0.233	0.234	0.236	0.235	0.240	0.243	0.243
	July	0.226	0.233	0.236	0.241	0.242	0.244	0.242	0.247	0.250	0.250
	Aug.	0.219	0.226	0.229	0.233	0.234	0.236	0.235	0.240	0.243	0.243
	Sept.	0.214	0.222	0.225	0.229	0.230	0.232	0.231	0.236	0.238	0.239
	Oct.	0.209	0.217	0.220	0.224	0.225	0.227	0.225	0.230	0.233	0.234
	Nov.	0.205	0.212	0.215	0.219	0.220	0.222	0.221	0.226	0.228	0.229
	Dec.	0.198	0.205	0.208	0.212	0.213	0.215	0.214	0.219	0.221	0.222
2008	*Jan.*	0.204	0.212	0.214	0.219	0.220	0.222	0.220	0.225	0.228	0.228
	Feb.	0.195	0.202	0.205	0.210	0.211	0.212	0.211	0.216	0.219	0.219
	Mar.	0.191	0.198	0.201	0.206	0.207	0.208	0.207	0.212	0.215	0.215
	April	0.180	0.188	0.191	0.195	0.196	0.198	0.196	0.201	0.204	0.204

RI Month		2014									
		Jan.	Feb.	Mar.	Apr.	May	Jun.	Jul.	Aug.	Sept.	Oct.
	May	0.174	0.182	0.185	0.189	0.190	0.192	0.190	0.195	0.198	0.198
	June	0.165	0.173	0.175	0.179	0.180	0.182	0.181	0.185	0.188	0.189
	July	0.167	0.174	0.177	0.181	0.182	0.184	0.182	0.187	0.190	0.190
	Aug.	0.163	0.170	0.173	0.177	0.178	0.180	0.179	0.183	0.186	0.186
	Sept.	0.157	0.164	0.167	0.171	0.172	0.174	0.172	0.177	0.179	0.180
	Oct.	0.160	0.168	0.170	0.175	0.175	0.177	0.176	0.181	0.183	0.184
	Nov.	0.169	0.177	0.180	0.184	0.185	0.187	0.185	0.190	0.193	0.193
	Dec.	0.186	0.194	0.197	0.201	0.202	0.204	0.202	0.207	0.210	0.210
2009	*Jan.*	0.202	0.210	0.213	0.217	0.218	0.220	0.218	0.223	0.226	0.227
	Feb.	0.195	0.202	0.205	0.210	0.211	0.212	0.211	0.216	0.219	0.219
	Mar.	0.195	0.203	0.206	0.210	0.211	0.213	0.212	0.216	0.219	0.220
	April	0.194	0.202	0.205	0.209	0.210	0.212	0.210	0.215	0.218	0.218
	May	0.187	0.195	0.197	0.202	0.203	0.204	0.203	0.208	0.211	0.211
	June	0.184	0.191	0.194	0.198	0.199	0.201	0.200	0.204	0.207	0.208
	July	0.184	0.191	0.194	0.198	0.199	0.201	0.200	0.204	0.207	0.208
	Aug.	0.178	0.186	0.188	0.193	0.194	0.195	0.194	0.199	0.201	0.202
	Sept.	0.173	0.181	0.183	0.188	0.189	0.190	0.189	0.194	0.196	0.197
	Oct.	0.169	0.177	0.180	0.184	0.185	0.187	0.185	0.190	0.193	0.193
	Nov.	0.166	0.174	0.176	0.181	0.181	0.183	0.182	0.187	0.189	0.190
	Dec.	0.159	0.166	0.169	0.173	0.174	0.176	0.174	0.179	0.182	0.182
2010	*Jan.*	0.159	0.167	0.169	0.173	0.174	0.176	0.175	0.179	0.182	0.183
	Feb.	0.152	0.160	0.162	0.167	0.167	0.169	0.168	0.172	0.175	0.176
	Mar.	0.145	0.152	0.155	0.159	0.159	0.161	0.160	0.164	0.167	0.168
	April	0.134	0.141	0.144	0.148	0.149	0.150	0.149	0.154	0.156	0.157
	May	0.130	0.137	0.140	0.144	0.144	0.146	0.145	0.149	0.152	0.153
	June	0.127	0.134	0.137	0.141	0.142	0.144	0.142	0.147	0.149	0.150
	July	0.130	0.137	0.140	0.144	0.144	0.146	0.145	0.149	0.152	0.153
	Aug.	0.125	0.132	0.135	0.139	0.140	0.142	0.140	0.145	0.147	0.148
	Sept.	0.121	0.128	0.131	0.135	0.136	0.138	0.136	0.141	0.143	0.144
	Oct.	0.119	0.126	0.128	0.132	0.133	0.135	0.134	0.138	0.141	0.141
	Nov.	0.114	0.121	0.123	0.127	0.128	0.130	0.129	0.133	0.136	0.136
	Dec.	0.106	0.113	0.116	0.120	0.120	0.122	0.121	0.125	0.128	0.128
2011	*Jan.*	0.103	0.110	0.113	0.117	0.117	0.119	0.118	0.122	0.125	0.125
	Feb.	0.092	0.099	0.102	0.105	0.106	0.108	0.107	0.111	0.114	0.114
	Mar.	0.086	0.093	0.096	0.100	0.101	0.102	0.101	0.105	0.108	0.108

RI Month		2014									
		Jan.	**Feb.**	**Mar.**	**Apr.**	**May**	**Jun.**	**Jul.**	**Aug.**	**Sept.**	**Oct.**
	April	0.078	0.084	0.087	0.091	0.092	0.093	0.092	0.096	0.099	0.099
	May	0.074	0.081	0.083	0.087	0.088	0.090	0.088	0.093	0.095	0.096
	June	0.074	0.081	0.083	0.087	0.088	0.090	0.088	0.093	0.095	0.096
	July	0.076	0.083	0.086	0.089	0.090	0.092	0.091	0.095	0.098	0.098
	Aug.	0.070	0.077	0.079	0.083	0.084	0.086	0.084	0.089	0.091	0.091
	Sept.	0.062	0.069	0.071	0.075	0.076	0.077	0.076	0.080	0.083	0.083
	Oct.	0.061	0.068	0.071	0.074	0.075	0.077	0.076	0.080	0.082	0.083
	Nov.	0.059	0.066	0.068	0.072	0.073	0.075	0.073	0.078	0.080	0.081
	Dec.	0.055	0.062	0.064	0.068	0.069	0.071	0.069	0.074	0.076	0.076
2012	*Jan.*	0.061	0.068	0.071	0.074	0.075	0.077	0.076	0.080	0.082	0.083
	Feb.	0.053	0.060	0.062	0.066	0.067	0.068	0.067	0.071	0.074	0.074
	Mar.	0.049	0.056	0.058	0.062	0.063	0.064	0.063	0.067	0.070	0.070
	April	0.042	0.048	0.051	0.054	0.055	0.057	0.056	0.060	0.062	0.063
	May	0.042	0.049	0.051	0.055	0.056	0.057	0.056	0.060	0.063	0.063
	June	0.045	0.051	0.054	0.057	0.058	0.060	0.059	0.063	0.065	0.066
	July	0.043	0.050	0.052	0.056	0.057	0.059	0.057	0.062	0.064	0.064
	Aug.	0.040	0.046	0.049	0.052	0.053	0.055	0.053	0.058	0.060	0.060
	Sept.	0.034	0.041	0.043	0.047	0.048	0.050	0.048	0.052	0.055	0.055
	Oct.	0.029	0.035	0.037	0.041	0.042	0.044	0.042	0.046	0.049	0.049
	Nov.	0.029	0.035	0.037	0.041	0.042	0.044	0.042	0.046	0.049	0.049
	Dec.	0.024	0.030	0.032	0.036	0.037	0.038	0.037	0.041	0.044	0.044
2013	*Jan.*	0.028	0.034	0.037	0.040	0.041	0.043	0.041	0.046	0.048	0.048
	Feb.	0.020	0.027	0.029	0.033	0.034	0.035	0.034	0.038	0.040	0.041
	Mar.	0.016	0.022	0.025	0.028	0.029	0.031	0.029	0.033	0.036	0.036
	Apr.	0.012	0.019	0.021	0.025	0.026	0.027	0.026	0.030	0.032	0.033
	May	0.010	0.017	0.019	0.023	0.024	0.025	0.024	0.028	0.030	0.031
	June	0.012	0.018	0.020	0.024	0.025	0.026	0.025	0.029	0.032	0.032
	July	0.012	0.018	0.020	0.024	0.025	0.026	0.025	0.029	0.032	0.032
	Aug.	0.006	0.013	0.015	0.019	0.020	0.021	0.020	0.024	0.026	0.027
	Sept.	0.003	0.009	0.012	0.015	0.016	0.017	0.016	0.020	0.023	0.023
	Oct.	0.003	0.009	0.012	0.015	0.016	0.017	0.016	0.020	0.023	0.023
	Nov.	0.002	0.008	0.011	0.014	0.015	0.017	0.015	0.019	0.022	0.022
	Dec.	Nil	0.006	0.009	0.012	0.013	0.015	0.013	0.017	0.020	0.020

RI Month	2014									
	Jan.	**Feb.**	**Mar.**	**Apr.**	**May**	**Jun.**	**Jul.**	**Aug.**	**Sept.**	**Oct.**
2014 *Jan.*	Nil	0.006	0.009	0.012	0.013	0.015	0.013	0.017	0.020	0.020
Feb.		Nil	0.002	0.006	0.007	0.008	0.007	0.011	0.013	0.014
Mar.			Nil	0.004	0.004	0.006	0.005	0.009	0.011	0.011
Apr.				Nil	0.001	0.002	0.001	0.005	0.007	0.008
May					Nil	0.002	0.000	0.004	0.007	0.007
June						Nil	Nil	0.003	0.005	0.005
July							Nil	0.004	0.006	0.007
Aug.								Nil	0.002	0.003
									Nil	0.000
										Nil

Foreign exchange rates

[¶12-000] Foreign exchange rates: general

HMRC publish annually currency exchange rates for the purposes of converting foreign currencies into sterling.

The currency exchange rates for the US dollar, German deutschmark, Japanese yen and euro are reproduced below.

Average exchange rates for year to 31 December

Average for year to 31 December	US $	DM	Yen	Euro
1989	1.6387	3.0786	225.64	
1990	1.7854	2.8749	257.45	
1991	1.7696	2.9247	237.69	
1992	1.7655	2.7528	230.90	
1993	1.5023	2.4828	166.9335	
1994	1.5318	2.4826	156.4429	
1995	1.5783	2.2603	148.283	
1996	1.5619	2.3506	169.593	
1997	1.638	2.8391	198.189	
1998	1.6573	2.9147	216.6834	1.4783[1]
1999	1.6181	2.9702	183.969	1.5207
2000	1.5163	3.2114	163.378	1.6427
2001	1.4401	3.1461	174.8889	1.6085
2002	1.5023	N/A	187.8315	1.5906
2003	1.6348	N/A	189.3354	1.4457
2004	1.8318	N/A	198.065	1.474
2005	1.8195	N/A	200.1041	1.4626
2006	1.8424	N/A	214.3005	1.4666
2007	2.0020	N/A	235.6273	1.4604
2008	1.8511	N/A	192.26	1.2586
2009	1.5633	N/A	146.366	1.1235
2010	1.5457	N/A	136.104	1.1664
2011	1.603844	N/A	128.003692	1.151701
2012	1.582875	N/A	126.15025	1.233473
2013	1.562598	N/A	151.646301	1.178398

Note

(1) Former European Currency Unit

Average exchange rates for year to 31 March

Average for year to 31 March	US $	DM	Yen	Euro
1985	1.2500	3.7300	305.00	
1986	1.3700	3.7100	285.00	
1987	1.4900	3.0300	238.00	
1988	1.7000	2.9800	234.76	
1989	1.7970	3.2460	229.33	
1990	1.6305	2.9144	235.64	
1991	1.8682	2.9090	258.31	
1992	1.7350	2.9113	230.80	
1993	1.6924	2.6526	218.72	
1994	1.5066	2.5203	162.2872	
1995	1.5553	2.4256	154.3941	
1996	1.5656	2.2375	150.75	
1997	1.5866	2.4642	178.8762	
1998	1.642	2.912	201.5651	
1999	1.6542	2.878	211.499	1.4647
2000	1.6114	3.0548	179.386	1.563
2001	1.4793	3.1886	163.482	1.6304
2002	1.432	3.1677	179.0169	1.6202
2003	1.5466	N/A	188.3036	1.5573
2004	1.6939	N/A	190.9326	1.4400
2005	1.8445	N/A	198.171	1.467
2006	1.79738	N/A	201.2374	1.4664
2007	1.8932	N/A	221.4527	1.475
2008	2.0080	N/A	229.3116	1.4178
2009	1.7138	N/A	173.793	1.2042
2010	1.5962	N/A	148.193	1.1298
2011	1.55345	N/A	133.404	1.1779
2012	1.5958134	N/A	126.098730	1.158234
2013	1.580925	N/A	130.738615	1.228351
2014	1.584390	N/A	158.325192	1.185417

[¶12-640] Foreign exchange rates 2013–14

		Average for the year to 31 December 2013		Average for the year to 31 March 2014	
Country	Unit of Currency	Sterling value of Currency Unit £	Currency Units per £1	Sterling value of Currency Unit £	Currency Units per £1
European Community	Euro	0.8486	1.1783981132075	0.8436	1.185417
Abu Dhabi	Dirham	0.1741	5.7432169811320	0.1717	5.823459
Afghanistan	Afghani	0.0118	84.465203773584	0.0114	87.572436
Albania	Lek	0.006	165.32826415094	0.006	166.511211
Algeria	Dinar	0.008	124.48918867924	0.0079	126.062557
Angola	Readj Kwanza	0.0068	147.99790188679	0.0066	150.756438
Antigua	E Caribbean Dollar	0.2368	4.2221226415094	0.2336	4.281115
Argentina	Peso	0.1176	8.5036377358490	0.1044	9.580773
Armenia	Dram	0.0016	638.99154716981	0.0015	649.094961
Aruba	Florin	0.3573	2.7991320754717	0.3523	2.838246
Australia	Dollar	0.6121	1.6336796296296	0.5887	1.698716
Austria	Euro	0.8486	1.1783981132075	0.8436	1.185417
Azerbaijan	New Manat	0.816	1.2255132075471	0.8049	1.24235
Bahamas	Dollar	0.64	1.5625982456140	0.6312	1.584390
Bahrain	Dinar	1.6963	0.5895075471698	1.6729	0.597748
Bangladesh	Taka	0.0082	122.25766037735	0.0081	123.287538
Barbados	Dollar	0.3197	3.1274698113207	0.315	3.174632
Belarus	Rouble	0.0001	13,870.637735840	0.0001	14,485.594230
Belgium	Euro	0.8486	1.1783981132075	0.8436	1.185417
Belize	Dollar	0.3192	3.1326905660377	0.3153	3.171282
Benin	CFA Franc	0.0013	773.00064150943	0.0013	777.458673
Bermuda	Dollar (US)	0.64	1.5625982456140	0.6312	1.584390
Bhutan	Ngultrum	0.011	91.217953703703	0.0104	95.733332
Bolivia	Boliviano	0.0926	10.804692452830	0.0913	10.95566
Bosnia-Herzegovinia	Marka	0.4339	2.3048415094339	0.4314	2.318132
Botswana	Pula	0.0766	13.061015094339	0.0734	13.623530
Brazil	Real	0.2975	3.3614094339622	0.2816	3.551688
Brunei	Dollar	0.5119	1.9534962264150	0.5013	1.994973
Bulgaria	Lev	0.4339	2.3048037735849	0.4314	2.318082
Burkina Faso	CFA Franc	0.0013	773.00064150943	0.0013	777.458673
Burundi	Franc	0.0004	2,445.3960377358	0.0004	2,463.063076

		Average for the year to 31 December 2013		Average for the year to 31 March 2014	
Country	**Unit of Currency**	**Sterling value of Currency Unit £**	**Currency Units per £1**	**Sterling value of Currency Unit £**	**Currency Units per £1**
Cambodia	Riel	0.0002	6,271.7741509434	0.0002	6,355.799423
Cameroon Republic	CFA Franc	0.0013	773.00064150943	0.0013	777.458673
Canada	Dollar	0.622	1.6076622641509	0.5998	1.667123
Cape Verde Islands	Escudo	0.0078	128.73862264150	0.0077	129.296134
Cayman Islands	Dollar	0.7799	1.2822886792452	0.7691	1.300207
Central African	CFA Franc	0.0013	773.00064150943	0.0013	777.458673
Chad	CFA Franc	0.0013	773.00064150943	0.0013	777.458673
Chile	Peso	0.0013	771.17207547169	0.0012	812.637711
China	Yuan	0.1039	9.6230905660377	0.1031	9.697792
Colombia	Peso	0.0003	2,912.1330188679	0.0003	3,041.423846
Comoros	Franc	0.0017	579.92037735849	0.0017	583.267134
Congo (Brazaville)	CFA Franc	0.0013	773.00064150943	0.0013	777.458673
Congo (DemRep)	Congo Fr	0.0007	1,401.7099245283	0.0007	1,447.820423
Costa Rica	Colon	0.0013	781.66175471698	0.0012	800.230134
Cote d'Ivoire	CFA Franc	0.0013	773.00064150943	0.0013	777.458673
Croatia	Kuna	0.1121	8.9216754716981	0.1111	8.997532
Cuba	Peso	0.6395	1.5637679245283	0.6307	1.585617
Cyprus	Euro	0.8486	1.1783981132075	0.8436	1.185417
Czech Republic	Koruna	0.0328	30.507841509434	0.032	31.288415
Denmark	Krone	0.1138	8.7880833962264	0.1131	8.841261
Djibouti	Franc	0.0037	273.37507547169	0.0036	277.324653
Dominica	E Caribbean Dollar	0.2368	4.2221226415094	0.2336	4.281115
Dominican Republic	Peso	0.0154	64.986096226415	0.015	66.857996
Dubai	Dirham	0.1741	5.7432169811320	0.1717	5.823459
Ecuador	Dollar	0.64	1.5625982456140	0.6312	1.584390
Egypt	Pound	0.0935	10.699456603773	0.0909	10.998159
El Salvador	Colon	0.0731	13.678796226415	0.0721	13.8699
Equatorial Guinea	CFA Franc	0.0013	773.00064150943	0.0013	777.458673
Eritrea	Nakfa	0.0451	22.180984905660	0.0446	22.413994

		Average for the year to 31 December 2013		Average for the year to 31 March 2014	
Country	**Unit of Currency**	**Sterling value of Currency Unit £**	**Currency Units per £1**	**Sterling value of Currency Unit £**	**Currency Units per £1**
Estonia	Euro	0.8486	1.1783981132075	0.8436	1.185417
Ethiopia	Birr	0.0342	29.216401886792	0.0333	29.991955
Fiji Islands	Dollar	0.3115	3.2101792452830	0.3028	3.302976
Finland	Euro	0.8486	1.1783981132075	0.8436	1.185417
Fr. Polynesia	CFP Franc	0.0071	140.62426415094	0.0071	141.435269
France	Euro	0.8486	1.1783981132075	0.8436	1.185417
Gabon	CFA Franc	0.0013	773.00064150943	0.0013	777.458673
Gambia	Dalasi	0.0187	53.476052830188	0.0178	56.026905
Georgia	Lari	0.0295	33.842681132075	0.0446	22.412782
Germany	Euro	0.8486	1.1783981132075	0.8436	1.185417
Ghana	Cedi	0.3117	3.2081641509434	0.2876	3.476582
Greece	Euro	0.8486	1.1783981132075	0.8436	1.185417
Grenada	E Caribbean Dollar	0.2368	4.2221226415094	0.2336	4.2811153
Guatemala	Quetzal	0.0813	12.298324528301	0.0803	12.446438
Guinea Bissau	CFA Franc	0.0013	773.00064150943	0.0013	777.458673
Guinea Republic	Franc	0.0001	10,966.441509434	0.0001	11,127.276923
Guyana	Dollar	0.0032	315.19879245283	0.0031	320.772346
Haiti	Gourde	0.015	66.817347169811	0.0146	68.409605
Honduras	Lempira	0.0318	31.413249056603	0.0314	31.841978
Hong Kong	Dollar	0.0825	12.125373584905	0.0813	12.297534
Hungary	Forint	0.0029	349.45062264151	0.0028	355.054096
Iceland	Krona	0.0052	191.53520754717	0.0053	188.893884
India	Rupee	0.011	91.217953703703	0.0104	95.7333320
Indonesia	Rupiah	0.0001	16,184.624528301	0.0001	17,358.536538
Iran	Rial	0.0001	19,284.292452830	0	22,404.017307
Iraq	Dinar	0.0006	1,815.7252830188	0.0005	1,841.446346
Ireland	Euro	0.8486	1.1783981132075	0.8436	1.185417
Israel	Shekel	0.1769	5.6537660377358	0.177	5.650203
Italy	Euro	0.8486	1.1783981132075	0.8436	1.185417
Jamaica	Dollar	0.0064	155.15284905660	0.0061	162.911096
Japan	Yen	0.0066	151.64630188679	0.0063	158.325192
Jordan	Dinar	0.9031	1.1073037735849	0.8911	1.122151
Kazakhstan	Tenge	0.0042	237.79622641509	0.004	247.49325

		Average for the year to 31 December 2013		Average for the year to 31 March 2014	
Country	**Unit of Currency**	**Sterling value of Currency Unit £**	**Currency Units per £1**	**Sterling value of Currency Unit £**	**Currency Units per £1**
Kenya	Schilling	0.0074	134.67341509434	0.0073	136.329173
Korea (North)	Won	0.492	2.0327169811320	0.4852	2.061119
Kuwait	Dinar	2.1619	0.4625490566037	2.1316	0.469126
Kyrgyz Republic	Som	0.0176	56.700590566037	0.0151	66.114298
Lao People's Dem Rep	Kip	0.0001	12,237.392452830	0.0001	12,452.840384
Latvia	Euro	1.2088	0.8272622641509	1.1007	0.908507
Lebanon	Pound	0.0004	2,357.4066037735	0.0004	2,390.3125
Lesotho	Loti	0.0669	14.953369811320	0.0626	15.973736
Liberia	Dollar (US)	0.64	1.5625982456140	0.6312	1.584390
Libya	Dinar	0.508	1.9686433962264	0.5034	1.986651
Lithuania	Litas	0.2458	4.0689075471698	0.2444	4.092365
Luxembourg	Euro	0.8486	1.1783981132075	0.8436	1.185417
Macao	Pataca	0.08	12.493056603773	0.0789	12.669376
Macedonia	Denar	0.0137	72.915816981132	0.0137	73.037817
Madagascar	Malagasy Ariary	0.0003	3,467.3888679245	0.0003	3,546.859615
Malawi	Kwacha	0.0018	567.30926415094	0.0017	604.846
Malaysia	Ringgit	0.2035	4.9132113207547	0.1974	5.066923
Maldive Islands	Rufiyaa	0.0416	24.031879245283	0.041	24.366065
Mali Republic	CFA Franc	0.0013	773.00064150943	0.0013	777.458673
Malta	Euro	0.8486	1.1783981132075	0.8436	1.185417
Mauritania	Ouguiya	0.0022	464.93481132075	0.0021	468.377980
Mauritius	Rupee	0.0208	48.083773584905	0.0206	48.5412192
Mexico	Mexican Peso	0.0501	19.946430188679	0.0489	20.439413
Moldova	Leu	0.051	19.610196226415	0.0491	20.384792
Mongolia	Tugrik	0.0004	2,366.3786792452	0.0004	2,534.994230
Montserrat	E Caribbean Dollar	0.2368	4.2221226415094	0.2336	4.281115
Morocco	Dirham	0.076	13.151809433962	0.0755	13.249678
Mozambique	Metical	0.0213	46.942524528301	0.0208	47.967882
Myanmar	Kyat	0.0007	1,446.2228301886	0.0007	1,516.657115
Nepal	Rupee	0.0069	145.63411320754	0.0065	152.856480
Netherland	Euro	0.8486	1.1783981132075	0.8436	1.185417
New Caledonia	CFP Franc	0.0071	140.62426415094	0.0071	141.435269
New Zealand	Dollar	0.5247	1.9058113207547	0.5175	1.932296

		Average for the year to 31 December 2013		Average for the year to 31 March 2014	
Country	**Unit of Currency**	**Sterling value of Currency Unit £**	**Currency Units per £1**	**Sterling value of Currency Unit £**	**Currency Units per £1**
Nicaragua	Gold Cordoba	0.0259	38.584190566037	0.0252	39.627757
Niger Republic	CFA Franc	0.0013	773.00064150943	0.0013	777.458673
Nigeria	Naira	0.004	248.79603773584	0.0039	254.236692
Norway	Norwegian Krone	0.1091	9.1654188679245	0.1054	9.485832
Oman	Rial	1.661	0.6020603773584	1.6381	0.610471
Pakistan	Rupee	0.0063	158.27356603773	0.0061	163.388115
Panama	Balboa	0.6395	1.5637679245283	0.6307	1.585617
Papua New Guinea	Kina	0.2777	3.6015	0.2601	3.844990
Paraguay	Guarani	0.0001	6,724.0109433962	0.0001	6,995.278653
Peru	New Sol	0.2375	4.2104452830188	0.229	4.367671
Philippines	Peso	0.0151	66.235656603773	0.0145	68.755323
Poland	Zloty	0.2025	4.9393320754717	0.2008	4.981088
Portugal	Euro	0.8486	1.1783981132075	0.8436	1.185417
Qatar	Riyal	0.1756	5.6933735849056	0.1732	5.773226
Romania	New Leu	0.1921	5.2050754716981	0.1897	5.270330
Russia	Rouble	0.0205	48.785824528301	0.0195	51.232159
Rwanda	Franc	0.001	1013.289	0.001	1046.674134
Saotome & Principe	Dobra	0	27,972.626415094	0	28,147.853846
Saudi Arabia	Riyal	0.1706	5.8626735849056	0.1682	6.045146
Senegal	CFA Franc	0.0013	773.00064150943	0.0013	777.458673
Serbia	Dinar	0.0075	133.13649056603	0.0074	135.015480
Seychelles	Rupee	0.0527	18.988941509434	0.0526	19.004840
Sierra Leone	Leone	0.0001	6,758.0890566037	0.0001	6,861.479807
Singapore	Dollar	0.5110	1.9533339622641	0.5015	1.994125
Slovakia	Euro	0.8486	1.1783981132075	0.8436	1.185417
Slovenia	Euro	0.8486	1.1783981132075	0.8436	1.185417
Soloman Islands	Dollar	0.0895	11.177784905660	0.0878	11.395278
Somali Republic	Schilling	0.0005	2,146.7824528301	0.0005	1,970.632884
South Africa	Rand	0.0666	15.011341509434	0.0626	15.977884
South Korea	Won	0.0006	1,710.2450943396	0.0006	1,729.588269
Spain	Euro	0.8486	1.1783981132075	0.8436	1.185417
Sri Lanka	Rupee	0.005	201.65239622641	0.0049	206.1235

		Average for the year to 31 December 2013		Average for the year to 31 March 2014	
Country	**Unit of Currency**	**Sterling value of Currency Unit £**	**Currency Units per £1**	**Sterling value of Currency Unit £**	**Currency Units per £1**
St Christopher &	E Caribbean Dollar	0.2368	4.2221226415094	0.2336	4.281115
St Lucia	E Caribbean Dollar	0.2368	4.2221226415094	0.2336	4.281115
St Vincent	E Caribbean Dollar	0.2368	4.2221226415094	0.2336	4.281115
Sudan Republic	Pound	0.1409	7.0985943396226	0.1294	7.730271
Surinam	Dollar	0.1938	5.1603622641509	0.1911	5.232471
Swaziland	Lilangeni	0.0669	14.953884905660	0.0626	15.974261
Sweden	Krona	0.0983	10.176862264150	0.0968	10.334775
Switzerland	Franc	0.6898	1.4496584905660	0.6859	1.457903
Syria	Pound	0.0064	156.19426415094	0.0053	188.354192
Taiwan	Dollar	0.0216	46.346854716981	0.0211	47.330036
Tajikistan	Somoni	0.0283	35.339220754717	0.0397	25.186496
Tanzania	Schilling	0.0004	2,528.7950943396	0.0004	2,566.585576
Thailand	Baht	0.0209	47.940149056603	0.0201	49.676876
Togo Republic	CFA Franc	0.0013	773.00064150943	0.0013	777.458673
Tonga Islands	Pa'anga (AUS)	0.6121	1.6336796296296	0.5887	1.698716
Trinidad/Tobago	Dollar	0.0997	10.030886792452	0.0983	10.169007
Tunisia	Dinar	0.3946	2.5344603773584	0.3857	2.593001
Turkey	Turkish Lira	0.3379	2.9591773584905	0.3149	3.175461
Turkmenistan	New Manat	0.2247	4.4500962264150	0.2216	4.512580
UAE	Dirham	0.1741	5.7432169811320	0.1717	5.823459
Uganda	Schilling	0.0002	4,055.1883018867	0.0002	4,041.717307
Ukraine	Hryvnia	0.0785	12.739381132075	0.0759	13.177934
Uruguay	Peso	0.0314	31.813079245283	0.0299	33.429732
USA	Dollar	0.64	1.5625982456140	0.6312	1.584390
Uzbekistan	Sum	0.0003	3,257.2273584905	0.0003	3,390.213269
Vanuatu	Vatu	0.0067	150.24737735849	0.0065	154.663769
Venezuela	Bolivar Fuerte	0.1076	9.2977339622641	0.1002	9.975996
Vietnam	Dong	0	32,865.616981132	0	33,421.130769
Wallis & Futuna Islands	CFP Franc	0.0071	140.62426415094	0.0071	141.435269
Western Samoa	Tala	0.2772	3.6078264150943	0.2712	3.687730
Yemen (Rep of)	Rial	0.003	336.21494339622	0.0029	340.972288
Zambia	Kwacha	0.0031	8.4061	0.1153	8.674986
Zimbabwe	Dollar	0.0017	591.43925490196	0.0017	600.03614

Table of Spot rates on 31 December 2013 and 31 March 2014

		31 December 2013		31 March 2014	
Country	Unit Of Currency	Sterling value of Currency Unit £	Currency Units per £1	Sterling value of Currency Unit £	Currency Units per £1
Australia	AUD Dollar	0.5402	1.8513	0.5559	1.7988
Canada	CAD Dollar	0.5682	1.7598	0.5434	1.8401
Denmark	DKK Krone	0.1115	8.9671	0.1107	9.031
European Community	EUR Euro	0.8319	1.202	0.8267	1.2096
Hong Kong	HKD Dollar	0.0779	12.8422	0.0773	12.9322
Japan	JPY Yen	0.0057	174.08	0.0058	171.691
Norway	NOK Norwegian Krone	0.0995	10.0483	0.1002	9.9813
South Africa	ZAR Rand	0.0576	17.3472	0.057	17.535
Sweden	SEK Krona	0.094	10.6374	0.0925	10.8091
Switzerland	CHF Franc	0.6789	1.473	0.679	1.4727
USA	USD Dollar	0.6038	1.6563	0.5998	1.6672

Residence of individuals

[¶13-000] Statutory residence: from 2013–14

(FA 2013, Sch. 45)

(Tax Reporter: ¶199-000ff.)

From 6 April 2013, with effect for the tax year 2013–14 and subsequent tax years, a new statutory residence test (SRT) applies to determine the residence of an individual for tax purposes. The test applies for the purposes of income tax, capital gains tax and so far as relevant inheritance tax and corporation tax.

Tests	**Status**
Automatic overseas test is satisfied	Not resident
Automatic UK residence test is satisfied (at least one of the automatic tests is satisfied **and** none of the automatic overseas tests are satisfied)	Resident
None of automatic overseas or automatic UK tests are satsifed: • sufficient ties test is satisfied • sufficient ties test is not satisfied	 • UK resident • Not resident

Automatic tests

An individual is automatically resident or not resident if they meet any of the four tests:

Automatic overseas test (any one)	**Automatic UK test (any one plus none of the overseas tests)**
Resident in the UK for one or more of the three previous tax years and spend fewer than 16 days in the UK in the current tax year	Spend at least 183 days in the UK during the tax year
Not resident in the UK for any of the previous three tax years and spend fewer than 46 days in the UK in the current tax year	A period of more than 90 days, part of which falls into the tax year, when the individual has a home in the UK, and no overseas home (disregarding any home at which they are present for fewer than 30 days in the tax year)

Automatic overseas test (any one)	Automatic UK test (any one plus none of the overseas tests)
Work full-time overseas in the tax year and spends fewer than 91 days in the UK in the tax year, incl. fewer than 31 working days	Work full-time in the UK in the current tax year
Die in the current tax year subject to conditions which include spending fewer than 46 days in the current tax year	Die in current tax year subject to conditions which include having been UK resident in the previous three tax years

Sufficient ties tests

Where none of the automatic overseas and none of the automatic UK tests are satisfied, an individual will need to look at the number of ties in conjunction with the number of days spent in the UK during the tax year and whether they have been resident in the previous three tax years to determine whether the sufficient ties test is satisfied. Ties to be considered are as follows:

- UK resident family;
- Substantive UK employment (including self-employment);
- Available accommodation in the UK;
- More than 90 days spent in the UK in either or both of the previous two tax years; and
- A country tie (but only if individual resident in one or more three previous tax years).

Days spent in the UK during the tax year	Number of ties that are sufficient	
	Not resident in previous three tax years	**Resident in any of the previous three tax years**
More than 15 but not more than 45	[Automatic overseas test is satisfied]	At least four
More than 45 but not more than 90	All four	At least three
More than 90 but not more than 120	At least three	At least two
More than 120	At least two	At least one

Definition of ties
Family tie (either): • Individual has a UK resident spouse (unless separated), or partner (if living together as husband and wife or civil partners); • Individual has a UK resident child under 18-years old (unless spends fewer than 61 days with the child in the tax year), (an individual will not be considered to have a family tie with a child who is UK resident and under 18 years who is in full-time education and would not be a UK resident if the time spent in full-time education were disregarded and the child spends fewer than 21 days in the UK outside term time (half-term counts as term time)).
Work tie Individual does more than three hours of work a day in the UK on at least 40 days in that year (whether continuously or intermittently). [NB. special rules apply as to what constitutes three hours work for workers on board a vehicle, aircraft or ship.]
Accommodation tie Individual has a place to live in the UK (including a home, holiday home, temporary retreat of other accommodation) that is: • available for a continuous period of 91 days or more during the year; and • the individual spends one or more nights there during the year; or • if it is at the home of a close relative (parent, grandparent, sibling, child or grandchild over 18 years old), the individual spends 16 or more nights there during the year.
90 day tie Individual spends more than 90 days (counting midnights) in the UK in either or both of the previous two tax years
Country tie **(applicable only where resident in any of previous three tax years)** UK is the country in which the individual was present at midnight for the greatest number of days in the tax year. If the number of days an individual is present in a country at midnight is the same for two or more countries in a tax year, and one of those countries is the UK, then the individual will have a country tie for that tax year if that is the greatest number of days spent in any country in that tax year.

[¶13-400] Split year treatment

(FA 2013, Sch. 45, Pt. 3)

(Tax Reporter: ¶199-375)

Under the SRT, an individual is either UK resident or non-UK resident for a full tax year and at all times in that tax year. However, if during a year that individual either starts to live or work abroad or comes from abroad to live or work in the UK, the tax year will be split into two parts if their circumstances meet specific criteria:

- A UK part for which they are charged to UK tax as a UK resident;
- An overseas part for which, for most purposes, they are charged to UK tax as a non-UK resident.

The taxpayer must be UK resident for a tax year under the SRT to meet the criteria for split year treatment for that year. They will not meet the split year criteria for a tax year for which they are non-UK resident under the SRT. Split year treatment only applies to an individual in their individual capacity and not to individuals acting as personal representatives. It applies in a limited way to individuals acting as trustee of a settlement.

[¶13-500] Abolition of ordinary residence

(FA 2013, Sch. 46)

(Tax Reporter: ¶199-975)

The concept of ordinary resident for tax purposes has been abolished for tax years 2013–14 onwards. Transitional provisions apply to ensure those who currently benefit form being ordinarily resident will continue to be able to benefit for a maximum of two complete tax years.

[¶13-600] Overseas workday relief

(ITEPA 2013, Pt. 2, Ch. 5)

(Tax Reporter: ¶199-960ff.)

Overseas workday relief is available to certain resident, but non UK-domiciled individuals with an employment the duties of which are carried out partly in the UK and partly overseas. If relevant conditions are met, the earnings which relation to the duties performed overseas are only taxable on the remittance basis and if not remitted, are not taxable – this is OWR. OWR is available to all non-UK domiciled individuals who arrive in the UK after 5 April 2013 having been non-UK resident for the previous three tax years. It will be available for the whole of the tax year that the individual becomes resident in the UK (or for the UK part of the year if that year is a split year) and for the following two tax years.

[¶14-000] Double tax treaties

The following table lists all the territories with which the UK has concluded agreements to avoid international double taxation and also facilitate the exchange of information to prevent tax evasion.

Albania (C)
Algeria (A)
Andorra (EC)
Anguilla (SIE/TIE)
Antigua and Barbuda (C/TIE)
Argentina (C)
Aruba (SIE/TIE)
Armenia (C)
Australia (C)
Austria (C)
Azerbaijan (C)
Bahamas (TIE)
Bahrain (C)
Bangladesh (C)
Barbados (C)
Belarus (C)(1)
Belgium (C)
Belize (C/TIE)
Bermuda (TIE/IGA)
Bolivia (C)
Bosnia-Herzegovina (C)(2)
Botswana (C)
Brazil (SA/AC/TIE)
British Virgin Islands (SIE/TIE/IGA)
Brunei (C)
Bulgaria (C)
Burma (C)
Cameroon (A)
Canada (C)
Cayman Islands (C/SIE/IGA)
Chile (C)(3)
China (C/A)
Croatia (C)(2)
Cyprus (C)
Czech Republic (C)
Denmark (C)
Dominica (TIE)
Egypt (C)
Estonia (C)(1)
Ethiopia (C/A)
Falkland Islands (C)
Faroe Islands (C)
Fiji (C)
Finland (C)
France (includes Guadeloupe, Guyane, Martinique and Réunion (C/EIG)
Gambia (C)
Georgia (C)
Germany (C)
Ghana (C)
Gibraltar (SIE/IGA)
Greece (C)
Grenada (C/TIE)
Guernsey (includes Alderney, Herm and Lithou) (C/TIE/IGA)
Guyana (C)
Hong Kong SAR (C/SA)
Hungary (C)
Iceland (C)
India (C/EIG)(3)
Indonesia (C)
Iran (A)
Ireland (C/EIG)
Isle of Man (SIE) (C/TIE/IGA)
Israel (C)
Italy (C/EIG)
Ivory Coast (Cote d'Ivoire) (C)
Jamaica (C)
Japan (C)
Jersey (SIE/C/TIE/IGA)
Jordan (C)
Kazakstan (C)
Kenya (C)
Kiribati and Tuvalu (C)
Korea (C)
Kuwait (C)
Latvia (C)
Lebanon (SA)
Lesotho (C)
Liberia (TIE)
Libya (C)
Liechtenstein (EC/TIE/C)
Lithuania (C)
Luxembourg (C)
Macedonia (C)
Malawi (C)
Malaysia (C)
Malta (C)
Marshall Islands (TIE)
Mauritius (C)
Mexico (C)
Moldova (C)
Monaco (EC)
Mongolia (C)
Montenegro (C)(2)
Montserrat (SIE/C/TIE/IGA)
Morocco (C)
Namibia (C)
Netherlands (C/EIG/BT)
Netherlands Antilles (SIE/TIE)
New Zealand (C)
Nigeria (C)
Norway (C)
Oman (C)
Pakistan (EIG unchecked(3)/C)
Panama (C)
Papua New Guinea (C)
Philippines (C)
Poland (C)
Portugal (C)
Qatar (C)
Romania (C)
Russia (C)
St. Christopher (St. Kitts) & Nevis (C/TIE)
St. Lucia (TIE)
St. Vincent and the Grenadines (TIE)
San Marino (EC/TIE)
Saudi Arabia (C/A)
Serbia (C)(2)
Sierra Leone (C)
Singapore (C)
Slovak Republic (C)
Slovenia (C)
Solomon Islands (C)
South Africa (C/EIG)
Spain (C)
Sri Lanka (C)
Sudan (C)
Swaziland (C)
Sweden (C/EIG)
Switzerland (TC/C/EC/EIG/EC)
Taiwan (C)
Tajikistan (C)(1)
Thailand (C)
Trinidad and Tobago (C)
Tunisia (C)
Turkey (C)
Turkmenistan (C)(1)
Turks & Caicos Islands (SIE/TIE/IGA)
Tuvula (UK/Gilbert and Ellice Islands) (C)
Uganda (C)
Ukraine (C)
Uruguay (TIE)
USA (C/EIG)
Uzbekistan (C)
Venezuela (C)
Vietnam (C)
Zaire (SA)
Zambia (C)
Zimbabwe (C)

These agreements may be of various types which are indicated below by the following letters:

- (C) – comprehensive agreements covering a wide range of areas of possible double taxation of income and capital gains;
- (SA) – agreements limited to shipping and air transport profits;
- (A) – agreements limited to air transport profits only;
- (AC) – agreements limited to salaries of aircrew only;
- (EIG) – agreements relating to tax on estates, inheritances and gifts;
- (SIE) – tax information exchange agreements: agreements relating to the EU Directive on taxation of savings income in the form of interest payments;
- (TIE) – tax information exchange agreements: bilateral agreements for co-operation in tax matters through exchange of information;
- (EC) – tax information exchange agreements concluded by the EC on behalf of its member states with third countries;
- (TC) – tax co-operation agreements;
- (BT) – convention in respect of bank taxes; and
- (IGA) – inter-governmental agreement to improve international tax compliance.

Notes

(1) The Convention of 31 July 1985 with the former USSR is regarded as continuing in force (see SP 04/01).

(2) The Convention of 5 November 1981 with the former Yugoslavia is regarded as continuing in force (see SP 03/07).

(3) The estate, inheritance and gifts agreements with India and Pakistan have not been formally terminated despite the fact that estate duties in those countries were abolished on 15 March 1985 and 29 July 1979 respectively.

Recognised exchanges

[¶15-000] Recognised stock exchanges

(ITA 2007, s. 1005)

With effect from 19 July 2007, a 'recognised stock exchange' is defined for the purposes of the Income Tax Acts as being one which is designated as such by an Order of the Commissioners for HMRC and which falls within one of two categories:

- 'recognised investment exchanges' designated by the Financial Conduct Authority (formerly the Financial Services Authority); and
- markets outside the UK (see below).

Designated 'recognised stock exchanges' by Order

Below is a list of stock exchanges designated as 'recognised stock exchanges' by Order of the Commissioners for HMRC, together with the date of recognition.

The Athens[(1)] Stock Exchange	14 Jun 1993
The Australian[(1)] Stock Exchange and any of its subsidiaries	22 Sep 1988
The Bahamas International Securities Exchange	19 April 2010
The Bermuda Stock Exchange	4 Dec 2007
The Bond Exchange of South Africa[(1)]	16 April 2008
The Cayman Islands Stock Exchange	4 Mar 2004
Channel Islands Securities Exchange Authority	20 Dec 2013
The Colombo[(1)] Stock Exchange	21 Feb 1972
The Copenhagen[(1)] Stock Exchange	22 Oct 1970
The Cyprus[(1)] Stock Exchange	22 June 2009
European Wholesale Securities Market	18 Jan 2013
Global Board of Trade	30 Jul 2013
GXG Official List	16 May 2013
GXG Main Quote[(1)]	23 Sep 2013
The Helsinki[(1)] Stock Exchange	22 Oct 1970
The Iceland[(1)] Stock Exchange	31 Mar 2006
ICAP Securities[(1)] & Derivatives Exchange Ltd	25 Apr 2013
The Johannesburg[(1)] Stock Exchange	22 Oct 1970
The Korea[(1)] Stock Exchange	10 Oct 1994
The Kuala Lumpa[(1)] Stock Exchange	10 Oct 1994
LIFFE[(1)] Administration and Management	26 Sept 2011
The London[(1)] Stock Exchange	19 July 2007
The Malta Stock Exchange	29 Dec 2005
The Mexico[(1)] Stock Exchange	10 Oct 1994

The MICEX[1] Stock Exchange	5 Jan 2011
The NASDAQ OMX Tallinn[1]	5 May 2010
The NASDAQ OMX Vilnius[1]	12 Mar 2012
The National Stock Exchange of Australia	19 Jun 2014
The New Zealand[1] Stock Exchange	22 Sep 1988
The Rio De Janeiro Stock Exchange	17 Aug 1995
The Sao Paulo[1] Stock Exchange	11 Dec 1995
The Singapore Exchange Limited (SGX)	7 Oct 2014 (30 Jun 1977)
The Stockholm[1] Stock Exchange	16 Jul 1985
The Stock Exchange of Mauritius[1]	31 Jan 2011
The Stock Exchange of Thailand[1]	10 Oct 1994
The Swiss Stock Exchange	12 May 1997
The Warsaw[1] Stock Exchange	25 Feb 2010

Note

[1] Markets of the above recognised exchanges on which securities would not meet HMRC definition of 'listed' are as follows:

- Athens Stock Exchange: The Alternative Market (EN.A)
- Australian Stock Exchange: The Sydney Futures Exchange (SFX)
- Bond Exchange of South Africa: Over-the Counter (OTC) market
- Colombo Stock Exchange: Diri Savi Board
- Copenhagen Stock Exchange (part of the OMX Nordic Exchange which is part of the NASDAQ OMX Group): First North
- Cyprus Stock Exchange: Emerging Companies Market (a Multi-lateral trading facility)
- GXG Main Quote: GXG Main Quote
- Helsinki Stock Exchange (part of the OMX Nordic Exchange which is part of the NASDAQ OMX Group): First North
- Iceland Stock Exchange (part of the OMX Nordic Exchange which is part of the NASDAQ OMX Group): First North
- ICAP Securities & Derivatives Exchange Ltd: ISDX Growth Market and ISDX Secondary Market
- Johannesburg Stock Exchange: Alt-X, Venture Capital Market (VCM) and Development Capital Market (DCM)
- Korean Stock Exchange: KOSDAQ and Korean Derivatives Market
- Kuala Lumpa Stock Exchange: ACE Market
- LIFFE Administration and Management (LIFFE A&M): London International Financial Futures and Options Market (LIFFE) the Derivatives Market
- London Stock Exchange: the Alternative Investment Market (AIM), Specialist Fund Market (SFM) and High Growth Segment (HGS)
- Mexico Stock Exchange: OTC Market
- MICEX Stock Exchange: Quotation list B, Quotation list V, Quotation list I, Over the Counter and unlisted security segments
- NASDAQ OMX Tallinn: First North
- NASDAQ OMX Vilnius: First North
- New Zealand Stock Exchange: NZAX Market (Alternative Market)
- Sao Paulo Stock Exchange: Over-the Counter (OTC) market
- Stockholm Stock Exchange (part of the OMX Nordic Exchange which is part of the NASDAQ OMX Group): First North
- Stock Exchange of Mauritius: Development and Enterprise Market (DEM)
- Stock Exchange of Thailand: Market for Alternative Investment (MAI) and the Thailand Futures Exchange (TFEX), and securities traded over the counter (OTC)
- Warsaw Stock Exchange: New Connect Market and Catalyst Market for Bonds (Retail Market) Multi-lateral Trading Facility (MTF)

In addition, a recognised stock exchange is any stock exchange in the following countries which is a stock exchange within the meaning of the law of the particular country relating to stock exchanges (or as specified below).

Austria[(1)]	22 Oct 1970
Belgium[(1)]	22 Oct 1970
Canada[(1)] (any stock exchange prescribed for the purpose of the Canadian Income Tax Act)	22 Oct 1970
France[(1)]	22 Oct 1970
Germany[(1)]	5 Aug 1971
Guernsey	10 Dec 2002
Hong Kong[(1)]	26 Feb 1971
Ireland[(1)], Republic of	22 Oct 1970
Italy	3 May 1972
Japan	22 Oct 1970
Luxembourg	21 Feb 1972
Netherlands[(1)]	22 Oct 1970
Norway	22 Oct 1970
Portugal	21 Feb 1972
Spain	5 Aug 1971
USA[(1)] (any exchange registered with the Securities and Exchange Commission of the United States as a national securities exchange)	22 Oct 1970

Note

[(1)] Markets of the above recognised exchanges on which securities would not meet HMRC definition of 'listed' are as follows:

- Austria: Third Market or Dritter Market
- Belgium: NYSE Alternext
- Canada: NEX
- France: NYSE Alternext
- Germany: Freiverkehr markets, Entry Markets (also known as open or unofficial markets)
- Hong Kong: The Growth and Enterprise Market (GEM)
- Ireland (Republic of): Enterprise Securities Market (ESM)
- Netherlands: NYSE Alternext
- USA: Over the counter transactions, Over the Counter Bulletin Board (OTCBB) and Pink Sheets

Alternative finance investment bonds

(ITA 2007, s. 564G; CTA 2009, s. 507; TCGA 1992, s. 151N)

'Alternative finance investment bonds' (Sharia compliant financial instruments commonly known as 'sukuk') must be listed on a recognised stock exchange. An alternative finance investment bond listed on an exchange recognised under ITA 2007, s. 1005 will meet this requirement. In addition, certain other exchanges are designated as recognised stock exchanges ***solely*** for the purposes of ITA 2007, s. 564G. These are listed below, together with the dates of recognition.

Abu Dhabi Securities Market	1 April 2007
Bahrain Stock Exchange	1 April 2007
Dubai Financial Market	1 April 2007
NASDAQ Dubai (formerley the 'Dubai International Financial Exchange')	1 April 2007
Labuan International Financial Exchange	1 April 2007
Saudi Stock Exchange (Tadawul)	1 April 2007
Surabaya Stock Exchange	1 April 2007

[¶15-050] Recognised futures exchanges

(TCGA 1992, s. 288(6))

The following futures exchanges have been designated by the Board of Her Majesty's Revenue and Customs as 'recognised futures exchanges' (when the Board recognises a futures exchange this is announced in the *London Gazette*):

Exchange	**Date**
International Petroleum Exchange of London London Metal Exchange	From 6 August 1985
London Gold Market London Silver Market	From 12 December 1985
CME Group (formerly Chicago Mercantile Exchange and Chicago Board of Trade[(3)]) Philadelphia Board of Trade New York Mercantile Exchange	From 19 December 1986
Montreal Exchange Mid-America Commodity Exchange	From 29 July 1987
Hong Kong Futures Exchange	From 15 December 1987
Commodity Exchange, Inc (COMEX)	From 25 August 1988
Sydney Futures Exchange Ltd	From 31 October 1988
OM Stockholm OMLX (formerly OM London)	From 18 March 1992
Euronext (London International Financial Futures and Options Exchange)[(1)]	From 22 March 1992
New York Board of Trade[(2)]	From 10 June 2004

Notes

[(1)] Euronext (merged with NYSE group in 2007 to form NYSE Euronext) acquired London International Financial Futures and Options Exchange in January 2002. On 22 March 1992, London International Financial Futures Exchange and the London Traded Options Market merged forming London International Financial Futures and Options Exchange. In 1996, the LIFFE merged with the London Commodity Exchange (formerly FOX). Markets incorporated within former London Commodity Exchange, recognised from 6 August 1985 include: Baltic International Freight Futures Exchange; London Cocoa Terminal Market; London Coffee Terminal Market; London Futures and Options Exchange; London Grain Futures Market; London Meat Futures Market; London Potato Futures Market; London Rubber Market; London Soya Bean Meal Futures Market and London Sugar Terminal Market.

[2] In June 2004, the New York Coffee Sugar and Cocoa Exchange (CS&CE) merged with the New York Cotton Exchange (NYCE) to form the New York Board of Trade. As a result of this merger, all previous exchanges and subsidiaries ceased to exist, including the Coffee, Sugar, & Cocoa Exchange, the New York Cotton Exchange, the Citrus Associates of the New York Cotton Exchange, the New York Futures Exchange (NYFE), and the FINEX Exchange. All markets are now referred to as the New York Board of Trade or NYBOT. [NY CS&CE was designated from 15 December 1987, and NYCE and Citrus Associates of the NYCE from 25 August 1988.]
[3] Chicago Board of Trade recognised from 24 April 1987.

[¶15-150] Recognised investment exchanges

(ITEPA 2003, s. 702)

(Tax Reporter; ¶494-300)

A 'recognised investment exchange' (RIE) is an investment exchange in relation to which a recognition order made by the Financial Conduct Authority (formerly Financial Services Authority) is in force (*Financial Services and Markets Act* 2000, s. 285ff.).

Where the Financial Conduct Authority does issue a recognition order for a 'recognised investment exchange' this has consequences for the rules relating to the operation of PAYE on the provision of 'readily convertible asset' for employees. If an employer provides an employee with an asset that can be sold, or otherwise realised, on a recognised investment exchange (RIE); the London Bullion Market; the New York Stock Exchange; or any market specified in PAYE Regulations, that asset is a 'readily convertible asset' and the employer is obliged to operate PAYE (ITEPA 2003, s. 696, 702. Similarly any asset, such as a gold bar, capable of sale or realisation on the London Bullion Market is a 'readily convertible asset'. As at November 2013, the FCA has currently issued recognition orders for the following RIEs:

Investment exchange	Effective date
UK	
ICE Futures Europe	22 November 2001
BATS Trading Limited	11 July 2013
ICAP Securities & Derivatives Exchange Limited	19 July 2007
LIFFE Administration and Management	22 November 2001
London Stock Exchange plc	22 November 2001
The London Metal Exchange Limited	22 November 2001
Overseas	
Australian Securities Exchange Limited	30 January 2002
Chicago Board of Trade [CBOT]	23 November 2001
EUREX [Zurich]	23 November 2001
ICE Futures U.S., Inc	17 May 2007
National Association of Securities Dealers Automated Quotations [NASDAQ]	23 November 2001
New York Mercantile Exchange Inc. [NYMEX Inc.]	23 November 2001
NYSE Liffe US	29 September 2009
SIX Swiss Exchange AG	23 November 2001
The Chicago Mercantile Exchange [CME]	23 November 2001

[¶15-200] Recognised growth markets

(FA 1986, s. 99A)

Finance Act 2014 introduces an exemption from stamp duty and stamp duty reserve tax for transfers of securities admitted to trading on recognised growth markets, with effect from 28 April 2014.

To qualify as a recognised growth market, a market must be a recognised stock exchange (see ¶15-000) and meet one of two conditions:

- a majority of companies trading on that market are companies with market capitalisations of less than £170m in the qualifying period; or
- the market's rules require that companies seeking admission demonstrate at least 20% compounded annual growth in revenue or employment over the three years preceding admission.

List of recognised growth markets

Name	**Effective date**
Alternative Investment Market	28 April 2014
Enterprise Securities Market (ESM)	28 April 2014
GXG Markets A/S	28 April 2014
High Growth Segment	28 April 2014
ICAP Securities and Derivatives Exchange Limited (ISDX)	28 April 2014

HMRC information

[¶15-450] Clearances and approvals

(Source: www.hmrc.gov.uk/cap/)

HMRC may be able to provide advance clearance or approval to some transactions. HMRC will not provide clearances on the following matters:

- application of the 'settlements legislation' in ITTOIA 2005, Pt. 5, Ch. 5; or
- the tax consequences of executing non-charitable trust deeds or settlements.

Clearances and the General Anti-Abuse Rule (GAAR)

HMRC will not give either formal or informal clearances that the GAAR does not apply. However, as part of its model of direct engagement with large businesses and wealthy individuals HMRC will discuss commercial arrangements and confirm where appropriate that it doesn't regard particular arrangements as tax avoidance.

Code of Practice on Taxation for Banks

A bank which adopts the Code of Practice on Taxation for Banks commits not to undertake any tax planning that achieves a tax result contrary to the intentions of Parliament. When approached by a bank under the code, Customer Relationship Managers will continue to give HMRC's view of whether a transaction is 'code compliant'.

[¶15-460] Non-statutory clearances

(Source: www.hmrc.gov.uk/cap/)

Transaction	Applications to:
Company migrations Notification of company migration and approval of arrangements for payment of tax liabilities in accordance with TMA 1970, s. 109B–109F (previously FA 1988, s. 130) (see SP 2/90).	Nicola Harris HM Revenue & Customs CTIS Business International, Foreign Profits Team 100 Parliament Street London SW1A 2BQ Telephone: 03000 543 476 E-mail link at: www.hmrc.gov.uk/cap/

General

Transaction	Applications to:
Controlled Foreign Companies Clearances in relation to Controlled Foreign Companies (CFC) in accordance with TIOPA 2010, Pt. 9A (new CFC rules) or ICTA 1988, s. 747–756 and Sch. 24–26 (old CFC Rules).	Electronically to Mary Sharp via link at: www.hmrc.gov.uk/cap/ and copied to the UK group's Customer Relationship Manager or Customer Co-ordinator. (No paper copies of an application are needed.)
	If it isn't possible to send applications for clearance electronically, applications should be sent to the following address: CTIS, Foreign Profits Team Registry (CFC clearances) 3rd floor 100 Parliament Street London SW1A 2BQ Telephone: 03000 585 623
Inward Investment Support service For information on inward investment and to discuss the tax implications of an investment.	Inward Investment Support HM Revenue & Customs CTIAA Business International 100 Parliament Street London SW1A 2BQ E-mail: inwardinvestmentsupport@hmrc.gsi.gov.uk.
Business Investment Relief Provisions For HMRC's view on whether a proposed investment can be treated as a qualifying investment as defined in ITA 2007, s. 809VC use the checklist at: www.hmrc.gov.uk/cap/annex-b.pdf	HM Revenue & Customs Business Investment Relief Team S1278 PO Box 202 Bootle L69 9AL Telephone: 03000 527 416 E-mail Cameron Wilson via link at: www.hmrc.gov.uk/cap/
Creative Industries Advice on the workings of the scheme as it applies to Film Tax, Animation Tax, High-end Television Tax and Video Games Development Reliefs.	Creative Industries Unit (Film, Television/ Animation and Video Games Tax Reliefs) Local Compliance S0717 PO Box 3900 Glasgow G70 6AA Telephone: 03000 510 191 E-mail link at: www.hmrc.gov.uk/cap/
Enterprise Investment Scheme (EIS), Seed Enterprise Investment Scheme (SEIS) and Venture Capital Trust (VCT) scheme Advice on the workings of these schemes, as well as providing non-statutory advance assurance to companies seeking investment under these schemes.	Local Compliance Small Company Enterprise Centre Admin Team SO777 PO Box 3900 Glasgow G70 6AA Telephone: 03000 588 907

Other non-statutory clearances

(Source: www.hmrc.gov.uk/cap/nscg.htm)

HMRC offer a further clearance service for customers and their advisers who need clarification on guidance or legislation in relation to a specific transaction that is not covered by a more appropriate clearance or approval route. HMRC will usually reply within 28 days.

HMRC will not provide advice under this service where:

- all the necessary information (per the checklists below) has not been provided;
- HMRC don't think that there are genuine points of uncertainty – they will explain why they think this and where the relevant online guidance can be found;
- the request is for HMRC to give tax planning advice, or to 'approve' tax planning products or arrangements;
- the application is about treatment of transactions which, in HMRC's view, are for the purposes of avoiding tax;
- HMRC are already checking the tax position for the period in question, in which case contact should be directed to the officer dealing with the check;
- any related return for the period in question is final;
- there's a statutory clearance applicable for the transaction.

Other Non-Statutory Clearances	Applications to:
All transactions other than Business Investment Relief and Business Property Relief See Annex A checklist at www.hmrc.gov.uk/cap/annex-a.pdf) – head the application letter 'Clearance service'.	HMRC Non-Statutory Clearance Team, 5th Floor Alexander House, 21 Victoria Avenue, Southend on Sea, Essex SS99 1AA E-mail: hmrc.southendteam@hmrc.gsi.gov.uk (HMRC Non-Statutory Clearance Team)
Advance assurance on Business Investment Relief for non-domiciled persons taxed on the remittance basis See Annex B checklist at www.hmrc.gov.uk/cap/annex-b.pdf – head the application letter 'Advance Assurance for Business Investment Relief'.	HM Revenue & Customs Business Investment Relief Team S1278 PO Box 202 Bootle L69 9AL
Inheritance Tax Business Property Relief clearances See Annex C checklist at www.hmrc.gov.uk/cap/annex-c.pdf	By e-mail to: mailpoint.e@hmrc.gsi.gov.uk (Trusts & Estates Technical Team (Clearances)). Please quote reference BP102/P1/08E By post to: HMRC Trusts & Estates Technical Team (Clearances) Ferrers House Castle Meadow Road Nottingham NG2 1BB

[¶15-470] Statutory clearance or approval

Transaction	Applications to:
Qualifying life assurance policies **ICTA 1988, Sch. 15** Applications to approve certification of qualifying life assurance policies.	Darryl Wall HM Revenue & Customs CTISA Corporation Tax and Business Income Tax Financial Services Team 3rd Floor 100 Parliament Street London SW1A 2BQ Telephone: 03000 585977 Fax: 020 7147 2641 E-mail: Darryl Wall link at: www.hmrc.gov.uk/cap/
Transfers of long-term business between life assurance companies **Under FA 2012, s. 133** Applications for clearance, including cases where the parties include non-UK resident companies or friendly societies	The transferor company's Customer Relationship Manager and to: HM Revenue & Customs CTISA Corporation Tax and Business Income Tax Financial Services Team 3rd Floor 100 Parliament Street London SW1A 2BQ Telephone: 03000 585911 Alternatively, by e-mail to Anthony Fawcett via link at: www.hmrc.gov.uk/cap/
Transactions in shares or debentures **Under ICTA 1988, s. 765 and 765A** The Treasury Consents regime was repealed by *Finance Act* 2009. Events or transactions taking place on or after 1 July 2009 are subject to a new reporting regime, detail of which can be found in HMRC's *International Manual* at INT700000.	

Transaction	Applications to:
Transfer pricing (advance pricing agreements) HMRC have run an Advanced Pricing Agreements programme since 1999 to assist businesses in identifying solutions for complex transfer pricing issues. HMRC issued Statement of Practice ('SP') 2/10 in December 2010 to update an earlier Statement of Practice (SP3/99) on Advance Pricing Agreements ('APAs'). The SP is intended as general guidance as to how HMRC interpret the APA legislation and how HMRC operate the UK APA Programme.	Dominic Vines (APA Team Leader) HM Revenue & Customs CTIS Business International East Spur, Euston Tower, 286 Euston Road, London NW1 3UH Telephone: 03000 585 861 Fax: 03000 543 795 E-mail Dominic Vines via link at: www.hmrc.gov.uk/cap/
Stamp Taxes Queries on Stamp taxes should be directed first to the Stamp Taxes Helpline and if the helpline is unable to answer the question, in writing to the Stamp Office. The Clearance and Counteraction Team (see below) does not handle applications for stamp duty land tax (SDLT) adjudications.	**Stamp Taxes Helpline** Tel: 0300 200 3510 Birmingham Stamp Office 9th Floor City Centre House 30 Union Street Birmingham B2 4AR
Statutory applications for advance clearance HMRC's Clearance and Counteraction Team, Counter-Avoidance handles requests where advance clearance is required under statutory provisions relating to any one or more of the following: ***Capital Gains:*** • share exchanges (TCGA 1992, s. 138(1)) • reconstruction involving the transfer of a business (TCGA 1992, s. 139(5)) • collective investment schemes: exchanges, mergers and schemes of reconstruction (TCGA 1992, s. 103K) • transfer of a UK trade between EU member states (TCGA 1992, s. 140B and 140D)	Please ensure a 'Market sensitive' application is marked for the attention of 'The Team leader', and send it to: HM Revenue & Customs CA Clearance SO528 PO Box 194 Bootle L69 9AA Telephone: 03000 589 004 Fax: 03000 589 802 E-mail: reconstructions@hmrc.gsi.gov.uk (Clearance and Counteraction Team)

Transaction	Applications to:
Other shares, securities, demergers and reorganisations • purchase of own shares by unquoted trading companies (CTA 2010, s. 1044) • demergers (CTA 2010, s. 1091) • EIS shares (acquisition by new company) (ITA 2007, s. 247(1)(f)) • Company reorganisation involving intangible fixed assets (CTA 2009, s. 831) • Transactions in securities (CTA 2010, s. 748 and ITA 2007, s. 701) ***Transactions in land*** • under CTA 2009, s. 237 (for corporation tax purposes) and ITTOIA 2005, s. 300 (for income tax purposes) – confirmation of the customer's view of the tax consequences of assigning a lease granted at under value • under CTA 2010, s. 831 (for corporation tax purposes) and ITA 2007, s. 770 (for income tax purposes). ***Company finance*** • CTA 2009, s. 426/7 (loan relationships transfers) and 437 (loan relationships: mergers) • CTA 2009, s. 677 (derivative contracts: transfers) and 686 (derivative contracts: mergers) ***Targeted Anti-Avoidance Rule 3 (Capital Gains)*** Informal clearances: companies and their representatives may make requests for advice about the legislation in TCGA 1992, s. 184G to 184H, including whether the provisions will apply to a planned series of transactions that may constitute an arrangement.	Where clearance is required under any one or more of the statutory provisions, a single letter should be sent to the Clearance and Counteraction Team, Counter-Avoidance at the address above. No extra copy is required as the same person will deal with each of the clearances asked for. A single response will be given covering all of these. Please make clear at the top of the letter what clearances are being requested. Please note the following points: • HMRC acknowledge only those applications that request an acknowledgement; • if a reply by e-mail is required, please write 'I confirm that I understand and accept the risks involved in using e-mail'. HMRC do not e-mail market sensitive applications; • enquiries about the progress of an application or making general enquiries should be made by telephone: 03000 589 004. Please allow ten days after receiving an acknowledgement before you contact to check progress; • HMRC regard information that could affect the price of a stock market quoted company and information concerning the financial affairs of well known individuals as sensitive; • in March, September and December HMRC receive high volumes of applications which increases turn around time. Please bear this in mind when applying during these times.

[¶15-500] HMRC forms

For 'find a form' search function see http://search.hmrc.gov.uk/kb5/hmrc/forms/home.page.

[¶15-550] HMRC leaflets and booklets

For a complete list see www.hmrc.gov.uk/leaflets/menu.htm.

[¶15-600] HMRC manuals

For a complete list see www.hmrc.gov.uk/thelibrary/manuals-a-z.htm.

[¶15-650] HMRC websites

HMRC home page

www.hmrc.gov.uk

The HMRC website contains full details of contact addresses and numbers, including in particular the following:

- Helplines and postal addresses for all taxes, national insurance and VAT queries: http://search2.hmrc.gov.uk/kb5/hmrc/contactus/home.page
- Dedicated helplines and contacts for authorised agents: www.hmrc.gov.uk/agents/contacting-effective.htm

Other useful parts of the HMRC website are:

HMRC self-assessment pages

www.hmrc.gov.uk/sa/index.htm

HMRC employers information

www.hmrc.gov.uk/employers/index.shtml

HMRC tax credits

www.gov.uk/browse/benefits/tax-credits

[¶15-800] Other useful websites

Adjudicator

www.adjudicatorsoffice.gov.uk/

Government Information Service
UK: www.direct.gov.uk
Scotland: www.scotland.gov.uk
Wales: www.wales.gov.uk

CIOT
www.tax.org.uk

ICAEW Tax Faculty
www.icaew.com/en/technical/tax/tax-faculty

Office of Public Sector Information – Statutory Instruments
www.legislation.gov.uk/uksi
For statutory instruments made by the National Assembly for Wales – www.legislation.gov.uk/wsi
For statutory instruments made by the Scottish Parliament – www.legislation.gov.uk/ssi

Parliament
UK: www.parliament.uk/
Scotland: www.scottish.parliament.uk/
Wales: www.assembly.wales/en/Pages/Home.aspx

Parliamentary Ombudsman
www.ombudsman.org.uk/

Treasury Home Page
www.hm-treasury.gov.uk/

Tribunals service
www.tribunals.gov.uk/tax/

Valuation Office Agency
www.voa.gov.uk/

Finance Acts

[¶15-950] Finance Acts

Year	Budget		Royal Assent	
1980	26 March	1980	1 August	1980
1981	10 March	1981	27 July	1981
1982	9 March	1982	30 July	1982
1983	15 March	1983	13 May	1983
1983 (No. 2)	15 March	1983	26 July	1983
1984	13 March	1984	26 July	1984
1985	19 March	1985	25 July	1985
1986	18 March	1986	25 July	1986
1987	17 March	1987	15 May	1987
1987 (No. 2)	17 March	1987	23 July	1987
1988	15 March	1988	29 July	1988
1989	14 March	1989	27 July	1989
1990	20 March	1990	26 July	1990
1991	19 March	1991	26 July	1991
1992	10 March	1992	16 March	1992
1992 (No. 2)	10 March	1992	16 July	1992
1993	16 March	1993	27 July	1993
1994	30 November	1993	3 May	1994
1995	29 November	1994	1 May	1995
1996	28 November	1995	29 April	1996
1997	26 November	1996	19 March	1997
1997 (No. 2)	2 July	1997	31 July	1997
1998	17 March	1998	31 July	1998
1999	9 March	1999	27 July	1999
2000	21 March	2000	28 July	2000
2001	7 March	2001	11 May	2001
2002	17 April	2002	24 July	2002
2003	9 April	2003	10 July	2003
2004	17 March	2004	22 July	2004
2005	16 March	2005	7 April	2005
2005 (No. 2)	16 March	2005	20 July	2005
2006	22 March	2006	19 July	2006
2007	21 March	2007	19 July	2007
2008	12 March	2008	21 July	2008
2009	22 April	2009	21 July	2009
2010	24 March	2010	8 April	2010
2010 (No. 2)	22 June	2010	27 July	2010
2010 (No. 3)	22 June	2010	16 December	2010
2011	23 March	2011	19 July	2011
2012	21 March	2012	17 July	2012
2013	20 March	2013	17 July	2013
2014	19 March	2014	17 July	2014

STAMP TAXES

Stamp duty land tax

[¶16-000] Stamp duty land tax rates

Note: See ¶26-200 for rates applicable in Scotland from 1 April 2015.

Applies to contracts entered into (or varied) after 10 July 2003 and completed after 30 November 2003 and to leases granted after that date.

SDLT also applies to transfers of an interest in land into or out of a partnership, and to an acquisition of an interest in a partnership where the partnership property includes an interest in land (from 22 July 2004). From 19 July 2006, SDLT additionally applies to transfers of partnership interests but only where the sole or main activity of the partnership is investing or dealing in interests in land.

From 4 December 2014 (contracts completing on or after), SDLT rates on residential property will only apply to the part of the property price that falls within each band (i.e. the former slab structure is replaced with a structure similar to that of income tax). Transitional rules will allow buyers who have already exchanged on a home but not completed before 4 December 2014 to choose whether to pay SDLT under the existing or new rules. Legislation to be included in the Stamp Duty Land Tax Bill 2014 (Autumn Statement 2014).

All land in UK

Period	Residential		Non-residential	
	Rate %	Band £	Rate %	Band £
On or after 4 December 2014	0 2 5 10 12 15(3)(4)	0–125,000 125,001–250,000 250,001–925,000 925,001–1,500,000 1,500,001 and over Over 500,000	0 1 3 4	0-150,000 150,001-250,000 250,001-500,000 Over 500,000

Period	Rate %	Residential £	Non-residential £
20 March 2014 to 3 December 2014	0 1 3 4 5 7 15(2)(3)	0–125,000 125,001–250,000 250,001–500,000 500,001–1,000,000 1,000,001–2,000,000 Over 2,000,000 Over 500,000	0–150,000 150,001–250,000 250,001–500,000 Over 500,000 N/A N/A N/A

Period	Rate %	Residential £	Non-residential £
22 March 2012 to 19 March 2014	0 1 3 4 5 7 15[2][3]	0–125,000 125,001–250,000 250,001–500,000 500,001–1,000,000 1,000,001–2,000,000 Over 2,000,000 Over 2,000,000	0–150,000 150,001–250,000 250,001–500,000 Over 500,000 N/A N/A N/A
6 April 2011 to 21 March 2012	0 1 3 4 5	0–125,000 125,001–250,000 250,001–500,000 500,001–1,000,000 Over 1,000,000	0–150,000 150,001–250,000 250,001–500,000 Over 500,000 N/A
1 January 2010 to 5 April 2011	0 1 3 4	0–125,000 125,001–250,000 250,001–500,000 Over 500,000	0–150,000 150,001–250,000 250,001–500,000 Over 500,000
3 September 2008 to 31 December 2009	0 1 3 4	0–175,000[1] 175,001–250,000 250,001–500,000 Over 500,000	0–150,000 150,001–250,000 250,001–500,000 Over 500,000
23 March 2006 to 2 September 2008	0 1 3 4	0–125,000 125,001–250,000 250,001–500,000 Over 500,000	0–150,000 150,001–250,000 250,001–500,000 Over 500,000
17 March 2005 to 22 March 2006	0 1 3 4	0–120,000 120,001–250,000 250,001–500,000 Over 500,000	0–150,000 150,001–250,000 250,001–500,000 Over 500,000
1 December 2003 to 16 March 2005	0 1 3 4	0–60,000 60,001–250,000 250,001–500,000 Over 500,000	0–150,000 150,001–250,000 250,001–500,000 Over 500,000

Notes

(1) From 3 September 2008 until 21 April 2009, the £175,000 threshold only applied to freehold or assigned leases with 21 years or more remaining. The £175,000 threshold does not apply to the residential element of a mixed use property.

[(2)] The 15% rate applies if the property is acquired by certain non-natural persons (e.g. companies, partnerships with corporate members and collective investment schemes) with effect from 21 March 2012. *Finance Act* 2014 reduces the threshold from £2m to £500,000 where the effective date is on or after 20 March 2014 with the £2m threshold continuing to apply, subject to exceptions, where contracts were entered into before that date.
[(3)] *Finance Act* 2013 introduced a number of reliefs to reduce the 15% rate to 7% with effect in relation to transactions with an effective date on or after 17 July 2013 (Royal Assent). The reliefs broadly match those where there is relief against the annual tax on enveloped dwellings. However, the SDLT reliefs will apply only if the property continues to satisfy the qualifying conditions throughout the following three years, otherwise, additional SDLT will become payable.
[(4)] *Finance Act* 2013 also introduced legislation to reform the stamp duty land tax rules for 'transfer of rights' with effect from 17 July 2013 (Royal Assent).

Lease rentals

		Net present value of rent	
Period	**Rate (%)**	**Residential**	**Non-residential**
From 1 January 2010	0	£0–£125,000	£0–£150,000
	1	Over £125,000	Over £150,000
3 September 2008 to 31 December 2009	0	£0–£175,000	£0–£150,000
	1	Over £175,000	Over £150,000
23 March 2006 to 2 September 2008	0	£0–£125,000	£0–£150,000
	1	Over £125,000	Over £150,000
17 March 2005 to 22 March 2006	0	£0–£120,000	£0–£150,000
	1	Over £120,000	Over £150,000
1 December 2003 to 16 March 2005	0	£0–£60,000	£0–£150,000
	1	Over £60,000	Over £150,000

Duty on premium is the same as for transfers of land (except special rules apply for premium where rent exceeds £1,000 annually (£600 annually before 12 March 2008).
Until 22 April 2009 if the net present value exceeded £175,000, the charge was on the excess over £125,000.
Finance Act 2013 simplifies reporting requirements that apply when a lease continues after the expiry of its fixed-term and where an agreement for the lease is substantially performed before the actual lease is granted and abolishes the rules on abnormal rent increases with effect from 17 July 2013 (Royal Assent).

[¶16-200] Stamp duty land tax penalties

Failure to deliver a land transaction return by the filing date (FA 2003, Sch. 10, para. 3 and 4)	£100 if return delivered within three months of filing date, otherwise £200. If not delivered within 12 months, maximum penalty of amount of tax chargeable
Failure to comply with a notice to deliver return within specified period (FA 2003, Sch. 10, para. 5)	Maximum of £60 for each day on which the failure continues after notification
Failure to keep or preserve records under FA 2003, Sch. 10, para. 9 or Sch. 11, para. 4	Maximum of £3,000 unless other documentary evidence provided

Error in taxpayers document (careless or deliberate) Error in taxpayers document attributable to another person (deliberately supplying false information or deliberately withholding information, with the intention to cause an inaccuracy) Failure to notify HMRC within 30 days that an assessment is an under assessment (FA 2007, Sch. 24) • careless • deliberate but unconcealed • deliberate and concealed	 Up to 30% potential lost revenue Up to 70% potential lost revenue Up to 100% potential lost revenue (subject to reductions for disclosure)
Failure to comply with an information notice (FA 2008, Sch. 36)	Initial penalty £300 Up to £60 per day for each day for continued failure Tax related penalty determined by Tribunal where significant tax at stake
Inaccurate information/documents provided in complying with an information notice (careless or deliberate)	Up to £3,000 for each inaccuracy

[¶16-250] Stamp duty land tax interest

The rates are as follows:

Period of application	Rate %	
	Underpayments	**Repayments**
From 29 September 2009	3.00	0.50
24 March 2009 to 28 September 2009	2.50	0.00
27 January 2009 to 23 March 2009	3.50	0.00
6 January 2009 to 26 January 2009	4.50	0.75
6 December 2008 to 5 January 2009	5.50	1.50
6 November 2008 to 5 December 2008	6.50	2.25
6 January 2008 to 5 November 2008	7.50	3.00
6 August 2007 to 5 January 2008	8.50	4.00
6 September 2006 to 5 August 2007	7.50	3.00
6 September 2005 to 5 September 2006	6.50	2.25

FA 2009, s. 101–104 and Sch. 53 and 54 contain provisions to harmonise interest regimes across all HMRC taxes and duties.

Stamp duty

[¶17-000] Stamp duty rates

Conveyance or transfer on sale of shares and securities

(FA 1999, Sch. 13, para. 3)

Instrument	Rate of tax after 26 October 1986[5] %
Stock transfer	0.5[1][2]
Conversion of shares into depositary receipts	1.5[3]
Take overs and mergers	0.5[1][2]
Purchase by company of own shares	0.5[1][2]
Letters of allotment	0.5

Notes

[1] Because duty at 0.5% is equivalent to £5 per £1,000 of consideration and duty is rounded up to the next multiple of £5 (FA 1999, s. 112(1)(b)), duty is effectively £5 per £1,000 (or part of £1,000) of consideration.

[2] Loan capital is generally exempt from transfer on sale duty subject to specific exclusions (designed to prevent exemption applying to quasi-equity securities) (FA 1986, s. 79).

[3] FA 1986, s. 67(3).

[4] FA 2008, s. 98 exempts transfers that would attract duty not exceeding £5. This applies to instruments executed on or after 13 March 2008 (i.e. where chargeable consideration less than £1,000).

[5] From 28 April 2014, transfers of securities admitted to trading on recognised growth markets are exempt from stamp duty (*Finance Act* 2014, Sch. 24). See ¶15-200 for a list of recognised growth markets.

[¶17-200] Stamp duty penalties

Type of document	Penalties applicable if document presented for stamping more than
Document executed in UK	30 days after execution
Document executed abroad relating to UK land and buildings	30 days after execution
Document executed abroad	30 days after document first received in UK[1]

Note

[1] Free standing penalty (see table further below) may apply if written information confirming date of receipt in UK is incorrect.

The maximum penalties are:

- £300 or the amount of duty, whichever is less; on documents submitted up to one year late; and
- £300 or the amount of duty, whichever is greater; on documents submitted more than one year late.

Mitigated penalties due on late stamping

The Stamp Office publishes tables of mitigated penalty levels that will be applied in straightforward cases at www.hmrc.gov.uk/sd/pay-penalties/penalties.htm#1.

From 1 October 2014

Length of delay	Penalty
Documents late by up to 12 months	10% of the duty, capped at £300
Documents late by 12 to 12 months	20% of the duty
Documents late by more than 24 months	30% of the duty

Before 1 October 2014

Months late	Up to £300	£305–£700	£705–£1,350	£1,355–£2,500	£2,505–£5,000	Over £5,000
Under 3	Nil	£20	£40	£60	£80	£100
Under 6	£20[1]	£40	£60	£80	£100	£150
Under 9	£40[1]	£60	£80	£100	£150	£200
Under 12	£60[1]	£80	£100	£150	£200	£300
Under 15		15% of the duty or £100 if greater				20% of the duty
Under 18		25% of the duty or £150 if greater				40% of the duty
Under 21		35% of the duty or £200 if greater				60% of the duty
Under 24		45% of the duty or £250 if greater				80% of the duty

Note

(1) Or the amount of the duty if that is less.

If a document is over 24 months late, the penalty is the higher of:

– the amount of stamp duty that's due

– £300.

Reasonable excuse

In all cases above, the penalties will not apply if the person responsible for stamping can show a 'reasonable excuse' for the failure to submit the document(s) within the time limit. Interest is due on any unpaid penalty.

[¶17-250] Stamp duty interest

In respect of instruments executed on or after 1 October 1999, interest is chargeable on stamp duty that is not paid within 30 days of execution of a stampable document, wherever execution takes place (SA 1891, s. 15A). Interest is payable on repayments of overpaid duty, calculated from the later of 30 days from the date of execution of the instrument, or lodgement with the Stamp Office of the duty repayable (FA 1999, s. 110). Interest is rounded down (if necessary) to the nearest multiple of £5. No interest is payable if that amount is under £25. The applicable interest rate is as prescribed under FA 1989, s. 178.

For interest periods from 1 October 1999 onwards, the rate of interest charged on underpaid or late paid stamp duty and SDRT exceeds that on repayments:

Period of application	Rate %	
	Underpayments	Repayments
From 29 September 2009	3.00	0.50
24 March 2009 to 28 September 2009	2.50	0.00
27 January 2009 to 23 March 2009	3.50	0.00
6 January 2009 to 26 January 2009	4.50	0.75
6 December 2008 to 5 January 2009	5.50	1.50
6 November 2008 to 5 December 2008	6.50	2.25
6 January 2008 to 5 November 2008	7.50	3.00
6 August 2007 to 5 January 2008	8.50	4.00
6 September 2006 to 5 August 2007	7.50	3.00
6 September 2005 to 5 September 2006	6.50	2.25
6 September 2004 to 5 September 2005	7.50	3.00[(1)]
6 December 2003 to 5 September 2004	6.50	2.25[(1)]
6 August 2003 to 5 December 2003	5.50	1.50[(1)]
6 November 2001 to 5 August 2003	6.50	2.25[(1)]
6 May 2001 to 5 November 2001	7.50	3.00[(1)]
5 February 2000 to 5 May 2001	8.50	4.00

Note

(1) Rates revised by HMRC (press release 5 September 2005).

FA 2009, s. 101–104 and Sch. 53 and 54 contain provisions to harmonise interest regimes across all HMRC taxes and duties.

Stamp duty reserve tax

[¶18-000] Stamp duty reserve tax rates

(FA 1986, s. 87, 93 and 96)

Principal charge

Subject matter of charge	Rate of tax %
Agreements to transfer chargeable securities[1] for money or money's worth	0.5
Renounceable letters of allotment	0.5
Shares converted into depositary receipts[2]	*1.5*
but transfer of shares or securities on which stamp duty payable	*1.0*
Chargeable securities[1] put into clearance system[2]	*1.5*
but transfer of shares or securities on which stamp duty payable	*1.0*

Notes

[1] Chargeable securities = stocks, shares, loan capital, units under unit trust scheme (FA 1986, s. 99(3)). From 28 April 2014, the definition of chargeable securities for SDRT purposes excludes securities admitted to trading on a recognised growth market (FA 1986, s. 99(4A) and 99A). See ¶15-200 for a list of recognised growth markets.

[2] Following the European Court of Justice judgment in HSBC Holdings Ltd and Vidacos Nominees v Commissioners for HM Revenue & Customs, HMRC accept that Article 11(a) of Council Directive 69/335/EEC of 17 July 1969 concerning indirect taxes on the raising of capital, as amended by Council Directive 85/303/EEC of 10 June 1985 (now Council Directive 2008/7/EC) ('the EC Capital Directive') must be interpreted as meaning that it prohibits the levying of a duty such as the charge to SDRT imposed by FA 1986, s. 96 on the issue of shares to a depositary receipt issuer or a clearance service located within the European Union.

[3] From 30 March 2014, the stamp duty reserve tax charge for which fund managers are liable when investors surrender their units in UK unit trust schemes or shares in UK OEICs is abolished. Previously, the charge was at the 0.5% rate. Non pro-rata in specie redemptions remain subject to the principle SDRT charge. (FA 2014, s. 114).

[¶18-050] Stamp duty reserve tax interest

(TMA 1970, s. 86; FA 1986, s. 92 and FA 1989, s. 178)

SDRT carries interest as follows:

- interest is charged on SDRT paid late;
- repayments of SDRT carry interest from the date that SDRT was paid; and
- similarly, SDRT is repaid with interest if an instrument is duly stamped within six years of the date of the agreement.

The same rates apply as for stamp duty – see above.

[¶18-100] Penalties

(FA 2007, Sch. 24)

The same penalties for errors apply to SDRT as apply for SDLT (see ¶16-200).

VALUE ADDED TAX

[¶19-000] Rates

(VATA 1994, s. 2)

(VAT Reporter: ¶18-014)

Period of application	Standard rate %	VAT fraction %	Reduced rate %	VAT fraction %
From 4 January 2011	20	1/6	5.0	1/21
1 January 2010 to 3 January 2011	17.5	7/47	5.0	1/21
1 December 2008 to 31 December 2009	15.0	3/23	5.0	1.21
1 April 1991 to 30 November 2008	17.5	7/47	5.0	1/21

Notes

Supplies of fuel and power for domestic, residential and charity non-business use and certain other supplies are charged at 5% (VATA 1994, Sch. 7A).

Imports of certain works of art, antiques and collectors' items are charged at an effective rate of 5% from 27 July 1999 (VATA 1994, s. 21(4)–(6)).

The zero rate has applied from 1 April 1973 to date.

[¶19-040] Flat-rate scheme

(VATA 1994, s. 26B; SI 1995/2518, reg. 55A–55V; Notice 733; HMRC 'Flat-rate scheme' manual)

(VAT Reporter: ¶55-350)

Generally, the percentage that applies to the flat-rate scheme (FRS) for small firms is cut by 1% for the first year of VAT registration.

Flat-rate percentages applying from 4 January 2011

Category of business	Appropriate percentage		
	From 4 Jan. 2011	1 Jan. 2010 to 3 Jan. 2011	1 Dec. 2008 to 31 Dec. 2009
Accountancy or book-keeping	14.5	13	11.5
Advertising	11	10	8.5
Agricultural services	11	10	7
Any other activity not listed elsewhere	12	10.5	9
Architect, civil and structural engineer or surveyor	14.5	13	11
Boarding or care of animals	12	10.5	9.5
Business services that are not listed elsewhere	12	10.5	9.5
Catering services including restaurants and takeaways	12.5	11	10.5
Computer and IT consultancy or data processing	14.5	13	11.5
Computer repair services	10.5	9.5	10
Dealing in waste or scrap	10.5	9.5	8.5
Entertainment or journalism	12.5	11	9.5
Estate agency or property management services	12	10.5	9.5
Farming or agriculture that is not listed elsewhere	6.5	6	5.5
Film, radio, television or video production	13	11.5	9.5
Financial services	13.5	12	10.5
Forestry or fishing	10.5	9.5	8
General building or construction services(1)	9.5	8.5	7.5
Hairdressing or other beauty treatment services	13	11.5	10.5
Hiring or renting goods	9.5	8.5	7.5
Hotel or accommodation	10.5	9.5	8.5
Investigation or security	12	10.5	9
Labour-only building or construction services(1)	14.5	13	11.5
Laundry or dry-cleaning services	12	10.5	9.5
Lawyer or legal services	14.5	13	12

Category of business	Appropriate percentage		
	From 4 Jan. 2011	1 Jan. 2010 to 3 Jan. 2011	1 Dec. 2008 to 31 Dec. 2009
Library, archive, museum or other cultural activity	9.5	8.5	7.5
Management consultancy	14	12.5	11
Manufacturing fabricated metal products	10.5	9.5	8.5
Manufacturing food	9	8	7
Manufacturing that is not listed elsewhere	9.5	8.5	7.5
Manufacturing yarn, textiles or clothing	9	8	7.5
Membership organisation	8	7	5.5
Mining or quarrying	10	9	8
Packaging	9	8	7.5
Photography	11	10	8.5
Post offices	5	4.5	2
Printing	8.5	7.5	6.5
Publishing	11	10	8.5
Pubs	6.5	6	5.5
Real estate activity not listed elsewhere	14	12.5	11
Repairing personal or household goods	10	9	7.5
Repairing vehicles	8.5	7.5	6.5
Retailing food, confectionary, tobacco, newspapers or children's clothing	4	3.5	2
Retailing pharmaceuticals, medical goods, cosmetics or toiletries	8	7	6
Retailing that is not listed elsewhere	7.5	6.5	5.5
Retailing vehicles or fuel	6.5	6	5.5
Secretarial services	13	11.5	9.5
Social work	11	10	8
Sport or recreation	8.5	7.5	6
Transport or storage, including couriers, freight, removals and taxis	10	9	8
Travel agency	10.5	9.5	8
Veterinary medicine	11	10	8
Wholesaling agricultural products	8	7	5.5
Wholesaling food	7.5	6.5	5
Wholesaling that is not listed elsewhere	8.5	7.5	6

Note

(1) 'Labour-only building or construction services' means building or construction services where the value of materials suppls than 10% of relevant turnover from such services; any other building or construction services are 'general building or construction services'.

Value Added Tax

[¶19-060] Farmer's flat-rate scheme

(VATA 1994, s. 54; SI 1995/2518, reg. 202 ff.; SI 1992/3220; SI 1992/3221; Notice 700/46; HMRC 'VAT – Agricultural flat-rate scheme' manual)

(VAT Reporter: ¶53-500)

The rate which applies to the farmers' flat-rate scheme is 4%.

[¶19-080] Registration limits

(1) Taxable supplies in the UK

(VATA 1994, Sch. 1; Notice 700/1)

(VAT Reporter: ¶43-025)

Period of application	Past turnover 1 year £	Future turnover 30 days £	Unless turnover for next year will not exceed £
From 1/4/14	81,000	81,000	79,000
1/4/13–31/3/14	79,000	79,000	77,000
1/4/12–31/3/13	77,000	77,000	75,000
1/4/11–31/3/12	73,000	73,000	71,000
1/4/10–31/3/11	70,000	70,000	68,000
1/5/09–31/3/10	68,000	68,000	66,000
1/4/08–30/4/09	67,000	67,000	65,000
1/4/07–31/3/08	64,000	64,000	62,000
1/4/06–31/3/07	61,000	61,000	59,000

Notes

Taxable supplies at both the zero rate and positive rates are included in the above limits.

All of a person's taxable supplies are considered, because it is 'persons' not 'businesses' who can or must register. If a person took over a business as a 'going concern', he is deemed to have made the vendor's supplies for the purposes of registration.

These limits are exclusive of VAT, as VAT is not chargeable unless a person is registered or liable to be registered.

The limit which applies for a particular past period is that which is in force at the end of the period.

There are two alternative tests of the liability to notify HMRC of a person's liability to register as a result of making taxable supplies:

(1) past 12 months turnover limit; and

(2) future 30 days turnover limit. Registration is required if there are reasonable grounds for believing that the value of taxable supplies in a period of 30 days will exceed the limit. This limit is the same as that for the past 12 months, but applies to 30 days from any time.

The following are excluded from the supplies for the purpose of applying the registration limits:

(1) the value of capital supplies (other than of land); and

(2) any taxable supplies which would not be taxable supplies apart from VATA 1994, s. 7(4), which concerns removal of goods to the UK.

Any supplies made at a previous time when the person was registered are disregarded if all necessary information was given to HMRC when the earlier registration was cancelled.

(2) Supplies from other member states (distance selling into the UK)

(VATA 1994, Sch. 2; Notice 700/1)

(VAT Reporter: ¶43-030)

Period of application	Cumulative relevant supplies from 1 January in year to any day in same year £
From 1/1/93 (VATA 1994, Sch. 2; Notice 700/1).	70,000

Generally, the value of relevant supplies is of those made by persons in other member states to non-taxable persons in the UK.

If certain goods, which are subject to excise duty, are removed to the UK, the person who removes the goods is liable to register in the UK because all such goods must be taxed in the country of destination. There is no de minimis limit.

(3) Acquisitions from other member states

(VATA 1994, Sch. 3; Notice 700/1)

(VAT Reporter: ¶43-035)

Period of application	Cumulative relevant supplies from 1 January in year to any day in same year £
From 1/4/14	81,000
1/4/13–31/3/14	79,000
1/4/12–31/3/13	77,000
1/4/11–31/3/12	73,000
1/4/10–31/3/11	70,000
1/5/09–31/3/10	68,000
1/4/08–30/4/09	67,000
1/4/07–31/3/08	64,000
1/4/06–31/3/07	61,000

Future prospects rule: a person is also liable to register at any time if there are reasonable grounds for believing that the value of his relevant acquisitions in the period of 30 days then beginning will exceed the given limit. This limit is the same as that for the period starting on 1 January above.

(4) Assets supplied in the UK by overseas persons

(VATA 1994, Sch. 3A; Notice 700/1)

(VAT Reporter: ¶43-045)

From 21 March 2000, any person without an establishment in the UK making or intending to make 'relevant supplies' must VAT register, regardless of the value of those supplies.

'Relevant supplies' are taxable supplies of goods, including capital assets, in the UK where the supplier has recovered UK VAT under:

- Directive 2008/9 for a person in a member state as regards VAT incurred in another member state; or
- Directive 86/560 (the thirteenth VAT directive) for claimants established outside the member states.

This applies where:

- the supplier (or his predecessor in business) was charged VAT on the purchase of the goods, or on anything incorporated in them, and has either claimed it back or intends to do so; or
- the VAT being claimed back was VAT paid on the import of goods into the UK.

(5) Electronic, telecommunication and broadcasting services

(VATA 1994, Sch. 3B and 3BA; Notice 700/1)

(VAT Reporter: ¶43-047)

A person can register if he makes or intends to make qualifying supplies, i.e. electronically supplied services to a person who belongs in the UK or another member state and who receives such services otherwise than for business purposes. The person who registers must have neither a business establishment nor a fixed establishment in the UK or in another member state in relation to any supply. Generally, the person must also be neither registered nor required to be registered for VAT in the UK or the Isle of Man or, under equivalent legislation, in another member state.

Digital services in the EU from 1 January 2015 (VAT MOSS)

From 1 January 2015, there are new place of supply rules for VAT on the supply of digital services by businesses to consumers in the EU. VAT on digital services will be paid in the consumer's country, not the supplier's country. It will be charged at the rate that applies in the consumer's country. Suppliers of digital services to EU consumers can either:

- register for VAT in each EU country; or
- register to use the VAT Mini One Stop Shop (VAT MOSS) online service.

VAT MOSS enables businesses to account for the VAT due on business-to-consumer (B2C) sales in other EU countries by submitting a single quarterly return and payment to HMRC. HMRC will send an electronic copy of the appropriate part of the return, and any payment, to each relevant country's tax authority.

(6) Non-established taxable persons

(VATA 1994, Sch. 1A; Notice 700/1)

(VAT Reporter: ¶43-049)

From 1 December 2012, if a person makes taxable supplies in the UK but has no establishment there, he must register for VAT regardless of the value of such supplies. Thus, non-UK established taxable persons (NETPs) no longer benefit from the UK VAT registration threshold.

A NETP is any person not normally resident in the UK, does not have a UK establishment and, in the case of a company, is not incorporated here.

[¶19-100] De-registration limits

(1) Taxable supplies in the UK

(VATA 1994, Sch. 1; Notice 700/11)

(VAT Reporter: ¶43-925)

Period of application	Future turnover £
From 1/4/14	79,000
1/4/13–31/3/14	77,000
1/4/12–31/3/13	75,000
1/4/11–31/3/12	71,000
1/4/10–31/3/11	68,000
1/5/09–31/3/10	66,000
1/4/08–30/4/09	65,000
1/4/07–31/3/08	62,000
1/4/06–31/3/07	59,000

Notes

A registered person ceases to be liable to be registered if at any time HMRC are satisfied that the value of his taxable supplies in the period of one year then beginning will not exceed the limit.

The value of supplies of capital assets is excluded from the supplies for the purpose of applying the de-registration limits.

The de-registration limits exclude VAT.

Taxable supplies at both the zero rate and positive rates are included in the above limits.

(2) Supplies from other member states (distance selling into the UK)

(VATA 1994, Sch. 2; Notice 700/11)

(VAT Reporter: ¶43-930)

Period of application	Past relevant supplies in last year to 31 December £	Future relevant supplies in immediately following year £
From 1/1/93	70,000	70,000

Generally, the value of supplies is of those made by persons in other member states to non-taxable persons in the UK.

(3) Acquisitions from other member states

(VATA 1994, Sch. 3; Notice 700/11)

(VAT Reporter: ¶43-940)

Period of application	Past relevant acquisitions in last year to 31 December £	Future relevant acquisitions in immediately following year £
From 1/4/14	81,000	81,000
1/4/13–31/3/14	79,000	79,000
1/4/12–31/3/13	77,000	77,000
1/4/11–31/3/12	73,000	73,000
1/4/10–31/3/11	70,000	70,000
1/5/09–31/3/10	68,000	68,000
1/4/08–30/4/09	67,000	67,000
1/4/07–31/3/08	64,000	64,000
1/4/06–31/3/07	61,000	61,000

(4) Assets supplied in the UK by overseas persons

(VATA 1994, Sch. 3A; Notice 700/11)

(VAT Reporter: ¶43-945)

If HMRC are satisfied that a person registered under VATA 1994, Sch. 3A has ceased to make relevant supplies, HMRC can de-register the person from the date on which he so ceased or from an agreed later date. However, HMRC must not de-register a person unless they are satisfied that he is not liable to be registered under another provision in VATA 1994.

(5) Electronic services

(VATA 1994, Sch. 3B and 3BA; Notice 700/11)

(VAT Reporter: ¶43-946)

HMRC cancel a person's registration under VATA 1994, Sch. 3B if he notifies them, or they determine, that he ceased to make, or have the intention of to make, qualifying supplies.

(6) Non-established taxable persons

(VATA 1994, Sch. 1A; Notice 700/11)

(VAT Reporter, ¶43-920)

HMRC may cancel the registration of a non-UK established taxable person (NETP) under VATA 1994, Sch. 1A if they are satisfied that:

(1) the person has ceased to make taxable supplies in the course or furtherance of a business; or

(2) the person is no longer a person in relation to whom condition C in Sch. 1A, para. 1 is met, i.e. the person has a business establishment, or another fixed establishment, in the UK in relation to any business carried on by him.

[¶19-120] Special accounting limits

Cash accounting scheme

(SI 1995/2518, reg. 56–65; Notice 731; HMRC 'VAT – Cash accounting scheme' manual)

(VAT Reporter: ¶55-450)

Period of application	Joining threshold (next 12 months supplies)[(1)] £	Leaving threshold (last 12 months supplies) £
From 1/4/07	1,350,000	1,600,000
1/4/04–31/3/07	660,000	825,000
1/4/01–31/3/04	600,000	750,000

Notes

[(1)] Includes zero-rated supplies, but excludes any capital assets previously used in the business. Exempt supplies are also excluded.

Outstanding VAT on supplies made and received while using the cash accounting scheme may be brought Into account on a cash basis for a further six months after withdrawal from the scheme, but only where withdrawal was voluntary or because the turnover threshold was exceeded.

Annual accounting scheme

(SI 1995/2518, reg. 49–55; Notice 732; HMRC 'VAT – Annual accounting scheme' manual)

(VAT Reporter: ¶55-300)

Period of application	Joining threshold (next 12 months supplies)[(1)] £	Leaving threshold (last 12 months supplies) £
From 1/4/06	1,350,000	1,600,000
1/4/04–31/3/06	660,000	825,000
1/4/01–31/3/04	600,000	750,000

Notes

[(1)] Positive and zero-rated supplies excluding any supplies of capital assets and any exempt supplies.

Persons with a taxable turnover of up to (from 10 April 2003) £150,000 may join the annual accounting scheme immediately, i.e. without having to be registered for at least 12 months.

Flat-rate scheme for small businesses scheme

(SI 1995/2518, reg. 55A–55V; Notice 733; HMRC 'Flat-rate scheme' manual)

(VAT Reporter: ¶55-350)

From 1 April 2009, the only test for eligibility to be admitted to the flat-rate scheme is the taxable turnover of the business, i.e. the £150,000 limit in the second column in the table below.

Period of application	Joining threshold (next 12 months taxable supplies)[1] £	Joining threshold (next 12 months business income)[2] £	Leaving threshold (flat-rate turnover at anniversary or next 30 days)
From 1/4/09	150,000	Test discontinued	230,000
10/4/03–31/3/09	150,000	187,500	225,000
25/4/02–9/4/03	100,000	125,000	150,000

Notes

[1] Zero-rated and positive-rated supplies excluding VAT. Exempt supplies are excluded.

[2] Total of business income excluding VAT.

Net VAT liability is calculated by applying a flat-rate percentage to the VAT-inclusive turnover. The flat-rate percentage depends on the trader sector. However from 1 January 2004, in the first year of VAT registration, the flat-rate percentage can be reduced by 1%, i.e. if the normal rate is 10%, then 9% applies.

If a user of the flat-rate scheme exceeds the annual exit threshold as a result of a one-off transaction, but in the subsequent year he expects his VAT-inclusive annual flat-rate turnover to be under £191,500 (before 4 January 2011: £187,500), he may remain in the scheme with HMRC's agreement (SI 1995/2518, Pt. VIIA; Notice 733).

[¶19-140] Zero-rated supplies

(VATA 1994, Sch. 8)

(VAT Reporter: ¶20-000)

A zero-rated supply is a taxable supply, but the tax rate is nil.

Group	
1.	Food (this includes most food for human and animal consumption – the exceptions are mainly food supplied in the course of catering, confectionary, pet foods and hot take-away food)[1][2]
2.	Sewerage services and water (except distilled and bottled water) but not if supplied to industry
3.	Books, pamphlets, newspapers, journals, maps, music, etc. (but not stationery and posters)
4.	Talking books for the blind and handicapped and wireless sets for the blind
5.	Construction of buildings, etc.
6.	Protected buildings[3]
7.	International services
8.	Transport
9.	Caravans and houseboats[4]
10.	Gold
11.	Bank notes
12.	Drugs, medicines, aids for the handicapped, etc.
13.	Imports, exports, etc.
14.	(repealed for supplies made after 30 June 1999) Tax-free shops
15.	Charities, etc.

Group	
16.	Clothing and footwear
17.	(for supplies made after 30 July 2009, but repealed for supplies made after 31 October 2010 when the reverse charge applies) Emissions allowances
18.	European Research Infrastructure Consortia (ERIC; from 1 January 2013)

Notes

Except for exported goods and certain transactions in commodities, generally a supply is not zero-rated *unless* it is specified in the zero-rated schedule (VATA 1994, Sch. 8). A supply which can be classified as zero-rated overrides exemption. A supply which is not outside the scope of VAT is standard-rated *unless* it falls within one of the categories of exempt or zero-rated or reduced-rate supplies.

(1) From 1 October 2012, food which is hot at the point of sale is standard-rated.

(2) From 1 October 2012, a new category of excepted items is inserted: 'Sports drinks for nutirition' in order to confirm standard-rating applies.

(3) From 1 October 2015, alterations of listed buildings are omitted from the list bringing their VAT treatment in line with other non listed buildings and repairs and maintenance for all buildings which are standard-rated.

(4) From 6 April 2013, criteria for zero-rating is amended to ensure 'holiday' caravans are consistently either standard-rated (tourers) or subject to the reduced rate of VAT (static, non-residential).

Value Added Tax

[¶19-160] Exempt supplies

(VATA 1994, Sch. 9)

(VAT Reporter: ¶27-000)

No VAT is chargeable on an exempt supply, but input tax cannot be reclaimed except as computed under the provisions on partial exemption.

Group	
1.	Land[1]
2.	Insurance
3.	Postal services (restricted after 30 January 2011 to supplies of public postal services and incidental goods made by the universal service provider)
4.	Betting, gaming, dutiable machine games and lotteries
5.	Finance
6.	Education
7.	Health and welfare
8.	Burial and cremation
9.	Subscriptions to trade unions, professional bodies and other public interest bodies
10.	Sport, sports competitions and physical education
11.	Works of art, etc.
12.	Fund-raising events by charities and other qualifying bodies
13.	Cultural services, etc.

Group	
14.	Supplies of goods where input tax cannot be recovered (from 1 March 2000)
15.	Investment gold (from 1 January 2000)
16.	Supplies of services by groups involving cost sharing (from 17 July 2012)

Notes

The descriptions of the zero-rated and exempt groups are for ease of reference only and do not affect the interpretation of the groups (VATA 1994, s. 96(10)). Some suppliers can unilaterally opt to tax certain land and buildings (VATA 1994, Sch. 10, para. 2–4).

(1) From 1 October 2012, self-storage facilities and rental of hairdressers' chairs are excluded from the exemption for land in order to confirm standard-rating applies.

[¶19-180] Reduced-rate supplies

(VATA 1994, Sch. 7A)

(VAT Reporter: ¶32-000)

VAT is chargeable at 5% on a reduced-rated supply

Group	
1.	Domestic fuel and power
2.	Installation of energy-saving materials
3.	Grant-funded installation of heating equipment or security goods or connection of gas supply.
4.	Women's sanitary products
5.	Children's car seats
6.	Residential conversions
7.	Residential renovations and alterations
8.	Contraceptive products (from 1 July 2006)
9.	Welfare advice or information (from 1 July 2006)
10.	Installation of mobility aids for the elderly (from 1 July 2007)
11.	Smoking cessation products (from 1 July 2007)
12.	Caravans (from 6 April 2013)
13.	Cable-suspended passenger transport systems (from 1 April 2013)

Notes

(1) The 'Listed Places of Worship Grants Scheme', which is administered by the Department for Culture, Media and Sport (DCMS), effectively leaves a listed place of worship bearing VAT at 5% on repairs by funding the difference between VAT at 5% and at the standard rate. This runs along with the scheme for UK charities which refunds the VAT charged on qualifying supplies made after 15 March 2005 in the construction, renovation and maintenance of certain memorials.

(2) From 6 April 2013, Group 12 'Caravans' is added to the list in VATA 1994, Sch. 7A by way of re-categorisation of 'holiday' (static, non-residential) caravans previously treated as zero-rated.

[¶19-200] Partial exemption

(SI 1995/2518, reg. 99–111; Notice 706; HMRC 'Partial exemption' manual)

(VAT Reporter: ¶19-400)

The law on partial exemption may restrict the amount of deductible input tax.

Where input tax cannot be attributed directly to taxable or exempt supplies (residual input tax), the standard method apportions the residual input tax according to the values of taxable and exempt supplies made in a period. In relation to input tax incurred after 17 April 2002, persons must adjust the input tax deductible under the standard method at the end of their tax year if that amount is substantially different from an attribution based on the use of purchases. 'Substantially' means in excess of:

- £50,000; or
- 50% or more of the value of the residual input tax and £25,000.

Where the residual input tax is less than £50,000 per year, the standard method can be used, unless the person is defined as a group undertaking under the Companies Acts and the residual input tax is greater than £25,000 per year.

Generally, the established de minimis limit for applying the partial exemption rules is as follows:

Period	Exempt input tax not exceeding
Tax years beginning after 30/11/94	• £625 per month on average; and • 50% of total input tax for prescribed accounting period

In order to establish whether the de minimis limit has been breached, for partial exemption years starting after 31 March 2010, some taxable persons need only carry out simplified tests, rather than carry out detailed partial exemption calculations. The simplest test is whether total input tax incurred by a taxable person is less than £625 per month on average. If so, as long as 50% or less of the turnover is exempt, the de minimis test is passed. If that test is failed, the next simplified test is to strip out all input tax that is directly and solely attributable to taxable supplies. If the remainder is less than £625 per month on average then, as long as the value of exempt supplies does not exceed one-half of the value of all supplies, the de minimis test is passed.

For accounting periods commencing after 31 March 2005, rounding up the recovery rate under the standard method to the next whole number is only allowed for persons incurring no more than £400,000 residual input tax per month on average. Other persons round to two decimal places.

HMRC's approval of a partial exemption special method from 1 April 2007 is subject to a declaration by the taxable person that to the best of his knowledge and belief the intended method is fair and reasonable.

[¶19-220] Capital goods scheme

(SI 1995/2518, reg. 112–116; Notice 706/2)

(VAT Reporter: ¶19-800)

The capital goods scheme affects the acquisition, etc. by a partially exempt person for use in a business of certain items as follows:

Item	Value	Adjustment period
Computers and computer equipment	£50,000 or more	Five years
Land and buildings	£250,000 or more	Ten years (five years where interest had less than ten years to run on acquisition)
Aircraft, ships, boats and other vessels (from 1 January 2011)	£50,000 or more	Five years

Where the capital goods scheme applies, any initial deduction of input tax is made in the ordinary way, but must then be reviewed over the adjustment period by reference to the use of the asset concerned.

[¶19-240] Particulars to be shown on a valid VAT invoice

(SI 1995/2518, reg. 14; Notice 700, para. 16.3ff. (August 2013))

(VAT Reporter: ¶55-800)

VAT invoices generally where supplied to a person who is also in the UK

VAT invoices must show:

- a sequential number based on one or more series which uniquely identifies the document;
- the time of supply (tax point);
- date of issue of the document (where different to the time of supply);
- trader's name, address and VAT registration number;
- customer's name and address;
- a description which identifies the goods or services supplied.

- for each **description**, the quantity of the goods or the extent of the services, and the rate of VAT and the amount payable, excluding VAT, expressed in any currency;
- the gross total amount payable, excluding VAT, expressed in any currency;
- the rate of any cash discount offered;
- the total amount of VAT chargeable, expressed in sterling;
- the unit price;
- the reason for any zero rate or exemption.

The final bullet point refers to the following types of supply:

- supplies subject to a second-hand margin scheme;
- supplies subject to the Tour Operators Margin Scheme (TOMS)
- intra-EC exempt supplies;
- intra-EC reverse charge supplies; and
- intra-EC zero-rated supplies.

Generally, VAT officers adopt a 'light touch' for about one year after any change to the requirements for a valid VAT invoice in order to give reasonable time to change procedures and help minimise the cost of change.

Persons providing VAT invoices for leasing certain motor cars must state on the invoice whether the car is a qualifying vehicle. This enables the lessee to claim the correct proportion of the VAT charged by the lessor.

The requirements for invoices concerning supplies intra-EU member states are in the *Value Added Tax Regulations* 1995 (SI 1995/2518, reg. 14(2)).

Also, a VAT invoice must be provided for an exempt supply made to a person in another member state for the purposes of that person's business.

Less detailed VAT and modified VAT invoices

For retail sales, a VAT invoice must be provided if the customer asks for one. However, it may be possible to issue a less detailed or modified VAT invoice as follows, otherwise a full VAT invoice must be issued:

Value of charge made for individual sale	**Less detailed invoice requirements**
is **£250 or less** (including VAT)	• name of supplier, address and VAT registration number; • the time of supply (tax point); • a description which identifies the goods or services supplied; • and for each VAT rate applicable, the total amount payable, including VAT and the VAT rate charged. Exempt supplies must not be included in this type of VAT invoice. To work out the amount of VAT in a VAT-inclusive price, multiply the sale price by the VAT fraction.
exceeds £250 and you are asked for a VAT invoice	must issue either a: • full VAT invoice; or • modified VAT invoice (see below).

Credit card sales

Where credit cards, such as Visa/Mastercard or Barclaycard, are accepted, the sales voucher given to the cardholder at the time of the sale may be adapted to serve as a less detailed VAT invoice.

Requirements
The credit card voucher should show: • retailer's name and address; • the charge made, including VAT; and • the date of sale.
Additional requirements: • VAT registration number; • rate of VAT; and • a description of the goods or services supplied.

Modified VAT invoice

Can be issued provided the customer agrees.

Requirements
• the VAT-inclusive value of each standard-rated or reduced-rated supply (instead of the VAT-exclusive values).
At the foot of the invoice, separate totals must be shown of: • VAT-inclusive value of the standard-rated or reduced rate supplies; • VAT payable on those supplies shown in sterling; • value, excluding VAT, of those supplies; • value of any zero-rated supplies included on the invoice; and • value of any exempt supplies included on the invoice.
In all other respects the invoice should show the details required for a full VAT invoice.

See Notice 700, for the rules on invoices concerning:

- petrol, derv, paraffin, and heating oil;
- credit cards;
- another form of modified VAT invoice for retailers;
- cash and carry wholesalers;
- computer invoicing; and
- calculation of VAT on invoices.

Continuous supplies of services

Certain additional particulars are required to be shown on a VAT invoice for a supply of continuous services, if the supplier chooses to use the advance invoicing facility (SI 1995/2518, reg. 90). Similar provisions apply for advance invoicing in respect of long leases (reg. 85) and in respect of supplies of water, gas, power, heat, refrigeration and ventilation (reg. 86).

[¶19-260] 'Blocked' input tax

(VATA 1994, s. 24)

(VAT Reporter: ¶19-004)

Any input tax charged on the following items is generally 'blocked', i.e. non-recoverable:

- motor cars, but (1) any person can recover input tax on motor cars used exclusively for business and (2) only 50% of VAT on car leasing charges is recoverable if lessee makes any private use of the car and if lessor recovered the VAT on buying the car;
- entertainment, except of employees. However, if there is a strict business purpose and if it is necessary for the business to make supplies, input tax is recoverable as regards entertaining overseas customers (HMRC Brief 44/2010 (2 November 2010));
- in the case of claims by builders, articles of a kind not ordinarily installed by builders as fixtures in new houses;
- goods supplied under the second-hand scheme;
- goods imported for private purposes;
- non-business element of supplies to be used only partly for business purposes. VAT incurred on supplies not intended for business use generally does not rank as input tax, so cannot be recovered. *Lennartz* accounting starting before 1 January 2011 should run its course. Generally, *Lennartz* accounting does not apply to VAT incurred after 31 December 2010; and
- goods and services acquired by a tour operator for re-supply as a designated travel service.

'Exempt input tax' is generally not recoverable by a partially exempt person.

[¶19-280] Input tax and mileage allowances (advisory fuel rates)

(SI 2005/3290)

(VAT Reporter: ¶19-071)

An employer can reclaim the VAT incurred by employees on fuel costs that are reimbursed by the employer on the basis of cost or via a mileage allowance. VAT can only be reclaimed by an employer on fuel which is used in the course of the business to make taxable supplies. However, the key practical change is that employers must obtain and retain a valid VAT invoice to support the reclaim. Generally, a retailer's invoice (also known as a 'less-detailed invoice') should suffice, because the amount of fuel that is purchased by an employee in a single supply is likely to be within the VAT-inclusive limit of £250 for a retailer's invoice.

Generally, the invoiced amount does not match the input tax claim for the fuel in any one claim period and invoices may concern more than one period. For example, if fuel is purchased towards the end of a period, it may not be fully used until a subsequent period. An invoice may cover more than one claim and this needs to be taken into account when checking the evidence to support claims. Another possible reason why the invoiced amount does not match the claim is that often some of the fuel is used by the employee for private journeys. Generally, the VAT can be reclaimed if the invoice(s) are for sufficient fuel to cover the claimed mileage, and cover the relevant period. Strictly, a claim cannot be supported by an invoice that is dated after the dates covered by the claim.

HMRC publish 'advisory fuel rates' to determine the business fuel cost, but rates set by recognised motoring agencies, such as the RAC and the AA, are usually acceptable. HMRC first published the rates in 2002 (www.hmrc.gov.uk/cars/fuel_company_cars.htm).

Transition to revised 'advisory fuel rate': one-month rule

For one month from the date of change, employers may use either the previous or new current rates, as they choose.

Engine size	Rate per mile		
	Petrol	Diesel	LPG
For journeys from 1 December 2014			
1400cc or less	13p	11p	9p
1401cc to 1600cc	16p	11p	11p
1601cc to 2000cc	16p	13p	11p
Over 2000cc	23p	16p	16p
For journeys from 1 September 2014			
1400cc or less	14p	11p	9p
1401cc to 1600cc	16p	11p	11p
1601cc to 2000cc	16p	13p	11p
Over 2000cc	24p	17p	16p
For journeys from 1 June 2014			
1400cc or less	14p	12p	9p
1401cc to 1600cc	16p	12p	11p
1601cc to 2000cc	16p	14p	11p
Over 2000cc	24p	17p	16p
For journeys from 1 March 2014			
1400cc or less	14p	12p	9p
1401cc to 1600cc	16p	12p	11p
1601cc to 2000cc	16p	14p	11p
Over 2000cc	24p	17p	17p
For journeys from 1 December 2013			
1400cc or less	14p	12p	9p
1401cc to 1600cc	16p	12p	11p
1601cc to 2000cc	16p	14p	11p
Over 2000cc	24p	17p	16p

Engine size	Rate per mile		
	Petrol	Diesel	LPG
For journeys from 1 September 2013			
1400cc or less	15p	12p	10p
1401cc to 1600cc	18p	12p	11p
1601cc to 2000cc	18p	15p	11p
Over 2000cc	26p	18p	16p
For journeys from 1 June 2013			
1400cc or less	15p	12p	10p
1401cc to 1600cc	17p	12p	12p
1601cc to 2000cc	17p	14p	12p
Over 2000cc	25p	18p	18p
For journeys from 1 March 2013			
1400cc or less	15p	13p	10p
1401cc to 1600cc	18p	13p	12p
1601cc to 2000cc	18p	15p	12p
Over 2000cc	26p	18p	18p
For journeys from 1 December 2012			
1400cc or less	15p	12p	11p
1401cc to 1600cc	18p	12p	13p
1601cc to 2000cc	18p	15p	13p
Over 2000cc	26p	18p	18p
For journeys from 1 September 2012			
1400cc or less	15p	12p	10p
1400cc to 1600cc	18p	12p	13p
1600cc to 2000cc	18p	15p	13p
Over 2000cc	26p	18p	17p
For journeys from 1 June 2012			
1400cc or less	15p	12p	11p
1400cc to 1600cc	18p	12p	13p
1600cc to 2000cc	18p	15p	13p
Over 2000cc	26p	18p	19p
For journeys from 1 March 2012			
1400cc or less	15p	13p	10p
1401cc to 1600cc	18p	13p	12p
1601cc to 2000cc	18p	15p	12p
Over 2000cc	26p	19p	18p

Engine size	Rate per mile		
	Petrol	Diesel	LPG
For journeys from 1 December 2011			
1400cc or less	15p	12p	10p
1401cc to 1600cc	18p	12p	12p
1601cc to 2000cc	18p	15p	12p
Over 2000cc	26p	18p	18p
For journeys from 1 September 2011			
1400cc or less	15p	12p	11p
1401cc to 1600cc	18p	12p	12p
1601cc to 2000cc	18p	15p	12p
Over 2000cc	26p	18p	18p
For journeys from 1 June 2011			
1400cc or less	15p	12p	11p
1401cc to 1600cc	18p	12p	13p
1601cc to 2000cc	18p	15p	13p
Over 2000cc	26p	18p	18p
For journeys from 1 March 2011			
1400cc or less	14p	13p	10p
1401cc to 2000cc	16p	13p	12p
Over 2000cc	23p	16p	17p

[¶19-300] VAT on private fuel (scale charges)

(VATA 1994, Sch. 6, para. B1; SI 2013/2911; Notice 700/64)

(VAT Reporter: ¶18-320ff.)

From 1 May 2014

Fuel scale charges for the 12-month period

CO_2 band	VAT fuel scale charge 12-month period £	VAT on 12-month charge £	VAT exclusive 12-month charge £
120 or less	627.00	104.50	522.50
125	939.00	156.50	782.50
130	1,004.00	167.33	836.67
135	1,064.00	177.33	886.67

CO_2 band	VAT fuel scale charge 12-month period £	VAT on 12-month charge £	VAT exclusive 12-month charge £
140	1,129.00	188.17	940.83
145	1,190.00	198.33	991.67
150	1,255.00	209.17	1,045.83
155	1,315.00	219.17	1,095.83
160	1,381.00	230.17	1,150.83
165	1,441.00	240.17	1,200.83
170	1,506.00	251.00	1,255.00
175	1,567.00	261.17	1,305.83
180	1,632.00	272.00	1,360.00
185	1,692.00	282.00	1,410.00
190	1,757.00	292.83	1,464.17
195	1,818.00	303.00	1,515.00
200	1,883.00	313.83	1,569.17
205	1,943.00	323.83	1,619.17
210	2,008.00	334.67	1,673.33
215	2,069.00	344.83	1,724.17
220	2,134.00	355.67	1,778.33
225 or more	2,194.00	365.67	1,828.33

Fuel scale charges for the 3-month period

CO_2 band	VAT fuel scale charge 3-month period £	VAT on 3-month charge £	VAT exclusive 3-month charge £
120 or less	156.00	26.00	130.00
125	234.00	39.00	195.00
130	251.00	41.83	209.17
135	266.00	44.33	221.67
140	282.00	47.00	235.00
145	297.00	49.50	247.50
150	313.00	52.17	260.83
155	328.00	54.67	273.33
160	345.00	57.50	287.50
165	360.00	60.00	300.00
170	376.00	62.67	313.33

CO_2 band	VAT fuel scale charge 3-month period £	VAT on 3-month charge £	VAT exclusive 3-month charge £
175	391.00	65.17	325.83
180	408.00	68.00	340.00
185	423.00	70.50	352.50
190	439.00	73.17	365.83
195	454.00	75.67	378.33
200	470.00	78.33	391.67
205	485.00	80.83	404.17
210	502.00	83.67	418.33
215	517.00	86.17	430.83
220	533.00	88.83	444.17
225 or more	548.00	91.33	456.67

Fuel scale charges for the 1-month period

CO_2 band	VAT fuel scale charge 1-month period £	VAT on 1-month charge £	VAT exclusive 1-month charge £
120 or less	52.00	8.67	43.33
125	78.00	13.00	65.00
130	83.00	13.83	69.17
135	88.00	14.67	73.33
140	94.00	15.67	78.33
145	99.00	16.50	82.50
150	104.00	17.33	86.67
155	109.00	18.17	90.83
160	115.00	19.17	95.83
165	120.00	20.00	100.00
170	125.00	20.83	104.17
175	130.00	21.67	108.33
180	136.00	22.67	113.33
185	141.00	23.50	117.50
190	146.00	24.33	121.67
195	151.00	25.17	125.83

CO_2 band	VAT fuel scale charge 1-month period £	VAT on 1-month charge £	VAT exclusive 1-month charge £
200	156.00	26.00	130.00
205	161.00	26.83	134.17
210	167.00	27.83	139.17
215	172.00	28.67	143.33
220	177.00	29.50	147.50
225 or more	182.00	30.33	151.67

1 May 2013 to 30 April 2014

Fuel scale charges for the 12-month period

CO_2 band	VAT fuel scale charge 12-month period £	VAT on 12-month charge £	VAT exclusive 12-month charge £
120 or less	675.00	112.50	562.50
125	1,010.00	168.33	841.67
130	1,080.00	180.00	900.00
135	1,145.00	190.83	954.17
140	1,215.00	202.50	1,012.50
145	1,280.00	213.33	1,066.67
150	1,350.00	225.00	1,125.00
155	1,415.00	235.83	1,179.17
160	1,485.00	247.50	1,237.50
165	1,550.00	258.33	1,291.67
170	1,620.00	270.00	1,350.00
175	1,685.00	280.83	1,404.17
180	1,755.00	292.50	1,462.50
185	1,820.00	303.33	1,516.67
190	1,890.00	315.00	1,575.00
195	1,955.00	325.83	1,629.17
200	2,025.00	337.50	1,687.50
205	2,090.00	348.33	1,741.67
210	2,160.00	360.00	1,800.00
215	2,225.00	370.83	1,854.17
220	2,295.00	382.50	1,912.50
225 or more	2,360.00	393.33	1,966.67

Fuel scale charges for the 3-month period

CO_2 band	VAT fuel scale charge 3-month period £	VAT on 3-month charge £	VAT exclusive 3-month charge £
120 or less	168.00	28.00	140.00
125	253.00	42.17	210.83
130	269.00	44.83	224.17
135	286.00	47.67	238.33
140	303.00	50.50	252.50
145	320.00	53.33	266.67
150	337.00	56.17	280.83
155	354.00	59.00	295.00
160	371.00	61.83	309.17
165	388.00	64.67	323.33
170	404.00	67.33	336.67
175	421.00	70.17	350.83
180	438.00	73.00	365.00
185	455.00	75.83	379.17
190	472.00	78.67	393.33
195	489.00	81.50	407.50
200	506.00	84.33	421.67
205	523.00	87.17	435.83
210	539.00	89.83	449.17
215	556.00	92.67	463.33
220	573.00	95.50	477.50
225 or more	590.00	98.33	491.67

Fuel scale charges for the 1-month period

CO_2 band	VAT fuel scale charge 1-month period £	VAT on 1-month charge £	VAT exclusive 1-month charge £
120 or less	56.00	9.33	46.67
125	84.00	14.00	70.00
130	89.00	14.83	74.17
135	95.00	15.83	79.17
140	101.00	16.83	84.17
145	106.00	17.67	88.33
150	112.00	18.67	93.33

CO_2 band	VAT fuel scale charge 1-month period £	VAT on 1-month charge £	VAT exclusive 1-month charge £
155	118.00	19.67	98.33
160	123.00	20.50	102.50
165	129.00	21.50	107.50
170	134.00	22.33	111.67
175	140.00	23.33	116.67
180	146.00	24.33	121.67
185	151.00	25.17	125.83
190	157.00	26.17	130.83
195	163.00	27.17	135.83
200	168.00	28.00	140.00
205	174.00	29.00	145.00
210	179.00	29.83	149.17
215	185.00	30.83	154.17
220	191.00	31.83	159.17
225 or more	196.00	32.67	163.33

1 May 2012 – 30 April 2013

Fuel scale charges for 12-month period

CO_2 band	VAT fuel scale charge, 12-month period £	VAT on 12-month charge £	VAT exclusive 12-month charge £
120 or less	665	110.83	554.17
125	1,000	166.67	833.33
130	1,065	177.50	887.50
135	1,135	189.17	945.83
140	1,200	200.00	1,000.00
145	1,270	211.67	1,058.33
150	1,335	222.50	1,112.50
155	1,400	233.33	1,166.67
160	1,470	245.00	1,225.00
165	1,535	255.83	1,279.17
170	1,600	266.67	1,333.33
175	1670	278.33	1,391.67
180	1,735	289.17	1,445.83
185	1,800	300.00	1,500.00

CO_2 band	VAT fuel scale charge, 12-month period £	VAT on 12-month charge £	VAT exclusive 12-month charge £
190	1,870	311.67	1,558.33
195	1,935	322.50	1,612.50
200	2,000	333.33	1,666.67
205	2,070	345.00	1,725.00
210	2,135	355.83	1,779.17
215	2,200	366.67	1,833.33
220	2,270	378.33	1,891.67
225 or more	2,335	389.17	1,945.83

Fuel scale charges for 3-month period

CO_2 band	VAT fuel scale charge, 3-month period £	VAT on 3-month charge £	VAT exclusive 3-month charge £
120 or less	166	27.67	138.33
125	250	41.67	208.33
130	266	44.33	221.67
135	283	47.17	235.83
140	300	50.00	250.00
145	316	52.67	263.33
150	333	55.50	277.50
155	350	58.33	291.67
160	366	61.00	305.00
165	383	63.83	319.17
170	400	66.67	333.33
175	416	69.33	346.67
180	433	72.17	360.83
185	450	75.00	375.00
190	467	77.83	389.17
195	483	80.50	402.50
200	500	83.33	416.67
205	517	86.17	430.83

CO_2 band	VAT fuel scale charge, 3-month period £	VAT on 3-month charge £	VAT exclusive 3-month charge £
210	533	88.83	444.17
215	550	91.67	458.33
220	567	94.50	472.50
225 or more	583	97.17	485.83

Fuel scale charges for 1-month period

CO_2 band	VAT fuel scale charge, 1-month period £	VAT on 1-month charge £	VAT exclusive 1-month charge £
120 or less	55	9.17	45.83
125	83	13.83	69.17
130	88	14.67	73.33
135	94	15.67	78.33
140	100	16.67	83.33
145	105	17.50	87.50
150	111	18.50	92.50
155	116	19.33	96.67
160	122	20.33	101.67
165	127	21.17	105.83
170	133	22.17	110.83
175	138	23.00	115.00
180	144	24.00	120.00
185	150	25.00	125.00
190	155	25.83	129.17
195	161	26.83	134.17
200	166	27.67	138.33
205	172	28.67	143.33
210	177	29.50	147.50
215	183	30.50	152.50
220	189	31.50	157.50
225 or more	194	32.33	161.67

[¶19-320] VAT publications having legal force

(VAT Reporter: ¶4-200)

Certain VAT publications that have legal force in whole or part are listed in Notice 747.

[¶19-340] VAT registration numbers: country code prefix

(SI 1995/2518, reg. 2(1); Notice 725, para. 16.19 (October 2012))

(VAT Reporter: ¶63-160)

Certain invoices should show the invoicer's registration number prefixed by the country code (also known as the alphabetical code).

Member state	Country code
Austria	AT
Belgium	BE
Bulgaria(2)	BG
Croatia(3)	HR
Cyprus(1)	CY
Czech Republic(1)	CZ
Denmark	DK
Estonia(1)	EE
Finland	FI
France	FR
Germany	DE
Greece	EL
Hungary(1)	HU
Ireland	IE
Italy	IT
Latvia(1)	LV
Lithuania(1)	LT
Luxembourg	LU
Malta(1)	MT
Netherlands	NL
Poland(1)	PL
Portugal	PT
Romania(2)	RO
Slovakia(1)	SK
Slovenia(1)	SI

Member state	Country code
Spain	ES
Sweden	SE
United Kingdom	GB

(1) This country joined the European Union on 1 May 2004.
(2) Bulgaria and Romania joined the EU on 1 January 2007.
(3) Croatia joined the EU on 1 July 2013.

[¶19-344] Territory of the EU

(Directive 2006/112, art. 5; Notice 60, para. 2.5; Notice 725, para. 2.4; Notice 741A, para. 21)

Member states
The territory of the EU for VAT purposes consists of the following member states: (1) Austria (including Jungholtz and Mittelberg); (2) Belgium; (3) Bulgaria (from 1 January 2007); (4) Croatia (from 1 July 2013); (5) Cyprus (from 1 May 2004, including the British Sovereign Base Areas of Akrotiri and Dhekelia); (6) Czech Republic (from 1 May 2004); (7) Denmark; (8) Estonia (from 1 May 2004); (9) Finland; (10) France (including Monaco); (11) Germany; (12) Greece; (13) Hungary (from 1 May 2004); (14) Ireland (the Republic of) (also known as Eire); (15) Italy; (16) Latvia (from 1 May 2004); (17) Lithuania (from 1 May 2004); (18) Luxembourg; (19) Malta (from 1 May 2004); (20) Netherlands (also known as Holland); (21) Poland (from 1 May 2004);

Value Added Tax

Member states	
(22)	Portugal (including the Azores and Madeira);
(23)	Romania (from 1 January 2007);
(24)	Slovakia (from 1 May 2004);
(25)	Slovenia (from 1 May 2004);
(26)	Spain (including the Balearic Islands);
(27)	Sweden; and
(28)	UK (including the Isle of Man).

Excluded territories

The following territories of member states are excluded from the 'territory of the country':

(1) re Cyprus: the United Nations buffer zone and the part of Cyprus to the north of the buffer zone where the Republic of Cyprus does not exercise effective control;

(2) re Denmark: the Faroe Islands and Greenland;

(3) re Finland: the Åland Islands;

(4) re France: Guadeloupe, French Guiana, Martinique, Mayotte, Réunion and Saint-Martin (French Republic);

(5) re Germany:
- (a) the Island of Heligoland; and
- (b) Büsingen,

(6) re Greece: Mount Athos (also known as Agion Oros);

(7) re Italy:
- (a) Campione d'Italia; and
- (b) the Italian waters of Lake Lugano and Livigno;

(8) re Netherlands: Antilles.

(9) re Spain:
- (a) the Canary Islands
- (b) Ceuta; and
- (c) Melilla; and

(10) re UK:
- (a) the Channel Islands; and
- (b) Gibraltar.

Included areas: Monaco and the Isle of Man

Monaco and the Isle of Man are not treated as 'third territories'. They are part of France and the UK respectively. Thus, transactions originating in or intended for:

(1) Monaco are treated as transactions originating in or intended for France; and

(2) the Isle of Man are treated as transactions originating in or intended for the UK.

Areas not within the EU

Andorra, San Marino, the Vatican City and Liechtenstein are not within the EU for VAT purposes.

[¶19-400] EC Sales List (ESL)

(SI 1995/2518, reg. 21–23)

(VAT Reporter: ¶64-800ff.)

VAT-registered businesses in the UK supplying goods and services to VAT-registered customers in another EU country must tell HMRC about those supplies using an EC Sales list. An EC sales list reports:

- details of each EU customer;
- the sterling value of supplies made to them; and
- the customer's country code.

Reporting of supplies to VAT-registered customers in other EU countries

Supplies of:	Value	Frequency
Goods	Over £35,000 threshold in current or four previous quarters	Monthly
Goods	Under £35,000 threshold in the current or previous four quarters	Quarterly
Services subject to reverse charge in customer's country	N/A	Quarterly (but monthly returns optional)
Goods and services where required to send monthly lists for goods	N/A	Monthly for all supplies or monthly for goods, and quarterly for services
Goods or services by traders submitting annual VAT returns	• taxable turnover does not exceed £145,000 • annual value of supplies to other EU countries is not more than £11,000 • sales do not include New Means of Transport	Annually (subject to application and approval by HMRC)
Goods only (not services)	• taxable turnover does not exceed £93,500 • supplies £11,000 or less • supplies exclude New Means of transport	Annually (subject to application and approval by HMRC)

ESL deadlines

Submission	Due date (following end of period)
Paper	Within 14 days
Electronic	Within 21 days

[¶19-450] Intrastat

(SI 1992/2790)

(VAT Reporter: ¶64-600)

All VAT-registered businesses show the total value of goods dispatched to other EU member states in box 8 and the total arrivals of goods acquired from other EU member states in box 9 of their VAT Return. In addition, those who trade in the EU above the Intrastat exemption threshold in force during the year must also complete a monthly Supplementary Declaration (SD). Larger businesses that trade above the Intrastat delivery terms threshold must also specify delivery terms information on their Supplementary Declarations. The table below shows recent thresholds:

Period	Acquisitions (Arrivals) £	Supplies (Dispatches) £	Delivery terms £
From 1 January 2014	1,200,000	250,000	24,000,000
From 1 January 2010	600,000	250,000	16,000,000
From 1 January 2009	270,000	270,000	16,000,000

Intrastat deadlines

Monthly submission	Due date (following end of period)
Online (only)	by 21st day following

Administration

[¶19-500] Civil penalties

(Notices 700/41 (Late registration penalty) and 700/50 (Default surcharge); HMRC 'Compliance handbook' manual; HMRC 'VAT – Civil penalties' manual)

(VAT Reporter: ¶59-600ff.)

Offence	Civil penalty
• **Dishonest conduct by a tax agent** (FA 2012, Sch. 38 from 1 April 2013)	• no less than £5,000; • no more than £50,000; • but the penalty may be reduced below £5,000 if there are special circumstances; • also HMRC may publish certain information about the tax agent if the penalty is more than £5,000.
• Failure of a data-holder to comply with a notice requiring **data to be provided to HMRC** (FA 2011, Sch. 23, Pt. 4 from 1 April 2012) • Inaccurate data provided	• a fixed penalty of £300 for the failure; • if the assessment of the £300 penalty has been notified, a further penalty of £60 for each subsequent day of default. If HMRC apply, the tribunal may increase the daily default penalty to £1,000 for each applicable day; • £3,000 if inaccurate data is provided.
• Failure of a company to notify HMRC of the name of its **senior accounting officer** for a financial year beginning after 20 July 2009 (FA 2009, s. 93 and Sch. 46, para. 7)	Penalty of £5,000
• Failure of a senior accounting officer (1) to take reasonable steps to ensure that the company establishes and maintains **appropriate tax accounting arrangements** or (2) to provide an accurate **certificate** to HMRC (FA 2009, s. 93 and Sch. 46, para. 4 and 5 in relation to financial years beginning after 20 July 2009)	Penalty of £5,000
• Failure of a third party to comply with a notice from HMRC requiring **contact details for a debtor** for the purpose of collecting VAT (FA 2009, Sch. 49, para. 5)	Penalty of £300
• Failure to make **quarterly returns** on time (FA 2009, Sch. 55 from a date **to be appointed** to replace the default surcharge)	• a fixed £100 penalty that escalates by £100 for each subsequent failure up to a maximum of £400 per failure; • a penalty of 5% of tax or £300 if greater at six and 12 months from the date of the failure • a penalty of up to 100% of tax or £300 if greater if, by failing to make the return, the taxpayer is deliberately withholding information to stop HMRC correctly assessing

<table>
<tr><th>Offence</th><th>Civil penalty</th></tr>
<tr><td>• Failure to make quarterly payments on time (FA 2009, Sch. 56 from a date to be appointed to replace the default surcharge)</td><td>• a penalty of 2% of the unpaid tax for a second failure during a penalty period;
• a penalty of 3% of the unpaid tax for a third failure during a penalty period with further failures attracting a maximum penalty of 4%;
• if any of the failures are prolonged, additional penalties of 5% of the unpaid tax are charged at six and 12 months from the date of the failure</td></tr>
<tr><td>• Deliberately obstructing an officer in the course of an inspection that has been pre-approved by the Tribunal</td><td>• a fixed £300 penalty (FA 2008, Sch. 36, para. 39); and
• daily penalties of up to £60 for continuing default (Sch. 36, para. 40)</td></tr>
<tr><td>• Failure to notify liability for registration or change in nature of supplies by person exempted from registration or certain acquisitions of goods in the UK from another member state (FA 2008, Sch. 41, para. 1, in relation to an obligation arising after 31 March 2010)[4]</td><td><table><tr><th>Type of failure</th><th>Percentage of the tax unpaid</th></tr><tr><td>Non-deliberate failure</td><td>30%</td></tr><tr><td>Deliberate but not concealed</td><td>70%</td></tr><tr><td>Deliberate and concealed</td><td>100%</td></tr></table></td></tr>
<tr><td>• Unauthorised issue of VAT invoice (FA 2008, Sch. 41, para. 2, in relation to an unauthorised issue of an invoice taking place after 31 March 2010)[4]</td><td>Penalty is the same as for the late notification penalty under Sch. 41, para. 1</td></tr>
<tr><td>• Error in taxpayer's document sent to HMRC (FA 2007, Sch. 24, para. 1)[1][2][4]</td><td>Maximum penalty, i.e. without disclosure,
• for careless action, 30% of the 'potential lost revenue' (PLR);
• for deliberate but not concealed action, 70% of the PLR; and
• for deliberate and concealed action, 100% of the PLR</td></tr>
<tr><td>• Failure to notify HMRC within 30 days of an underassessment (FA 2007, Sch. 24, para. 2)[1]</td><td>30% of the potential lost revenue[2]</td></tr>
<tr><td>• Inaccuracy delays tax (FA 2007, Sch. 24, para. 8)</td><td>5% of the delayed tax for each year or a percentage of the delayed tax, for each separate period of delay of less than one year, equating to 5% p.a.[2]</td></tr>
<tr><td>• Evasion of VAT due on imports (FA 2003, s. 25)</td><td>Amount of import VAT evaded</td></tr>
</table>

Offence	Civil penalty	
• Contravention of HMRC rules relating to **exports** (FA 2003, s. 26; *Customs (Contravention of a Relevant Rule) Regulations* 2003 (SI 2003/3113))	Penalty of up to £2,500	
• Default **surcharge** (VATA 1994, s. 59 but from a date **to be appointed** to be replaced by the penalty in FA 2009, Sch. 55 and 56)	1st default in surcharge period	2%
	2nd	5%
	3rd	10%
	4th or later	15%
	If a return is late, but either no VAT is due or the VAT is paid on time, although a default is recorded, no surcharge is assessed.	
	HMRC generally only issue a surcharge assessment at the 2% or 5% rate if the assessment is at least £400. The surcharge may be suspended while there is an agreement for deferred payment (FA 2009, s. 108).	
	There is no automatic default surcharge for persons with an annual turnover of up to £150,000. Generally, by concession, such persons are first offered help and advice when they are late with a VAT payment. Small businesses are often allowed two defaults before a default surcharge is assessed: a first default should trigger a letter and a second default should trigger a surcharge liability notice.	
	The penalty regime in FA 2009, Sch. 55 and 56 is due to replace the default surcharge and apply to taxpayers who fail (1) to file their VAT returns on time or (2) to pay their VAT liabilities in full and on time. The revised penalties will treat late payment of VAT and late-filed returns separately and try to encourage filing and payment by the correct dates by imposing an escalating series of penalties, depending on the number of failures within a penalty period. Further penalties arise if there is a prolonged delay in filing returns or paying the VAT due. A late payment penalty may be avoided where the taxpayer has agreed a 'time to pay' arrangement with HMRC.	

Offence	Civil penalty	
• Incorrect **certificates** as to zero-rating and reduced-rate certificates re fuel and power, etc. (VATA 1994, s. 62)	VAT chargeable if certificate had been correct minus any VAT actually charged.	
• Inaccurate **EU sales statement** or **reverse charge sales statement** (VATA 1994, s. 65)	£100 for a material inaccuracy on a statement submitted within two years of a penalty notice (itself issued after a second materially inaccurate statement)	
• **Failure to submit** EU sales statement or reverse charge sales statement (VATA 1994, s. 66)	1st default including that to which the default notice relates	£5 per day
	2nd	£10 per day
	3rd	£15 per day
	(Maximum: 100 days – minimum: £50)	
• Breach of **walking possession agreement** (VATA 1994, s. 68)	50% of the VAT due or amount recoverable	
• Breach of **regulatory provision** (VATA 1994, s. 69) (The penalty cannot be imposed without a prior written warning (VATA 1994, s. 76(2)))	Failure to preserve records: £500	
	• **Submission of return or payment is late**	
	Number of relevant failures in two years before the failure	**Greater of:**
	0	£5 or 1/6 of 1% of VAT due
	1	£10 or 1/3 of 1% of VAT due
	2 or more	£15 or 1/2 of 1% of VAT due
	• **Other breaches**	
	Number of relevant failures in two years before the failure	**Prescribed daily rate**
	0	£5
	1	£10
	2 or more	£15
	Penalty: the number of days of failure (100 maximum) multiplied by above prescribed daily rate (minimum penalty £50)	

Offence	Civil penalty	
• Failure to comply with requirements of scheme for **investment gold** (VATA 1994, s. 69A)	20% of the value of the transaction concerned	
• Breach of **record-keeping requirements** imposed by a direction (VATA 1994, s. 69B)	Penalty: the number of days of failure (30 maximum) multiplied by £200 daily rate	
• Failure to notify acquisition of **excise duty goods** or **new means of transport** (VATA 1994, s. 75)	**Period of failure**	**Percentage of relevant VAT**
	Three months or less	5%
	Over three months but not over six months	10%
	Over six months	15%
• **Failure to pay** on time correct amount of a relevant tax (such as VAT) (SI 2013/1894; formerly SI 1997/1431)	Taking control of goods (from 6 April 2014; formerly distress)	
• Failure of certain persons to use an **electronic return system** to make a VAT return (SI 1995/2518, reg. 25A)	**Annual VAT-exclusive turnover**	**Penalty**
	£22,800,001 or more	£400
	£5,600,001 to £22,800,000	£300
	£100,001 to £5,600,000	£200
	£100,000 and under	£100

Note

(1) The penalty under FA 2007, Sch. 24, para. 1 and 2 is calculated on the '**potential lost revenue**' (PLR) by reference to:

(a) the amount of VAT understated;

(b) the nature of the behaviour giving rise to the understatement; and

(c) the extent of the taxpayer's disclosure.

Penalised behaviour	Maximum penalty, without disclosure, based on PLR	Minimum penalty, with prompted disclosure, based on PLR	Minimum penalty, with unprompted disclosure, based on PLR
Careless	30%	15%	Nil
Deliberate but not concealed	70%	35%	20%
Deliberate and concealed	100%	50%	30%

If HMRC think it right, because of special circumstances, they may reduce a penalty. 'Special circumstances' excludes:

(a) ability to pay; or

(b) the fact that the PLR from one taxpayer is balanced by a potential over-payment by another.

The penalty regime includes the concept of suspended penalties for careless (not deliberate) action for up to two years where the taxpayer shows that his compliance has improved. In due course, any such suspended penalty is cancelled or becomes payable. Apparently, suspension will only be used for weaknesses in the system for accounting for VAT and not for a one-off error.

The 'potential lost revenue' (PLR) in respect of an inaccuracy in a VAT return is the additional amount due or payable in respect of VAT as a result of correcting the inaccuracy or assessment. If an inaccuracy resulted in VAT being declared later than it should have been ('the delayed tax'), the PLR is:

(a) 5% of the delayed tax for each year of the delay; or
(b) a percentage of the delayed tax, for each separate period of delay of less than a year, equating to 5% per year, i.e. the 5% is calculated pro rata for part-years.

(2) The penalty under FA 2007, Sch. 24 for incorrect returns, etc. applies from the **appointed date** which, subject to the transitional provisions in SI 2008/568 (C. 20), art. 3, is:

- 1 April 2008 in relation to relevant documents relating to tax periods commencing on or after 1 April 2008;
- 1 April 2008 in relation to assessments falling within FA 2007, Sch. 24, para. 2 for tax periods commencing on or after 1 April 2008;
- 1 July 2008 in relation to relevant documents relating to claims under the thirteenth VAT directive for years commencing on or after 1 July 2008;
- 1 January 2009 in relation to relevant documents relating to claims under the eighth VAT directive for years commencing on or after 1 January 2009;
- 1 April 2009 in relation to documents relating to all other claims for repayments of relevant tax made on or after 1 April 2009 which are not related to a tax period;
- 1 April 2009 in relation to documents given where a person's liability to pay relevant tax arises on or after 1 April 2009.

The penalty for under-assessment by HMRC applies from 1 April 2008 in relation to assessments under FA 2007, Sch. 24, para. 2 for tax periods commencing on or after that date, but no person is liable to the penalty in respect of a tax period for which a return is required to be made before 1 April 2009.

(3) HMRC may waive certain interest and surcharges on VAT that was paid late and was payable by those who were adversely affected by designated **national disasters**, e.g. certain severe flooding (FA 2008, s. 135).

(4) HMRC may publish certain details of **deliberate tax defaulters** as regards return periods starting after 31 March 2010 and for failing to meet obligations that arise after 31 March 2010 (FA 2009, s. 94).

However, there is no publication of the details of an offender who made a full disclosure, either unprompted or prompted in a time considered appropriate by HMRC.

Criminal offences relating to VAT

(1) Knowingly engaged in fraudulent evasion

If a person is knowingly concerned in, or in the taking of steps with a view to, the fraudulent evasion of VAT by him or another person, he is liable:

- on summary conviction, to a penalty of the statutory maximum (£5,000) or of three times the amount of the VAT, whichever is the greater, or to imprisonment for a term not exceeding six months or to both; or
- on conviction on indictment, to a penalty of any amount or to imprisonment for a term not exceeding seven years or to both

(VATA 1994, s. 72).

HMRC must prove fraud to criminal standards of proof, i.e. beyond reasonable doubt, rather than on a balance of probabilities.

The circumstances in which HMRC consider prosecution under the criminal law are described in Notice 700, para. 27.4.3 (May 2012).

A tax evader may be charged with 'false accounting' or the common law offence of cheating the Public Revenue (*Theft Act* 1968, s. 32(1)).

(2) Supplementary declarations (Intrastats)

As regards supplementary declarations, a failure to submit a declaration under the Intrastat system can result on summary conviction in a fine up to £2,500 (level 4 on the standard scale) (SI 1992/2790, reg. 6).

(3) Impersonating an officer

It is a criminal offence to impersonate a HMRC officer with a view to obtaining:

- admission to premises;
- information; or
- any other benefit.

On summary conviction the penalty is imprisonment for up to 51 weeks, a fine not exceeding level 5 on the standard scale (£5,000), or both (CRCA 2005, s. 30).

[¶19-530] Reckonable dates

(VATA 1994, s. 74; FA 2009, s. 101; Notice 700/43)

(VAT Reporter: ¶60-630)

The reckonable dates for VAT are:

- *interest on overdue VAT*: due date for submission of return (usually last day of month following end of return period);
- *interest on VAT incorrectly repaid*: seven days after issue of instruction directing payment of amount incorrectly repaid.

From 1 September 2008, HMRC may charge interest on a voluntary disclosure of underdeclared VAT even if the underdeclaration error is below the disclosure threshold. However, underdeclaration errors properly corrected on a return still avoid an interest charge.

Proposed harmonisation of interest charged by HMRC

From a date to be appointed, interest charged on late paid VAT and certain other taxes is to be harmonised (FA 2009, s. 101 and Sch. 53).

[¶19-560] Interest on underpaid VAT (default interest)

(VATA 1994, s. 74; Notice 700/43; HMRC 'VAT default interest' manual)

(VAT Reporter: ¶60-630)

Period of application	Days in period	Interest %
From 29/9/09	–	3.0
24/3/09–28/9/09	189	2.5
27/1/09–23/3/09	56	3.5
6/1/09–26/1/09	21	4.5
6/12/08–5/1/09	31	5.5
6/11/08–5/12/08	30	6.5

Period of application	Days in period	Interest %
6/1/08–5/11/08	305	7.5
6/8/07–5/1/08	153	8.5
6/9/06–5/8/07	334	7.5
6/9/05–5/9/06	365	6.5
6/9/04–5/9/05	365	7.5
6/12/03–5/9/04	275	6.5
6/8/03–5/12/03	122	5.5

Proposed harmonisation of interest charged by HMRC

From a date to be appointed, interest charged on late paid VAT and certain other taxes is to be harmonised (FA 2009, s. 101 and Sch. 53).

[¶19-590] Interest on overpaid VAT (statutory interest)

(VATA 1994, s. 78)

(VAT Reporter: ¶60-680)

Interest on overpaid VAT (statutory interest) arises in certain cases of official error.

Such interest is not free of income or corporation tax.

Period of application	Interest rate %
From 29/9/09	0.5
27/1/09–28/9/09	0
6/1/09–26/1/09	1
6/12/08–5/1/09	2
6/11/08 – 5/12/08	3
6/1/08–5/11/08	4
6/8/07–5/1/08	5
6/9/06–5/8/07	4
6/9/05–5/9/06	3
6/9/04–5/9/05	4
6/12/03–5/9/04	3
6/8/03–5/12/03	2
6/11/01–5/8/03	3

Proposed harmonisation of interest on overpaid VAT

From a date to be appointed, interest on overpaid VAT and certain other taxes is to be harmonised (FA 2009, s. 102 and Sch. 54).

INSURANCE PREMIUM TAX

[¶20-000] Rates

(FA 1994, Pt. III; Notice IPT 1; HMRC 'Insurance premium tax' manual)

Insurance premium tax (IPT) is imposed on certain insurance premiums where the risk is located in the UK.

Period of application	Standard rate %	Higher rate %
From 4 January 2011	6.0	20.0
1 July 1999 to 3 January 2011	5.0	17.5
1 April 1997 to 30 June 1999	4.0	17.5
1 October 1994 to 31 March 1997	2.5	n/a

Note
From 1 August 1998, the higher rate applies to all travel insurance.

[¶20-100] Error correction

(SI 1994/1774, reg. 13)

If the underdeclarations or overdeclarations on previous returns do not exceed a limit, such errors may be corrected on the return for the period in which the errors are discovered.

For accounting periods starting after 30 June 2008, the limit is the greater of £10,000 and 1% of the net IPT turnover as per Box 10 on the IPT return. However, this is subject to an upper limit of £50,000.

The previous limit was a single figure of £2,000.

LANDFILL TAX

[¶21-000] Rates

(FA 1996, s. 42; Notices LFT 1; HMRC 'Landfill tax' manual)

Note: See ¶26-300 for rates applicable in Scotland from 1 April 2015.

Landfill tax was introduced on 1 October 1996 and is collected from landfill site operators.

Landfill tax aims to encourage diversion of waste disposal from landfill sites.

Type of waste	Rate (per tonne) £
Inactive waste liable to lower rate	
From 1 April 2015	2.60[1]
From 1 April 2008	2.50
1 October 1996 to 31 March 2008	2.00
Active waste liable to standard rate	
From 1 April 2015	82.60[1]
1 April 2014 to 31 March 2015	80.00
1 April 2013 to 31 March 2014	72.00
1 April 2012 to 31 March 2013	64.00
1 April 2011 to 31 March 2012	56.00
1 April 2010 to 31 March 2011	48.00
1 April 2009 to 31 March 2010	40.00
1 April 2008 to 31 March 2009	32.00
1 April 2007 to 31 March 2008	24.00
1 April 2006 to 31 March 2007	21.00
1 April 2005 to 31 March 2006	18.00
1 April 2004 to 31 March 2005	15.00
1 April 2003 to 31 March 2004	14.00
1 April 2002 to 31 March 2003	13.00
1 April 2001 to 31 March 2002	12.00

Note

[1] Rates per *Finance Act* 2014.

[¶21-150] Error correction

(SI 1996/1527, reg. 13)

If the underdeclarations on previous returns do not exceed a limit, such errors may be corrected on the return for the period in which the errors are discovered.

For accounting periods starting after 30 June 2008, the limit is the greater of £10,000 and 1% of net VAT turnover as per Box 6 on the VAT return for the return period. However, this is subject to an upper limit of £50,000. If the person is not required to be VAT-registered, there is a single limit of £10,000.

The previous limit was a single figure of £2,000.

AGGREGATES LEVY

[¶22-000] Rates

(FA 2001, s. 16; Notices AGL 1 and AGL 2; HMRC 'Aggregates levy' manual)

Aggregates levy seeks to incorporate the environmental costs imposed by aggregates extraction into the price of virgin aggregate, and to encourage the use of alternative materials such as wastes from construction and demolition.

Generally, 'aggregate' is rock, gravel or sand and whatever occurs or is mixed with it as well as, in certain circumstances, spoil, offcuts and by-products.

Period of application	Rate (per tonne) £
From 1 April 2014	2.00
1 April 2009 to 31 March 2014	2.00
1 April 2008 to 31 March 2009	1.95
1 April 2002 to 31 March 2008	1.60

[¶22-100] Error correction

(SI 2002/761)

If the undercalculations or overcalculations on previous returns do not exceed a limit, such errors may be corrected on the return for the period in which the errors are discovered.

For accounting periods starting after 30 June 2008, the limit is the greater of £10,000 and 1% of net VAT turnover as per Box 6 on the VAT return for the return period. However, this is subject to an upper limit of £50,000. If the person is not required to be VAT-registered, there is a single limit of £10,000.

The previous limit was a single figure of £2,000.

CLIMATE CHANGE LEVY

[¶23-000] Rates: climate change levy

(FA 2000, Sch. 6)

CCL is a tax on the taxable supply of specified energy products ('taxable commodities') for use as fuels (that is for lighting, heating and power) by business consumers including consumers in industry, commerce, agriculture, public administration and other services. CCL does not apply to taxable commodities supplied for use by domestic consumers or to charities for non-business use. There are four groups of taxable commodities, as follows:

- electricity;
- natural gas when supplied by a gas utility;
- liquid petroleum gas (LPG) and other gaseous hydrocarbons in a liquid state; and
- coal and lignite; coke, and semi-coke of coal or lignite; and petroleum coke.

CCL is charged at a specific rate per unit of energy. There is a separate rate for each of the four categories of taxable commodity. The rates are based on the energy content of each commodity and are expressed in kilowatt-hours (kWh) for gas and electricity, and in kilograms for all other taxable commodities. The rates, including the reduced rate for participants of the climate change agreement scheme and for gas in Northern Ireland where a lower rate for gas applies, are set out in the following tables:

[¶23-090] Main rates from 1 April 2015

(*Finance Act* 2014)

Commodity	**Rates from 1 April 2015**[(1)]
Electricity	£0.00554 per kilowatt hour
Natural gas	£0.00193 per kilowatt hour
Liquefied petroleum gas	£0.01240 per kilogram
Any other taxable commodity	£0.01512 per kilogram

Note

(1) Rates per *Finance Act* 2014.

[¶23-100] Rates from 1 April 2014

(FA 2000, Sch. 6, para. 42)

Taxable commodity supplied	Unit	Rate from 1 April 2014		
		Rate	Reduction on main commodity rate for holders of a CCA	Lower rate when used in approved metal recycling process
Electricity	per kWh	£0.00541	10%	20% of full electricity rate
Natural gas	per kWh	£0.00188	35%	20% of main gas rate
Liquefied petroleum gas and other gaseous hydrocarbons in a liquid state	per kilogram[(1)]	£0.01210	35%	20% of main LPG, etc. rate
Any other taxable commodity	per kilogram	£0.01476	35%	20% of rate for other taxable commodities

Note

[(1)] For CCL purposes, the conversion rate of 2,000 litres per tonne is to be used when converting litres of butane and propane to kilograms.

[¶23-200] Rates from 1 April 2013

(FA 2000, Sch. 6, para. 42)

Taxable commodity supplied	Unit	Rate from 1 April 2013		
		Rate	Reduction on main commodity rate for holders of a CCA	Lower rate when used in approved metal recycling process
Electricity	per kWh	£0.00524	10%	20% of main electricity rate
Natural gas (in GB)	per kWh	£0.00182	35%	20% of main gas rate
Natural gas (in Northern Ireland)	per kWh	0.00064 until 31 October 2013 (then GB rate applies)	n/a up to 31 October 2013 then 35%	n/a up to 31 October 2013 then 20% of main gas rate for GB

Taxable commodity supplied	Unit	Rate from 1 April 2013		
		Rate	Reduction on main commodity rate for holders of a CCA	Lower rate when used in approved metal recycling process
Liquefied petroleum gas and other gaseous hydrocarbons in a liquid state	per kilogram[(1)]	£0.01172	35%	20% of main LPG, etc. rate
Any other taxable commodity	per kilogram	£0.01429	35%	20% of rate for other taxable commodities

Note

[(1)] For CCL purposes, the conversion rate of 2,000 litres per tonne is to be used when converting litres of butane and propane to kilograms.

[¶23-300] Rates from 1 April 2012

Taxable commodity supplied	Unit	Rate from 1 April 2012		
		Rate	Reduction on main commodity rate for holders of a CCA	Lower rate when used in approved metal recycling process
Electricity	per kWh	£0.00509	35%	20% of main electricity rate
Natural gas (in GB)	per kWh	£0.00177	35%	20% of main gas rate
Natural gas (in Northern Ireland)	per kWh	£0.00062	Not available	Not available
Liquefied petroleum gas and other gaseous hydrocarbons in a liquid state	per kilogram[(1)]	£0.01137	35%	20% of main LPG, etc. rate

Taxable commodity supplied	Unit	Rate from 1 April 2012		
		Rate	Reduction on main commodity rate for holders of a CCA	Lower rate when used in approved metal recycling process
Any other taxable commodity	per kilogram	£0.01387	35%	20% of rate for other taxable commodities

Note

(1) For CCL purposes, the conversion rate of 2,000 litres per tonne is to be used when converting litres of butane and propane to kilograms.

[¶23-500] Carbon price floor

(FA 2000, Sch. 6)

From 1 April 2013, supplies of solid fossil fuels, gas and liquefied petroleum gas (LPG) used in most forms of electricity generation are liable to newly created carbon price support (CPS) rates of climate change levy. The commodities liable to the CPS rates of CCL when they become the subject of a deemed supply for use in electricity generation on or after 1 April 2013 are:

- gas of a kind supplied by a gas utility;
- LPG; and
- coal and other solid fossil fuels (petroleum coke; lignite; coke and semi-coke of coal or lignite).

Electricity is not a CPS rate commodity and does not become the subject of a deemed supply if used in electricity generation. The CPS rates of CCL do not apply to offshore (outside the UK's 12-mile territorial limit) electricity generation.

[¶23-600] Carbon price support (CPS) rates of CCL from 1 April 2013

(FA 2000, Sch. 6; FA 2013, Sch. 42, para. 24; FA 2014, s. 97 and 98)

CPS rates of CCL	2016–17[1]	2015–16[1]	2014–15	2013–14
Natural gas (£ per kilowatt hour)	0.00331	0.00334	0.00175	0.00091
LPG (£ per kilogram)	0.05280	0.05307	0.02822	0.01460
Coal and other taxable solid fossil fuels (£ per gross gigajoule)	1.54790	1.56860[1]	0.81906[1]	0.44264

Note

[1] Rates per *Finance Act* 2014.

AIR PASSENGER DUTY

[¶24-000] Rates

(FA 1994, s. 30)

Air passenger duty (APD) is an excise duty which is due on chargeable passengers being carried from a UK airport on chargeable aircraft.

The rate of APD depends on the passengers' final destination which are allocated into bands based on the distance between London and the capital city of the destination country/territory. Each destination band has three rates of duty depending on the class of travel and the type of aircraft used.

Air Passenger Duty Rates From 1 April 2015[1][4]				
Period	**Bands (approximate distance in miles from the UK)**	**Reduced rate (lowest class of travel)** £	**Standard rate (other than the lowest class of travel)[2]** £	**Higher rate[3]** £
2015–16	Band A (0–2,000 miles)	13	26	78
	Band B (over 2,000 miles)	71	142	426

Notes

[1] Rates per *Finance Act* 2014. *Finance Act* 2014 also reduces the number of destination bands from four to two by merging the former bands B, C and D and sets the higher rates that apply to aircraft with an authorised take off weight of 20 tonnes or more and with fewer than 19 seats at six times the reduced rate (previously twice the standard rate).

[2] If any class of travel provides a seat pitch in excess of 1.016 metres (40 inches) the standard rate is the minimum rate that applies.

[3] The higher rate applies to flights aboard aircraft of 20 tonnes and above with fewer than 19 seats.

[4] From 1 May 2015, economy tickets for children under 12 will be exempt from the reduced rate of APD. The exemption will be extended to include children under 16 from 1 March 2016 (Autumn Statement 2014)

Air Passenger Duty Rates[1][2]								
Bands (approximate distance in miles from the UK)	**Reduced rate (lowest class of travel)**			**Standard rate (other than the lowest class of travel)[3]**			**Higher rate[4]**	
From	**1 April 2012 £**	**1 April 2013 £**	**1 April 2014 £**	**1 April 2012 £**	**1 April 2013 £**	**1 April 2014 £**	**1 April 2013 £**	**1 April 2014 £**
Band A (0–2000 miles)	13	13	13	26	26	26	52	52
Band B (2,001–4,000 miles)	65	67	69	130	134	138	268	276
Band C (4,001–6,000 miles)	81	83	85	162	166	170	332	340
Band D (over 6,000 miles)	92	94	97	184	188	194	376	388

Notes:

[1] From 1 April 2013, APD has applied to all flights aboard aircraft 5.7 tonnes and above.

[2] From 1 January 2013, the rates for direct long-haul flights from NI were devolved to the Northern Ireland Executive, and set at £0. Direct long haul journeys from NI are those where the first part of the journey is to a destination outside Band A.

[3] If any class of travel provides a seat pitch in excess of 1.016 metres (40 inches), the standard rate is the minimum rate that applies.

[4] The higher rate applies to flights aboard aircraft of 20 tonnes and above with fewer than 19 seats.

[¶24-100] Destinations by band

(FA 1994, Sch. 5A)

Band A			
Country/Territory	**Capital City**	**Country/Territory**	**Capital City**
Albania	Tirana	Malta	Valletta
Algeria	Algiers	Moldova	Chisinau
Andorra	Andorra la Vella	Monaco	Monaco
Austria	Vienna	Montenegro	Podgorica
Belarus	Minsk	Morocco	Rabat
Belgium	Brussels	Netherlands	Amsterdam
Bosnia & Herzegovina	Sarajevo	Norway	Oslo
Bulgaria	Sofia	Poland	Warsaw
Corsica	Ajaccio	Portugal	Lisbon
Croatia	Zagreb	Romania	Bucharest
Cyprus	Nicosia	Russian Federation (West of the Urals)	Moscow
Czech Republic	Prague		
Denmark	Copenhagen	San Marino	San Marino
Estonia	Tallinn	Sardinia	Cagliari
Faroe Islands	Torshavn	Serbia	Belgrade
Finland	Helsinki	Sicily	Palermo
France	Paris	Slovakia	Bratislava
Germany	Berlin	Slovenia	Ljubljana
Gibraltar	Gibraltar	Spain	Madrid
Greece	Athens	Svalbard	Longyearbyen
Greenland	Nuuk	Sweden	Stockholm
Hungary	Budapest	Switzerland	Bern
Iceland	Reykjavik	The Azores	Ponta Delgada
Ireland	Dublin	The Balearic Islands	Palma
Isle of Man	Douglas	The Canary Islands	Santa Cruz de Tenerife
Italy	Rome	The Channel Islands	Encompassing the Bailiwick of Guernsey and the Bailiwick of Jersey
Kosovo	Pristina		
Latvia	Riga		
Libya	Tripoli		
Liechtenstein	Vaduz	Tunisia	Tunis
Lithuania	Vilnius	Turkey	Ankara
Luxembourg	Luxembourg	Ukraine	Kiev
Macedonia	Skopje	United Kingdom	London
Madeira	Funchal	Vatican City	Vatican City

Band B			
Country/Territory	**Capital City**	**Country/Territory**	**Capital City**
Afghanistan	Kabul	Kazakhstan	Astana
Armenia	Yerevan	Kuwait	Kuwait City
Azerbaijan	Baku	Kyrgyzstan	Bishkek
Bahrain	Manama	Lebanon	Beirut
Benin	Porto-Novo	Liberia	Monrovia
Bermuda	Hamilton	Mali	Mali
Burkina Faso	Ouagadougou	Mauritania	Nouakchott
Cameroon	Yaounde	Niger	Niamey
Canada	Ottawa	Nigeria	Abuja
Cape Verde	Praia	Oman	Muscat
Central African Republic	Bangui	Pakistan	Islamabad
Chad	N'Djamena	Qatar	Doha
Congo, Democratic Republic of	Kinshasa	Russian Federation (East of the Urals)	Moscow
Congo, Republic of	Brazzaville		
Djibouti	Djibouti	Saint Pierre & Miquelon	Saint-Pierre
Egypt	Cairo	Sao Tome and Principe	Sao Tome
Equatorial Guinea	Malabo	Saudi Arabia	Riyadh
Eritrea	Asmara	Senegal	Dakar
Ethiopia	Addis Ababa	Sierra Leone	Freetown
Gabon	Libreville	Republic of South Sudan	Juba
Gambia	Banjul	Sudan	Khartoum
Georgia	Tblisi	Syria	Damascus
Ghana	Accra	Tajikistan	Dushanbe
Guinea	Conakry	Togo	Lome
Guinea-Bissau	Bissau	Turkmenistan	Ashgabat
Iran	Tehran	Uganda	Kampala
Iraq	Baghdad	United Arab Emirates	Abu Dhabi
Israel	Jerusalem	United States	Washington D.C.
Ivory Coast	Yamoussoukro	Uzbekistan	Tashkent
Jordan	Amman	Yemen	Sanaa

Band C			
Country/Territory	**Capital City**	**Country/Territory**	**Capital City**
Angola	Luanda	Lesotho	Maseru
Anguilla	The Valley	Macao SAR	–
Antigua & Barbuda	Saint John's	Madagascar	Antananarivo
Aruba	Oranjestad	Malawi	Lilongwe
Bahamas	Nassau	Maldives	Male
Bangladesh	Dhaka	Martinique	Fort de France
Barbados	Bridgetown	Mauritius	Port Louis
Belize	Belmopan	Mayotte	Mamoudzou
Bhutan	Thimphu	Mexico	Mexico City
Bonaire	Kralendijk	Mongolia	Ulaanbaatar
Botswana	Gabarone	Montserrat	Plymouth
Brazil	Brasilia	Mozambique	Maputo
British Indian Ocean Territories		Namibia	Windhoek
		Nepal	Kathmandu
British Virgin Islands	Road Town	Nicaragua	Managua
Burma	Rangoon	Panama	Panama City
Burundi	Bujumbura	Puerto Rico	San Juan
Cayman Islands	George Town	Reunion	Saint Denis
China	Beijing	Rwanda	Kigali
Colombia	Bogota	Saba	The Bottom
Comoros	Moroni	Saint Barthelemy	Gustavia
Costa Rica	San Jose	Saint Helena, Ascension and Tristan da Cunha	Jamestown
Cuba	Havana	Saint Kitts & Nevis	Basseterre
Curacao	Willemstad	Saint Lucia	Castries
Dominica	Roseau	Saint Martin	Marigot
Dominican Republic	Santa Domingo	Saint Vincent Grenadines	Kingstown
Ecuador	Quito	Seychelles	Victoria
El Salvador	San Salvador	Sint Eustatius	Oranjestad
French Guiana	Cayenne	Sint Maarten	Philipsburg
Grenada	Saint George's	Somalia	Mogadishu
Guadeloupe	Basse Terre	South Africa	Pretoria
Guatemala	Guatemala	Sri Lanka	Colombo

Band C			
Country/Territory	**Capital City**	**Country/Territory**	**Capital City**
Guyana	Georgetown	Suriname	Paramaribo
Haiti	Port-au-Prince	Swaziland	Mbabane
Honduras	Tegucigalpa	Tanzania	Dar es Salaam
Hong Kong SAR	–	Thailand	Bangkok
India	New Delhi	Trinidad & Tobago	Port of Spain
Jamaica	Kingston	Turks & Caicos Islands	Grand Turk
Japan	Tokyo	Venezuela	Caracas
Kenya	Nairobi	Vietnam	Hanoi
Korea, North	Pyongyang	Virgin Islands	Charlotte Amalie
Korea, South	Seoul	Zambia	Lusaka
Laos	Vientiane	Zimbabwe	Harare

VEHICLE EXCISE DUTY

[¶25-000] Rates

(VERA 1994, Sch. 1)

VED bands and rates for cars registered on or after 1 March 2001 (graduated VED)

		2014–15		2013–14		2012–13	
VED band	CO_2 emissions (g/km)	Standard rate[1] £	First year rate[1] £	Standard rate[1] £	First year rate[1] £	Standard rate[1] £	First year rate[1] £
A	Up to 100	0	0	0	0	0	0
B	101–110	20	0	20	0	20	0
C	111–120	30	0	30	0	30	0
D	121–130	110	0	105	0	100	0
E	131–140	130	130	125	125	120	120
F	141–150	145	145	140	140	135	135
G	151–165	180	180	175	175	170	170
H	166–175	205	290	200	285	195	275
I	176–185	225	345	220	335	215	325
J	186–200	265	485	260	475	250	460
K[2]	201–225	285	635	280	620	270	600
L	226–255	485	860	475	840	460	815
M	Over 255	500	1,090	490	1,065	475	1,030

Notes

[1] Alternative fuel discount 2010–11 onwards: £10 for all cars.

[2] Includes cars emitting over 225g/km registered before 23 March 2006.

VED bands and rates for vans registered on or after 1 March 2001

Vehicle registration date	2014–15 £	2013–14 £	2012–13 £
Early Euro 4 and Euro 5 compliant vans	140	140	135
All other vans	225	220	215

VED bands and rates for cars and vans registered before 1 March 2001 (pre-graduated VED)			
Engine size	**2014–15 £**	**2013–14 £**	**2012–13 £**
1549cc and below	145	140	135
Above 1549cc	230	225	220

VED bands and rates for motorcycles			
Engine size	**2014–15 £**	**2013–14 £**	**2012–13 £**
Not over 150cc	17	17	16
151cc and 400cc	38	37	36
401cc to 600c	58	57	55
Over 600cc	80	78	76

VED bands and rates for motor tricycles			
Engine size	**2014–15 £**	**2013–14 £**	**2012–13 £**
Not over 150cc	17	17	16
All other tricycles	80	78	76

VED bands and rates for trade licences			
Vehicle type	**2014–15 £**	**2013–14 £**	**2012–13 £**
Available for all vehicles	165	165	165
Available only for bicycles and tricycles (weighing no more than 450kg without a sidecar)	80	78	76

VED and levy bands and rates for articulated vehicles and rigid vehicles without trailers							
VED band (letter) and rate (number)	**Total VED and Levy**		**VED rates**		**Levy rates**		
	12 months	**6 months**	**12 months**	**6 months**	**Levy bands**	**12 months**	**6 months**
	£	**£**	**£**	**£**	**£**	**£**	**£**
A0	165.00	90.75	165.00	90.75	n/a	0	0
B0	200.00	110.00	200.00	110.00			
A1	165.00	91.00	80.00	40.00	A	85	51
A2	169.00	93.00	84.00	42.00			
A3	185.00	101.00	100.00	50.00			
A4	231.00	124.00	146.00	73.00			
A5	236.00	126.50	151.00	75.50			

VED band (letter) and rate (number)	Total VED and Levy		VED rates		Levy rates		
	12 months	6 months	12 months	6 months	Levy bands	12 months	6 months
	£	£	£	£	£	£	£
B1	200.00	110.50	95.00	47.50	B	105	63
B2	210.00	115.50	105.00	52.50			
B3	230.00	125.50	125.00	62.50			
C1	450.00	249.00	210.00	105.00	C	240	144
C2	505.00	276.50	265.00	132.50			
C3	529.00	288.50	289.00	144.50			
D1	650.00	360.00	300.00	150.00	D	350	210
E1	1,200.00	664.00	560.00	280.00	E	640	384
E2	1,249.00	688.50	609.00	304.50			
F	1,500.00	831.00	690.00	345.00	F	810	486
G	1,850.00	1,025.00	850.00	425.00	G	1000	600

VED and Levy amounts payable for rigid vehicles with trailers (vehicles WITH Road Friendly Suspension)

HGV axles	Levy band	Trailer weight category	Total weight of HGV and trailer, not over	VED band (letter) and rate (number)	VED rates		Levy rates	
					12 months	6 months	12 months	6 months
					£	£	£	£
Two	B(T)	4,001–12,000kg	27,000kg	B(T)1	230.00	115.00	135	81
		Over 12,000kg	33,000kg	B(T)3	295.00	147.50		
			36,000kg	B(T)6	401.00	200.50		
			38,000kg	B(T)4	319.00	159.50		
			–	B(T)7	444.00	222.00		
	D(T)	4,001–12,000kg	30,000kg	D(T)1	365.00	182.50	450	270
		Over 12,000kg	38,000kg	D(T)4	430.00	215.00		
			–	D(T)5	444.00	222.00		
Three	B(T)	4,001–12,000kg	33,000kg	B(T)1	230.00	115.00	135	81
		Over 12,000kg	38,000kg	B(T)3	295.00	147.50		
			40,000kg	B(T)5	392.00	196.00		
			–	B(T)3	295.00	147.50		
	C(T)	4,001–12,000kg	35,000kg	C(T)1	305.00	152.50	310	186
		Over 12,000kg	38,000kg	C(T)2	370.00	185.00		
			40,000kg	C(T)3	392.00	196.00		
			–	C(T)2	370.00	185.00		
	D(T)	4,001–10,000kg	33,000kg	D(T)1	365.00	182.50	450	270
			36,000kg	D(T)3	401.00	200.50		
		10,001–12,000kg	38,000kg	D(T)1	365.00	182.50		
		Over 12,000kg	–	D(T)4	430.00	215.00		

HGV axles	Levy band	Trailer weight category	Total weight of HGV and trailer, not over	VED band (letter) and rate (number)	VED rates		Levy rates	
					12 months	6 months	12 months	6 months
					£	£	£	£
Four	B(T)	4,001–12,000kg	35,000kg	B(T)1	230.00	115.00	135	81
		Over 12,000kg	–	B(T)3	295.00	147.50		
	C(T)	4,001–12,000kg	37,000kg	C(T)1	305.00	152.50	310	186
		Over 12,000kg	–	C(T)2	370.00	185.00		
	D(T)	4,001–12,000kg	39,000kg	D(T)1	365.00	182.50	450	270
		Over 12,000kg	–	D(T)4	430.00	215.00		
	E(T)	4,001–12,000kg	44,000kg	E(T)1	535.00	267.50	830	498
		Over 12,000kg	–	E(T)2	600.00	300.00		

VED and Levy amounts payable for rigid vehicles with trailers (vehicles WITHOUT Road Friendly Suspension)

HGV axles	Levy band	Trailer weight category	Total weight of HGV and trailer, not over	VED band (letter) and rate (number)	VED rates		Levy rates	
					12 months	6 months	12 months	6 months
					£	£	£	£
Two	B(T)	4,001–12,000kg	27,000kg	B(T)1	230.00	115.00	135	81
		Over 12,000kg	31,000kg	B(T)3	295.00	147.50		
			33,000kg	B(T)6	401.00	200.50		
			36,000kg	B(T)10	609.00	304.50		
			38,000kg	B(T)7	444.00	222.00		
			–	B(T)9	604.00	302.00		
	D(T)	4,001–12,000kg	30,000kg	D(T)1	365.00	182.50	450	270
		Over 12,000kg	33,000kg	D(T)4	430.00	215.00		
			36,000kg	D(T)8	609.00	304.50		
			38,000kg	D(T)5	444.00	222.00		
			–	D(T)7	604.00	302.00		
Three	B(T)	4,001–10,000kg	29,000kg	B(T)1	230.00	115.00	135	81
			31,000kg	B(T)2	289.00	144.50		
		10,001–12,000kg	33,000kg	B(T)1	230.00	115.00		
		Over 12,000kg	36,000kg	B(T)3	295.00	147.50		
			38,000kg	B(T)5	392.00	196.00		
			–	B(T)8	542.00	271.00		

HGV axles	Levy band	Trailer weight category	Total weight of HGV and trailer, not over	VED band (letter) and rate (number)	VED rates		Levy rates	
					12 months	6 months	12 months	6 months
					£	£	£	£
	C(T)	4,001–10,000kg	31,000kg	C(T)1	305.00	152.50	310	186
			33,000kg	C(T)4	401.00	200.50		
		10,001–12,000kg	35,000kg	C(T)1	305.00	152.50		
		Over 12,000kg	36,000kg	C(T)2	370.00	185.00		
			38,000kg	C(T)3	392.00	196.00		
			–	C(T)5	542.00	271.00		
	D(T)	4,001–10,000kg	31,000kg	D(T)1	365.00	182.50	450	270
			33,000kg	D(T)3	401.00	200.50		
			35,000kg	D(T)8	609.00	304.50		
		10,001–12,000kg	36,000kg	D(T)1	365.00	182.50		
			37,000kg	D(T)2	392.00	196.00		
		Over 12,000kg	38,000kg	D(T)4	430.00	215.00		
			–	D(T)6	542.00	271.00		
Four	B(T)	4,001–12,000kg	35,000kg	B(T)1	230.00	115.00	135	81
		Over 12,000kg	–	B(T)3	295.00	147.50		
	C(T)	4,001–12,000kg	37,000kg	C(T)1	305.00	152.50	310	186
		Over 12,000kg	–	C(T)2	370.00	185.00		
	D(T)	4,001–10,000kg	36,000kg	D(T)1	365.00	182.50	450	270
			37,000kg	D(T)5	444.00	222.00		
		10,001–12,000kg	39,000kg	D(T)1	365.00	182.50		
		Over 12,000kg	–	D(T)4	430.00	215.00		
	E(T)	4,001–10,000kg	38,000kg	E(T)1	535.00	267.50	830	498
			–	E(T)3	604.00	302.00		
		10,001–12,000kg	–	E(T)1	535.00	267.50		

Rigid goods vehicle – WITHOUT trailer				
Revenue weight of vehicle, kg		2 axles	3 axles	4 or more axles
Over	Not over			
3,500	7,500	A0	A0	A0
7,500	11,999	B0	B0	B0

Vehicle Excise Duty

Revenue weight of vehicle, kg Over	Not over	2 axles	3 axles	4 or more axles
11,999	14,000	B1	B1	B1
14,000	15,000	B2		
15,000	19,000	D1		
19,000	21,000		B3	
21,000	23,000		C1	
23,000	25,000		D1	C1
25,000	27,000			D1
27,000	44,000			E1

Rigid vehicles – WITH trailer				
Weight of rigid (not trailer), kg Over	Not over	Two-axled rigid	Three-axled rigid	Four-axled rigid
11,999	15,000	B(T)	B(T)	B(T)
15,000	21,000	D(T)		
21,000	23,000	E(T)	C(T)	
23,000	25,000		D(T)	C(T)
25,000	27,000			D(T)
27,000	44,000		E(T)	E(T)

Articulated vehicles – Tractive unit with three or more axles				
Revenue Weight of Vehicle, kg Over	Not over	One or more semi-trailer axles	Two or more semi-trailer axles	Three or more semi-trailer axles
3,500	11,999	A0	A0	A0
11,999	25,000	A1	A1	A1
25,000	26,000	A3		
26,000	28,000	A4		
28,000	29,000	C1		
29,000	31,000	C3		
31,000	33,000	E1	C1	
33,000	34,000	E2	D1	
34,000	36,000			C1
36,000	38,000	F	E1	D1
38,000	44,000	G	G	E1

<table>
<tr><th colspan="5">Articulated vehicles – Tractive unit with two axles</th></tr>
<tr><th colspan="2">Revenue Weight of Vehicle, kg</th><th rowspan="2">One or more semi-trailer axles</th><th rowspan="2">Two or more semi-trailer axles</th><th rowspan="2">Three or more semi-trailer axles</th></tr>
<tr><th>Over</th><th>Not over</th></tr>
<tr><td>3,500</td><td>11,999</td><td>A0</td><td>A0</td><td>A0</td></tr>
<tr><td>11,999</td><td>22,000</td><td>A1</td><td rowspan="3">A1</td><td rowspan="6">A1</td></tr>
<tr><td>22,000</td><td>23,000</td><td>A2</td></tr>
<tr><td>23,000</td><td>25,000</td><td>A5</td></tr>
<tr><td>25,000</td><td>26,000</td><td rowspan="2">C2</td><td>A3</td></tr>
<tr><td>26,000</td><td>28,000</td><td>A4</td></tr>
<tr><td>28,000</td><td>31,000</td><td>D1</td><td>D1</td></tr>
<tr><td>31,000</td><td>33,000</td><td rowspan="2">E1</td><td>E1</td><td rowspan="2">C1</td></tr>
<tr><td>33,000</td><td>34,000</td><td>E2</td></tr>
<tr><td>34,000</td><td>38,000</td><td>F</td><td>F</td><td>E1</td></tr>
<tr><td>38,000</td><td>44,000</td><td>G</td><td>G</td><td>G</td></tr>
</table>

SCOTTISH TAXES

[¶26-000] Scottish Taxes

(*Scotland Act* 1998, *Scotland Act* 2012)

The establishment of the Scottish Parliament and the Scottish Government was provided for in the *Scotland Act* 1998 (as amended by the *Scotland Act* 2012). The Scottish Parliament was officially convened on 1 July 1999. The *Scotland Act* 1998 does not specify which matters are devolved to the Scottish Parliament, rather it specifies those matters that are reserved to the UK Parliament and those matters not reserved are devolved to the Scottish Parliament. Schedule 5 to the Act (as amended) sets out those matters which are reserved to the UK Parliament and all other issues are deemed to be devolved. The Scottish Parliament has primary legislative powers, i.e. the power to pass Acts.

The *Scotland Act* 1998, Pt. IV also introduced a tax-varying power, with effect from 6 May 1999 (SI 1998/3178), to enable the Scottish parliament to vary the rate of income tax levied on the income of Scottish tax-payers by up to 3%. However, this power has never been used and is replaced with a new power to set a Scottish rate of income tax (SRIT) (see below) by the *Scotland Act* 2012.

The *Scotland Act* 2012 also amends the *Scotland Act* 1998 to fully devolve the power to raise taxes on land transactions and on waste disposal to landfill which are expected to take effect from April 2015, at which point the existing stamp duty land tax and landfill tax will not apply in Scotland. The Act also provides powers for new taxes to be created in Scotland and for additional taxes to be devolved.

The Smith Commission was established on 19 September 2014 as a cross-party process to decide what new powers should be transferred to the Scottish Parliament. The Smith Commission reported on 27 November 2014 and the Government has announced it will prepare draft legislative clauses to implement the Heads of Agreement. These include: the personal allowance remaining reserved; the first ten percentage points of the standard rate of VAT being assigned to the Scottish Government; and Aggregates Levy and Air Passenger Duty being fully devolved.

Administration of devolved taxes

The devolved taxes will be collected by Revenue Scotland, Scotland's new tax authority established by the *Revenue Scotland and Tax Powers Act* 2014 (see below).

The *Tribunals (Scotland) Act* 2014, which received Royal Assent on 15 April 2014, makes provision for the establishment of the First-tier Tribunal for Scotland and the Upper Tribunal for Scotland.

The *Revenue Scotland and Tax Powers Act* 2014, which received Royal Assent on 24 September 2014:

- establishes Revenue Scotland and provides for its general functions and responsibilities (Pt. 2);
- makes provision about the use and protection of taxpayer and other information (Pt. 3);
- establishes the Scottish Tax Tribunals (the First-tier Tax Tribunal for Scotland and the Upper Tax Tribunal for Scotland) to exercise functions in relation to devolved taxes (Pt. 4);
- puts in place a general anti-avoidance rule (Pt. 5);
- contains provisions on the self-assessment system, the checking of tax returns by Revenue Scotland and claims for repayment of tax (Pt. 6);
- makes provision for Revenue Scotland's investigatory powers (Pt. 7);

- sets out the matters in relation to which penalties may be imposed (Pt. 8);
- makes provision about the interest payable on unpaid tax, on penalties and on tax repayments (Pt. 9);
- contains provisions on debt enforcement by Revenue Scotland (Pt. 10); and
- sets out the system for the review, mediation and appeal of Revenue Scotland decisions (Pt. 11).

[¶26-100] Scottish Income Tax

(*Scotland Act* 1998; ITA 2007, s. 6A and 11A)

(Tax Reporter: ¶148-160)

The *Scotland Act* 2012 replaces the tax varying power contained in the *Scotland Act* 1998 with a new power to set a Scottish rate of income tax (SRIT) (*Scotland Act* 1998, Pt. 4A). The new SRIT is to be administered by HM Revenue & Customs for Scottish taxpayers and is expected to be implemented in April 2016.

Annually, the Scottish Parliament will levy a Scottish rate of income tax which will be used for the purpose of calculating the rates of income tax to be paid by Scottish taxpayers. The basic, higher and additional rates of income tax paid by Scottish taxpayers will be calculated by reducing the basic, higher and additional rates of income tax levied by the UK Government by ten percentage points and adding the 'Scottish rate' (the rate set by the Scottish Parliament) across the (reduced) rates.

For example, if the UK basic rate, higher and additional rates of income tax were 20%, 40% and 45% respectively and the Scottish rate of income tax were 11%, then the rates applied to Scottish taxpayers for basic, higher and additional rates of income tax would be 21%, 41% and 46%. The Scottish basic, higher and additional rates of income tax will be charged on non-savings income of those defined as Scottish taxpayers. A Scottish taxpayer is broadly an individual who in any tax year is treated as resident in the UK for income tax purposes, and Scotland is the part of the UK with which he has the 'closest connection' during that year (*Scotland Act* 1998, s. 80D–80F, as inserted by the *Scotland Act* 2012, s. 25).

The Scottish Budget published on 9 October 2014 announced that "all Scottish taxpayers will see their rate of UK income tax on non-savings, non-dividend income reduced by 10 pence in the pound across each income tax band from April 2016".

DEVOLVED TAXES

Land and Buildings Transaction Tax (LBTT)

[¶26-200] Proposed LBTT rates from 1 April 2015

(*Land and Buildings Transaction Tax (Scotland) Act* 2013)

The Scottish LBTR has a progressive rate structure, which means that the rates shown in the table below are marginal rates, payable on the portion of the total value which falls within each band. Tax bands and percentage tax rates are to be set by order of the Scottish Ministers.

Residential transactions	Rate[1] %	Non-residential transactions	Rate[1] %	Non-residential leases	Rate[1] %
Up to £135,000	nil	Up to £150,000	nil	Up to £150,000	nil
£135,001 to £250,000	2.0	£150,001 to £350,000	3.0	Over £150,000	1.0
£250,001 to £1,000,000	10.0	Over £350,000	4.5		
Over £1,000,000	12.0				

Note

(1) Rates per draft Scottish budget 2015–16 published on 9 October 2014.

Scottish Landfill Tax

[¶26-300] Proposed SLT rates from 1 April 2015

(*Landfill Tax (Scotland) Act* 2014)

Rates are to be specified by order of the Scottish Ministers.

	Standard rate[1] (per tonne)	Lower rate[1] (per tonne)	Scottish Landfill Communities Fund Credit rate[1]
From 1 April 2015	£82.60	£2.60	5.6%

Note

(1) Rates per draft Scottish budget 2015–16 published on 9 October 2014.

SCOTTISH LAW

[¶26-500] Succession Scotland

Prior rights of surviving spouse, on intestacy, in dwelling house and furniture

(*Succession (Scotland) Act* 1964, s. 8–9; SSI 2011/436)

Prior rights apply where the deceased dies intestate leaving a spouse or civil partner. The surviving spouse or civil partner takes as follows:

Period	House £	Furniture £	Cash (children survive) £	Cash (no children) £
From 01.02.2012	473,000	29,000	50,000	89,000
01.06.2005–31.01.2012	300,000	24,000	42,000	75,000
01.04.1999–31.05.2005	130,000	22,000	35,000	58,000

Legal rights

(HMRC Manuals: IHTM12221)

Legal rights vest in beneficiaries by force of law and apply whether the deceased dies testate or intestate. Accordingly, rights by any provision in the deceased's Will or rules of intestacy can only take effect once legal rights have been met. Prior rights may reduce or extinguish the estate that would otherwise be available to settle legal rights. Legal rights apply to the deceased's moveable estate only (which includes money, shares, cars, furniture, jewellery but excludes heritable property (land and buildings)).

Surviving family	Right of surviving spouse or civil partner	Right of children	Deceased's part[(1)]
Spouse or civil partner and children	One-third	One-third	One-third
Spouse or civil partner but no children	One-half	N/A	One-half
Children but no spouse or civil partner	N/A	One-half	One-half
Neither spouse, civil partner or children	N/A	N/A	Whole moveable estate

Note

[(1)] The balance of the estate is the part which the deceased was free to dispose of by will, or which passes under the rules of intestacy.

Distributions under intestacy

(*Succession (Scotland) Act* 1964, s. 2)

After prior and legal rights have been satisfied, the remainder of the estate, both heritable and moveable devolves in the following order:

Surviving family	Beneficiaries take:
Children	Whole estate
Parents and brothers/sisters Either of, or both, parents and also by brothers or sisters, but not by any prior relative	Surviving parent(s) take half; Surviving brothers and sisters take half
Brother and sisters Brothers or sisters, but not any prior relative	Surviving brothers and sisters take whole estate
Parents Either of, or both, parents, but not survived by any prior relative	Surviving parent(s) take whole estate
Spouse Husband or a wife, but not any prior relative	Spouse takes whole estate
Uncles or aunts Uncles or aunts (being brothers or sisters of either parent of the intestate), but not any prior relative	Surviving uncles and aunts take whole estate
Grandparents A grandparent or grandparents (being a parent or parents of either parent of the intestate), but not any prior relative	Surviving grandparent(s) take whole estate

Surviving family	Beneficiaries take:
Great uncles or aunts Brothers or sisters of any of his grandparents (being a parent or parents of either parent of the intestate), but not by any prior relative	Surviving brothers and sisters (or grandparents) take whole estate
Other ancestors Where not survived by any prior relative, the ancestors of the intestate (being remoter than grandparents) generation by generation successively, without distinction between the paternal and maternal lines, shall have right to the whole of the intestate estate; so however that, failing ancestors of any generation, the brothers and sisters of any of those ancestors shall have right thereto before ancestors of the next more remote generation.	

INDEX

References are to paragraph numbers.

Paragraph

A

Accommodation
. national minimum wage 4-720
. working abroad, rates 4-520

Accounting schemes
. value added tax
. . annual accounting 19-120
. . cash accounting 19-120
. . flat-rate scheme 19-120

Additional rate of income tax 1-006; 1-008; 1-009; 1-010; 1-020

Advertising hoardings
. capital allowances 8-410

Advisory fuel rates
. company cars 4-180

Age allowances 1-100

Aggregates levy
. errors in returns 22-100
. rate 22-000

Agricultural buildings allowances 8-600

Agricultural property relief 6-400

Aircraft
. buildings for testing engines, capital allowances 8-410
. roll-over relief 5-050

Air passenger duty
. destinations bands 24-100
. rates 24-000

Alternative finance investment bonds (sukuk) 15-000

Amusement parks
. capital allowances 8-410

Animation
. corporation tax relief 7-125

Annual accounting scheme
. value added tax 19-120

Annual exemption
. capital gains tax 5-000
. inheritance tax 6-200

Paragraph

Annual investment allowances
. plant and machinery 8-100

Annual tax on enveloped dwellings 7-350
. ATED-related capital gains tax charge 5-020

Armed forces
. State benefits 10-550

Arrears of tax
. official error 1-650

Artists – see Creative artists

Assured tenancy allowances 8-800

Attendance allowance 10-550

Authorised unit trusts
. corporation tax 7-000

Averaging profits
. full and marginal averaging 2-000

B

Back to work bonus 10-550

Bank levy 7-300

Barristers
. cash basis and simplified expenses or accruals basis 2-010

Basic rate of income tax . . . . . . 1-006—1-030

Bathroom fittings
. capital allowances 8-410

Beneficial loans – see Employment-related loans

Benefits – see Employee benefits; State benefits

Bereavement allowance 10-500

Bereavement payment 10-550

Bicycles
. mileage allowance payments 4-200
. used cycles, valuation table 4-380

Blind person's allowance 1-100

Budget (The)
. dates 15-950

Paragraph

Burglar alarm systems
. capital allowances 8-410

Business premises renovation allowances 8-800

Business profits
. cash basis for small businesses 2-010
. flat rate expenses. 2-020
. full and marginal averaging 2-000
. time limits for claims and elections 2-100

Business property relief 6-400

Bus services 4-360

C

Capital allowances
. agricultural buildings and structures 8-600
. assured tenancy allowances 8-800
. business premises renovation 8-800
. claims and elections, time limits 8-950
. dredging 8-800
. dwelling-houses let on assured tenancies 8-800
. enterprise zones
.. commercial buildings or structures 8-650
.. designated areas 8-650
.. hotels 8-650
.. plant and machinery 100 per cent allowances 8-550
. flat conversion 8-800
. hotels 8-600
. industrial buildings 8-600
. know-how 8-800
. mineral extraction 8-800
. patents 8-800
. plant and machinery – see Plant and machinery allowances
. research and development 8-800
. set-off on special leasing, time limits 8-950
. short life assets 8-950
. sports pavilions 8-600
. transfers between connected persons, time limits 8-950

Capital gains tax
. annual exempt amount 5-000
. arrears of tax due to official error 1-650
. ATED-related gains 5-020
. charities 5-050
. chattel exemption 5-000
. claims and elections, time limits 5-950

Paragraph

. deferral, time limits 5-950
. disincorporation relief 5-050
. due dates 1-300
. employee shareholders status 5-050
. employee share ownership 5-050
. enterprise investment scheme 5-050
. entrepreneur's relief 5-050
. exemptions 5-050
. gifts to the nation 1-200; 5-050
. gilt-edged securities, exemption from tax 5-200
. identification of securities 5-300
. indexation allowance pre-5 April 1998 . . . . . 5-050; 11-020
. interest
.. certificates of tax deposit 1-600
.. overdue tax 1-450; 1-500
.. relevant date 1-450
.. repayment of tax 1-450; 1-500
. leases
.. premiums for short leases 5-150
.. wasting assets 5-100
. non-natural persons, disposal of high value residential property 5-020
. payment dates 1-300
. penalty provisions 1-350; 1-400
. personal representative's expenses 5-350
. personal tax returns, filing date 1-250
. private residence relief 5-050
. rates 5-000
. retail prices index 11-020
. roll-over relief, classes of assets 5-050
. securities of negligible value 5-250
. seed enterprise investment scheme 5-050
. self-assessment, due dates 1-300
. social investment tax reliefs 5-050

Capital goods scheme
. value added tax 19-220

Caravans
. capital allowances 8-410

Carer's allowance 10-500

Cars – see also Vans
. advisory fuel rates 4-180
. alternative fuel cars 4-035
. benefit charges
.. appropriate percentage pre-5 April 2012 4-012

Paragraph

. . appropriate percentages post-6 April 2012 4-002
. . lower thresholds pre-5 April 2012 4-010
. . relevant thresholds post-6 April 2012 4-000
. bi-fuel gas and petrol cars 4-035; 4-040
. capital allowances 8-210; 8-500
. compressed natural gas (CNG) 4-040
. CO2 emissions
. . appropriate percentage pre-5 April 2012 4-012
. . appropriate percentages post-6 April 2012 4-002
. . diesel cars, appropriate percentage 4-015
. . lower thresholds pre-5 April 2012 4-010
. . qualifying low emissions cars 4-020
. . relevant thresholds post-6 April 2012 4-000
. . ultra-low emission cars 4-025
. . zero 4-030
. diesel cars 4-015
. electric cars 4-030; 4-035; 4-040
. E85 fuel 4-035; 4-040
. fuel benefit charges 4-140
. . type of fuel, key letters 4-160
. hire charges 7-200
. . post-6 April 2009 2-050
. . pre-6 April 2009 2-060
. hybrid electric and petrol cars 4-035; 4-040
. leased, hire charges 7-200
. . post-6 April 2009 2-050
. . pre-6 April 2009 2-060
. liquid petroleum gas (LPG) 4-040
. mileage allowance payments 4-200
. passenger payments 4-220
. qualifying low emissions cars 4-020
. statutory mileage rates 4-200
. ultra-low emission cars 4-025
. value added tax
. . advisory fuel rates 19-280
. . mileage allowances 19-280
. . private fuel scale charges 19-300
. zero emissions 4-030

Cash accounting scheme
. value added tax 19-120

Cash basis
. barristers 2-010

Paragraph

. excluded business 2-010
. excluded persons 2-010
. excluded trades 2-010
. small business profits 2-010

Certificates of tax deposit
. interest rates 1-600

Charities
. capital gains tax 5-050
. gifts
. . inheritance tax 6-100
. . payroll giving scheme 4-980
. . plant and machinery 1-150
. . property settled by gift 1-150
. . shares and securities 1-150
. . trading stock 1-150
. payroll giving scheme 4-980

Chattel exemption 5-000

Childcare
. cap on relief post-April 2011 4-815
. vouchers 4-810

Children
. child benefit 10-550
. . high income earners 1-110
. investment plans, CTFs/junior ISAs 3-350
. settlements on 3-550
. special allowance 10-550
. tax credits
. . child tax credit 10-100; 10-550
. . working tax credit, child care element 10-000

Christmas bonus 10-550

Civil partners – see Husband and wife and civil partners

Claims and elections
. capital allowances, time limits 8-950
. capital gains tax, time limits 5-950
. corporation tax, time limits 7-900
. group relief 7-900
. income tax, time limits 2-100; 3-700
. losses 7-900
. . time limits 2-100

Clearances
. clearances and approvals 15-450
. non-statutory clearances 15-460
. statutory clearance or approval 15-470

Climate change levy
. carbon price floor 23-500
. rates .... 23-000—23-300

Index

Paragraph

..CPS rates 23-600

Close companies
.loans to participators 7-000
..interest on overdue tax 7-550

Close investment holding companies
.corporation tax 7-000

Clothing and tools allowances 4-750

Cold stores
.capital allowances 8-410

Cold weather payment 10-550

Commercial buildings or structures
.capital allowances 8-650

Community care grant 10-550

Community investment tax relief 3-465

Company purchase of own shares
.stamp duty 17-000

Company share option plans (CSOP)
.market value of shares 4-610
.maximum options 4-610

Company vehicles and fuel – see Cars; Vans

Computer equipment 4-820

Corporation tax
.administration, in 7-000
.animation, additional relief 7-125
.associated companies 7-000
.augmented profits, meaning 7-000
.authorised unit trusts 7-000
.bank levy 7-300
.car hire 7-200
.claims, time limits 7-900
.close investment holding companies . . . 7-000
.disincorporation relief 5-050
.distributions 7-000
.due and payable dates 7-450
.effective marginal rates 7-000
.elections, time limits 7-900
.filing deadlines 7-400
.film, additional relief 7-125
.franked investment income 7-000
.gifts to the nation 7-150
.indexation allowance 11-000; 11-450
.instalment payments 7-450
.interest
..overdue tax 7-550; 7-700
..overpaid tax 7-650; 7-700
.liquidation 7-000
.loans to participators 7-000
.main rate 7-000
.marginal relief 7-000
.open-ended investment companies 7-000
.patent profits election (patent box) 7-050
.patents 7-000
.pay and file 7-700
.penalties
..documents 7-500
..failure to notify chargeability 7-500
..notification of commencement of trade 7-500
..records 7-500
..returns or accounts 7-500
.repayment, rate of interest 7-700
.research and development, additional relief, expenditure credits 7-100
.retail prices index 11-000; 11-450
.ring fence profits 7-000
.small profits rate 7-000
.taxable total profits, meaning 7-000
.television, additional relief 7-125
.video games, additional relief 7-125

Council tax benefit 10-550

Creative artists
.averaging profits 2-000
..time limits 2-100

Crisis loan 10-550

Cycles – see Bicycles

D

Dates for payment of tax
.capital gains tax 1-300
.corporation tax 7-450
.income tax 1-300
.inheritance tax 6-750
.self-assessment 2013—14 1-300

Death
.capital gains tax claims 5-950
.inheritance tax – see Inheritance tax
.personal representative's expenses 5-350

Decorative assets
.capital allowances 8-410

Deductions
.unincorporated businesses, deductions allowable at fixed rate . . . 2-020

Paragraph

Deep discount securities
. cap on income tax relief. 1-120

Delivery of accounts
. inheritance tax 6-700

Dependent adults' benefits 10-500

De-registration limits
. value added tax 19-100

Disabled persons
. disability living allowance. 10-550
. severe disablement allowance. 10-550

Disincorporation relief 5-050

Display equipment
. capital allowances 8-410

Dividend income
. income tax rate . . . . 1-006—1-030

Documents
. penalties – see Penalties

Double tax treaties 14-000

Dredging allowances 8-800

Dry docks
. capital allowances 8-410

Due dates of tax – see Dates for payment of tax

Dwelling-houses let on assured tenancies
. capital allowances 8-800

E

EC Sales list (ESL) 19-400

Educational courses
. tax-free payments 4-850

Educational establishments
. gifts
. . plant and machinery. 1-150
. . trading stock. 1-150

Elections – see Claims and elections

Employee benefits
. bus services. 4-360
. cars – see Cars
. company vehicles and fuel – see Cars
. computer equipment 4-820
. educational courses, tax-free payments 4-850
. loans – see Employment-related loans
. medical treatment 4-805
. mobile phones 4-800
. National Insurance contributions. 9-350
. relocation allowance 4-830

Paragraph

. termination payments 4-840
travel and subsistence – see Travel and subsistence

Employee ownership trusts
. capital gains tax relief 5-050
. income tax exemption 4-695
. inheritance tax exemption 6-355

Employee share schemes – see Share schemes

Employee shareholders shares. 4-690; 5-050

Employment and support allowance . . . 10-500; 10-550

Employment income
. benefits – see Employee benefits
. PAYE – see PAYE
. payroll giving scheme 4-980
. share schemes – see Share schemes
. statutory adoption pay. 10-800
. statutory maternity pay 10-700
. statutory paternity pay. 10-750
. statutory sick pay. 10-650

Employment loss relief
. cap on income tax relief. 1-120

Employment-related loans
. official rate of interest. 4-400
. . average rates 4-405
. . foreign currency loans 4-420
. threshold 4-390

Enterprise investment scheme (EIS). . . 3-400; 5-050

Enterprise management incentives (EMI)
. maximum options 4-620
. qualifying company 4-620

Enterprise zones
. capital allowances
. . commercial buildings or structures 8-650
. . hotels 8-650
. . industrial buildings 8-650
. . plant and machinery 100 per cent allowances 8-550
. designated 8-650

Entrepreneur's relief
. gains eligible for. 5-000; 5-050

Ewe and suckler cow premium quotas
. roll-over relief 5-050

Excepted estates
. inheritance tax 6-700

Excepted settlements
. inheritance tax 6-700

Exchange rates. 12-000; 12-640

Paragraph

Exemptions
. capital gains tax 5-050
. inheritance tax 6-200
. value added tax 19-160

Exhibitions
. capital allowances 8-410

Expenses
. barristers, simplified expenses 2-010
. incidental overnight expenses 4-540
. personal representatives 5-350
. travel and subsistence
.. day subsistence rates 4-500
.. incidental overnight expenses and benefits 4-540
.. overseas rates 4-520

F

False statements
. penalties 1-350

Farming and market gardening
. agricultural buildings allowances 8-600
. averaging profits 2-000
.. time limits 2-100
. quotas, roll-over relief 5-050
. relief for fluctuating profits 2-000
. value added tax flat-rate scheme 19-060

Film
. corporation tax relief 7-125

Finance Acts dates 15-950

Fire alarm systems
. capital allowances 8-410

First-year allowances – see Plant and machinery allowances

Fish quotas
. roll-over relief 5-050

Fish tanks and fish ponds
. capital allowances 8-410

Fixed sum deductions
. repairing and maintaining equipment ... 4-750

Fixtures
. plant and machinery allowances 8-450

Flat conversion allowances 8-800

Flat-rate expenses 4-750

Floodlight towers
. capital allowances 8-410

Paragraph

Foreign currency loans
. official rate of interest 4-420

Foreign exchange rates 12-000; 12-640

Foreign gains
. delayed remittances 5-950

Foreign social security payments 10-550

Forms
. PAYE return deadlines 4-940

Fuel scale charges – see Cars

Funeral payment 10-550

Furnished holiday lettings
. time limits for averaging elections 3-700

Futures exchanges 15-050

G

Gas and sewerage systems
. capital allowances 8-410

Gifts
. benefit of public or nation
.. corporation tax reduction 7-150
.. income tax/capital gains tax reduction 1-200; 5-050
.. inheritance tax exemption 6-350
. capital gains tax, time limits for hold-over gain 5-950
. charity
.. payroll giving scheme 4-980
.. plant and machinery 1-150
.. property settled by gift 1-150
.. shares and securities 1-150
.. trading stock 1-150
. inheritance tax 6-200
.. charities, lower rate tax 6-000

Gilt-edged securities
. capital gains tax exemption 5-200
. non-residents holding, FOTRA status ... 3-300

Glass houses
. capital allowances 8-410

Goodwill
. roll-over relief 5-050

Groups of companies
. group relief, time limits for elections and claims 7-900
. surrender of company tax refund, time limits 7-900

Guardian's allowance 10-550

Paragraph

H

High income earners
. child benefit charge ... 1-110
. personal allowance ... 1-100

Higher rate of income tax ... 1-006—1-030

HMRC
. forms ... 15-500
. leaflets and booklets ... 15-550
. manuals ... 15-600
. websites ... 15-650

Hoists
. capital allowances ... 8-410

Hold-over relief
. time limits for elections and claims ... 5-950

Home
. use for business/business premises, deductions allowed at fixed rate ... 2-020

Hotels
. capital allowances ... 8-600; 8-650

Housing benefit ... 10-550

Hovercraft
. roll-over relief ... 5-050

Husband and wife and civil partners
. age allowance ... 1-100
. married couple's allowance ... 1-100
. transfers between ... 6-300

I

Identification of securities
. disposals by individuals/trustees and companies ... 5-300

Incapacity benefit ... 10-500; 10-550

Incidental overnight expenses and benefits ... 4-540

Income support ... 10-550; 10-600

Income tax
. additional rate ... 1-006—1-020
. arrears of tax due to official error ... 1-650
. basic rate ... 1-006—1-030
. benefits – see Employee benefits
. cap on loss relief ... 1-120
. claims and elections, time limits ... 2-100; 3-700

Paragraph

. company vehicles and fuel – see Cars
. creative artists, relief for fluctuating profits ... 2-000
. . time limits ... 2-100
. dividend income ... 1-006—1-030
. elections, time limits ... 2-100; 3-700
. employment income – see Employment income
. farming and market gardening, relief for fluctuating profits ... 2-000
. . time limits ... 2-100
. gifts to the nation ... 1-200; 5-050
. higher rate ... 1-006—1-030
. interest
. . overdue tax ... 1-450; 1-500
. . relevant date ... 1-450
. . repayment of tax ... 1-450; 1-500
. investment income – see Investment income
. leases, premiums for short leases ... 5-150
. PAYE – see PAYE
. payment dates ... 1-300
. penalties ... 1-350
. personal allowances and reliefs ... 1-100
. personal tax returns, filing date ... 1-250
. savings income ... 1-006—1-030
. Scottish rate ... 26-100
. starting rate ... 1-006–1-030
. state benefits
. . non-taxable ... 10-550
. . taxable ... 10-500
. trust rate ... 1-006—1-030

Incorporation relief
. disapplication ... 5-950

Indexation allowance
. capital gains on corporation tax ... 11-000; 11-450
. capital gains tax pre-5 April 1998 ... 5-050; 11-020
. retail prices index ... 11-000; 11-450

Individual savings accounts (ISAs)
. adult and junior ... 3-350

Industrial buildings allowance ... 8-600

Industrial death benefit ... 10-500

Industrial injuries benefit ... 10-550

Paragraph

Inheritance tax
. agricultural property relief 6-400
. annual exemption. 6-200
. business property relief 6-400
. delivery of accounts. 6-700
. due dates 6-750
. election for UK domicile. 6-325
. employee ownership 6-355
. excepted estates 6-700
. excepted lifetime transfers, no account required. 6-700
. excepted settlements 6-700
. exemptions 6-200
. fall in value relief
. . interests in land 6-550
. . qualifying investments 6-550
. . quoted securities sold 6-550
. gifts
. . annual exemption. 6-200
. . in consideration of marriage/civil partnership 6-250
. . non UK domiciled spouse/civil partner. . . 6-300
. . small 6-200
. gifts to charities, lower rate tax 6-000
. gifts to the nation 6-350
. instalment option 6-500
. intestate rules. 6-475
. . Scotland 26-500
. lifetime transfers. 6-000
. . delivery of accounts 6-700
. . due dates for payment 6-750
. nil rate band
. . lifetime transfers. 6-000
. . transfers on death/within seven years before death 6-050
. penalties. 6-800
. pre-owned assets
. . chattels. 6-650
. . intangible property in settlor interested trusts 6-650
. . land. 6-650
. prescribed rates of interest 6-850
. quick succession relief. 6-450
. rates 6-000
. taper relief 6-600
. transfers by spouses/civil partners 6-300
. transfers on death
. . delivery of accounts 6-700
. . due dates for payment 6-750
. transfers on death/within seven years before death 6-050
. UK domicile election 6-325
. values below which no account required. 6-700

Paragraph

Instalment payments
. corporation tax. 7-450
. inheritance tax 6-500

Insurance premium tax
. errors in returns 20-100
. higher rate 20-000
. returns, error correction 20-100
. standard rate 20-000

Intellectual property
. corporation tax. 7-050

Interest
. capital gains tax
. . certificates of tax deposit. 1-600
. . overdue tax. 1-450; 1-500
. . relevant date. 1-450
. . repayment of tax. 1-450; 1-500
. certificates of tax deposit 1-600
. corporation tax
. . overdue tax. 7-550; 7-700
. . overpaid tax 7-650; 7-700
. . repayment. 7-650; 7-700
. employment-related loans 4-400
. . average rates 4-405
. . foreign currency loans 4-420
. gilt-edged securities, FOTRA status 3-300
. income tax
. . overdue tax. 1-450; 1-500
. . overpaid tax 1-450; 1-500
. . relevant date. 1-450
. inheritance tax 6-850
. loans, cap on income tax relief 1-120
. National Insurance contributions
. . overdue. 9-650
. . overpaid 9-650
. official rate 4-400
. . average rates 4-405
. . foreign currency loans 4-420
. PAYE paid late 4-948
. prescribed rates, inheritance tax 6-850
. repayments of income tax and capital gains tax 1-550
. SAYE option schemes 4-680
. stamp duty. 17-250
. stamp duty land tax 16-250
. stamp duty reserve tax 18-050
. value added tax
. . overpaid 19-590
. . reckonable date 19-530

Paragraph

..statutory 19-590
..underpaid 19-560

Intestate rules
.inheritance tax 6-475
.Scotland......................... 26-500

Intrastat declarations............... 19-450

Invalidity benefit 10-550

Investment exchanges.............. 15-150

Investment income
.community investment tax relief 3-465
.enterprise investment scheme......... 3-400
.gilt-edged securities held by non-residents, FOTRA status 3-300
.individual savings accounts........... 3-350
.pensions – see Pension schemes
.seed enterprise investment scheme 3-420
.settlements on children 3-550
.social investment tax relief............ 3-430
.venture capital trusts 3-450

Invoices
.value added tax 19-240

In-work credit 10-550

In-work emergency discretion
.fund payment..................... 10-550

In-work emergency fund payment 10-550

J

Jetties
.capital allowances 8-410

Jobseeker's allowance.............. 10-600

K

Kitchen fittings
.capital allowances 8-410

Know-how allowances............... 8-800

L

Land and buildings
.installation of plant or machinery, capital allowances 8-410
.roll-over relief...................... 5-050
.stamp duty land tax – see Stamp duty land tax

Land and buildings transaction tax (Scotland)
.rates 26-200

Paragraph

Landfill tax
.errors in returns 21-150
.inactive/active waste, lower/standard rate 21-000
.Scottish rates.................... 26-300

Lease premiums
.capital gains tax.................... 5-150
.income tax 5-150
.short leases 3-500; 5-150

Leases
.premiums – see Lease premiums
.stamp duty land tax................ 16-000
.wasting assets 5-100

Letters of allotment
.stamp duty...................... 17-000
.stamp duty reserve tax 18-000

Life assurance relief................. 1-100

Lifetime transfers – see Inheritance tax

Lloyd's underwriters
.roll-over relief...................... 5-050

LLPs – salaried members rules........ 2-030

Loans
.close companies to participators....... 7-000
.employment-related loans............ 4-400
..average rates 4-405
..foreign currency 4-420
..threshold......................... 4-390
.irrecoverable loans to traders, claims ... 5-950

Lorry drivers
.subsistence allowances.............. 4-550

Losses – see also Trading losses
.cap on income tax relief.............. 1-120
.enterprise investment scheme share disposals....................... 3-400

M

Machinery and plant – see Plant and machinery allowances

Main residence
.determination, time limits............. 5-950

Manufacturing or processing equipment
.capital allowances 8-410

Married couple's allowance........... 1-100

Maternity allowance................ 10-550

Maternity payment 10-550

Paragraph

Medical treatment exemption 4-805

Mergers
. stamp duty 17-000

Mileage allowance payments 4-200

Milk quotas
. roll-over relief 5-050

Mineral extraction allowances 8-800

Mineral leases
. deemed disposal/reacquisition 5-950

Mobile telephones 4-800

Motor cycles
. mileage allowance payments. 4-200

Moveable buildings
. capital allowances 8-410

N

National Insurance contributions
. Class 1 9-000
. . contracted-out rebate 9-000
. . defined benefits schemes, rebates for 9-000
. . primary (employee) contributions 2009–10 9-050
. . primary (employee) contributions 2010–11 9-045
. . primary (employee) contributions 2011–12 9-040
. . primary (employee) contributions 2012–13 9-035
. . primary (employee) contributions 2013–14 9-030
. . primary (employee) contributions 2014–15 9-025
. . primary (employee) contributions 2015–16 9-020
. . reduced rates 9-000
. . return deadlines 9-400
. . secondary (employer) contributions 2009–10 9-050
. . secondary (employer) contributions 2010–11 9-045
. . secondary (employer) contributions 2011–12 9-040
. . secondary (employer) contributions 2012–13 9-035
. . secondary (employer) contributions 2013–14 9-030

Paragraph

. . secondary (employer) contributions 2014–15 9-025
. . secondary (employer) contributions 2015–16 9-020
. . state pension age 9-000
. . £2,000 employment allowance. 9-000
. . Class 1A 9-350
. . return deadlines 9-400
. Class 1B. 9-450
. Class 2 9-500
. Class 3 9-550
. Class 3A. 9-570
. Class 4 9-600
. company vehicles and fuel 9-350
. employee benefits 9-350
. . return deadlines 9-400
. overdue, interest rates 9-650; 1-500
. overpaid, interest rates 9-650; 1-500
. penalties. 9-400
. repayments, interest rates 9-670
. return deadlines for Class 1 and 1A. 9-400
. voluntary contributions 9-550

National Loans Funds
. stocks and bonds charged on 5-200

National minimum wage
. accommodation offset. 4-720
. post-1 October 2010 4-700

Negligible values
. securities 5-250
. time limits. 5-950

Non-domiciles
. election for UK domicile. 6-325

Non-residents
. gilt-edged securities, FOTRA status 3-300

O

Offences – see Penalties

Official rate of interest 4-400; 4-405; 4-420

Open-ended investment companies
. corporation tax. 7-000

Ordinary residence 13-500

Overdue/overpaid tax
. interest – see Interest
. penalties – see Penalties

Overseas workday relief 13-600

Paragraph

P

P11D and P9D returns
. deadlines 4-940
. penalties. 4-942

P14 returns
. deadlines 4-940

P35 returns
. deadlines 4-940

P38 and P38A returns
. deadlines 4-940

P46 returns
. deadlines 4-940

P60 returns
. deadlines 4-940

Partial exemption
. value added tax 19-200

Partition walls
. capital allowances 8-410

Partnerships: salaried members rules . . . 2-030

Patents
. capital allowances 8-800
. corporation tax. 7-050

Pay and file
. corporation tax. 7-700

PAYE
. codes 4-920
. coding out limits. 4-925
. electronic filing penalties
. . P35 and P14. 4-965
. . P45 4-962
. late payments, interest. 4-948
. monthly accounting periods 4-975
. payroll giving scheme 4-980
. penalties
. . incorrect returns 4-945
. . late filing 4-942
. . late payment. 4-946
. quarterly accounting periods. 4-976
. real time information returns 4-978
. . correction of errors. 4-938
. . forms 4-932
. . mandatory use 4-930
. . penalties. 4-942; 4-945
. . submissions and deadlines 4-930
. . unchanged procedures 4-935
. returns
. . deadlines 4-940

Paragraph

. . incorrect, penalties. 4-945
. . late, penalties 4-942
. settlement agreements, Class 1B National Insurance contributions 9-450
. student loan deductions
. . repayment conditions, post-2012 student loans 4-985
. surcharges 4-970
. thresholds 4-900

Payment of tax
. capital gains tax. 1-300
. corporation tax, due and payable dates. 7-450
. income tax 1-300
. inheritance tax
. . due dates 6-750
. . instalment option 6-500
. self-assessment. 1-300

Payroll giving scheme 4-980

Penalties – see also Interest
. capital gains tax. 1-350; 1-400
. chargeability, failure to notify 1-350
. corporation tax
. . documents 7-500
. . failure to notify chargeability. 7-500
. . failure to notify commencement of trade 7-500
. . records 7-500
. . returns or accounts 7-500
. cumulative 1-350
. documents, failure to produce. 1-350
. false statements. 1-350
. inaccuracies in returns or documents . . . 1-350
. individuals 1-350
. inheritance tax 6-800
. interest on 1-350
. late payment of income tax 1-400
. late returns. 1-350
. National Insurance contributions Class 1 and Class 1A returns. 9-400
. offshore territories 1-360
. PAYE
. . electronic filing 4-962; 4-965
. . incorrect returns. 4-945
. . late filing 4-942
. . late payment
. . . penalties for late monthly or quarterly payments. 4-946
. . . penalty dates. 4-946
. . late returns 4-940

Paragraph

..real time information returns 4-942; 4-945
.reasonable excuse defence 1-350
.records, failure to keep 1-350
.reductions 1-350
.stamp duty 17-200
.stamp duty land tax 16-200
.stamp duty reserve tax 18-100
.tax at risk 1-350
.value added tax 19-500
.withholding information 1-350

Pension credit 10-550

Pension schemes
.personal pension schemes – see Personal pension schemes
.post-6 April 2006 – see Registered pension schemes
.retirement annuity contracts – see Retirement annuities
.State retirement pensions 10-500
..pensionable ages 3-175
..weekly rates 3-200

Pensionable ages 3-150; 3-175; 10-550

Personal allowance 1-100

Personal pension schemes
.early retirement ages 3-150
..profession or occupation, list of 3-150

Personal reliefs 1-100

Personal representatives
.capital gains
..tax rate 5-000
.expenses 5-350

Petrol and diesel – see Cars

Pipelines, ducts or tunnels
.capital allowances 8-410

Places of worship
.value added tax 19-180

Plant and machinery
.fixed, roll-over relief 5-050
.gifts to charities and educational establishments 1-150

Plant and machinery allowances
.air cooling/air purification 8-400
.annual investment allowances 8-100
.assets treated as buildings 8-420
.balancing allowances and charges 8-000

Paragraph

.cars 8-210; 8-500
.cold water systems 8-400
.electrical systems 8-400
.energy-saving assets 8-210
.enterprise zones 8-550
.environmentally beneficial assets 8-210
.excluded structures and other assets 8-430
.expenditure unaffected by statutory restrictions 8-410
.first-year allowances
..availability 8-200
..cars 8-210
..energy-saving assets 8-210
..environmentally beneficial assets 8-210
..exclusions 8-200; 8-220
..gas refuelling stations 8-210
..ring fence trade 8-210
..small and medium-sized enterprises 8-200
..temporary allowances 8-200
..zero-emission goods vehicles 8-210
..100 per cent 8-210
.fixtures 8-450
.gas refuelling stations 8-210
.integral features 8-400
.lifts/escalators and moving walkways 8-400
.long-life assets 8-400
.ring fence trade 8-210
.short life assets 8-950
.solar shading 8-400
.space/water heating systems 8-400
.thermal insulation 8-400
.ventilation systems 8-400
.writing-down allowances 8-300
.zero-emission goods vehicles 8-210

Post-cessation expenses
.claims, time limits 2-100; 5-950

Post-cessation relief
.cap on income tax relief 1-120
.claims, time-limits for 3-700

Potato quotas
.roll-over relief 5-050

Pre-eminent property
.gifts to the nation
..corporation tax reduction 7-150
..income tax/capital gains tax reduction 1-200; 5-050
..inheritance tax exemption 6-350

Paragraph

Premiums for leases – see Lease premiums

Pre-owned assets
. chattels 6-650
. intangible property in settlor interested trusts 6-650
. land 6-650

Private residence relief 5-050

Professions or occupations
. early retirement ages 3-150

Property business
. cap on income tax relief.............. 1-120
. losses, claims and elections 3-700
. post-cessation relief.................. 3-700

Property tax
. enveloped dwellings 7-350

Purchase of own shares
. stamp duty....................... 17-000

Q

Quick succession relief
. inheritance tax 6-450

Quotas
. roll-over relief..................... 5-050

R

Railways or tramways
. rails/sleepers and ballast, capital allowances 8-410

Real time information returns – see PAYE

Re-basing of assets
. time limits for claims 5-950

Recognised futures exchanges....... 15-050

Recognised growth markets......... 15-200

Recognised investment exchanges . . . 15-150

Recognised stock exchanges........ 15-000

Records
. corporation tax, penalties 7-500
. income tax, penalties................ 1-350

Reduced earnings allowance 10-550

Reduced rate supplies
. value added tax................... 19-180

Refrigeration or cooling equipment
. capital allowances.................. 8-410

Paragraph

Registered pension schemes
. annual allowance................... 3-000
. death benefits charge 3-000
. deregistration charge................ 3-000
. ill-health lump sum.................. 3-000
. lifetime allowance 3-000
. lump sums........................ 3-000
. minimum pension age............... 3-000
. short service refund lump sums........ 3-000
. unauthorised payments.............. 3-000

Registration limits
. value added tax................... 19-080

Re-investment relief
. time limits........................ 5-950

Relocation allowance................ 4-830

Remission of tax
. official error 1-650

Renovation of business premises
. capital allowances.................. 8-800

Rental income
. lease premiums 3-500

Rent-a-room relief 1-100

Repairing and maintaining equipment
. fixed sum deductions................ 4-750

Repayment of tax
. interest
. . capital gains tax 1-450; 1-500
. . corporation tax.............. 7-550; 7-650; 7-700
. . income tax 1-450; 1-500

Replacement of business assets – see Roll-over relief

Research and development
. capital allowances.................. 8-800
. corporation tax relief 7-100

Reservoirs
. capital allowances.................. 8-410

Residence
. ordinary residence 13-500
. overseas workday relief............. 13-600
. private residence relief............... 5-050
. statutory residence test 13-000
. . split year treatment................ 13-400

Retail prices index 11-000; 11-450

Retirement ages
. personal pension schemes 3-150

Index

Paragraph

. profession or occupation, list of 3-150
. retirement annuity contracts 3-150
. state pensionable ages 3-175

Retirement allowance 10-550

Retirement annuities
. early retirement ages 3-150
. . profession or occupation, list of 3-150

Return to work credit 10-550

Returns
. corporation tax filing deadlines 7-400
. PAYE – see PAYE
. penalties 1-350
. personal tax returns, submission dates 1-250
. real time information – see PAYE

Roll-over relief
. classes of assets 5-050
. disincorporation relief 5-020
. time limits 5-950

S

Sandwich courses
. tax-free payments 4-850

Sanitary ware
. capital allowances 8-410

Satellites, space stations and spacecraft
. roll-over relief 5-050

Savings income
. income tax rates . . . . 1-006—1-030
. individual savings accounts 3-350

SAYE share schemes
. bonus rates 4-640
. early leaver rates 4-660
. interest rates 4-680
. simplification of scheme rules 4-635

Scholarships
. tax-free payments 4-850

Scottish law
. succession 26-500

Scottish taxes 26-000
. income tax 26-100
. land and buildings transaction tax 26-200
. landfill tax 26-300

Securities – see Shares and securities

Seed enterprise investment scheme . . 3-420; 5-050

Paragraph

Self-assessment
. returns
. . submission date 1-250
. . withdrawal of notice to file 1-250

Self-employed
. National Insurance contributions
. . Class 2 9-500
. . Class 4 9-600

Self-employment credit 10-550

Settlements on children 3-550

Severe disablement allowance 10-550

Sewerage systems
. capital allowances 8-410

Share loss relief
. cap on income tax relief 1-120

Shares and securities
. employee share schemes – see Share schemes
. gifts to charities 1-150
. identification 5-300
. negligible value 5-250
. same day acquisitions 5-950
. stamp duty 17-000
. stamp duty reserve tax 18-000

Share schemes
. company share option plans 4-610
. employee shareholders shares 4-690; 5-050
. enterprise management incentives 4-620
. SAYE
. . bonus rates 4-640
. . early leaver rates 4-660
. . interest rates 4-680
. . simplification of scheme rules 4-635
. share incentive plans 4-600

Sharia compliant financial instruments 15-000

Ships
. roll-over relief 5-050

Silage clamps
. capital allowances 8-410

Silos
. capital allowances 8-410

Slurry pits
. capital allowances 8-410

Small and medium-sized enterprises (SMEs)
. plant and machinery allowances 8-200;

Paragraph

. research and development, corporation tax relief 7-100

Small businesses
. cash basis 2-010

Small companies
. corporation tax small profits rate 7-000

Social fund payments 10-550

Social investment tax relief
. capital gains tax reliefs 3-430; 5-050
. income tax relief 3-430

Sound insulation
. capital allowances 8-410

Sports pavilions
. capital allowances 8-600

Stamp duty
. company purchase of own shares 17-000
. conversion of shares into depositary receipts 17-000
. conveyance or transfer on sale of shares and securities 17-000
. interest 17-250
. letters of allotment 17-000
. penalties 17-200
. purchase of own shares 17-000
. recognised growth markets 15-200
. take overs and mergers 17-000
. transfers of stock 17-000

Stamp duty land tax
. all land in UK 16-000
. interest 16-250
. land in disadvantaged areas 16-000
. lease rentals 16-000
. penalties 16-200
. zero-carbon homes, exemption 16-000

Stamp duty reserve tax
. interest 18-050
. letters of allotment 18-000
. penalties 18-100
. recognised growth markets 15-200
. shares and securities 18-000

Starting rate of income tax . . . . 1-006—1-030

State benefits
. cap 10-625
. non-taxable 10-550
. taxable 10-500

State pension credit 10-550

Paragraph

State retirement pension
. pension age 3-175
. taxable benefit 10-500
. weekly rates 3-200

Statutory adoption pay 10-800

Statutory maternity pay 10-700

Statutory paternity pay 10-750

Statutory redundancy pay 10-550

Statutory residence test 13-000
. split year treatment 13-400
. ordinary residence 13-500
. overseas workday relief 13-600

Statutory sick pay 10-650

Stock exchanges 15-000

Stocks and bonds – see also Shares and securities
. charged on National Loans Funds 5-200

Storage equipment and storage tanks
. capital allowances 8-410

Strong rooms and safes
. capital allowances 8-410

Student loans
. PAYE deductions 4-985

Subsistence – see Travel and subsistence

Surcharges
. PAYE 4-970
. value added tax 19-500

Swimming pools
. capital allowances 8-410

T

Take overs
. stamp duty 17-000

Taper relief
. inheritance tax 6-600

Tax codes 4-920

Tax credits
. child tax credit 10-550
. . baby element 10-100
. . family element 10-100

Paragraph

.. income thresholds and withdrawal rates 10-100
.. individual element..... 10-100
. universal credit..... 10-900
. working tax credit
.. basic element 10-000
.. child care element 10-000
.. disability element 10-000
.. lone parent element 10-000
.. maximum rates..... 10-000
.. second adult element..... 10-000
.. 30-hour element..... 10-000
.. 50-plus element 10-000

Tax information exchange agreements 14-000

Telecommunication and surveillance systems..... 8-410

Telephones
. mobile telephones 4-800

Television
. corporation tax relief 7-125

Terminal losses
. carry-back, time limits 2-100

Termination payments 4-840

Thermal insulation
. capital allowances 8-300; 8-400; 8-410

Time limits
. elections and claims
.. capital gains tax 5-950
.. corporation tax..... 7-900
.. income tax 2-100; 3-700

Tools and clothing
. allowances..... 4-750

Trading losses
. cap on income tax relief..... 1-120
. carry-back/carry-forward, time limits 2-100; 7-900
. current and preceding year set-off, time limits 2-100
. elections and claims
.. capital gains tax 5-950
.. corporation tax..... 7-900
.. income tax 3-700
.. income tax, time limits 2-100
. set-off, time limits 7-900

Paragraph

Trading stock
. gifts to charities and educational establishments 1-150
. valuation, transfer on cessation of trade 7-900

Transfers of stock
. stamp duty..... 17-000

Transfers on death – see Inheritance tax

Travel and subsistence
. day subsistence rates 4-500
. incidental overnight expenses and benefits..... 4-540
. lorry drivers approved amounts..... 4-550
. overseas rates 4-520

Trusts
. capital gains tax
.. rate 5-000
. income tax rate ..... 1-008—1-030

U

UK domicile election 6-325

Unincorporated businesses
. cash basis 2-010
. deductions allowable at fixed rate..... 2-020
. disincorporation relief 5-050

Universal credit
. cash basis for unincorporated businesses 2-010
. rates..... 10-900

Unpaid tax
. interest – see Interest

Unquoted trading company
. losses..... 7-900
.. time limits for set-off..... 3-700

V

Vaccine damage..... 10-550

Value added tax
. annual accounting scheme 19-120
. blocked input tax..... 19-260
. capital goods scheme 19-220
. cars
.. advisory fuel rates 19-280
.. mileage allowances 19-280

Paragraph

. . private fuel scale charges 19-300
. cash accounting scheme 19-120
. civil and criminal offences and
penalties 19-500
. default interest 19-560
. default surcharge 19-500
. de-registration
. . acquisitions from other member
states 19-100
. . assets supplied in UK by overseas
persons 19-100
. . electronic services 19-100
. . non-established taxable persons 19-100
. . supplies from other member
states 19-100
. . taxable supplies 19-100
. digital services from
1 January 2015 19-080
. EC sales list (ESL) 19-400
. EU territories 19-344
. exempt supplies 19-160
. farmers, flat-rate scheme 19-060
. flat-rate scheme
. . farmers 19-060
. . small firms 19-040; 19-120
. fraudulent evasion 19-500
. input tax blocked 19-260
. interest
. . default 19-560
. . overpaid 19-590
. . reckonable date 19-530
. . statutory 19-590
. . underpayments 19-560
. Intrastat declarations 19-450
. invoices 19-240
. Member states 19-344
. offences and penalties 19-500
. partial exemption 19-200
. penalties 19-500
. places of worship 19-180
. publications having legal force 19-320
. rates
. . fractions 19-000
. . fuel and power 19-000
. . reduced rate 19-000
. . standard rate 19-000
. . works of art/antiques and
collectors' items 19-000
. . zero rate 19-000
. reckonable dates 19-530
. reduced rate supplies 19-180

Paragraph

. registration
. . acquisitions from other member
states 19-080
. . assets supplied in UK by overseas
persons 19-080
. . electronic services 19-080
. . non-established taxable persons 19-080
. . supplies from other member states . . . 19-080
. . taxable supplies 19-080
. registration numbers, country code
prefix 19-340
. surcharges 19-500
. zero-rated supplies 19-140

Vans
. benefit charges 4-300
. fuel benefit charges 4-345
. mileage allowance payments 4-200
. passenger payments 4-220

Vehicle excise duty
. rates 25-000

Venture capital trusts (VCTs) 3-450

Video games
. corporation tax relief 7-125

Vouchers
. childcare 4-810
. . cap on relief post-April 2011 4-815

W

War injuries 10-550

War widow's pension 10-550

Wasting assets
. leases 5-100

Websites 15-650; 15-800

White goods
. capital allowances 8-410

Widow's/Widower's pension 10-500

Winter fuel payment 10-550

Working tax credit
. basic element 10-000
. child care element 10-000
. disability element 10-000
. lone parent element 10-000
. maximum rates 10-000
. non-taxable 10-550
. second adult element 10-000
. 30-hour element 10-000
. 50-plus element 10-000

Paragraph

Works transport services 4-360

Writing-down allowances
. cars 8-300
. cushion gas 8-300
. integral features 8-300
. long life asset expenditure 8-300
. solar panels 8-300
. special rate. 8-300; 8-300
. standard rate 8-300
. thermal insulation. 8-300

Z

Zero-rated supplies
. value added tax 19-140

Zoo cages
. capital allowances 8-410